The Complete Idiot's Reference Card

Dr. Mel's Forecast at a Glance

Cloud Type	Appearance	General Conditions	Forecast
Cirrus	Thin, wispy high clouds	Clouds scattered, wind from the west or southwest, barometer steady or falling	Generally fair with a warming trend
		Clouds increasing, barometer falling	Rain or snow within 24 hours
Cirro-stratus and alto-stratus	Thickening cirrus clouds, alto-stratus clouds are lower and create haloes	Clouds increasing with falling barometer	Precip. likely in 24 hours
		Rising barometer and freshening westerly breeze	Skies gradually clearing
Cirro-cumulus and alto-cumulus	Small puffy cloud masses with the cirro-cumulus being the higher cloud	Clouds thickening and barometer falling	Precip. likely within 12 hrs. Snow possible in winter with a NE wind
	Appears with cirro-stratus and alto-stratus	Barometer rising and wind ranging between north and west	A storm just missing, skies clearing
Nimbo-stratus	Low, grey rain cloud	Rain in area, barometer falling, wind generally from east	Rain to continue for next 6-12 hrs.
		Barometer rising, wind becomes westerly	Clearing is imminent
Stratus	Low, fog cloud. Cloud touching ground	Barometer rising or steady, wind light heating	Fog will lift with daytime
		Wind fresh and gusty from the south or east and barometer falling	Fog will persist for at least the next several hours
Cumulus	Puffy, billowy clouds	Clouds scattered and not increasing, wind generally from west or north. Barometer steady or rising or falling slowly	Continued fair weather for at least the next 24 hrs.
		Developing into towers and increasing. Barometer falling, wind generally from west or southwest	Possible showers and thunder-storms within 2-4 hrs.

alpha
books

Dr. Mel's Forecast at a Glance...continued

Cloud Type	Appearance	General Conditions	Forecast
Cumulo-nimbus	Towering cumulus clouds with dark grey base, having an explosive mushroom-cloud appearance	Barometer falling rapidly, increasing wind generally from the southwest	Thunderstorm is imminent, possible severe weather with hail; tornadoes possible if cloud mass is rotating
Mostly clear	Deep blue	Wind northerly or from west, barometer rising	Continued fair weather for the next 24-48 hrs.

Did You Know?

Highest world temperature: 136°F; El Azizia, Libya; September 13, 1922
Highest average annual temperature: 94°F; Dallol, Ethiopia
Lowest world temperature: –129°F; Vostok, Antarctica; July 21, 1983
Most abrupt temperature change: –4° to +45°F in 2 minutes; Spearfish, SD; between 7:30 and 7:32 a.m. on August 29, 1936
Greatest 24-hour temperature range: +44° to –56°F; Browning, MT; January 23–24, 1916
Highest recorded wind gust: 231 mph; Mt. Washington, NH; April 12, 1934
Highest average 24-hour wind: 129 mph; Mt. Washington, NH; April 11–12, 1934
Most rainy days: 335 days/yr, 460"/yr; Mount Wai'ale'ale, Kauai, Hawaii
Highest average rain: 467.4"/yr; Mawsynram, India
Greatest 12-month rainfall: 1,042"; Cherrapungi, India; August 1, 1860–July 31, 1861
Lowest average annual rainfall: 0.03"; Arica, Chile

Exceptional cloudbursts:

1 hour	15.78"	August 1, 1977	Muduuocaidang, Mongolia
42 minutes	12"	June 22, 1947	Holt, Missouri
20 minutes	8.1"	July 7, 1889	Curtea-de-Arges, Roumania
15 minutes	7.8"	May 12, 1916	Plumb Point, Jamaica
8 minutes	4.96"	May 15, 1920	Fussen, Bavaria
1 minute	1.23"	July 4, 1956	Unionville, MD

Largest single hailstone: 1.67 lbs., 7.5" diameter; Coffeyville, KA; September 30, 1970
Largest tornado outbreak: 148 tornadoes; Midwest, Ohio Valley; April 3–4, 1974
Greatest recorded annual snowfall: 1224.5"; Paradise Ranger Station, Washington; 1971–72
Greatest 24-hour snowfall: 74"; Silver Lake, CO; April 14–15, 1921

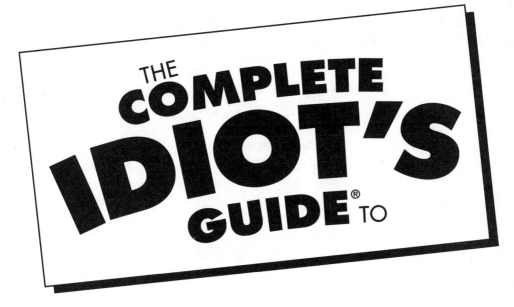

THE **COMPLETE IDIOT'S GUIDE**® TO

Weather

by Dr. Mel Goldstein

alpha books

A Division of Macmillan General Reference
A Pearson Education Macmillan Company
1633 Broadway, New York, NY 10019-6785

Macmillan General Reference books may be purchased for business or sales promotional use. For information please write: Special Markets Department, Macmillan Publishing USA, 1633 Broadway, New York, NY 10019.

International Standard Book Number: 0-02-862709-1
Library of Congress Catalog Card Number: 99-63423

01   00   99   8   7   6   5   4   3

Interpretation of the printing code: The rightmost number of the first series of numbers is the year of the book's printing; the rightmost number of the second series of numbers is the number of the book's printing. For example, a printing code of 99-1 shows that the first printing occurred in 1999.

Printed in the United States of America

Alpha Development Team

Publisher
Kathy Nebenhaus

Editorial Director
Gary M. Krebs

Managing Editor
Bob Shuman

Marketing Brand Manager
Felice Primeau

Acquisitions Editors
Jessica Faust
Michelle Reed

Development Editors
Phil Kitchel
Amy Zavatto

Assistant Editor
Georgette Blau

Production Team

Development Editor
Phil Kitchel

Production Editor
Carol Sheehan

Copy Editor
Lynn Northrup

Cover Designer
Mike Freeland

Photo Editor
Richard H. Fox

Illustrator
Theresa Varga

Book Designers
Scott Cook and Amy Adams of DesignLab

Cartoonist
Brian Mac Moyer

Indexer
Craig Small

Layout/Proofreading
Angela Calvert
Julie Trippetti

Contents at a Glance

Part 1: What Is This Thing Called Weather?   1

1   What Should I Wear?   3
    A look at some basic weather forecasting techniques.

2   Partly to Mostly Cloudy   13
    *How clouds form and what the different types of clouds
    mean.*

3   Bring On the Rain   29
    Why it rains and a look at rainmaking experiments.

4   Going in Circles   41
    The development of atmospheric circulations and storms.

5   There's No Place Like Home   57
    *The formation and characteristics of thunderstorms and
    tornadoes.*

6   On Another Front   69
    *The development of air masses, fronts, and frontal
    cyclones.*

7   Hurricanes: The Greatest Storms on Earth   87
    How these storms develop and their unique characteristics.

8   Blowing Cold and Hot: The Big Ones   99
    A look back at some of the most notable storms in history.

9   El Niño: The Grown-Up Child   113
    *The formation and impact of El Niño and other ocean
    circulations.*

Part 2: The Weather and Us   125

10 Warning: The Weather Can Be Hazardous to
    Your Health   127
    *The impact of weather on health—the aches, the pains, the
    colds, and the blues.*

11 Air Pollution   137
    The major air pollutants, their sources and effects.

12 Control of Pollution   153
    *An examination of the politics, economics, and science of
    air pollution control.*

13 Ozone—The Good and the Bad   165
    *The formation of the ozone layer and a look at the hole
    over our heads.*

Part 3: Climate and Global Change   **175**

14 Well-Seasoned   177
Earth-sun relationships, seasons, and heat budgets.

15 Staying in Circulation   191
The nature and development of global wind patterns.

16 Climatology   203
The hottest, the coldest, the wettest, and the driest—and why.

17 Are You Planning to Move?   215
Taking a look at the climate of some of the fastest-growing areas in the United States.

18 Climates Are Made to Be Broken   227
The changes of climate through the ages.

19 Making the Change Happen   239
The causes of climate change.

20 The Greenhouse Wars   253
The great debate—are we warming, and if so, what does it all mean?

Part 4: Now for the Real Forecast   **265**

21 Measuring the Atmosphere   267
Monitoring and measuring the weather's warmth, its chill, and its bluster.

22 Radar and Satellites   281
Looking at some of the modern tools for analyzing the weather.

23 Let's See How It's Done   291
Going to work with a meteorologist and watching a forecast being put together.

24 Prediction by Numbers   305
The history of computers in meteorology and techniques of computer forecasting.

25 Making a Career Out of It   315
To be a meteorologist, or not to be—that is the question.

Appendixes

A Weather-Speak Glossary   325

B Earth and Climate History   333

C Weather Maps   335

D Computer Forecasting   339

Index   343

Contents

Part 1: What Is This Thing Called Weather?   **1**

1 What Should I Wear?   **3**

Your 50-Year Forecast 3
How Did He Do That? 4
Playing the Odds 5
Getting Down to Basics 6
    Red Skies at Night 7
    Blue Skies, Too 8
    Know Which Way the Wind Blows 9
    Halos and Rings 9
    Storm Signals 10
Forecasting from the Beginning 10
Going for the Gold 12

2 Partly to Mostly Cloudy   **13**

Moisture and Humidity 13
    A Sense of Humid 16
    Is It the Heat or the Humidity? 17
In the Clouds 20
    Cloud Formation 20
    Cloud Classification 21
Ten Major Cloud Types 22
    High Clouds 23
    Middle Clouds 24
    Low Clouds 24
    Foggy Notions 24
Clouds with Vertical Development 25
Forecasting by Clouds 26

3 Bring On the Rain   **29**

Droplet to Drop...How Rain Happens 29
Let's See What Sticks 30
Ice to the Rescue 31
Is There Enough Ice? 31
Types of Precipitation 31
    Snow 32
    Sleet and Hail 32
    Freezing Rain 33

Fooling the Clouds 34
   Age of Experimentation 35
   Raining on Our Parade 36
So Why Does It Rain? 36
Those Ups and Downs 38

4 Going in Circles 41

Storms 'R' Us 41
Feeling the Pressure 42
Origin of Pressure 43
Normal Variation 45
High Points and Low 47
What Makes the Weather Go 'Round 48
What's in a Name? 51
Scales of Motion 52
Is It Getting Worse? The Naughty '90s 54

5 There's No Place Like Home 57

Thunderstorms 57
   Stability and Instability 58
   Lapse Rates 59
   Lightning Strikes 60
Avoid the Ash 62
Doing the Twist 63
The Chase 66
Staying Safe in a Storm 67

6 On Another Front 69

Mass Appeal 69
   Birth of an Air Mass 70
   Going Hot and Cold 71
   Feeling the Chill 72
   Too Cold for Comfort 73
   By the Sea 73
   Putting On the Heat 73
   How Dry It Is 75
Putting Up a Front 75
Front Row 76
Frontal Attack 78
   There's a Storm a-Brewin' 80
   It Looks Like Rain 80
   Stalled in Its Tracks 81

Storms on the Front 81
   Formation and Life Cycle 82
   Of Nor'easters and Sou'westers 83
Telling What's Next 84

7 Hurricanes: The Greatest Storms on Earth   87

It's Different in the Tropics 88
How It Happens 89
The Name Game 92
Hurricane Forecasting 93
The Triple Threat 94
Another Big One Coming? 96
Taming the Tiger 97

8 Blowing Cold and Hot: The Big Ones   99

Winter Gone South 99
Big-City Snows 100
Storm of the Century? 101
The Greatest One of All 102
Modern Winter of Deep Snows 104
Galveston Storm Surge 106
The Great New England Hurricane 106
The Fabulous '50s and Super '60s 107
Camille 108
Of Agnes, Gloria, and Hugo 109
The Amazing Andrew 110

9 El Niño: The Grown-Up Child   113

New Kid on the Block? 113
The Connection Between the Sea and the Atmosphere ... 114
Here Comes the Kid 117
Child's Play 118
Global Weather Extremes 119
   The Wet Coast 119
   South America 120
   Western Pacific 120
   June in January 120
   Southern Floods and Tornadoes 121
   Atlantic Hurricane Season 122
La Niña: The Kid's Sister 122
   Girl Power 122
   Fire and Ice 122
What's Next? 123

Part 2: The Weather and Us 125

10 Warning: The Weather Can Be Hazardous to Your Health 127

Weather and Health 128
My Aching Back.. 129
If You Can't Stand the Heat….. 129
Catching the Common Cold 131
Those Nasty Allergies 133
SAD and Other Moods 134

11 Air Pollution 137

The Main Players 137
Here's the Dirt 138
Pollution Emissions 140
It's a Gas 141
A Silent Killer 144
Out of the Blue 146
VOCs... 147
Photochemical Smog... 149

12 Control of Pollution 153

Politics of Control 153
  It's a Nuisance 153
The Regulations 154
How Are We Doing? 156
Engineering Techniques 158
  Change of Fuels 158
  Getting the Dirt Out 158
  Degassing 159
The Infernal Combustion Engine 160
Weathering the Pollution.. 161
  Horizontal Dispersal 161
  Vertical Mixing 162
  Those Dirty Highs 163
Economics of Control—Can We Afford It? 164

13 Ozone—The Good and the Bad 165

Old Sol 165
  Atomic-Powered Fireball 166
  Crazy with the Heat 167
Atmospheric Structure.. 168

The Good Ozone 170
Ozone Hole—Here Today, Gone Tomorrow? 171
Changes in Ozone 173

Part 3: Climate and Global Change   175

14 Well-Seasoned   177

The Earth in Motion 177
The Seasons 179
Sun Matters 181
Scattering, Reflection, and Absorption 181
Radiation Budget 182
Balancing the Global Heat Budget 184
Local Heat Budgets 185
Ocean and Land Heating 185
Monsoons 186
Ups and Downs 188

15 Staying in Circulation   191

What Do We See—On the Average? 192
The Doldrums 193
The Horse Latitudes 193
Polar Front 194
What Sets Up the Global Pattern? 195
Unicell 196
Tri-Cell 197
Bi-Cell 198
Ocean Circulations 199

16 Climatology   203

Guess This Climate 203
Now Try to Guess This Climate, Too 204
Zone 1 205
Zone 2 205
Zone 3 206
Zone 4 206
Can You Name Continent X? 207
Climate Classification 208
Tropical Moist Climates (A) 208
Dry Climates (B) 210
Mid-Latitude, Moist Subtropical Climates (C) 210
Moist Continental Climates (D) 211
Polar Climates (E) 211

Mapping It All Out 212
Going to Extremes 212

17   Are You Planning to Move?   215

Ideal Climate 215
Economics of Relocation 215
  A Dew Point Reminder 217
  Bring on the Chill 218
Climates of Selected Areas 219
  Houston, Texas 219
  Atlanta, Georgia 220
  Phoenix, Arizona 220
  Denver, Colorado 221
  Orlando, Florida 222
  Salt Lake City, Utah 222
  Las Vegas, Nevada 223
  Raleigh-Durham, North Carolina 223
  Fresno, California 224
  Cincinnati, Ohio 224

18   Climates Are Made to Be Broken   227

Aging with a Glow 227
  The Atomic Clock Is Ticking 227
  Carbon Dating 228
  Uranium Dating 230
It's a Very Old Earth 230
Evidence of Climate Change 232
The Last Two Million Years 233
The Last 500,000 Years 234
Climate of the Last 3,000 Years 235
The Climate of the Twentieth Century 236

19   Making the Change Happen   239

What's the Problem with Understanding
  Climate Change? 239
Plate Tectonics: Get My Drift? 240
Changes in Earth's Orbit 241
  Eccentricity of Earth's Orbit 242
  The Wobbling Earth 243
  The Tilted Earth 243

Changes in Solar Output 244
Volcanism 248
Carbon Dioxide and the Greenhouse Effect 249

20 The Greenhouse Wars   253

The Players.. 253
Have We Really Warmed? 254
So, Where Are We Going? 258
What If We Really Do Warm Up? 260
The Negatives of Greenhouse Warming 261
But There Are Positives 262
So What Should We Do? 263

Part 4: Now for the Real Forecast   265

21 Measuring the Atmosphere   267

The Take on Temperature 267
Is the Pressure Getting to You? 271
The Wind in the Willows 272
It's Not the Heat, It's the Humidity 273
Measuring the Rain 275
Placing the Instruments 276
Upper Air Observations 276
Putting the Data Together... 278

22 Radar and Satellites   281

Radar—Scanning the Skies 281
Doppler—The New Generation 284
Satellites—A Far-Out Look.. 286
The Modern Era 288
Putting It All Together... 289
So, Are the Forecasts Going to Be Better? 290

23 Let's See How It's Done   291

Sunday Night—The Night Before the Forecast 291
Early Monday Morning—Getting In to Work 293
Now for the Real Work.. 293
Checking Out the Data 293
Looking at the Surface Maps 294
Going Into the Upper Air 296
Bring on the Machines 300
What About the Five-Day Forecast? 302
Are We Ready? 303

24 Prediction by Numbers 305

Richardson's Experiment 306
Want to Try the Math? 306
Newton's Law 306
Ideal Gas Law 307
Thermodynamics 307
The Dilemma 308
The Computer Age 308
A Brief History of the Computer 309
Putting the Machines to Work 310
Too Much of a Good Thing 312
The Machines Are Getting Better 313

25 Making a Career Out of It 315

Opening the Mail 315
What Would I Do? 316
Forecasting 316
Broadcasting 316
Consulting 317
Air Quality 317
Computer Programming 318
Research and Development 318
Teaching 319
Forensics 319
Other Areas of Specialization 319
How Much Will I Earn? 320
How Do I Become a Meteorologist? 321
Will I Find a Job? 322

Appendices

A Weather-Speak Glossary 325

B Earth and Climate History 333

C Weather Maps 335

D Computer Forecasting 339

Index 343

Foreword

Surely, the most frequently uttered statement about weather is, "Everybody talks about the weather, but nobody does anything about it." Well, I can't claim that Dr. Mel Goldstein has "done" anything about the weather, but in *The Complete Idiot's Guide® to Weather* he "talks about" it in a way that is certain to greatly enhance your understanding and appreciation of the subject.

I've been a television weather forecaster since 1972, but I've never seen a weather book quite like this one. Dr. Mel has truly found the proper balance between information and entertainment. Along the way we are entertained by a delicious mixture of meteorological meaning and merriment. As he teaches us about dew points, Dr. Mel also reveals his "sense of humid"; as he defines low clouds, he also shares some "foggy notions"; and while demystifying halos, rainbows, and red sunsets, he also demonstrates that he knows "which way the wind blows."

In this book, Dr. Mel covers everything you need to know about meteorology, yet he does it in a reader-friendly, non-intimidating fashion. He explains the basic cloud formations, describes how storms form, delves into weather history, outlines the tools of the forecasting trade, and even shares some fascinating bits of weather lore.

This fact-filled, fun-filled book will acquaint you with the natural forces that generate our weather systems, and it will quote some of the great writers and philosophers of the ages on their musings about weather. Everything you could ask of a weather book is here, and more. If you're fascinated by record-setting weather conditions, this book will satisfy that appetite. Curious about the origin of popular expressions of weather lore? This book holds the answers. Looking for some basic instruction on how to do your own at-home forecasting? Dr. Mel is your guy.

I invite you to join Dr. Mel in a memorable journey that will inform, enlighten, entertain, and inspire. I feel certain that you will discover, as I did, that *The Complete Idiot's Guide® to Weather* is for everyone. No matter what the level of your knowledge—from the trained meteorologist to the youngster who wants to know why raindrops fall—there is something in this book for you. As a really good book should, this one leaves the reader hoping for a sequel. I look forward to Volume Two.

—Spencer Christian

Introduction

Congratulations—you are no longer an idiot! If you have picked up this book, I know that you can go the distance.

The weather is a fabric that is woven around every aspect of our lives. After writing 4,378 newspaper columns about the weather, I am convinced that a weather connection exists within everything that we experience. Our health, our economy, our comfort, safety, and even politics can be tied to the weather. And amazingly, the weather is really easy to understand. In no time at all, you could be like those television weather wizards, smiling while they point to that famous blank blue wall. (Why does this sound like a television commercial? I guess I've been doing that too long, too.)

The understanding of the weather always begins with a look outside. Technology has revolutionized the way we gather information, but Harold Gibson, the former head of the New York City office of the National Weather Service, once said, "The best weather instrument is a pair of human eyes." Many years earlier, Ralph Waldo Emerson was thinking along the same lines when he said, "The sky is the daily bread of our eyes." By looking, thinking, and developing our own insight, we can predict the weather with exceptional accuracy. *The Complete Idiot's Guide® to Weather* begins with that look outside, and then we add basic fundamentals, along with technology.

We'll be looking closely at that entire meteorological tapestry. We'll examine El Niño, climate change, air pollution, and changing weather patterns. We'll also look at the social, political, and economic influences of the weather. In other words—everything under the sun, including the sun.

The appendices provide plenty of reference material, including basic forecast methods from just looking at the clouds to examining weather maps and interpreting computer outputs. World weather records are included within the text. I tried not to leave too much out.

What You'll Learn in This Book

The *Complete Idiot's Guide® to Weather* is divided into four parts:

Part 1, "What Is This Thing Called Weather?" goes into the basic fundamentals of meteorology. We start off with weather forecasting, and that is unusual. Most books will save that for later, once the fundamentals are learned. But let's do it differently and have some fun. This, as they say, is not brain surgery. After a look at basic forecasting techniques, we jump into the nitty-gritty of weather—clouds, rain, and storms. And what about El Niño, and its sister, La Niña?

Part 2, "The Weather and Us," looks at how the weather influences every aspect of our lives. We'll examine how the weather affects our physical and mental health. Air pollution is a big topic, and we'll look at the major pollutants and their sources and effects. Also, how well are we controlling that pollution, and what about the ozone layer?

Part 3, "Climate and Global Change," focuses on one of the hottest topics around. We look at the factors that contribute to climate, including the sun, the earth's motion around the sun, the oceans, and land masses. We look at some of the extremes around the world and classify the different climates. Is there an ideal climate? Are you planning to retire? Last but not least, we look at the greenhouse effect and examine the changes of recent decades. Are we really warming? What can we expect during the twenty-first century?

Part 4, "Now for the Real Forecast," goes into all the basics that contribute to a modern weather forecast. We have the fundamentals down, and now, we take off into the world of modern weather prediction. We look at the ways the atmosphere is observed with balloons, satellites, and radar. What about the weather map and all those lines and arrows? How about that jet stream? And how about those computer projections? If all this convinces you that there's nothing like the weather, and you want to pursue it as a career, you'll find information on requirements and opportunities. I'm convinced that after you have gotten through these chapters, you'll be able to go up against the best of them!

In addition to the text, you'll find more interesting facts in the following sidebars:

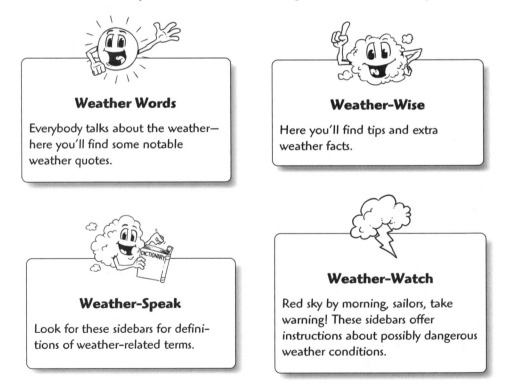

Weather Words

Everybody talks about the weather—here you'll find some notable weather quotes.

Weather-Wise

Here you'll find tips and extra weather facts.

Weather-Speak

Look for these sidebars for definitions of weather-related terms.

Weather-Watch

Red sky by morning, sailors, take warning! These sidebars offer instructions about possibly dangerous weather conditions.

Braving the Elements

These sidebars contain real-life anecdotes and stories about famous storms and famous survivors.

Acknowledgments

A sincere thanks is given to my colleague at WTNH-TV, Theresa Varga, who created the figures for this book.

Also, a huge thanks to my wife, Arlene, who worked tirelessly in the researching, organizing, and typing of the text. Arlene's efforts made this book possible.

Special Thanks to the Technical Reviewer

The Complete Idiot's Guide® to Weather was reviewed by an expert who double-checked the accuracy of what you'll learn here, to help us ensure that this book gives you everything you need to know about the weather. Special thanks are extended to Gary Lessor.

Mr. Lessor began working as a meteorologist at the Weather Center at Western Connecticut State University in 1990, where he distinguished himself as someone who just didn't make mistakes. He went on to become assistant to the director at the Center, where he currently supervises students, consults with numerous corporations, prepares daily weather pages for a number of newspapers, and broadcasts on several radio stations.

Trademarks

All terms mentioned in this book that are known to be or are suspected of being trademarks or service marks have been appropriately capitalized. Alpha Books and Macmillan General Reference cannot attest to the accuracy of this information. Use of a term in this book should not be regarded as affecting the validity of any trademark or service mark.

Part 1

What Is This Thing Called Weather?

Welcome to Weather World. Wherever we turn, we hear about storms, droughts, heat waves, and cold snaps. But as complex as the weather seems, it can be sorted out and nicely understood.

That's what we're about to do. We start the ball rolling with a look at some basic forecast methods, and then we examine the elements that make the weather happen. The essential principles of meteorology are here, including humidity, precipitation, storms of all sizes and intensities, and of course, El Niño. Did you ever wonder why it rains? You'll find out here, and look at how successful rainmaking experiments have been. We'll look at the development and characteristics of air masses, fronts, thunderstorms, tornadoes, and hurricanes; learn what makes the weather go around; and even study clouds.

After reading these chapters, you'll know as much meteorology as the best of them!

Chapter 1

What Should I Wear?

In This Chapter

➤ The very long-range forecast

➤ Differences between weather and climate

➤ Weather lore that works

➤ Forecasting in days of old

Very often, books on weather save the best for last. Before you finally get to weather forecasting, you've had to master volumes of basics. But this series offers room for creativity. Why not start with dessert and get to the rest of the menu later? Let's begin with forecasting, at least a little bit about it. We'll then give you all the background you could want, and then revisit it in later chapters. For now, then, our first task is to take a look outside.

Your 50-Year Forecast

I know what you're thinking—he's the biggest idiot of all. How can anyone forecast 50 years in advance when most forecasts seem to depart from reality in just 50 hours?

Well, as I was putting this book together, my boss at the TV station asked how I might contribute to a special called "Taken By Storm: 50 Years of Weather." The station is marking its 50th anniversary, and there were specials in the works commemorating 50 years of everything, including the weather. So, in addition to a historical wrap-up of major weather events, I suggested a segment on the weather expected for the next 50 years. He had that "Are you nuts?" look on his face, but really, that ultra-long-range forecast isn't as far out as it might seem.

The following table shows that long-range prediction for some of the larger cities around the country. All you have to do is find the city closest to your location, and check the numbers. The forecast of sunny and cloudy days is included among the predictions for all the other meteorological possibilities over the next 50 years. I bet the forecast comes close to at least 90 percent accuracy.

City	Sun	Clouds	Days with 90	Days with 0	Rain/Snow	Inches of Precipitation	Inches of Snow
Atlanta, GA	10,950	7,300	950	-	5,800	2,433	75
Birmingham, AL	10,555	7,700	2,000	-	5,900	2,673	60
Boston, MA	10,200	8,050	550	50	6,400	2,077	2,095
Buffalo, NY	8,050	10,200	100	200	8,400	1,759	4,430
Chicago, IL	9,850	8,400	1,050	350	6,150	1,673	2,035
Denver, CO	12,450	5,800	1,600	500	4,400	730	3,005
Detroit, MI	9,400	8,850	750	100	6,550	1,574	1,585
Hartford, CT	9,350	8,900	1,000	300	6,400	2,150	2,655
Houston, TX	9,950	8,300	4,150	0	5,400	2,353	20
Kansas City, MO	10,400	7,850	1,900	250	5,200	1,833	985
Los Angeles, CA	14,550	3,700	1,000	0	1,700	739	T
Miami, FL	12,400	5,850	1,600	0	6,450	2,960	-
Minneapolis, MN	9,950	8,300	700	1,700	5,650	1,331	2,290
New Orleans, LA	11,550	6,700	3,350	-	5,700	2,946	10
New York, NY	11,600	6,650	800	10	6,050	2,178	1,455
Philadelphia, PA	10,250	8,000	950	3	5,800	2,059	1,015
Phoenix, AZ	14,750	3,500	8,250	-	1,700	370	T
San Diego, CA	13,350	4,900	150	-	2,050	485	T
Seattle, WA	6,850	11,400	150	-	8,050	2,015	760
Washington, DC	10,350	7,900	1,850	-	5,600	2,000	840

The next 50 years.

Weather Words

"There is really no such thing as bad weather, only different kinds of good weather."

—John Ruskin

How Did He Do That?

Long-range forecasting is just an application of climate to weather. *Weather* is a snapshot of current conditions—the temperature, humidity, wind, and precipitation. But *climate* represents those weather conditions averaged over decades. The weather is always changing. Some days are hot, some are wet; but as they say, "One swallow doesn't make a summer," and one balmy day in winter, or even a whole balmy season, doesn't make a tropical climate.

In today's hot debate about greenhouse warming, current weather conditions are often confused with climate. The decades of the 1980s and 1990s have set some record warm temperatures, but is that a sign of climate change, or just normal variability of weather?

We'll revisit that steamy topic later, but there's no doubt that a knowledge of climate is important for weather forecasting. And that 50-year forecast is simply a compilation of average annual conditions multiplied by 50. Over the long haul, climate changes slowly, even glacially. In fact, *persistence* is one of the most accurate short-range forecast techniques. So, for example, if Atlanta receives an average of 219 sunny days each year, then over the next 50 years, this southern city should experience about 10,950 sunny days. I know that will be close—give or take a few days for leap years. The 50-year forecast is that simple. Of course, if there's a sudden climate change, you'll need an update, but I have 50 years to work on that.

Certainly, our first forecast doesn't exactly tell us what to wear for the next 18,250 days, but we're just getting started.

Weather-Speak

People often think the words "weather" and "climate" can be used interchangeably, but that's not so. **Weather** refers to current conditions of temperature, precipitation, humidity, and wind. **Climate** is an average of those conditions as they've occurred over decades.

Playing the Odds

You can narrow down the forecast still more by working with climatology. For example, New York City receives precipitation an average of 121 days each year, or on about one-third of each year. If you predict that the weather will be good each day, your forecast will be correct 67 percent of the time. You can forget about calculus, weather maps, satellite loops, radar—all of it. Just predict that it will never rain in New York, and you'll be right two-thirds of the time. And what's wrong with 67 percent accuracy? If you were a baseball player and hit .670 every season, you wouldn't just be put in the Hall of Fame, a new hall of fame might be built in your honor!

Of course, areas other than the stormy mid-latitudes will provide an even higher accuracy rate. In Los Angeles, rain only falls about 10 percent of the time. If you say it will never rain in southern California, you'll be correct 90 percent of the time. Who needs the evening weather? The table on the next page lists the percent of the time that precipitation normally occurs at the various major cities. Find the city nearest you, and impress your neighbors and relatives.

Weather-Speak

Persistence is the assumption that weather patterns do not change rapidly. Even in mid-latitudes, where change is always expected, persistence can be surprisingly accurate. If you predict that today's weather will be repeated tomorrow, you'll be correct 67 percent of the time in places like Boston, New York, or Chicago. If you predict that in Los Angeles during the summer, you'll be correct 98 percent of the time.

Percentage of rainy days.

City	% of days with precipitation
Atlanta, GA	32%
Birmingham, AL	32%
Boston, MA	35%
Buffalo, NY	46%
Chicago, IL	34%
Denver, CO	24%
Detroit, MI	36%
Hartford, CT	35%
Houston, TX	30%
Kansas City, MO	28%
Los Angeles, CA	9%
Miami, FL	35%
Minneapolis, MN	31%
New Orleans, LA	31%
New York, NY	33%
Philadelphia, PA	32%
Phoenix, AZ	9%
San Diego, CA	11%
Seattle, WA	44%
Washington, DC	31%

Weather-Wise

Weather forecasting has become big business on the evening news. Surveys of viewer interest show that local weather is the most popular portion of the news. Whenever the weather acts up and makes headlines, local newscasts as much as double their ratings. Along those lines, weathercasters are the most recognized personalities in a local television market.

Getting Down to Basics

Although this introduction to weather forecasting may seem flip, it is meant to show the importance of understanding climate in the weather-prediction process. And when you look outside and observe the weather over a period of time, your skills sharpen even more. In my weather office, I would much rather consult with someone who works outside as a farmer or a construction worker than talk to a new post-doc in meteorology. Experience combined with climate become key to figuring out what might be next. Ever since there was weather and people, those analogs were formed, and often passed along from one generation to another. It's called weather lore, and much of it really makes sense. I have my favorites.

Braving the Elements

The most famous weather day is February 2nd, known as Candlemas Day, as well as Groundhog Day. For centuries, Candlemas Day was thought to mark an important point in winter, possibly a turning point. "If Candlemas Day be fair and bright, winter will have another flight. But if Candlemas brings clouds and rain, winter is gone and won't come again." Later, bears, badgers, and woodchucks were brought into it, and if they saw their shadows, six more weeks of winter would follow. Supposedly, the critters would be afraid of their shadows, and would return to their dens. Of course, those shadows could be seen only if Candlemas Day were bright and clear. Does this work? Not really, except that you can't trust a quiet spell during the normally harshest part of the season. A quiet February can lead to a very rough March.

Red Skies at Night

Here's a nugget of weather wisdom that goes back to the beginning of time:

Sky red in the morning
Is a sailor's sure warning.
Sky red at night
Is the sailor's delight.

References to this useful forecasting tip can even be found in some versions of St. Matthew's gospel—and it should be the gospel for anyone who needs a quick idea of what the weather's about to do. There's a good reason why this saying has stood the test of time: It works.

Normally, the weather moves from west to east. If clouds and storms are approaching, the first sign will be an increasingly threatening western sky. Now, sunlight consists of all the colors of the rainbow, including red, which represents the longest wavelength of the spectrum. When the sun is low on the horizon, all the other colors can be scattered and diffused away by atmospheric molecules including dust and water vapor—but the longest wavelength, red, lingers. So, at sunrise or sunset, the sky tends to be red.

The red sky at night is a delight because it can only appear if skies are clear in the west—or at least if clouds have broken in the west while the sun goes down. Because the weather moves from west to east, that clear or clearing sky is coming this way.

Just the opposite is true in the morning, when an overcast western sky and a clear or partly cloudy eastern horizon will cause the sky to turn red as the sun comes up. If the sky were overcast in the east, those red rays of sunlight wouldn't appear. Again, because the weather moves toward the east, the heavier western horizon clouds are on the way, and sailors should take warning.

Blue Skies, Too

> *When the sky is blue,*
> *It will be true*
> *When the sky turns white,*
> *Get ready for a fight.*

I just made that one up, because who wants to read a book about weather and never know why the sky is blue?

Sunlight contains all the colors of the rainbow, with each color having a different wavelength. The shortest wavelength, blue, is preferentially scattered the most by microscopic molecules and particles suspended in the air. When the air is really dry and clean, that scattering is most effective, and as that light is scattered, the sky takes on a brilliant shade of blue. If the particles are too large—if the air is packed with pollution and moisture—there is no preferential scattering, and the sky looks hazy and murky. So, when the weather is going to really shine, often with a crisp, clean breeze out of the northwest, that deep blue sky is there for all to see. But frequently, when the wind comes from the moist southwest direction, the sky turns hazy or cloudy, the weather becomes less comfortable, the air quality diminishes, and storms often begin to appear.

Braving the Elements

Are you dreaming of a White Christmas? For most of the Northern Hemisphere, a White Christmas really is a dream, with the odds of snow cover for December 25 being far less than 50-50. But, according to weather lore, "A green Christmas makes a fat churchyard." The thought is that a warm Christmas and winter will eventually lead to sickness and disease. Because the weather is always busy balancing its extremes, a warm winter will eventually be balanced by colder weather—perhaps during the spring and growing season. Resulting crop failures will cause food shortages and possibly contribute to that fatter churchyard.

Know Which Way the Wind Blows

When the wind is from the west,
The weather is at its best.

Or the flip side:

When the wind is from the east,
It is good for neither man nor beast.

Now, this does not hold universally true, but except for the west coasts of continents, the west wind comes from land areas, and it is a dry wind. The weather is generally settled. But when the wind is from the east, the weather turns overcast and stormy. Because of the counter-clockwise circulation around storms, as they approach, the wind comes out of the east. That east wind gathers moisture from the ocean and skies eventually open up. Few ancients had anything good to say about east winds. Aristotle and his student, Theophrastus, warned about it. Even in Exodus, it was written, "The east wind brought the locusts." Still, an east wind can be very exciting as a storm gathers and makes its approach. Storm lovers and cyclopaths look forward to those days with an east wind. When the rain blows in from the east, "It is four and twenty hours at least." In other words, a day of rain is on the way.

Halos and Rings

The literature is rich with references to halos around the Moon or Sun being predictors of approaching storms. Those halos form when high, thin clouds are present. (We will be flying through all types of clouds in later chapters.) These particular clouds are so high that they always consist entirely of ice crystals, and they are called "cirrus" clouds. That is a Latin word meaning thin, wispy, or feathery. When light passes through the ice crystals, the light bends, as if going through a prism. All types of optical effects are possible: rainbows, or double or triple moons and suns. The most common is a ring or halo.

Weather-Wise

The month of March is named after Mars, the Roman god of war, and for good reason. It's one of the most belligerent months on the calendar. Sharp temperature contrasts create strong winds, and often the biggest storm of the winter appears in early March. The Great Blizzard of 1888 was a March product. In 1970, when Easter arrived in late March, so too, did a massive snowstorm in the Northeast. The refrain of the day was "In your Easter bonnet, with all the snow upon it."

Weather Words

"For I fear a hurricane;
Last night the Moon had a golden ring,
And tonight no Moon we see."

—Longfellow's observation in "Wreck of the Hesperus"

Weather-Wise

Here is some wisdom of the ages that applies to the timing for hurricanes, the greatest storms on Earth: "June—too soon. July—standby. August—look out you must. September—remember. October—all over." These storms develop in the tropics and feed off the warm oceans. During June, the waters are just warming up, and often it is too soon for storms in the Atlantic, although they can form then, especially in the Gulf of Mexico. By August and early September, the oceans reach their highest temperatures, and the hurricane season peaks.

Weather-Speak

A **temperature inversion** occurs when the air near the ground is much colder than the air above. Instead of falling with elevation, the temperature rises with elevation. This takes place most often during a calm, dry, and cloudless night. **Refraction** is the bending of light as it passes from one medium into another.

Because those high, thin clouds frequently precede a storm by about 24 hours or so, those halos are solid indicators that the weather will take a stormy turn. Not all storms are preceded by cirrus clouds, but those that stay around for a day or so seem to always telegraph their approach by first sending in those clouds. A major change in weather is on the way.

Storm Signals

Now that we have observed the color of the sky, watched for halos, and kept an eye on the wind, it is time to stop and listen.

> *Sound traveling far and wide,*
> *A stormy day will betide.*

The next time you go for a walk, listen to the different sounds. There are days when distant sounds can be heard sharply and distinctly. Often as a storm approaches, warmer air pushes overhead while colder air clings to the surface. The air actually warms the higher up you go. That's called a *temperature inversion* because the normal temperature profile is inverted. It usually gets colder in the upper layers of the atmosphere.

At any rate, the speed of sound increases with increasing temperature, and the sound waves themselves bend when going from a layer of one temperature to a layer of another temperature. That behavior is called *refraction* and is similar to what happens to light when it goes through ice crystals, as in cirrus clouds. When warmer air overlies colder air, upward directed sound waves will bend back to the ground. The sound is focused to where you are standing, and a distant train whistle or the hoot of an owl will seem much closer.

Forecasting from the Beginning

Our brief exploration into forecasting pretty much follows the techniques and methods developed by early weather wizards. From the earliest of times, hunters, farmers, warriors, shepherds, and sailors learned the importance of being able to tell what the weather might be up to next. Ancient civilizations appealed to the gods of the sky. The Egyptians looked to Ra, the sun god. The Greeks sought out the all-powerful Zeus. Then there was Thor, the god of thunder and lightning in ancient Nordic times. Some societies, such as the Aztecs, used human sacrifice to satisfy the rain god, Tlaloc. Native American and Australian Aborigines performed rain dances. Those who were able to predict the weather and influence its production were held in highest esteem. After all, they were very well connected.

One of the earliest scientific approaches to weather prediction occurred around 300 B.C. with Aristotle's work, "Meteorologica." The ancient Greeks invented the term *meteorology*, which means the study of atmospheric disturbances or meteors. Aristotle tried to explain the weather through the interaction of earth, fire, air, and water. His pupil, Theophrastus, really went to work and wrote the ultimate weather text, "The Book of Signs," which contained a collection of weather lore and forecast signs. Amazingly, it served as the definitive weather book for 2,000 years! (What if they're still reading *this* book 2,000 years from now?)

Theophrastus' weather lore included colors of the sky, rings and halos, and even sound. Hippocrates was also very much involved with the weather. His work, "On Airs, Waters, and Places," became a medical classic and it linked good health with favorable weather conditions. The opening of his work begins with the advice that those who wish to investigate medicine must first begin with an understanding of seasons and weather.

Weather forecasting advanced little from these ancient times to the Renaissance. Then, beginning in the fifteenth century, Leonardo da Vinci designed an instrument for measuring humidity, a hygrometer. Later, Galileo Galilei invented the thermometer, and his student Evangelista Torricelli came up with the barometer for measuring air pressure. Now the atmosphere could be monitored. Then Sir Isaac Newton derived the physics and mathematics that accurately described the atmosphere. Newton's work on motion remains the "Book of Signs" of modern meteorology. To this day, those principles form the foundation of all computer analyses and predictions.

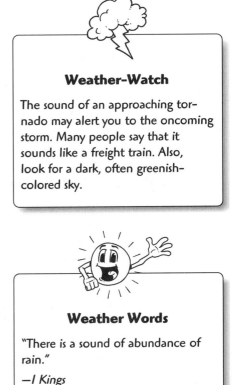

Weather-Watch

The sound of an approaching tornado may alert you to the oncoming storm. Many people say that it sounds like a freight train. Also, look for a dark, often greenish-colored sky.

Weather Words

"There is a sound of abundance of rain."

—*I Kings*

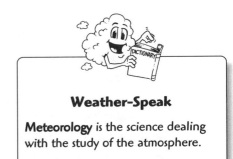

Weather-Speak

Meteorology is the science dealing with the study of the atmosphere.

11

Braving the Elements

Warning! Forecasters are not always held harmless for their predictions. In Taiwan, the head of the weather service was jailed for not warning of an approaching typhoon. His office predicted that the storm would miss the island. It didn't. In Israel, a weathercaster was sued by a viewer who claimed a surprise shower messed up her hair, gave her the flu, made her miss four days of work, and caused mental anguish. In the United States, the families of fishermen lost in a surprise storm off Boston sued the National Weather Service. Also, the state of Connecticut has been sued by the family of a girl who was killed by a falling tree during a severe storm in July 1989. The girl was attending a group outing at a state park when the storm struck.

Going for the Gold

So, how does it feel to already be a weather forecaster who'll be correct most of the time? We've just touched on a few basic principles that have been developed over the eons. Still, regardless of the accuracy provided by these tried-and-true techniques, you'll want to sharpen those skills even more. It would be nice to predict with confidence the specific nature of the weather at least several days in advance. Red sunsets, halos, climatology, and the odds can carry you far, but if you really want to go for the prize, you need to learn more of the basics—the basics first uncovered during the Renaissance and built upon during our space and computer age.

We've been working on dessert, but there's so much more on the weather menu. What about those basic laws of meteorology and the application of technology? And what about the ways in which weather affects our lives—our economy, politics, and health? By the time you finish the upcoming chapters, you'll know far more than which way the wind is blowing. You could even be ready to take my job.

The Least You Need to Know

➤ Climate is the weather averaged over the long term.

➤ Because of the scattering of light, the sky is blue.

➤ As light moves through clouds that contain ice crystals, the light bends, and that creates halos and rings.

➤ Forecasting in ancient times consisted of examining the signs of nature.

➤ In even changeable regions, forecast accuracy can be as high as 67 percent by simply using the prediction technique of persistence.

Chapter 2

Partly to Mostly Cloudy

In This Chapter

➤ Putting on the heat and humidity

➤ Making a point about dew point

➤ Clouds—putting the squeeze on water vapor

➤ Wooly fleece, mare's tails, and cat feet

One of the great wonders of the universe is that our planet is surrounded by a unique blend of compounds, including water in its vaporous state. Actually, water is pretty big on our planet. Over 75 percent of the earth's surface consists of water. Maybe this should be called planet Ocean rather than planet Earth. There really is water everywhere, and the big forecasting challenge each day is to determine whether some of that invisible vapor will transform into falling rain. "To rain, or not to rain…." That really is the question weather forecasters deal with daily.

Moisture and Humidity

In all my years of teaching and talking about the weather, I have never encountered a concept more difficult to grasp than humidity. If you make it through the next few pages, the rest of the book will be a breeze. Let's start off by recognizing that water can exist in three different states: solid, liquid, and vapor. All states consist of the molecule H_2O; the only difference concerns the spacing of the molecules. The following figure depicts these different states. As a solid, the water molecules are closest together. As a vapor, the molecules are farthest apart. So, the whole story here hinges on what makes these molecules drift apart, or come together. Any guesses?

Change of phase.

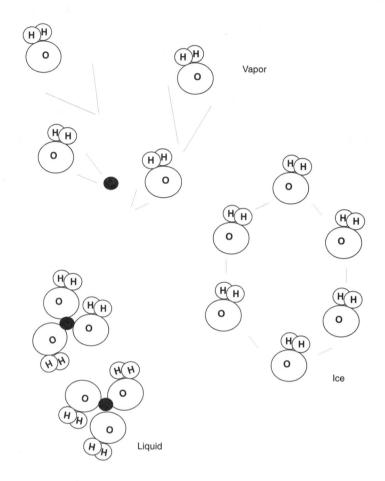

How about temperature? Think of the molecules as popcorn in a popper. When the heat is first turned on, the kernels are just sitting there, solidly, on the bottom of the popper. But then, as heat is added and the temperature increases, the kernels start popping, and the popped corn moves around. Like popcorn, water vapor molecules are bouncing around, thanks to heat in the atmosphere. The water molecules are far enough apart that the vapor is invisible. The vapor itself comes from the water that is evaporated from the earth's surface, including oceans and lakes.

If the heat is reduced, the temperature lowers, and the molecules no longer move around as much. They stick. They become visible, turning into water. The water can take the form of a visible plume of steam, like a cloud, or just raindrops that form pools of water on the ground. If the temperature lowers even more, the molecules become closer. Eventually, you can even walk—or at least skate—on that water. It turns to ice. So, the whole process is a function of temperature.

If the temperature is warm, the atmosphere has a greater capacity to hold water in its vaporous state than if it were cold. During the winter months, the water-vapor content of the atmosphere is as much as four times greater in the tropics than in mid-latitudes such as New York, Boston, or Chicago. In the summertime, the differences become less.

Vapor can change into visible water in one other way: Vapor molecules can also come closer together if *more* vapor is tossed into the mix. As more molecules congregate, they get a little cozy with each other, and eventually transform into visible water. So even if the temperature stays the same, the molecules can be crowded, and then change over to regular water.

Let's combine both concepts. For any given temperature, the air has a particular capacity for water vapor. If that capacity is exceeded, the excess spills out as liquid water. The concept is similar to filling a glass with soda. If the glass is full, pouring more soda into the glass (or somehow shrinking the glass) will cause the soda to spill over the sides of the glass. In the atmosphere, that spillage is made possible by the addition of more water vapor, beyond the particular capacity, or by lowering the capacity through lowering of temperature.

This may be the right moment for a real popcorn and soda break! But this is as difficult as it gets. The rest just builds on the basic concept. The following figure shows these concepts.

Humidity factors.

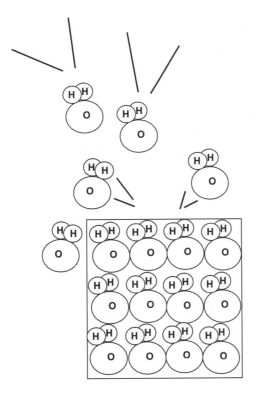

A Sense of Humid

Relative humidity becomes the ratio between the actual amount of water vapor present to the capacity that the air has at a particular moment. Just to be an optimist, if the glass is half-filled, the relative humidity is 50 percent. If the glass is three-quarters filled, the relative humidity is 75 percent. Again, the relative humidity will depend on how tall a glass might be (capacity) and how full that glass might be. The relative humidity will increase if more vapor collects in the atmosphere, or if the temperature is lowered. If the water-vapor content remains the same, the humidity becomes dependent on the temperature. An increasing temperature will lower the relative humidity. A lowered temperature will increase the relative humidity. You see this happening all the time.

Braving the Elements

Here's a little quiz: What was the most deadly weather disaster in New England history? The blizzard of 1888? Not exactly. How about the big floods of 1955? No, try again. The Great New England Hurricane of 1938? Wrong again. It was actually the heat wave of 1911. For nearly half the month of July, the thermometer soared into the 90s and low 100s. The humidity also increased, and the combination caused at least 2,000 deaths during that month alone. A similar heat wave took the lives of more than 700 people during July 1995 in Chicago. Across the entire United States, about 1,250 deaths were attributed to the 1980 heat wave. Overall, more than 20,000 deaths due to heat waves have occurred in the United States since the mid–1930s.

For example, you go to bed at night, and the lawn and car are dry. Skies are clear, yet, in the morning, everything is wet with dew. Where did the water come from? That's easy. It didn't rain, but the temperature cooled at night, and eventually the lowered capacity matched the amount of vapor present. Additional cooling brought the capacity *below* the amount of vapor present. The excess spilled over. Dew formed—the *dew point* was reached. So dew point is the temperature at which the vapor goes over to a liquid. In this whole humidity and dew-point concept, just keep thinking of a glass getting smaller and smaller. Eventually it matches the level of its contents, and finally it spills over.

The point at which the glass is totally filled is called *saturation*. When it is filled to overflowing, the condition is called *condensation*. So when saturation is reached, the temperature equals the dew point, and the relative humidity becomes 100 percent. Any increase in water vapor, or decrease in temperature, will result in condensation.

Is It the Heat or the Humidity?

Probably both, but the relative humidity alone is the poorest indicator of comfort. For example, if the temperature lowers, the humidity will automatically increase and could reach 100 percent. But if the temperature is low enough, nobody seems terribly uncomfortable. Then there are days when the relative humidity checks in at a seemingly comfortable 40 percent, but the air is stifling. During those days, the temperature reaches close to or over 90 degrees in the afternoon. Amazingly, in the morning on such a day, the relative humidity would be higher, but you probably wouldn't be complaining, because the temperature would be lower in the morning. Comfort levels seem to be a combination of both temperature and humidity, with the moisture content of the air playing a huge role. The dew point is an excellent indicator of comfort.

Weather-Speak

Dew point is the temperature at which the vapor in the atmosphere becomes liquid. The point at which the atmosphere is totally filled is called **saturation**. When it is filled to overflowing, the condition is called **condensation**.

The dew point reflects the water vapor content in the air, and that water vapor influences the natural cooling mechanism of our bodies: sweating.

When the weather heats up, a gland in our brain called the hypothalamus tries to regulate the body temperature by setting off our 10 million sweat glands. Water, in the form of perspiration, springs up on our bodies. When that moisture evaporates, we cool down because the process of evaporation always extracts heat. Why do you think your skin feels cool when alcohol is rubbed on it? Because alcohol evaporates very rapidly.

If the air is filled with water vapor, it can't hold much additional water. So, when the dew point is high, the water vapor content is high, and less perspiration can evaporate into the air. Our bodies can't cool as effectively. Dew point readings in the 60s indicate moderately uncomfortable weather. When the dew point climbs over 70 degrees, the air becomes very uncomfortable, and as it approaches 80 degrees, it becomes tough to breathe, even for normally healthy people. Of course, when the temperature becomes high, the effect of a high dew point is magnified. The high temperature makes our bodies perspire, and the high dew point works against the natural cooling mechanism.

In hot weather, rapid water and salt loss can cause a chemical imbalance that leads to heat cramps. Additional water loss and increased temperature brings on heat exhaustion, which causes fatigue, headache, nausea, and even fainting. If the body temperature reaches 106 degrees, heat stroke becomes possible. The body completely shuts down, and this can be fatal.

Braving the Elements

The hottest temperature ever recorded in the United States occurred on July 10, 1913 at Greenland Ranch, California, where the temperature reached 134 degrees. In Libya, the world's highest temperature was recorded at 136 degrees. Based on an average annual temperature of 77.8 degrees, Key West, Florida, holds the distinction of being the hottest city in the United States. Miami is the second hottest with an average of 75.9 degrees. Yet, Chicago experiences more days with 90-degree temperatures than Miami. The U.S. city with the highest one-time recorded temperature is Phoenix, Arizona, with a blistering 118 degrees. In Europe, Seville takes the hot temperature honors with a 117-degree reading. And if you are planning to head for Djibouti, Djibouti (near Ethiopia), travel light. That west-African city has the distinction of being the hottest in the world, with an average temperature of 86 degrees.

A *heat index* is commonly used to describe comfort levels, and it combines temperature and humidity. The table on the next page shows that index and its effects. The index is represented by an apparent temperature, or what the air may feel like to most people because of the combination of temperature and moisture. That temperature is derived by combining the air temperature with the relative humidity, and the relationship is shown in the following figure.

For example, if the temperature is 90 degrees and the relative humidity is 50 percent, the heat index, or apparent temperature, is 93 degrees. At that level, the following table tells us that sunstroke, heat cramps, and exhaustion become possible with prolonged exposure and physical activity. What level of activity is dangerous really depends on the age and health of an individual, but for most people, an apparent temperature of 90 degrees sends a warning to slow down.

Weather-Speak

The **heat index** describes what the air feels like given the combination of temperature and humidity.

Heat index.

Relative Humidity (%)

Air Temperature (°F)	10	20	30	40	50	60	70	80	90	100
76		60	63	67	70	73	76	79	82	85
78		63	67	70	74	76	79	82	85	89
80	62	66	70	73	77	80	83	86	90	93
82	63	68	73	76	80	83	86	90	93	97
84	66	71	76	79	83	86	90	94	98	103
86	68	73	78	82	86	90	94	98	103	
88	70	76	81	85	89	93	98	102	108	
90	73	79	84	88	93	97	102	108		
92	75	82	87	91	96	101	106	112		
94	77	84	90	95	100	105	111			
96	79	87	93	98	103	110	116			
98	82	90	96	101	107	114				
100	85	92	99	105	111	118				
102	87	95	102	108	115	123				
104	90	98	106	112	120					

Apparent Temperature

Apparent temperature.

Relative Humidity (%)

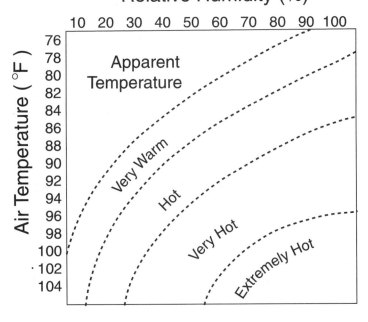

Apparent Temperature

Very Warm

Hot

Very Hot

Extremely Hot

You may not be roaming the countryside with charts and tables in your pocket, but if you plan to be physically active, you can at least keep an eye or ear to the weather people when they give the dew point. A dew point of 70 or more will deliver a heat index of near or over 90 degrees with even modest heating. Dew points that soar through the 70s will likely give a heat index of 100 or more. Dew points of 80 are just plain oppressive to everyone. Let that be an excuse to sit under a shady tree or go to an air-conditioned mall.

In the Clouds

Hopefully, all this talk about humidity hasn't put you in a fog—but that's the topic we discuss next. Fog is just a cloud that has touched the ground. It's one of 10 basic cloud types, and if you master those cloud forms, you can tell quite a bit about what the weather is up to. The clouds decorate the sky, and the patterns tell a story.

Cloud Formation

How do the clouds get there? Well, we are experts on humidity now, and it might seem that if the humidity climbs to 100 percent over a portion or slice of the atmosphere, condensation will take place, and clouds will have no choice but to form. Not so fast. There are some glitches along the way. For one, droplets are small and round. How small? About one ten-thousandth of an inch or less—microscopic. A powerful surface tension exists among the water molecules that form the small curved surfaces, and any vapor that goes into the liquid state must overcome this surface tension. That's not so easy. In fact, the force needed to overcome such tension is simply not available in the atmosphere. Left alone, water vapor would never form cloud droplets. There would never be clouds, there would never be rain, and I would be a pharmacist now like my mother wanted.

Dirt to the rescue! Or at least small, microscopic particles. Thanks to particles suspended in the air, cloud droplets are able to form. Certain *hygroscopic* particles, such as salt, attract water vapor. Even when the atmosphere looks crystal clear, these small particles float around us. In a volume that is no larger than an index finger, there are up to 150,000 of these particles, called *condensation nuclei*. Thanks to them, water vapor is able to overcome that curvature effect, condensation can take place, droplets form, and eventually, we have a rainy day. So many of these particles are present that cloud droplets can form at a relative humidity that is even slightly less than 100 percent. These particles are about one-one hundredth the size of cloud droplets, and they come from smokestacks, volcanoes, forest fires, and ocean spray. The following figure shows the spectrum of sizes between these tiny nuclei, cloud droplets, and raindrops.

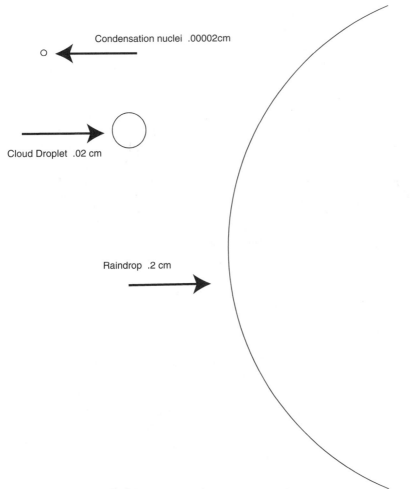

Condensation nuclei .00002cm

Cloud Droplet .02 cm

Raindrop .2 cm

Spectrum of atmospheric elements.

Cloud Classification

The first effort to make some order out of the patterns in the sky occurred in the very early nineteenth century. The French naturalist Lamarck first introduced a system, but shortly after, an English chemist, Luke Howard, worked on a scheme that became widely accepted. Howard became known as the "father of British meteorology" and his pioneering work won him all kinds of distinctions, including having a poem written for him by Goethe. In those days, Latin was big, and Howard's system was based on four major cloud types named according to the way they looked. Toward the end of the century, Howard's original system was expanded into 10 principal cloud forms, and

21

Weather-Speak

Cirrus clouds are thin, wispy, high clouds. **Stratus** comes from the Latin meaning "layer"; these clouds are flat and stay close to the ground. **Cumulus** comes from the Latin for "puffy." Those are the fleecy-looking clouds that paint the sky on a pleasant, quiet day. **Nimbus** comes from the Latin for "rain-bearing." Any cloud that delivers rain is a nimbus cloud.

Weather-Wise

Since the late 1950s, clouds have been observed by satellites. Two types of satellites look down on our clouds: POES (Polar Orbiting Environmental Satellites) and GOES (Geostationary Orbiting Environmental Satellites). The POES move around the poles. The GOES provide the pictures for television weather shows. They move around the earth at the same speed that the earth rotates, so they seem to hover over one location above the earth, near the equator at a height of 23,000 miles.

that classification scheme has remained essentially unchanged for the past 100 years.

The four basic cloud types are *cirrus, stratus, cumulus,* and *nimbus.* Cirrus comes from the Latin for "thin," "wispy," or "curl of hair." And that is how cirrus clouds appear from the ground. Sometimes they are called mare's tails. They are high clouds, consisting of ice crystals because they are at elevations of 20,000 feet and higher. At those heights, water droplets freeze into ice crystals. These clouds often tell us that change is on the way. A storm may be approaching, or warmer air could be knocking on the door. Stratus comes from the Latin meaning "layer." These clouds are flat and stay close to the ground. Cumulus comes from the Latin for "puffy." Those are the fleecy-looking clouds that help paint the sky on a pleasant, quiet day. But these clouds are noted for their strong vertical development. They can form towers, and when they do, watch out. The sky can open up into a violent thunderstorm. Nimbus comes from the Latin for "rain-bearing." Any cloud that delivers rain is a nimbus cloud.

These are the four basic cloud types. There are also combinations that show up at different elevations. The classification scheme that so far has been based solely on a cloud's appearance now becomes a little more sophisticated. The types are combined and categorized into groups of high, middle, low clouds, and clouds that extend through all elevations.

Ten Major Cloud Types

In Biblical times, Job asked, "Can any understand the spreadings of the clouds?" We're certainly trying. In modern times, we understand that clouds represent the basic building blocks to our weather. The foundation consists of 10 major cloud types. In addition to cirrus, stratus, cumulus, and nimbus clouds, there are cirrostratus, cirrocumulus, altostratus, altocumulus, stratocumulus, nimbostratus, and cumulonimbus clouds. The following table places these cloud types into the four major cloud groups.

Major Cloud Groups

Cloud Group	Cloud Type
High clouds	Cirrus
	Cirrostratus
	Cirrocumulus
Middle Clouds	Altostratus
	Altocumulus
Low Clouds	Stratus
	Stratocumulus
	Nimbostratus
Clouds with Vertical Development	Cumulus
	Cumulonimbus

High Clouds

These clouds are found at elevations of 20,000 feet (6,000 meters) and higher. The cold air at these elevations causes the small cloud droplets to freeze into ice crystals. Actually, because the droplets are so small, they can exist in liquid form below 32 degrees, and they are called supercooled. The ice crystals act as prisms and cause light to separate into its many colors. High clouds can deliver some spectacular optical effects, including a red sky in the morning and at night. Cirrus clouds are in this grouping, and these are joined by *cirrostratus* clouds, which appear as thin sheets across the sky. The thin, feathery cirrus clouds thicken to form cirrostratus. The Sun or the Moon will shine through cirrostratus and often form a halo. Cirrus clouds can also thicken into small, rounded cotton-ball-like masses, the *cirrocumulus* clouds. Sometimes these look like scales of a fish, so a sky filled with cirrocumulus is called a "mackerel sky." When a storm advances, these high clouds are first to arrive. They are great clues to impending weather changes.

Warm air often streams ahead of storms, and this warm, less dense air is forced to rise over colder surface air. That warmer air can extend a thousand miles from a particular storm center, and as it rises to great heights, it cools and forms the high clouds. First those thin, wispy cirrus clouds appear. Then they thicken to cirrostratus and cirrocumulus. At that point, halos and rings form around the Sun

Weather-Watch

The earliest sky watchers said, "Mackerel sky and mare's tails make lofty ships carry low sails." The mare's tails are the cirrus clouds, which, combined with cirrocumulus, often indicate the approach of wind and rain—so it's time for the low sails. Other variations include, "Mackerel scales, furl your sails," and, "A mackerel sky, not twenty-four hours dry."

and Moon, and storms can be just 24 hours away. Later, as the storm grows closer, the clouds thicken and begin to lower.

Middle Clouds

Generally, middle clouds form at elevations ranging from about 6,500 feet (2,000 meters) to 20,000 feet (6,000 meters). Because these clouds are lower than the high-flying type, they can consist of both water droplets and ice crystals. The "alto" clouds fall in this category: *altostratus* and *altocumulus*.

The altostratus clouds are similar to cirrostratus except that they are thicker and lower. More of the Sun or Moon will be obscured. Unlike cirrostratus, these clouds do not produce halos, and enough light is obscured to produce few, if any, shadows on the ground.

Likewise, altocumulus clouds are thicker and lower versions of cirrocumulus. The tiny cotton ball appearance thickens into larger round masses, and because of the thickness, the sky appears gray rather than white. After the high cirrus clouds give way to this middle group of clouds, we know that rain is only a few hours away.

Weather Words

There is a proverb that says, *"Every cloud has a silver lining."*

Low Clouds

These clouds form at elevations below 6,500 feet (2,000 meters) and consist mostly of water, except during the winter when snow becomes a possibility. Stratus clouds, which are the fog clouds, fall into this category. When low stratus clouds begin to deliver rain, they are called *nimbostratus*. This cloud is dark, gray, and appears flat at the base. The storm has arrived when nimbostratus appears. The precipitation is steady, not showery. Usually, the rain will come down at a light to moderate rate, and it will last a good part of the day, or even longer. When nimbostratus appears, it's time to curl up with a big, thick, Russian novel.

Sometimes, stratus clouds form rounded, puffy masses, and these clouds are called *stratocumulus*. These differ from altocumulus because there are larger round masses, and the sky can appear very dark and ominous. These clouds are the most difficult to determine—whenever I can't exactly figure out what a particular cloud is, it turns out to be stratocumulus. It can be confused with other low cloud types. Stratocumulus will often form when a stratus layer is heated, and the atmosphere begins to overturn. That process of overturning from heating is called *convection,* and it becomes an important factor in the next category of clouds.

Foggy Notions

First, though, let's look at a unique cousin of the cloud. Fog is a form of stratus cloud. Although fog can creep along on little cat feet, many types of fog exist.

The basic mechanism that causes fog is simply anything that can bring the relative humidity up to 100 percent. Usually, when the air cools to the dew point, fog will roll in. That cooling may occur during a clear, calm night. The accumulated heat of the day will radiate from the earth, and the temperature near the ground cools. It could cool all the way down to the dew point. That type of fog is called *radiation fog* because it is brought about by *radiational cooling*—by cooling caused by the radiating of heat from the ground. This type of fog frequently forms in valleys, because there the wind has the best chance of being light. If the wind is gusty, that type of fog will not form because the atmosphere remains mixed, and will not likely cool as easily to the dew point.

Another type of fog occurs when warm air is brought over a colder surface. The warm air will be cooled on contact with the colder surface, and as its temperature lowers to the dew point, fog will develop. This fog often appears during a winter thaw when warm air streams over a frozen or snow-covered surface. Fog is often said to be a great snow-eater. But it doesn't come along and chomp away at the snow. The warm air, which contributes to the fog, melts the snow away.

Fog that develops over the ocean and in coastal areas often forms in a similar way. Warm air streams over a colder ocean surface. As soon as the air is cooled to its dew point, fog will shroud the ocean surface and adjacent shores. If the air is tropical with plenty of water vapor and a high dew point, it will not take much to cool it to its dew point. (Of course, if the water is cold, that also helps.) Early summer is a favorite time for coastal fog. This entire fog category is called *advection fog* because warm air is advected, or brought to, colder regions.

Weather Words

"When clouds appear like rocks and towers,
The earth's refreshed by frequent showers.
When mountains and cliffs in the clouds appear,
Some sudden and violent showers are near."

—G. Herbert

Clouds with Vertical Development

So far, we have looked at clouds that can be found at specific levels of the atmosphere. There are others that can be found extending through all elevations, and these are the ones associated with strong upward atmospheric currents. These updrafts spread the moisture through a large column of the atmosphere, and the clouds appear to have a puffy, even tower-like structure. Convection plays a big role in delivering these updrafts. In fact, these clouds are often called *convective clouds,* and the rain that falls from them is frequently referred to as *convective precipitation.* Just like a boiling pot of water, the atmosphere can cook on a hot summer's day, causing these convective clouds to appear. The precipitation is often heavy, but not necessarily long-lasting. As they say, "The sharper the rain, the shorter the shower."

The basic cumulus clouds fall into this category. Sometimes these puffy clouds are limited in vertical development. They look innocent enough and take on different shapes. These are fair-weather clouds, and just the normal heating of the day is enough to set the stage for these clouds to pop up overhead. But on other occasions, the upward motions are large and the cumulus clouds develop towers, which can cluster and grow into a full-blown thunderstorm within an hour. Those towering cumulus clouds that deliver rain, lightning, and thunder are called cumulonimbus. They can extend from just a few thousand feet above the ground to levels of 50,000 feet or higher. The bigger they grow, the more violent the weather becomes. Hail will often fall from these clouds. Even tornadoes are possible when cumulonimbus clouds appear.

Weather Words

"It sits looking over the harbor and city on silent haunches and then moves on."

—"Fog," Carl Sandburg

Weather-Wise

If you want an inexpensive radar for thunderous occasions, try an AM-band radio. Even before those towers develop into rip-roaring thunderstorms, static will be given off that can be picked up on the AM-band, especially in the low frequencies, between stations. It really works, and after a while, you'll be able to relate the intensity of the static to the proximity of the storm.

Forecasting by Clouds

I'm constantly looking at the sky. Sure, the computer offers a lot of information and insight, but the first step in any forecast is observation. How does the sky appear? Is it deep blue or is it hazy? That immediately tells me about the humidity, because with increasing moisture, the sky will lose its ability to scatter blue light. As the humidity increases, the sky has that hazy appearance.

Are cirrus clouds drifting by? That by itself is okay, but if the cirrus clouds appear to be thickening into cirrostratus on the western horizon, I know changes are about to occur. And if the thicker cirrostratus covers the sky, and if that gives way to cirrocumulus, I would bet my last thermometer that something is up. The changes might indicate a warming trend or that some rain is a short 24 hours away. If the clouds continue to lower to those altostratus and altocumulus types, without knowing anything else, I would take out the umbrella.

Of course, sometimes the sky doesn't give solid clues, and we must wait to see more before we can confidently predict the weather's next moves. For example, there will be days when innocent-looking cumulus clouds appear during the middle or late morning. The clouds seem to be capable of doing absolutely no wrong. But then, without much notice, the cumulus clouds develop into towers, and that is when we should begin to pay attention. Thunderstorms can rapidly form. These convective storms do not announce their arrival 24 or 36 hours in advance—they're not bringing your normal rainy day. But if the dew point is in the 60s or above, and those cumulus clouds start building towers by late morning, I would pay attention to the sky throughout the day.

The following table gives you the lowdown on how you can forecast the weather based on cloud appearance.

Cloud Type	Description	Forecast
Cirrus	Scattered, high thin clouds	Mostly fair, but watch for cirrostratus or altostratus
Cirrostratus and altostratus	Halo around Sun or Moon, sometimes a rainbow effect	Precipitation within 24 hours if clouds are increasing; if clouds are decreasing, Moon becomes more discernible, skies clearing
Cumulus	Scattered puffy clouds	Fair
Cumulus congestus	Cumulus increasing and covering sky, also forming in towers	Showers within 2–4 hours
Cumulonimbus	Tall, mountainous clouds with a flat anvil top	Rain, thunderstorm imminent
Cirrocumulus and altocumulus	High, puffy, cotton-ball-shaped clouds	Precipitation within 12–24 hours if increasing and accompanied by cirrostratus and altostratus clouds
Jet contrails	Trails of condensed vapor from high-flying jets	Fair weather, but watch for increasing cirrus or cirrostratus
Mammatus	Puffy rolls of dark clouds, frequently at the bottom of a cumulonimbus cloud	Violent thunderstorms, even tornadoes, are imminent; watch for rotation
Stratocumulus	Long, dark, rolling cloud; no precipitation with it	Remaining overcast, or slow clearing
Stratus	Low cloud upon ground, or fog	No precipitation by itself; clearing likely if fog developed overnight; otherwise, remaining cloudy

Air-pressure trends and wind are also important, and later we will explore those variables. But if you know your cloud types, it's like knowing your chords if you want to play jazz. It's a good beginning.

The Least You Need to Know

➤ The relative humidity increases with decreasing temperature.

➤ The dew point is a good index of comfort level.

➤ Excessive heat and humidity have claimed thousands of lives.

➤ Cloud droplets form on microscopic nuclei.

➤ Ten major cloud types make up much of what we see overhead.

➤ Different cloud forms provide different clues of upcoming weather.

Chapter 3

Bring On the Rain

In This Chapter

➤ Good to the last droplet

➤ Droplets that stick together, fall together

➤ Raindrops on ice

➤ Not just raining on our parade

"The rain it raineth every day, upon the just and unjust feller, but mostly on the just, because the unjust hath the just's umbrella." Umbrellas aside, rain is very democratic. In general, the weather is a great equalizer, and although a rainy day isn't always welcomed, that rain can serve many purposes. As the ancient weather watchers said, "Some rain, some rest. Fine weather isn't always the best." We can't live by sunshine alone.

In this chapter, we try to get a handle on the precipitation process. We'll "pore" over both the natural and the artificial rainmaking techniques. Most importantly, we learn why it really does rain, and given the complexity of this topic, that's quite an accomplishment.

Droplet to Drop...How Rain Happens

In Chapter 2 we discussed how clouds form. Our next challenge is to understand how clouds turn into rainmakers. Thanks to those microscopic condensation nuclei, clouds form. Condensation allows droplets to grow to a size of about .001 inch, or about .002 centimeter. But a raindrop can be a hundred, even a thousand times larger. Cloud droplets have a lot of growing to do to approach rainmaker status. It takes about one million cloud droplets to deliver a single raindrop. If the relative humidity is high enough, those droplets could grow to a full-sized drop.

But there is a problem with the obvious. Those cumulus clouds could grow into a rip-roaring downpour within an hour. Yet, the condensation process alone would take days to generate drops large and heavy enough to fall. Something else is needed. If no other process was at work, we might have clouds, but we would never have rain. Water, water everywhere, but not a drop falls down. We need to find a process that will allow droplets to grow at least a hundred-fold in the time frame of a single hour.

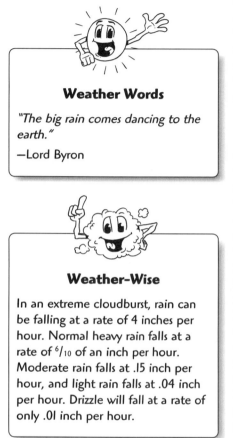

Weather Words

"The big rain comes dancing to the earth."

—Lord Byron

Weather-Wise

In an extreme cloudburst, rain can be falling at a rate of 4 inches per hour. Normal heavy rain falls at a rate of $^6/_{10}$ of an inch per hour. Moderate rain falls at .15 inch per hour, and light rain falls at .04 inch per hour. Drizzle will fall at a rate of only .01 inch per hour.

Let's See What Sticks

One natural rainmaking process involves the joining together, or *coalescence,* of the small droplets. Little droplets stick together and become bigger droplets, until they're heavy enough to fall to the ground. That sounds easy enough, but because of the way air streams around small objects, if the droplets are less than .002 centimeter, the efficiency of collision becomes very small. The following figure shows that air stream. A large droplet might approach a smaller one, but it does not necessarily collide because of the air motion, especially if the large droplet isn't much bigger. The smaller one just deflects the bigger one. Unfortunately, in most clouds over land areas, only one in every 10 million droplets is initially at that .002-centimeter threshold level. Over the oceans, giant salt nuclei do generate larger cloud droplets, and coalescence works quite well. But over land masses, where most of us live, it would never rain. So...why does it rain?

Air stream over droplets.

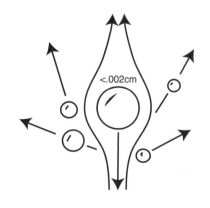

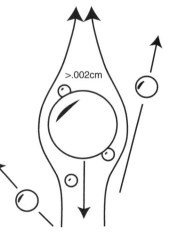

Ice to the Rescue

Ice acts as a magnet for water vapor. Ice really is nice. When ice crystals are around, water vapor thinks the relative humidity is 10 to 20 percent higher than when just water droplets are in the neighborhood. Toss ice into a cloud, and suddenly the pressure of the vapor becomes so great that it simply rushes onto the surface of the ice, and the crystal grows rapidly—until it becomes sufficiently heavy to fall. It could melt during descent, and if so, it would turn into a large droplet that more easily coalesces with smaller ones. The ice crystals get the droplet to grow initially, and then coalescence takes over.

Weather-Speak

Coalescence is the joining together of small droplets into larger droplets.

Is There Enough Ice?

Well, not exactly. (There's always a problem, isn't there?) Water droplets don't form ice just because the temperature is at 32 degrees Fahrenheit or 0 degrees Celsius. If the droplets are microscopic, they can stay in liquid form at temperatures as low as 40 below; which, by the way, is where the Fahrenheit temperature scale matches the Celsius one. Clouds aren't necessarily cold enough. Ice may be just what we need for droplet growth, but there appears to be a shortage of ice within clouds. But come on! It *does* rain. So, something else must be going on.

Fortunately for reservoirs and wells, that 40-below-freezing threshold only exists for *pure* water—and since when is water really pure? Thanks to suspended particles, the temperature at which liquid droplets freeze within clouds is closer to 12 below Celsius or 10 degrees Fahrenheit, which is far more attainable at cloud elevation. So, it rains! But if the atmosphere were absolutely crystal clear and pure, it simply would never rain.

Weather-Wise

The first person to break the ice on this theory was Alfred Wegener, of continental-drift fame, in the early 1900s. In the 1930s, it was refined by Swedish meteorologist Tor Bergeron. Within a few years, German meteorologist Walter Findeison made additional contributions. So, the ice-nucleation theory has become known as the Wegener-Bergeron-Findeison process. Sometimes it's called the Bergeron process for short.

Types of Precipitation

Precipitation can take on many different forms. The temperature plays a major role in determining the various types of precipitation, and also important are the motions within the atmosphere. Raindrops aren't the only elements that could be falling upon our heads.

31

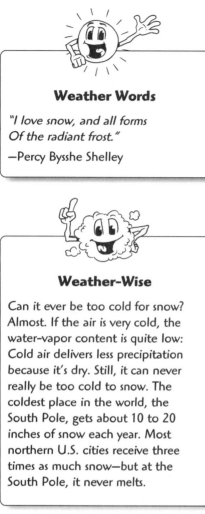

Weather Words

*"I love snow, and all forms
Of the radiant frost."*

—Percy Bysshe Shelley

Weather-Wise

Can it ever be too cold for snow? Almost. If the air is very cold, the water-vapor content is quite low: Cold air delivers less precipitation because it's dry. Still, it can never really be too cold to snow. The coldest place in the world, the South Pole, gets about 10 to 20 inches of snow each year. Most northern U.S. cities receive three times as much snow—but at the South Pole, it never melts.

Weather-Speak

Sleet is frozen rain and occurs during the winter. As rain falls into a cold layer near the ground, it sometimes will refreeze into ice pellets. That's sleet.

Snow

Precipitation can take many forms. Ice crystals can link to each other and form snowflakes. John Burroughs once said, "I was born with a chronic anxiety about the weather." Most people share that anxiety, and—once you're out of school—few elements of weather bring on as much anxiety as snow. Although snow is beautiful, it is disruptive to traffic and communities. My own students who work part-time at grocery stores say they can tell how much snow I'm predicting based on the length of the checkout lines. The perceived need for loaves of bread and quarts of milk is directly proportional to the amount of snow that is in the forecast.

Snow has been a focus of study for centuries. In the sixteenth century, Swedish historian Olaus Magnus was the first to study individual snow crystals. Later, Descartes and even Kepler studied the shapes and sizes of snowflakes. But not until the turn of the twentieth century did William Bentley put together a detailed catalogue of snowflake forms. Bentley was an American farmer who was completely fascinated by snowflakes, and from age 20, he dedicated 40 years of his life to building a collection of 6,000 photographs of snow crystals—all different. An infinite variety of crystal shapes exists. Two snowflakes can look alike, but there is no shortage of different forms. Temperature and humidity determine the shape of snowflakes, along with the nature of the nuclei around which the crystals form.

Sleet and Hail

These two elements are confused more than any other precipitation types. Both are pieces of ice, but there are major differences between the two. If rain freezes into pellets while falling to the ground, those pellets are called *sleet*. Sleet occurs in the winter when warm air streams over a cold layer. Rain falls from the warm layer, then the drops pass through a shallow freezing layer that isn't exceptionally cold, so snowflakes are unable to form—just those pellets. During many winter storms, the precipitation will begin as snow, but as the warm air reaches overhead, the snow changes to sleet. As the warmer air becomes even more dominant, the sleet changes to rain. Just before the change from snow to sleet, the snowflakes become thick and heavy.

Braving the Elements

In an attempt to control hail, in 1896 Albert Stiger, Austrian wine grower, invented a hail cannon, which consisted of a cast-iron mortar. A metal smokestack was attached to the muzzle to act as a sound box that would increase the noise even more. Stiger's hail cannon became popular throughout the world because of the apparent diminishing of hailstorms during the first season of operations in Austria. By 1900, 7,000 of these devices were in use in northern Italy alone. During that year, 11 deaths and 60 serious injuries were attributed to the hail explosions. By 1902, the concept was discredited after two years of intensive barrages by the Austrian and Italian governments. Both areas experienced disastrous storms during those years of explosive experimentation.

Sleet is quite different from *hail,* which is a warm-weather phenomenon. Hail forms when ice slowly descends through a cumulonimbus cloud. Strong updrafts allow layer after layer of ice to build up until the hail becomes so heavy that it overcomes the updrafts and falls to the ground. The hail can be tossed around the clouds as well, between melting and freezing layers, so layers of clear and opaque ice form—something like an onion skin.

Freezing Rain

When rain freezes on contact with surfaces that are below freezing, it's called "freezing rain." The air may be warm aloft, too warm for snow or sleet. But because of a stubborn cold wind at ground level, the rain forms a sheet of ice on the ground. A glaze of ice coats roads and walkways. When the ice build-up becomes extensive, widespread power outages occur. The weight of the ice can cause tree limbs to break as well as power lines.

Weather-Speak

Hail forms in thunderstorms when small ice crystals collect vapor and slowly descend through the cloud. Strong updrafts allow the ice particle to remain suspended for long periods and it can grow to a large size. Because of the turbulence within a thunderstorm cloud, these ice particles can be tossed up and down, allowing successive layers of ice to form.

Braving the Elements

During the winter of 1997–98, historic ice storms struck northern New England and Canada. Millions were without power for weeks when a stream of tropical air spread northward while a very shallow pool of cold air hung tough at the ground. Another record-setting ice storm occurred in the Northeast in December 1973. During that storm, the temperature ranged from 20 degrees at ground level to 50 degrees at 5,000 feet. That storm provided the setting for a 1997 film named, you guessed it, *The Ice Storm.* Kevin Kline and *Sigourney Weaver* starred in the film.

Fooling the Clouds

Now that we have a handle on the processes nature uses in delivering a rainy day, what about those artificial rainmaking efforts? Do they really work?

In days of old, prior to the twentieth century, rainmaking efforts involved the ringing of bells, the explosive firing of cannons, ritual drum beating, and dancing. Sometimes the rain came—just often enough for people to keep trying. Hail cannons were exploded in Europe, and even earlier, Native American tribes made rain dances famous, but these rainmaking efforts had already been going on for centuries by groups of people from all over the world. Armies have fallen and civilizations have risen based on the success or failure of these efforts.

In modern times, weather modification methods haven't been quite so explosive. Based on the concept that "ice is nice," in the early 1940s, Vincent Schaefer, an atmospheric physicist, tried to produce more ice crystals in the clouds. How did he do that?

Well, dry ice, which is frozen carbon dioxide, has a temperature of more than 100 degrees below zero. So, if dry ice is put into a cloud, the cloud's temperature will be lowered enough to cause ice crystals to appear even if ice nuclei aren't present in abundant quantities. At first, big chunks of dry ice were tossed out of airplanes. Predictably, they just crashed to the ground—sometimes through roofs. Later, the ice was crushed into small pieces and sprayed into the cloud. It worked! (Sort of.)

Weather-Watch

The single costliest hailstorm in U.S. history occurred in 1990 in Denver, Colorado, where damage came to $600–$700 million. In 1984 in Munich, Germany, a hailstorm caused one billion dollars' worth of damage. The largest documented hailstone occurred in Coffeyville, Kansas, on September 3, 1970. The hail weighed 1.67 pounds and it measured 7.5 inches.

At first, the planes would fly figure-8 formations through the cloud, and the droplets would fall, leaving the shape of an eight.

Braving the Elements

Sometimes, the rainmaking efforts seemed a bit *too* successful. During the early 1900s, San Diego was suffering a punishing drought when a self-proclaimed rainmaker came into town promising results. The city hired J. S. Stingo, whose device seemed to produce more rain than anyone had ever imagined. The skies opened up, flash flooding occurred, and Stingo was run out of town—and sued. The entire experience became the focus of a play, and later a movie, *The Rainmaker,* starring Burt Lancaster.

On the very day after Schaefer's first dry-ice experiment in a cloud, Bernard Vonnegut, brother of famed writer Kurt Vonnegut, figured out that a certain chemical, silver iodide, has crystal faces similar to real ice. He proposed that if silver iodide were sprayed into a cloud, the cloud would think that ice is present, and the tiny water vapor molecules would quickly attach themselves to the crystals. He was right. Even if extremely low temperatures were not present, ice would quickly form on the silver iodide, and then the natural precipitation process could do its thing. Coalescence would become possible as the ice crystal and droplet size rapidly increased. The silver iodide served as a magnet for water vapor, just as if ice were present. The cloud was "fooled" into raining!

Silver iodide could be sprayed into a cloud from generators at ground level, or injected into clouds from planes. It was easier to work with than dry ice, and became widely used in experiments through the 1950s and 1960s. But there is one problem with silver iodide: If the crystal faces are exposed to the Sun, they lose their magical attracting properties.

Age of Experimentation

The concept of fooling a cloud into raining caught on very quickly, and numerous rainmaking experiments were conducted for more than 25 years. Although the theory was solid, the reality was a little different. Sometimes, rain did occur. Changes always seemed to happen, but the changes were temporary, and the question always remained whether that rain would have occurred naturally. The most optimistic experiments showed a 10- to 30-percent increase in rainfall following *cloud seeding.* That could be significant, especially in areas short of water. But overall, the results have been mixed, and while scientists can modify clouds, their ability to make it rain at will leaves a lot to be desired.

Cloud-seeding experiments have included more than rainmaking. Hail, which generates about one billion dollars' worth of damage each year in the United States, has been the object of considerable study. The idea has been to generate numerous smaller hailstones rather than the fewer large ones that cause the damage. In theory, more ice crystals would mean less water vapor for the bigger, chunky hailstones, but in practice, after seeding, clouds sometimes generated more and bigger hail.

Hurricane seeding experiments have also had mixed results. The concept has been to generate rain outside the steamy core of the storm. That rain generation would release heat and cause the pressure distribution of the storm to become less organized. Without a central hot core, the storm should weaken. But again, the results haven't been clear. Sometimes, the storm diminished in intensity, and other times, it actually increased. After decades of experimentation, the hurricane modification work was discontinued. The project is discussed further in Chapter 7.

Weather-Speak

Cloud seeding is a process that introduces silver iodide or dry ice into a cloud for producing rain. **Hurricane seeding** places silver iodide into the clouds just outside the eye wall of the storm. The eye wall is the ring of squalls wrapped around the center of the hurricane. This seeding is an attempt to diffuse the storm's winds.

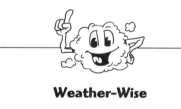

Weather-Wise

In the 1960s, one seeded hurricane eventually hit Cuba, and the Cuban government accused the CIA of plotting the entire event.

Raining on Our Parade

Although early rainmaking experiments offered some promise, they yielded confusing and disappointing results. We're a long way off in making it rain, or not rain, on somebody's parade. And in modification experiments, the socioeconomic questions always lead to plenty of debate. During a severe drought in New York during the 1960s, resort owners in the Catskill mountains sued New York City for its rainmaking efforts. The city needed more water in the storage areas of upstate New York, but in that region, resort owners wanted those sunny days! In Pennsylvania, weather modification experiments have been banned. More than half the states in the United States have laws controlling the weather controllers.

So Why Does It Rain?

Wait a minute! After all this, we still don't know why it rains? Talk about beating around the bush! I guess that's what you'd expect from someone who's been a college professor for three decades. But we're almost there.

In order for it to rain, the air must be saturated: The relative humidity must be 100 percent, or very close to it. How does that happen? By lowering the temperature, or bringing in more water vapor. But if we just bring in more water vapor, and nothing else happens, we're still just stuck with microscopic droplets. So, let's focus on lowering the temperature. The temperature can be lowered by a colder wind, possibly coming from the north. But those north winds contain less water vapor, so the temperature may lower, but the humidity could remain the same.

Braving the Elements

How hard can it rain? Very hard! On June 22, 1947, 12 inches of rain fell in just 42 minutes over Holt, Missouri. That is about 25 percent of the normal annual rainfall for Holt, and it happened in less than an hour. On July 4, 1956, 1.23 inches of rain fell in just 60 seconds in Unionville, Maryland. On July 3, 1976, 10 inches of rain fell in four hours across Big Thompson Canyon, Colorado. Flash flooding killed 80 people. On June 9, 1972, 15 inches of rain fell in five hours over the Black Hills of North Dakota. More than 200 people were swept away by the waters. In Calama, Chile, no rain fell for 400 years, then, on February 10, 1972, the skies opened up during the mid-afternoon. Catastrophic floods and mud slides swept through that region. The wettest inhabited location in the world is Buenaventura, Colombia, where an average of 265.47 inches of rain falls each year. The driest inhabited location is Aswan, Egypt, where the average annual rainfall comes to just .02 inch.

The temperature could also be lowered if a column of air *rises*. As an air column rises, there is less atmosphere around it and the pressure outside the column is reduced. So, the column expands as it goes up. That expansion will lower the temperature because the air molecules will not hit each other as frequently. Eventually, the relative humidity will reach 100 percent, and the rising column loses no water vapor. Rising air seems to be the surest way of getting a cloud to form.

Also, as the air rises, the moisture is distributed over a wide region. There are plenty of droplets available for coalescence, and if the rising takes the cloud to great heights, ice will form—even during the summer, even in tropical latitudes. So, rising air delivers the best environment for cloud droplets to grow into raindrops. The figure on the next page shows the dynamics involved with natural rainmaking.

And that is the message of this chapter, even this book. Upward motions make rain happen, and the faster the air goes up, the harder the rain comes down. Everything else that occurs within the atmosphere simply builds on this basic principle.

Rising air and rain.

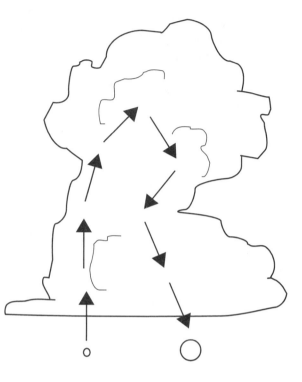

Those Ups and Downs

The following table shows the range of upward motions for different weather phenomena. A typical rainy day might be generated by relatively gentle upward motion—a couple centimeters per second. That would normally occur over 12 or 24 hours, possibly longer. The intensity of the precipitation would be directly related to the magnitude of that rising motion. The sky would first be covered by cirrus clouds, which would then thicken, lower, and eventually lead to nimbostratus clouds.

Weather with Associated Rising Currents

Particle Type	Upward Velocity (m/sec)
Condensation Nuclei	0.0000001
Cloud Droplet	0.01
Large Cloud Droplet	0.27
Drizzle	0.70
Small raindrop	4.0
Average raindrop	6.5
Large raindrop	9.0

In contrast to this slow and gentle process, the upward motions can be violent in those tall, cumulonimbus clouds that bring thunderstorms and even tornadoes. The vertical velocity can be a thousand times greater—20 meters per second, or 40 miles per hour—with updrafts approaching 100 miles per hour. Large hail takes shape in these clouds because the upward motion keeps the ice suspended for an extended time and the ice has a chance to build up. Eventually, it has no choice but to fall.

Of course, if the air motions are downward, the sky is clear and the weather is dry. Spells of bright weather are directly related to that subsiding motion. Instead of condensation taking place, evaporation occurs. Ahead of a storm, the air is rising, but after the storm passes, the atmosphere is sinking, which is why skies clear soon after a storm center moves away. *Subsidence* is not without its weather headaches. If the atmosphere always sinks, desert conditions will prevail. The desert zones around the earth occur where the air is sinking. Also, serious air-pollution levels appear when subsidence is present. Air pollutants are unable to rise through the stable atmosphere created by the subsidence.

We can explain much about the weather just by knowing the nature of the atmosphere's vertical motion. Throughout the coming chapters, we take a look at the mechanisms that cause that upward and downward motion to occur. But if you close this book without learning anything else, be assured that you now understand a lot about meteorology. You know why it rains.

Weather-Speak

Subsidence is the sinking of air, usually associated with a high pressure area.

The Least You Need to Know

➤ The weather turns rainy when the air rises.

➤ The intensity of a storm is directly related to the strength of the vertical motions.

➤ An entire spectrum of upward motions exists for different types of weather.

➤ The growth of small droplets into raindrops is a process that has obstacles along the way.

➤ Rainmaking experiments have had mixed results.

Chapter 4

Going in Circles

In This Chapter

➤ Kicking up a storm

➤ Highs and lows of weather

➤ Putting a spin on the weather

➤ Storms of all sizes

➤ The wild weather of the naughty nineties

Now that you understand why the sky is blue and why it rains, you are, without question, more meteorological than most. You are at least ready to stand in front of a camera, point to a blank blue wall, and smile. After all, that's what we television people make a career doing. Benjamin Franklin once said, "Some people are weather wise, and some are otherwise." *You* are no longer in that "otherwise" category.

The next big step is to look at how the atmosphere puts it all together. In many respects, meteorology is not only a study of things that bump in the night—and day— but a study of things that go in circles. Those circles come in many different sizes, and the nature of the weather that's unleashed really depends on the circles that are put into motion. But through it all, there is one common theme: If the atmosphere goes up, the rain comes down. We'll look at how the weather twist contributes to those ups and downs.

Storms 'R' Us

The earth is a storm factory, where monsoons, hurricanes or typhoons, tornadoes, and blizzards are all made fresh daily. Thanks to unequal heating between the equator and

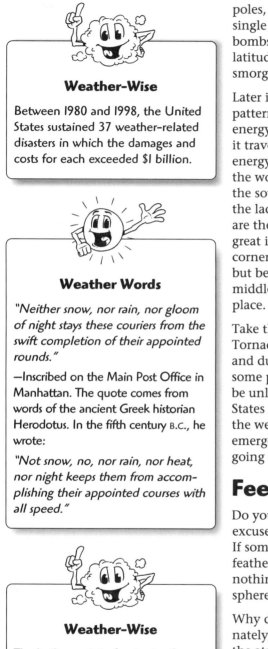

Weather-Wise

Between 1980 and 1998, the United States sustained 37 weather-related disasters in which the damages and costs for each exceeded $1 billion.

Weather Words

"Neither snow, nor rain, nor gloom of night stays these couriers from the swift completion of their appointed rounds."

—Inscribed on the Main Post Office in Manhattan. The quote comes from words of the ancient Greek historian Herodotus. In the fifth century B.C., he wrote:

"Not snow, no, nor rain, nor heat, nor night keeps them from accomplishing their appointed courses with all speed."

Weather-Wise

The boiling point of water is a function of pressure. At the surface, water boils at 212 degrees. But at 100,000 feet, water boils at only 40 degrees.

poles, phenomenal amounts of energy are unleashed. A single thunderstorm has the power of *millions* of nuclear bombs. The production never ceases, and in mid-latitudes, where most people live, the atmospheric smorgasbord offers quite a variety.

Later in this book we'll focus on global-circulation patterns, but for now, think of it this way: All the heat energy taken in at the equator has to go someplace, and it travels toward the poles. The greatest exchange of that energy takes place at around 45 degrees latitude, near the world's population centers. So, all the excess heat of the southern latitudes must travel 45 degrees to balance the lack of heat in the polar regions. The mid-latitudes are the Times Square of the atmosphere. Through this great intersection, everything must pass. Sure, every corner of the earth experiences wild and wacky weather, but because of the meteorological intersection across the middle, every conceivable form of weather will take place.

Take the United States. Everything happens here: Tornadoes, floods, hurricanes, snowstorms, hailstorms, and dust storms are all part of our normal weather. In some parts of the nation, the entire weather glossary can be unleashed in a single year. The northeastern United States is especially vulnerable to just about anything the weather might cook up. A former director of an emergency-operations center once said to me, "If it's going to happen, it will happen here."

Feeling the Pressure

Do you grow tired at the end of the day? I have an excuse for you. Blame it on the atmospheric pressure. If something floats, it's supposed to be lighter than a feather, but the atmosphere is floating, and there's nothing feathery about it: Ten to twenty *tons* of atmosphere rests on the average adult.

Why don't we collapse under such pressure? Fortunately, our bodies exert from within an equal pressure to the atmosphere. So, 10 tons of air may be resting on you, but another 10 tons are pushing outward from inside your body. Nobody really collapses, and hardly anyone is even aware of the heavy air. But if you had an operation, an injury, or maybe a connective-tissue disease (such as arthritis), your body might not be in exact, natural balance with the surroundings. You really can feel it when the pressure changes within the atmosphere. The following figure shows that balance.

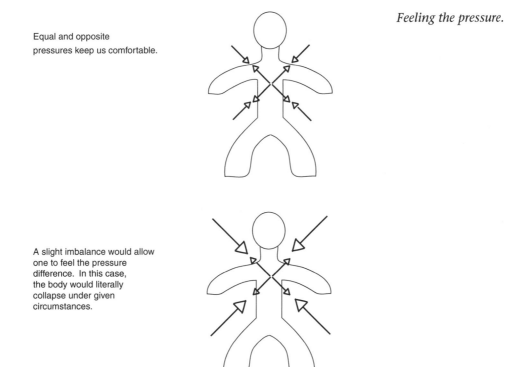

Feeling the pressure.

Equal and opposite pressures keep us comfortable.

A slight imbalance would allow one to feel the pressure difference. In this case, the body would literally collapse under given circumstances.

The atmosphere itself is very sensitive to its own variations, and a slight change—even 1 percent or less—is enough to get winds blowing and storms coming into circulation.

Origin of Pressure

Because the atmosphere consists of a group of gases, it must have some weight. The figure on the next page shows the composition of the atmosphere—and are we ever lucky! There's just the right mix of oxygen and nitrogen to support life, and achieving that mix was no easy matter.

If the earth were closer to the Sun, the intense heat would cause the gases to escape—just like vapor escapes from a boiling pot of water. On Venus, the temperature is as high as 900 degrees. Mercury has an average temperature of 500 degrees. If the earth were smaller, its gravitational pull would be reduced, and like on the Moon, the atmosphere would be lost in space.

Composition of the atmosphere.

Permanent Gases	
Nitrogen	78.08%
Oxygen	20.95%
Argon	0.93%
Neon	0.0018%
Helium	0.0005%
Methane	0.0001%
Hydrogen	0.00005%
Xenon	0.000009%
Variable Gases	
Water vapor	0-4%
Carbon dioxide	0.034%
Ozone	0.000004%
Carbon monoxide	0.00002%
Sulfur dioxide	0.000001%
Nitrogen dioxide	0.000001%
Dust, soot, etc.	0.00001%

If the earth were *larger*, lots of nasty gases would stay within the atmosphere because of the stronger gravitational pull. For example, the most common gas in the universe is hydrogen, but our atmosphere doesn't hold much hydrogen. What is present combines with oxygen to simply form low concentrations of water vapor. Hydrogen and many of its compounds are too light to be held down by the earth's gravitational pull. So, they escape—which is a good thing, because those hydrogen compounds, such as methane and ammonia, are noxious. (What's more, hydrogen is explosive.) These gases are found around larger planets like Jupiter, and that's why life can't be supported there.

So, we have the amazing good fortune to have a planet that's just the right size and just the right distance from the Sun. This unique arrangement—the combination of distance and size—is also responsible for our weather, including pressure and its variations.

Pressure itself is the weight of a column of air per unit of surface area. It is a force per unit area, and that force is a function of the atmosphere's weight relative to the gravitational pull of the planet.

Weather-Wise

Temperatures at the equator on Mars are comparable to the temperature found in the polar regions on Earth, but on the Martian poles the temperature plunges to about 180 degrees below zero. That's cold enough to freeze carbon dioxide and form an ice cap of dry ice.

Normal Variation

Atmospheric pressure is amazingly stable. On the average, the atmosphere weighs about 15 pounds per square inch. Pressure is also expressed in a metric unit, the millibar (mb). The *bar* is a basic unit of pressure, and a *millibar* is one-one thousandth of a bar. The average sea-level pressure reading is 1013.2 millibars. I like millibars, but the most common unit is expressed in inches of mercury, and relates to how high a column of mercury will rise within a tube where there's an absence of atmosphere. Normal sea-level pressure comes to 29.92 inches. Those tubes are called *barometers.*

An *aneroid* barometer contains no liquid. The term "aneroid" comes from the Greek meaning "without liquid." A little box within the instrument will expand or contract when the pressure around it decreases or increases. As the volume changes, a dial moves right or left, showing the pressure. This is the type of barometer found in most homes, and the pressure reading is also expressed in terms of inches. The figure on the next page illustrates these barometers, which we'll discuss in more detail when we look at the instruments in a weather station.

Weather-Speak

A **barometer** is an instrument used to measure the pressure of the atmosphere. The two kinds of barometers are aneroid and mercurial. The **aneroid** has a metallic surface and a pointer, with a graduated scale. The **mercurial** has mercury in a graduated glass tube.

Braving the Elements

The highest pressure ever recorded was 1083.8 millibars (32.005 inches) at Agata, Siberia, on December 31, 1968. The temperature was as low as 50 degrees below zero. The extremely cold, dense air contributed to that very high pressure. The lowest sea–level pressure ever recorded was 870 millibars (25.69 inches), on October 12, 1979, about 1,000 miles east of the Philippines within typhoon "Tip." In the United States, the lowest pressure was 26.35 inches in the hurricane of 1935 that crossed the Florida Keys. The absolute lowest pressure has yet to be measured—it would occur within a tornado. The chances of a barometer being in a tornado and withstanding the fury of the storm are slim to none.

Generally, at ground level, the atmospheric pressure doesn't fluctuate by more than a few percent—between 30.50 inches and 29.50. Because the air is rising when it rains, the pressure will be lower. The deepest storm will seldom have a pressure below 29 inches, although some hurricanes can have a pressure below 28 inches. The strongest dry areas of high pressure seldom exceed a pressure of 31 inches. So, a relatively small fluctuation of pressure can deliver a hugely different type of weather.

Because pressure results from the earth's gravitational pull, higher elevations will experience reduced pressures—the gravity is less up there. The figure at the top of the following page shows the variation of pressure for different elevations.

By the way, the actual pressure is not as important as the *change* in pressure. Changes in pressure indicate shifts in vertical motion. Those words around the rim of barometers saying, "Clear, Stormy, Rain" don't mean a thing. You don't even have to worry about setting a barometer to a particular standard. Just watch the change, or variation, and the change in pressure will give you solid clues about what is about to occur.

Barometers.

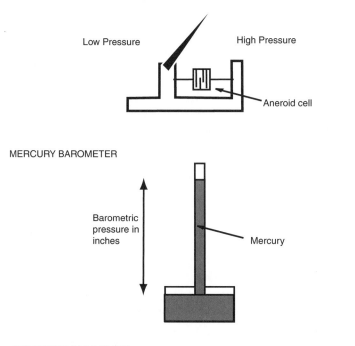

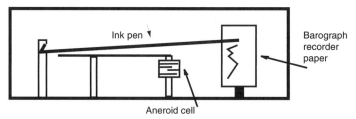

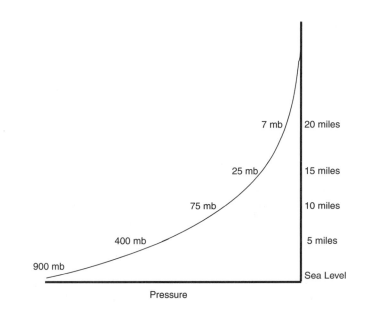

Pressure and elevation.

7 mb   20 miles

25 mb   15 miles

75 mb   10 miles

400 mb   5 miles

900 mb   Sea Level

Pressure

High Points and Low

Here we are talking about pressure, and the subject of vertical motions appears, once again. Well, why not? Take a look at the next figure to see what's going on.

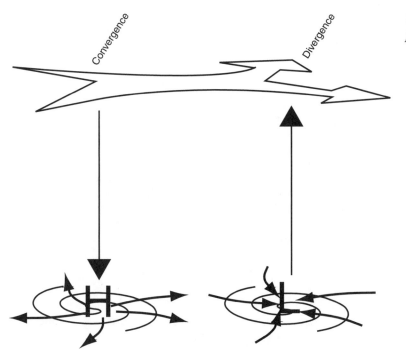

Origins of high and low pressure.

Let's think about it. If rising air causes rain, what causes the rising motion? A force in the atmosphere, at high levels, that takes the air out and away. The atmosphere is really a three-dimensional layer cake, and motions aloft don't always resemble what's occurring at ground level. An outflow of air in the upper atmosphere is one of the most common mechanisms for drawing the atmosphere upward and setting off those vertical motions that lead to rain.

That high-level *divergence* of air is something weather forecasters are always looking for. Heating can cause the atmosphere to rise, too, and *converging* currents near the ground can deliver lift as well. Also, as air runs into a mountain, it lifts. All of these bring about precipitation, but whenever the atmosphere is lifted away from the earth's surface, and that air is drawn away at high levels, the pressure in the atmospheric column will be lowered. Low pressure, therefore, is always associated with stormy weather.

On the other hand, if the atmosphere is forced to sink toward the earth's surface, the weight of the air will be greater, and the pressure will rise. The skies might have been stormy, but as the barometer begins to rise, the skies will clear. High pressure, therefore, is associated with a sunny day.

Of course, there are always exceptions. I can remember my share of high-pressure systems when rain was falling. That occurred when the area of high pressure was really shallow and air was actually rising above it. But overall, rising air goes along with lowering pressure, and sunny sinking motions happen with high-pressure areas. Those pressure areas are really defined by the vertical motions.

Weather-Speak

Convergence in the atmosphere occurs when air comes together at a particular location. That would take place if opposing winds meet over that point. Convergence would also occur if more air enters a region than departs. **Divergence** describes the opposite process where more air leaves than arrives.

What Makes the Weather Go 'Round

While high and low pressure areas are defined by sinking and rising air, they are also characterized by spinning motions. In the Northern Hemisphere, high pressure areas spin clockwise and low pressure areas spin counterclockwise. Just the opposite spin is put on the atmosphere in the Southern Hemisphere. It's all because of a mysterious force called *Coriolis force*. I can't begin to tell you how often I've wanted to write about the Coriolis force, which makes the atmosphere go in circles. This is one of the most important elements of weather—and one of the most poorly explained. Throughout my learning years I badgered my teachers and seldom felt comfortable with their explanations of

Weather-Speak

The **Coriolis force** is an apparent force due to the rotation of the earth. Moving objects, such as wind, are deflected to the right in the Northern Hemisphere and to the left in the Southern Hemisphere.

this magical mechanism. I've seen record players that turn the wrong way, carousels, and other assorted spinning devices used to explain why the atmosphere goes in circles. Usually, my head was spinning instead, clockwise and counterclockwise. Let's see if we can offer up a simpler explanation.

The Coriolis force is named for Gaspard Coriolis, a nineteenth-century French scientist who figured out why weather systems spin. (For purists, he really didn't discover a force—more of an effect—so sometimes the spinning factor is called the Coriolis *effect.*) In any case, we begin with the knowledge that the earth is in motion. It is rotating on its axis. It goes around once a day. The atmosphere is attached to the earth because of gravity, so it goes around once a day, too, otherwise we would pass through the entire world's weather in just 24 hours. The following figure shows what's going on.

If you've got a globe handy, you might want to refer to it as you read this. Near the equator, where the earth is obviously widest, the outer edge of the earth's atmosphere is moving faster than it does around the poles. So, the atmosphere is given more west-to-east spin at the equator than, for example, at a latitude of 45 degrees north.

Weather-Wise

Bob Dylan claims you don't need a weatherman to know which way the wind blows: A north wind blows *from* the north. By the way, if you stand with your back to the wind and extend your right arm to the right of your body, it points toward high pressure. Your left arm, extended to the left side of your body, will point toward low pressure. In the Southern Hemisphere, it's the opposite. The weather can be as simple as knowing right from left.

Coriolis force.

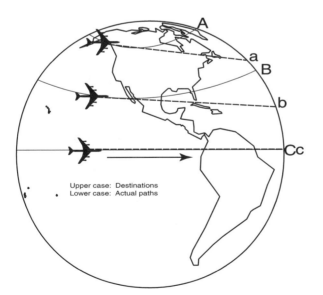

Upper case: Destinations
Lower case: Actual paths

Let's say a system is moving north toward your town. It picks up a greater eastward momentum due to the extra force at the equator. So that system may have been heading straight toward you, but it arrives to the east, because of that eastward push. The eastward momentum, or motion, that system had near the equator is conserved, so the atmosphere is moving faster to the east than the earth is at that latitude. And this is what Coriolis force is all about.

Weather-Wise

The earth's rotation has been slowed by meteorological and tidal forces. A leap second was added Monday, June 30, 1997 to get the astronomical clock into sync with the standard atomic clock.

Weather-Speak

A balance between the pressure force and the Coriolis force is called **geostrophic.** The pressure force causes the air to move from high to low pressure. In the Northern Hemisphere the Coriolis force causes that motion to turn to the right. When that right directed motion is balanced by the pressure force, the flow is geostrophic.

In our example, the air arrives to the east (or the right) of its original heading. Now, check what happens in the Southern Hemisphere. The same principle applies, but because up is down in the Southern Hemisphere, the pocket shifts to the west of its original destination. You can try this out for motions in the opposite directions, too, and it works.

If you look in the direction that the air is moving, it will always shift to the right of its original path in the Northern Hemisphere, and to the left in the Southern Hemisphere. This is a relative force, relative to the motion of the earth. If the earth weren't rotating, and if it were a block, not a ball, there would be no Coriolis effect, and the weather would never go around in circles.

Now let's bring pressure into the mix (see the figure on the next page). The air will naturally flow from pockets of high pressure to pockets of low pressure—just like what occurs when the air in a blown-up balloon (under high pressure) is released (into low pressure). The air is trying to go from high pressure to low, but Coriolis says, "Not so fast." The air gets spun to the right in the Northern Hemisphere and to the left in the Southern Hemisphere. North of the equator the air spins clockwise around the area of high pressure. Around the area of low pressure, the air turns counterclockwise.

In the atmosphere, there is nearly a balance between the Coriolis force and the force generated by the air moving from high to low pressure areas. This balance is called *geostrophic*, and it is a setup that is very simple but often very appropriate. In the early days of computer forecasting, motions were assumed to be geostrophic, and the predictions weren't bad.

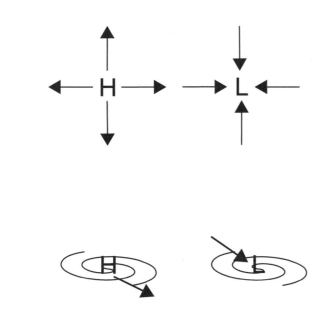

Circulation of highs and lows.

What's in a Name?

In ancient Greece, *Boreas* was the name of the north wind—a wind that blows out of the north. *Notos* was a south wind. *Zephyros* came from the west, and *Apeliotes* was an east wind. Although the wind is no longer deified, it does receive plenty of local attention, and there are infinite regional names.

For example, in the European Alps, the *Fohn* describes a dry wind that comes down a mountain. A similar wind in the United States is called a *chinook*. A *haboob* is a desert wind strong enough to kick up a sandstorm, and a *khamsin* is an oppressively hot wind that blows across Egypt. A *sirocco* is a hot, dry south wind that moves along the north coast of Africa, from the Sahara. In the Persian Gulf area, a *shamal* is a hot, dry northwest wind. The *mistral* is a dry, cold north wind that reaches the Mediterranean coasts of France and Spain. In the United States, there are the famous *Santa Ana* winds—hot, dry winds that move down through the Santa Ana Pass into southern California. And this is only a partial list.

Weather people don't think of the wind as "the wind," but as isolated patterns of atmospheric motion, or circulation patterns, which are divided into four "scales of motion."

Weather-Wise

English poet Christina Rossetti once asked, "Who has seen the wind?" Maybe we can't see the wind, but we can certainly feel its impact. The pressure exerted by the wind increases with the square of the wind speed. So, the pressure becomes four times greater every time the wind speed doubles. A 100-mph wind is four times as punishing as a 50-mph wind; a 75-mph wind is more than twice as powerful as a 50-mph wind.

Weather-Speak

Because the earth is rotating, the atmosphere also rotates, and that rotation creates **circulations** of different sizes. Circulation is simply the atmosphere moving in a closed path.

Scales of Motion

In the study of atmospheric motions, little swirls are observed to feed on bigger swirls, which feed on, or spin off, even larger ones. This swirling feeding frenzy is just part of our daily weather, and splitting the atmosphere into its many spinning components really helps us understand what's going on. These *scales of motion* start from the smallest *circulation* blowing through a pile of leaves to the largest circulation extending from one end of the globe to another. Each is distinguished by its size and structure, and each generates different forms of weather, depending on—you guessed it—its vertical velocity. The following figure shows the spectrum of atmospheric motions, along with the different characteristic forms of weather.

Scales of motion.

Microscale

Mesoscale

Synoptic scale

New York City

All the circulations we experience can be grouped into these different categories:

➤ Microscale

➤ Synoptic

➤ Mesoscale

➤ Global

The small, *microscale circulations,* or eddies, don't really do much to our weather, but a somewhat bigger sea breeze can make a big difference on a summer's day. A sea breeze develops when the land areas become warmer than the ocean surface. The land heats up more than the ocean on a summer day because of the mixing that constantly occurs in the water. The surface of the water may heat up, but the mixing prevents the ocean surface from being warmer than the land. The warm air over the land is more buoyant, and it rises. So, low pressure develops over the land, and relatively high pressure occurs over the water. The air flows from high to low pressure, from cooler sea to warmer land, and that's a sea breeze.

At night, the land areas lose their heat more effectively than the well-mixed ocean surfaces, so the opposite circulation develops, and that becomes a land breeze. The wind blows from land to sea. The land breeze is usually much weaker than the sea breeze, but it can be a source for mosquitoes, which drift toward the shore. They are poised and ready to crash any beach party. The figure on the next page shows the sea- and land-breeze circulations. Another example of a microscale circulation is a mountain breeze. Again, unequal heating is responsible for the flow.

The next category is called *synoptic,* from the Greek meaning "at the same time." Within that scale, observations are taken at the same time around the world and put together on a weather map for analysis. The synoptic scale is sometimes referred to as the *medium scale.* The normal weather patterns shown on television and in the newspaper belong to the synoptic scale, and that scale includes the typical high- and low-pressure systems. Hurricanes also belong to this scale. Upward motions can be as gentle as a couple of centimeters per second (less than .02 mph), but that's enough to deliver a rainy or snowy day. The motions are slight, but very effective.

The *mesoscale* circulations include thunderstorms and tornadoes. This is the most violent scale. Within this category, the vertical motions can be as high as 50 mph.

The largest scale are the *global* circulations, which govern seasonal weather conditions and even climate. The vertical motions are slight, but they do much in determining whether a rain forest or a desert climate will exist. These global wind patterns are discussed in Chapter 15. They occur at all levels of the atmosphere.

The atmosphere is always in motion. Its different scales are operating at all times. But lately it may seem that those circulations have gone to extremes.

Sea and land breezes.

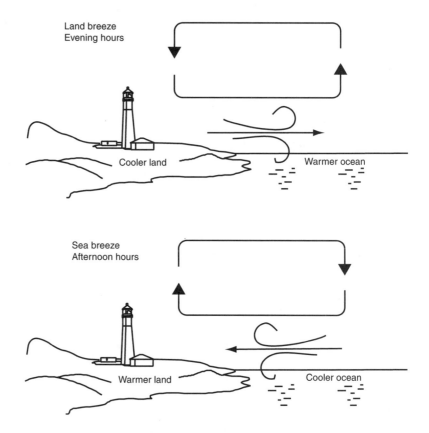

Land breeze
Evening hours

Cooler land

Warmer ocean

Sea breeze
Afternoon hours

Warmer land

Cooler ocean

Is It Getting Worse? The Naughty '90s

The weather seems to be capturing plenty of headlines in recent years, and there seems to be a consensus that the weather has gone beyond its normal limits. That impression is not universally accepted by scientists. Still, there are reasons to feel that the weather has become extreme.

Based on land-station readings, the world seems to have experienced its six warmest years on record during the 1990s. Satellite data is not so conclusive, but thousands of fixed land stations and ocean buoys have registered extreme warmth during most of the 1990s. Also, the first half of 1998 delivered the highest global temperature on record—and records have been kept since 1860! Most of the warmth has occurred in the tropical latitudes and the Northern Hemisphere. And certainly, where there is warmth, there is fire.

Storms have occurred with great frequency and intensity. The 1990s brought the most costly meteorological disaster on record when Hurricane Andrew slammed into southern Florida in 1992. Damage came to more than $20 billion. The decade also brought one of the coldest and snowiest winters on record, with the 1995–96 season delivering almost three times as much snow as normal to the eastern portion of the United States.

Overall, between 1948 and 1994, the four highest years for insured property losses occurred from 1991 to 1994.

The 1998 spring tornado season was the most active on record. Extreme drought prevailed in Asia, helping to destabilize economies and governments. Mild weather occurred in January across much of the United States. Flowers blossomed in February, and in March, a summer-style "heat wave" occurred across the Northeast, along with punishing rains. The highest global temperature on record was also delivered in 1998. And the 1998 hurricane season brought the most deadly storm since 1780 into the Atlantic basin. Hurricane Mitch raked Central America, claiming at least 9,000 lives. In the United States, weather disasters were responsible for the deaths of 460 people, more than twice the annual average.

The number of violent storms and the extremes in temperature and precipitation provide a strong case for suspecting that something strange is going on. But something strange *always* seems to be happening with the weather! The droughts of the 1930s, the bitter cold winters of 1917 and 1934, the hurricane of 1938, the floods and storms of the 1950s—all were extreme occurrences.

The nineteenth century had its extremes, too, with the blizzard of 1888 and the "year of no summer" in 1816, just to name two occurrences. The eighteenth century brought tremendous cold and snow. The period became known as the "little ice age," yet at the turn of that century, Thomas Jefferson wrote about a period of great warmth where the snow no longer lingered as it did in former years. He wrote about a global warming, which he attributed to the burning and clearing of forests for settlements and cities. Still, a few years later, the weather cooled once again, the mini-ice age returned, and snow fell in southern New England in June of that famous summer in 1816. Even during the warmth of 1998, snow fell in northern New England during a June cold snap.

The weather is always going to extremes. I call it the "Law of Weather Averages." If you gamble at a casino table, you have the option of leaving with your winnings at any time. But if you stay too long, you will certainly lose. At the weather table, we don't have the option of walking away. We're there for the duration. We may have a hot streak, but in time, we're bound to go ice-cold again. Of course, there may be subtle changes in the overall climate, too, but we'll sort that one out later. Many of the extremes attributed to global change are probably more related to *weather* than *climate*.

In the pages that follow, we'll look at the various scales of atmospheric motions, examine their characteristics, and learn how to predict their development. Thunderstorms, tornadoes, blizzards, and hurricanes are on the way!

Weather-Wise

During the 1990s, 29 billion-dollar weather disasters have hit the United States. In 1998 alone, there were four such disasters including the severe weather during the winter and spring in the Southeast, the drought and heat wave of the summer, and Hurricanes Bonnie and Georges.

The Least You Need to Know

➤ The earth's atmosphere has a special mix of gases brought about by a unique set of factors.

➤ Wind develops because of differences in atmospheric pressure.

➤ Atmospheric pressure fluctuates in a small but significant range.

➤ Because the earth rotates, the Coriolis force develops, causing weather systems to spin.

➤ The weather in recent decades has gone through tremendous extremes, but that could be entirely normal.

There's No Place Like Home

In This Chapter

➤ It's electrifying

➤ When lightning strikes

➤ Putting a spin on thunderstorms

➤ Chasing down tornadoes

➤ Staying safe

Although the mesoscale level of weather action is small in stature, it certainly is huge in impact. The most violent weather on the face of the earth takes place within this scale. Tall cumulonimbus clouds turn into violent thunderstorms, delivering strong winds, torrential rains, and damaging lightning. At the extreme, these clouds can begin to spin and form tornadoes. This severe weather strikes throughout the world, but the United States seems to be world capital for violent thunderstorms and tornadoes. A unique convergence of forces makes them happen with amazing frequency.

Thunderstorms

These powerhouses have their origins in a strong, volatile atmosphere. The atmosphere has nicely figured out a way to make those tall, towering clouds form. The essential requirement is for rapid upward motions to develop.

It is all based upon Archimedes' bathtub experience. He was the ancient thinker who, while taking a bath, discovered that the deeper he went into the water, the more water was displaced, and the more that was displaced, the less he seemed to weigh. According to legend, he ran directly from the bathtub through the streets of Syracuse screaming, "Eureka!"

What he found was the basic principle of buoyancy: Something that is less dense, surrounded by something more dense, will float. People float, and ships float on water because they are able to displace enough water to have a volume that is less dense than the surrounding water. A cork rises in a basin of water because of that very principle. A cloud, or a pocket of air, can act in the same way as a cork.

Stability and Instability

If some object is given a shove and it keeps going, its condition is said to be unstable. In the opposite sense, if the object comes back, the condition is stable.

Braving the Elements

"The calm before the storm," is a proverb that seems to make plenty of meteorological sense. Before Hurricane Andrew slammed across southern Florida, the skies were partly cloudy, the wind was light, and the temperatures were mild. But in a few short hours, one of the most intense hurricanes in U.S. history was bearing down in that very same area. Sinking motions on the periphery of the storm account for both the calm before, and after, the storm.

In the atmosphere, if a pocket of air rises and just keeps going, the air is unstable. Of course, as the pocket rises, the pressure around it is reduced, so it expands. That expansion automatically causes a cooling. Now, cooler air has a greater density than warmer air, so the pocket will tend to return to the ground from where it originated. But if the air outside the pocket is cooling faster because of particular weather conditions, then the pocket will have a free ride. As it continues upward, it will eventually condense (when its relative humidity reaches 100 percent). A cloud is born. If the cloud stays warmer than its surroundings, it will grow bigger and bigger. Soon, the cloud will reach as high as 30,000 feet, then 40,000 or 50,000 feet. At that point, we're into some real severe weather!

The following figure sorts out Archimedes' principle applied not to taking a bath, but to looking at the atmosphere.

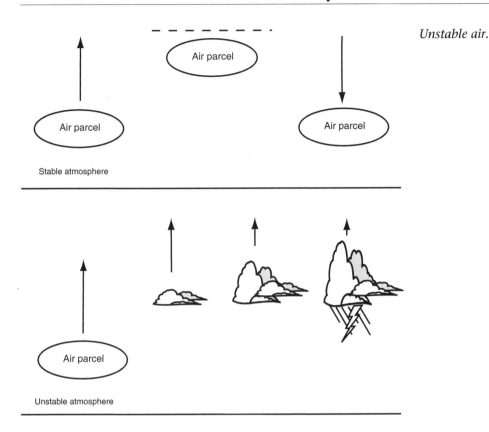

Unstable air.

Lapse Rates

The change in temperature with elevation is the *lapse rate.* The rising pocket has one lapse rate; the air surrounding it has another. They could be equal, but they're usually not. The pocket's lapse rate is simply a function of the rate of expansion, and that is predictable and known. If the pocket is dry, it will cool at a rate of 5.5 degrees for every thousand feet it rises. That is called the *dry adiabatic lapse rate.* "Adiabatic" means no change in heat—the temperature changes not because a fire was lit or because ice was tossed in, but because the volume of the pocket changed. The molecules became farther apart, so the temperature went down. I know we're getting in pretty deep, but do you know what you just learned? The First Law Of Thermodynamics!

Once the pocket forms a cloud, the cooling rate will decrease because the condensation process releases some heat. The cooling rate becomes about

Weather-Speak

The change in temperature with elevation is the **lapse rate.** If a pocket of air is dry, it will cool at a rate of 5.5 degrees for every thousand feet it rises. That is called the **dry adiabatic lapse rate.**

3 degrees for every thousand feet of lift. That's called the *moist adiabatic lapse rate,* but because some heat is absorbed in the process, it is not truly adiabatic. So, it is sometimes called a pseudo-adiabatic lapse rate.

In any case, if the pocket's lapse rate is less than the environment's lapse rate, the pocket will not cool as much, it will be warmer, less dense, and…Eureka! A storm is born.

Weather-Speak

If a rising pocket is saturated, it will cool at a lower rate of about 3 degrees Fahrenheit. That is called the **moist adiabatic lapse rate.**

The environment's lapse rate is measured every day by sending balloons equipped with instruments into the atmosphere. The temperature throughout the atmosphere is monitored. That observed environmental lapse rate is then compared with the theoretical rates for rising pockets of air, and a determination of stability is made. If the environment is really cold in the upper levels of the atmosphere, and the air near the ground is especially warm, there's a good chance these pockets will be warmer than their surroundings. The pockets will have a free rise to the top, and look out! Nature's most violent weather will develop. The upward motions can reach expressway speeds.

Lightning Strikes

A thunderstorm is made possible by both electronics and dynamics. We just looked at some of those dynamics. Now, bring on the electronics.

The figure on the following page shows the progression of events that allows those tall clouds with strong updrafts to become electrifying. The atmosphere normally has small, electrically charged gases called *ions*. Those ions have a net negative charge in the upper reaches of the atmosphere, and because opposites attract, those negative charges induce positive charges on the surface of the earth. The positive charges collect at the surface. That is called a *fair weather field* because it occurs when the weather is quiet.

Now let's put one of those tall, towering clouds into that atmosphere. Because of the earth's original field, cloud droplets and ice crystals will line up, with negative charges

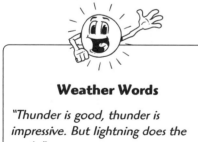

Weather Words

"Thunder is good, thunder is impressive. But lightning does the work."

—Mark Twain

at the base and positive charges on top—again, opposites attract. The earth's original positive charge induces a negative charge at the lower end of these elements. The upper atmosphere's negative charge induces a positive charge on the top end of these droplets. The next step gets a bit tricky, and it is not so clearly understood.

Magically, these cloud elements begin to separate, with the positive charge on the top of the droplets and ice crystals transferring to the bottom of the droplets and ice rising within the cloud. This transfer of charge and separation is mysterious, but ice seems to be an effective agent for the transfer. In any case, positive charges cluster in the top of the clouds, and negative charges collect at the base. There are smaller pockets of positive charge at the cloud base, but overall, the charge is negative there.

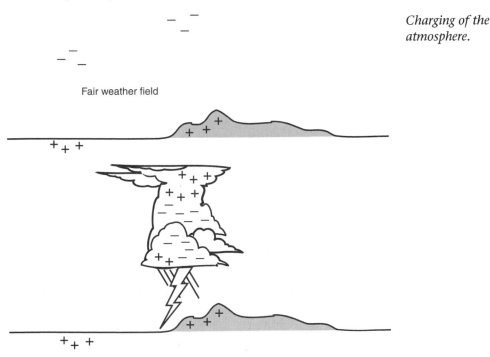

Charging of the atmosphere.

Now that a net negative charge is induced at the base of a cloud, a new, net positive charge is forced at the ground. No longer is it a fair weather field. When the difference in charge becomes strong enough, a current begins to flow, step by step, from the cloud toward the ground. When the entire channel is carved out, the final surge of electricity is sent from the ground up to the cloud, and that is the lightning stroke. The current reaches 100,000 amps. That energy is huge.

So, the lightning that appears to travel from cloud to ground actually goes from ground to cloud. Other lightning discharges will remain within a cloud or go from cloud to cloud. The entire process—going from a puffy cumulus cloud to a rip-roaring lightning storm—can unfold within an hour.

The temperature of that channel can hit 54,000 degrees, causing the atmosphere to rapidly expand. After expanding, the atmosphere quickly contracts. A shock wave is set off, and that expanding and collapsing channel becomes the source of the thunder. Mark Twain was right. Lightning really does the work. Without lightning, there wouldn't be thunder. And without a cloud, there couldn't be lightning.

Lightning can take on many different forms and shapes:

➤ **Sheet lightning** This is cloud-to-cloud lightning that represents discharges from one cloud to another.

➤ **Forked lightning** This is caused by the lightning's path to the ground being broken or jagged.

➤ **Heat lightning** Sometimes on a hot night lightning appears to be occurring at some distance while skies are mostly clear overhead. With heat lightning, a thunderstorm is still in progress, but at a great distance.

➤ **Ball lightning** This is mysterious. It looks like a furry, luminous sphere that moves and floats around. This type of lightning has yet to be explained to everyone's satisfaction.

➤ **St. Elmo's Fire** This is a glow that appears on the tip of masts, wings of airplanes, and around power lines. St. Elmo was the Bishop of Gaeta, Italy, in the fourth century. He became the patron saint of fire, and his protection was called upon by mariners.

Weather-Wise

Lightning travels at the speed of light—186,000 miles each second. Sound travels about 0.2 mile per second. So, you will see lightning sooner than you will hear its accompanying thunder. For every five-seconds between lightning and thunder, a storm is one mile away. So, if your room lights up, and you count to 15 before you hear thunder, the storm is 3 miles away. When lightning is really close, the thunder happens at nearly the same time, and is it loud!

Weather Words

"Avoid the ash, it attracts the flash. Stay away from the oak, it draws the stroke."

Most recently, a new form of lightning has been noted from spacecraft. Charged spikes originate from the tops of clouds and extend into space. Also, sometimes the sky is observed to have a green tinge during violent storms. The origin of that green color is mysterious; some say it's related to the presence of hail.

Avoid the Ash

Lightning is responsible for about a hundred deaths each year in the United States. Exposed objects are most susceptible to a lightning strike. No, it really isn't a good idea to sit under an apple tree—or any tree—during a thunderstorm. Some trees such as ash and oak have a high water content, and these are the absolute worst. Because water is a good conductor of electricity, those trees especially should be avoided.

On the subject of water, stay off (and out of) the water when thunderstorms are threatening. You are much more exposed to lightning over the open water than over land. Also, the turbulence associated with thunderstorms is enough to make plenty of waves. Stay away from metal objects, too.

If you are in an open area and suddenly feel a tingling sensation, or your hair begins to stand on end, lightning is about to hit you. Crouch down toward the ground in a small ball. By crouching, you reduce your surface area and the area exposed to the electrical field.

The best advice during a thunderstorm is to go indoors, don't talk on the phone, don't take a bath or shower, and stay away from windows. An all-metal automobile will offer protection by creating a shell around which the electricity will be deflected. But if the car has a plastic exterior, that shell will be broken, and the protection is lost. Also, you might want to turn off your computer. Lightning could cause a shocking experience, not to mention the loss of your data files.

Weather-Watch

People already struck by lightning do not carry an electrical charge. They can be handled safely and should be taken care of immediately. Prompt mouth-to-mouth resuscitation, cardiac massage, and prolonged artificial respiration can revive a person who may appear to be dead.

Braving the Elements

Can lightning strike twice? It sure can—even the same *person.* Roy "Dooms" Sullivan, a ranger at Shenandoah National Park, had the distinction of being struck *seven* different times by lightning. He survived, but he lost the nail of his big toe in 1942 and his eyebrows in July 1969. In July 1970, he was burned on his left shoulder. His hair caught on fire in April 1972, and again in August 1973. He was struck on his ankle in June 1976, and in June 1977, he received chest and stomach burns.

Doing the Twist

Thunderstorms have a way of going to extremes. If the atmosphere is very unstable and some mechanism is present to evacuate the air rising through a thunderstorm, those upward motions will become even greater. Eventually, thanks to sharp wind variations called *wind shear* and the spinning Earth itself, the column within the thunderstorm cloud begins to rotate, usually counterclockwise. A *funnel* drops from the base of the cloud, and when it touches down, it becomes a *tornado.* Winds in a tornado can reach over 300 mph.

Often, a cluster of thunderstorm cells will be rotating when a tornado appears. Those clusters are called *mesoscale convective complexes,* and the individual strong

Weather-Wise

One of the largest tornado out-breaks on record occurred in 1965 on Palm Sunday. About three dozen tornadoes spread over five Midwest states. More than 250 people were killed. But even that was topped in April 1974, when nearly 150 tornadoes occurred over 16 states. The death toll reached 307, with 6,000 injured.

thunderstorms are called *supercells*. The rotation of these complexes might be the source of the rotation that gets those air columns to do the twist. A tornado is sometimes called a *twister*, or, in the United States, a *cyclone*. A cyclone, however, is technically any counterclockwise circulation. In the Indian Ocean, cyclones refer to hurricanes.

Tornadoes are powerful, but they're relatively small. They may not be much wider than the length of a football field, although a few might be as much as a mile wide. Most tornadoes will move along a path of a few miles and last just minutes before dissipating, but some have traveled a hundred miles or more. Usually those long-distance runners are accompanied by other funnels, and an entire family of storms will shake loose. The following table shows a commonly used Fujita Scale, which relates damage to tornadoes of different intensities. The scale was named after T. Theodore Fujita, a meteorologist who has devoted years to the study of severe weather.

Fujita Scale

Scale	Category	MPH	Results
F0	Weak	40-72	Branches break, sign posts damaged
F1	Weak	73-112	Trees snap, windows break
F2	Strong	113-157	Large trees uproot, weak structures destroyed
F3	Strong	158-206	Cars overturn, framed structures sustain severe damage
F4	Violent	207-260	Framed structures flattened
F5	Violent	261-318	Cars lifted and moved great distances, steel-reinforced structures severely damaged

The United States has the distinction of experiencing more tornadoes than any other country in the world. Tornadoes have occurred in every state, even Alaska, but the vast majority are unleashed within the Midwest. The following figure shows a map with the number of tornadoes that have occurred per square mile for each state over a 25-year period. The greatest concentration of activity occurs in a swath from Indiana to Texas, and then eastward along the Gulf Coast to Florida. A special set of circumstances makes tornadoes more likely to happen here.

Average Number of Tornadoes by State
1961-1990

Distribution of tornadoes.

The United States is caught between the cooler weather systems of Canada and the tropical air farther south. Especially during the springtime, some of that warm air pushes northward through Texas and the lower Plains. The air is extremely unstable, packed with warmth and moisture. That volatile air is just waiting for a spark to be delivered, and it usually is during the spring, when cold air masses still linger over North America and clash with the surging warmer air.

This large density difference between the extremes sets the air in motion. The lighter, warmer air is lifted. At the same time, strong winds associated with the pattern appear above the ground, and these draw the air away from the top of the rising column. The column continues to destabilize with more warm, moist air rushing northward near the surface. Severe thunderstorms erupt, and eventually, they form tornadoes. The figure on the next page gives you an idea how the process unfolds.

Weather-Wise

Tornadoes destroy normal wind-measuring instruments, but researchers can now use Doppler radar to measure the wind speed.

Formation of tornadoes.

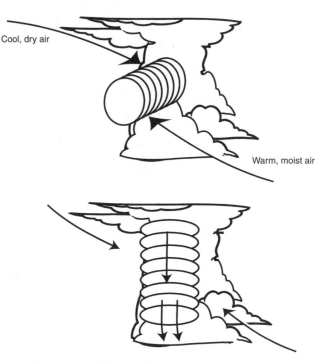

Cool, dry air

Warm, moist air

Circulation forced downward by strong downdrafts within the thunderstorm.

Although the spring is the most common time for these vicious storms, they can occur throughout the year, with southern states first experiencing the action during the winter; the Midwest, during the spring; and the northern states, during the summer. July is a big tornado month for the Northeast. If conditions favor the development of a damaging thunderstorm, the National Weather Service issues a *severe thunderstorm watch*. If conditions are expected to be extremely volatile, a *tornado watch* is posted. When the storm becomes imminent, the watch is upgraded to a *tornado warning*.

The Chase

Weather people enjoy bad weather. Something about a turbulent sky makes their day. I often half-jokingly tell people that if I wake up and the sun is shining, my day is ruined. The excitement of the weather—the storms, the changes—attract a certain type of individual, sometimes called a weather nut, who actually enjoys chasing violent weather. Recently much attention has been given to these storm chasers, including at least one

Weather-Speak

Whenever thunderstorms are expected to deliver winds of at least 58 mph and at least $3/4$-inch hail, a **severe thunderstorm watch** is issued. If the storm is spotted on radar, or observed, it's considered imminent, and a **severe thunderstorm warning** is posted. If conditions favor tornado development, a **tornado watch** goes up. If a tornado is sighted, or its signature shows up on radar, a **tornado warning** is issued, with information about where the storm is occurring and its direction of movement.

major Hollywood film, about the personalities involved. Of course, there's a scientific side to storm chasing, too.

Meteorologists at the National Severe Storms Laboratory in Norman, Oklahoma, have elevated storm chasing to a science. An instrument package called TOTO is placed in the path of a severe thunderstorm or tornado. (No, it's not named after Dorothy's dog in *The Wizard of Oz*—it stands for Totable Tornado Observatory.)

Braving the Elements

On October 3, 1979, a devastating twister as powerful as any Midwest twister hit Connecticut and swept through Bradley International Airport and the Poquonock section of Windsor. It seemed to be a fluke. It developed in New England during the fall.

The goal is to collect wind, temperature, pressure, moisture, and electrical data as a storm approaches. The activity is filmed and tracked on sophisticated radar systems. The data will be analyzed after the storm has passed. Unlike the Hollywood version of tornado chasing, the real-life effort does not involve people heading directly into the storm. The information becomes important in understanding how these storms develop.

One storm-chasing project is called **Subvortex.** Two mobile radar units are mounted on two flatbed trucks. In addition, a number of vehicles equipped with instruments and computers set out for the target region. That location is initially determined by satellite data, and the team will drive hundreds of miles to be at the right place at the right time. Hydraulic stabilizing legs try to keep the trucks steady as the storm approaches. After the storm moves away, the equipment is quickly packed up, and the chase continues.

Staying Safe in a Storm

In a tornado, winds are so great that brick and concrete walls can collapse. Roofs are pulled off buildings. In the past, the advice was to open a

Weather-Wise

The first official tornado forecast was issued on March 25, 1948. The storm was predicted by Air Force Capt. Robert C. Miller and Maj. Ernest J. Fawbush. Precautions were taken based on the forecast, which preceded the storm by several hours. Although the storm slammed through Tinker Air Force Base in Oklahoma and caused considerable damage, lives were saved by the warning.

window opposite to the wind, so the indoor and outdoor pressure would be equalized. That's no longer considered wise. The thought is that opening a window actually increases the force on the opposite wall and will hasten the building's destruction. Also, the wind is always shifting in a tornado, so it's tough to know which window to open! Keep the windows closed.

Stay *away* from the windows, too! If a tornado warning is issued, go into a basement or an interior room on the lowest floor. A hallway, closet, or bathroom will have enough reinforcement to protect you from collapsing walls. If you are outside, don't try to outrun one of these storms. If the sky is threatening and you are driving, leave your car and find some indoor shelter. If you must be outdoors and the storm nears, find some protection in an underpass, or just lie flat in a ditch or other low area.

There is nothing small-time or mediocre about the mesoscale. From thunderstorms to tornadoes, it contains the most violent weather on Earth.

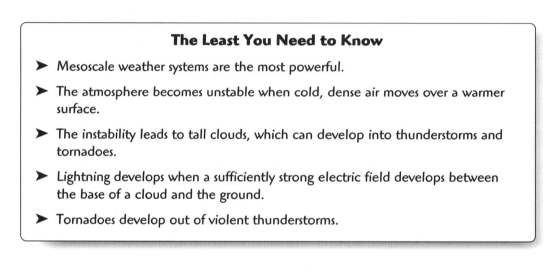

The Least You Need to Know

➤ Mesoscale weather systems are the most powerful.

➤ The atmosphere becomes unstable when cold, dense air moves over a warmer surface.

➤ The instability leads to tall clouds, which can develop into thunderstorms and tornadoes.

➤ Lightning develops when a sufficiently strong electric field develops between the base of a cloud and the ground.

➤ Tornadoes develop out of violent thunderstorms.

Chapter 6

On Another Front

In This Chapter

➤ How the typical rainy day happens

➤ When two air masses meet

➤ Front and center

➤ Making that prediction

Tornadoes and thunderstorms are the violent products of larger circulations that set off a huge variety of weather—from the all-day drizzle to the blinding blizzard, and even the rip-roaring hurricane. These larger circulations are part of the medium or synoptic scale, and they essentially account for the majority of weather that makes headlines. Air masses, fronts, and high- and low-pressure systems all make up this thing called weather.

Mass Appeal

Although the weather is very changeable and always seems to show great variations, there are huge bodies of air that have surprisingly uniform characteristics. These can extend for hundreds, even a thousand miles, and they are called *air masses*.

The temperature and humidity within these air masses will not exactly be constant, but the variations are slight enough so that the air masses can be called warm, cold, dry, or moist. A single air mass offers its own weather. At the same time, when two opposing air masses collide, the weather goes into a spin, and the skies open up.

Birth of an Air Mass

Air masses form over particular source areas, taking on the characteristics of the surface over which they form. Air masses develop over polar regions, tropical regions, oceanic areas, and continents. A large high-pressure system is associated with the development of these air masses. In a high-pressure area, the air is *diverging*—moving away from a particular center. That divergence allows for uniformity—the same air spreads out over a wide area, rather than different air converging toward a particular place. If the air converged toward a center, then, different types of air would be on a collision course, and great differences in temperature and humidity would occur. But if the air diverges, the mass of air will tend toward uniformity. The figure below shows how these air masses form.

Weather-Speak

An **air mass** is a very large body of air that has uniform moisture and temperature characteristics. One air mass can cover one-half of the United States.

Also, in polar regions, clear skies and light winds become important for bringing down the temperature of the air mass. That combination delivers what is called *radiational cooling*. It allows heat to escape during the long polar nights. If skies are overcast, or if the wind is mixing the air, heat is trapped near the ground, and the air mass will not be able to cool as effectively. The figure on the next page shows how this radiational cooling takes place.

Air mass formation.

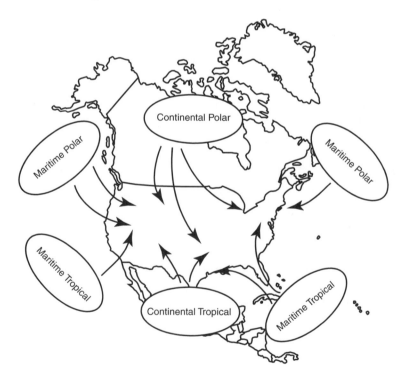

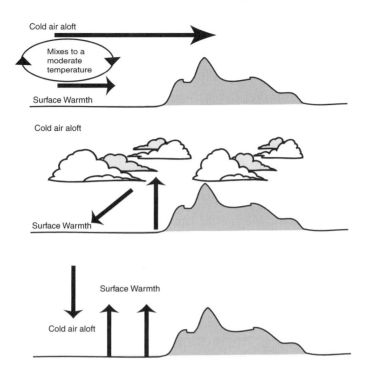

Radiational cooling.

But while mixing may inhibit air mass formation over the far north, it will help bring moisture into the air, and that becomes important for air masses that take shape over the oceans.

Going Hot and Cold

Air masses are given names based upon their source regions:

➤ **Arctic (A)**

➤ **Polar (P)**

➤ **Tropical (T)**

➤ **Equatorial (E)**

➤ **Maritime (M)**

➤ **Continental (C)**

Weather-Speak

Radiational cooling is cooling that occurs at night. The ground will cool more quickly than the air above it. It is most effective when skies are clear and winds are light.

The arctic and polar air masses are cold for a particular time of year, tropical and equatorial air masses are warm, maritime systems are moist, and continental are dry. The arctic systems are colder then the polar air masses, and they form in the northern-most regions of the earth. The equatorial air masses form over the equator and are the warmest and most humid air masses on the face of the earth.

71

Then there are the combination platters:

- ➤ **Continental polar (cP)**   A polar air mass that forms over the continents.
- ➤ **Maritime polar (mP)**   A polar air mass that forms over the oceans.
- ➤ **Maritime tropical (mT)**   An extremely humid air mass.
- ➤ **Continental tropical (cT)**   An air mass that is desert-dry.

The following table outlines the type of weather that occurs with the different air masses. The actual weather will be different for different locations, but there are similarities within each air mass. The letter abbreviations are used to indicate air mass type on a weather map.

Air Mass Weather

	Land (continental)	Water (maritime) (m)
Polar (P)	Cold, dry, stable (cP)	Cool, moist, unstable (mP)
Tropical (T)	Hot, dry, stable (aloft) unstable (surface) (cT)	Warm, moist, unstable (usually) (mT)

Feeling the Chill

Continental polar air masses usually bring relatively chilly conditions, especially during the winter months. During the summer, a continental polar experience offers a delightful break in heat and humidity. In North America, these air masses form over central and northern Canada and sweep southward. Winds are from the northwest and the air is dry. Little precipitation will normally fall within these air masses and skies will at least be partly cloudy. But there are always exceptions.

The major variation on the theme occurs during the winter, when these air masses move over relatively warmer bodies of water, such as the Great Lakes. The cold, heavier air will overturn, and that turbulence will pick up moisture from the lakes. Then, as this unstable air runs into hills on the *lee side* of the lakes, the lifting releases the moisture, and heavy bursts of snow, called snow squalls, will develop. The intensity of the snow squalls is a function of the difference in temperature between the air and water, as well as the amount of lifting that takes place. These snow squalls can deliver several feet of snow; the process is called the *lake effect* (see the next figure).

Weather-Speak

The **lee side** is the shore toward which the wind is blowing. If the wind is from the west, the lee side would be on the eastern shore. Local snowstorms form on the lee side of a lake as the cold, dry air picks up moisture from the lake. The air runs into hills and rises. It then releases moisture in the form of snow squalls. This is called the **lake effect.**

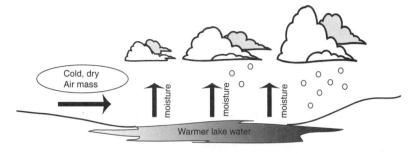

Lake-effect snow.

Too Cold for Comfort

Arctic air masses have characteristics similar to continental polar air masses, except that they are more extreme. These form near the poles and deliver record cold temperatures. Usually, the weather is dry within these air masses, but the turbulence becomes severe over warmer surfaces, and snow squalls can be especially punishing in localized areas. The lake effect goes to the extreme, and snow depths are measured not in feet, but yards!

Occasionally, a strong arctic high-pressure system will form over northern Siberia and then spread across the polar region southward into the United States. That type of weather system is sometimes called the Siberian Express.

By the Sea

Maritime polar air masses form over the colder oceans. These can deliver low clouds and fog, but commonly, the air sinks within these air masses so that skies clear. The wind is generally onshore. During the summer, these air masses deliver cool conditions to shore areas. Other than some drizzle, the weather is usually precipitation-free when these air masses stand by themselves. Within medium-scale low-pressure systems, this air mass is often tapped for its moisture, but when maritime polar air masses are simply associated with a high-pressure system, the weather is free of rain or snow.

Weather-Wise

In January 1977, the Buffalo, New York area was especially hard hit when weeks of heavy snow fell during a series of arctic outbreaks. That ice-age month even brought snow to southern Florida. The temperature during that month averaged 10 degrees below normal across much of the eastern states. Glaciers would make a major advance if that temperature departure from normal were sustained over decades.

Putting On the Heat

Tropical air masses either form over the warm, tropical oceans, or over deserts. The moist maritime tropical air masses are steamy with mostly fair weather, but locally heavy thunderstorms can develop when there is some lifting mechanism present. The air is humid and very unstable. The atmosphere is filled with moisture, like a sponge, and if something occurs to squeeze that sponge, look out! The air could run into a mountain and be lifted, and on the windward side of the mountain, the air will rush upslope and pour down. On the opposite side, the air will be sinking, and the precipitation will disappear.

Any mechanism that lifts the tropical air will unleash torrents of rain, but for the most part, the weather in maritime tropical air masses is hazy with sunshine burning through the haze. Dew-point temperatures are generally above 70 degrees during the summer months. These air masses cause great discomfort and are associated with strong high-pressure systems that push northward. The famous "Bermuda High" and the "Azores High" are sources for maritime tropical air. The following figure shows the setup for one of these heat-wave patterns.

In the winter, a surge of maritime tropical air over a cold, snow-covered surface will be responsible for thick fog. Winter thaws always occur when these air masses stream northward.

Weather-Wise

Hawaii has the distinction of holding the world's record for the most amount of rainfall, but only on the windward side of Mt. Waialeale.

Heat-wave pattern.

How Dry It Is

Continental tropical air masses are extremely hot, but dry. These develop over the deserts and can expand into regions such as the Midwest. Skies are clear, and the high pressure system associated with these air masses can be especially persistent. The great droughts develop within these systems. Sometimes these hot, dry high-pressure areas will appear during the spring over portions of the Plains, and that's a bad sign. As the sun becomes stronger and the summer months arrive, the high pressure itself strengthens. A desert-dry summer then settles across a huge area.

Braving the Elements

During the spring of 1998, a blistering, hot continental tropical air mass developed over central Mexico. Fires flared across Mexico and smoke spread into Texas. Then that same weather system moved across the Gulf states to Florida, where disastrous fires developed. At one point, more than one hundred miles of Interstate 95 was closed to traffic because of the fires. Disaster officials were actually hoping for a tropical storm. The pattern was very unusual for Florida, which normally receives copious summertime rains within maritime tropical air masses.

An equatorial air mass is the tropical equivalent of an arctic air mass. It goes to the extreme. It is extremely warm and humid, very much like a maritime tropical system, except more so. The dew-point temperature can reach the incredible 80s in these air masses.

Putting Up a Front

What happens when two different air masses meet? You get a *front*. The figure on page 77 gives you an idea how a front is formed. Air masses with contrasting characteristics are pushed together by the winds, so that along a particular line, the weather will change noticeably and sometimes, dramatically. As soon as a front passes a particular location, the weather could change from a steamy maritime tropical air mass to a dry, cold continental polar air mass. The transition seldom happens without stormy weather developing. Only rarely is all quiet on the weather front.

Front Row

The naming of fronts is very straightforward. If colder or drier air overtakes warmer, more moist air, that's a *cold front.* Here, a continental polar air mass, or a maritime polar air mass, pushes aside a tropical air mass. Sometimes, a continental polar air mass will overtake a maritime polar air mass, and the transition zone is also called a cold front. The temperature could even increase following the passage of a cold front, but the common element is density. A cold front really marks the boundary between more-dense air and less-dense air, with the more-dense air mass overtaking the less-dense air mass.

Most commonly, that involves colder, heavier air overtaking warmer, less dense air. But sometimes, especially during the spring and summer, the continental polar air mass will be warmer than a maritime air mass, because the oceans are cooler than land masses during the warmer time of year. The weather, even in a tropical air mass, could be cloudy and hazy with limited sunshine. The air temperature might be in the 80s, but then a cold front comes through and the temperature turns warmer!

How can that be? Well, the continental polar air mass is drier, and therefore more dense. Air filled with water vapor will weigh less than drier air—the water-vapor molecules weigh less than the other common atmospheric gases. The temperature may not always drop following a cold front's passage, but the dew point always will.

A *warm front* leads the way of a tropical air mass. It will push aside a more-dense air mass, typically continental polar or maritime polar. Because a warm front involves less-dense air overtaking more-dense air, it travels more slowly than a cold front. It's tough for something light to shove aside something heavier, so a warm front may plow along at about 20 or 30 mph, while a cold front will move forward at 40 or 50 mph. The figure on the next page shows a cross-section through a typical cold and warm front.

In a warm front, the tropical air mass gently rides up over the adjacent cold air mass. In a cold front, the polar air wedges through the lighter air over a much shorter distance. The different lift experienced by the air along the different fronts really accounts for the different types of weather that develop.

Because a cold front can move twice as fast as a warm front, in the course of weather events, cold fronts will be

Weather-Speak

A **cold front** is a front where a colder air mass overtakes and replaces a warmer air mass. A **warm front** is a front where a warm air mass overtakes and replaces a cold air mass.

Weather-Speak

An **occluded front** is a front caused by a cold front overtaking a warm front, and the warm air is lifted above the earth's surface. A **stationary front,** on the other hand, is not moving.

able to catch up with warm fronts. The fronts will cross paths with the cold front catching up. The fronts go through a merger. I don't know if their stock rises after a merger like on Wall Street, but on Weather Street, the air rises, and we get our dividends in the form of precipitation. This merged front is called an *occluded front.* Take a look at the figure on the next page to see how the fronts get it together.

If a front is no longer moving, it's called a *stationary front.* The continental polar air mass, or the tropical air mass, just doesn't have enough push to move the opposing air mass out of the way. Stationary fronts become real headaches for weather forecasters because the weather turns stormy near the front, and the pattern offers few signs of change.

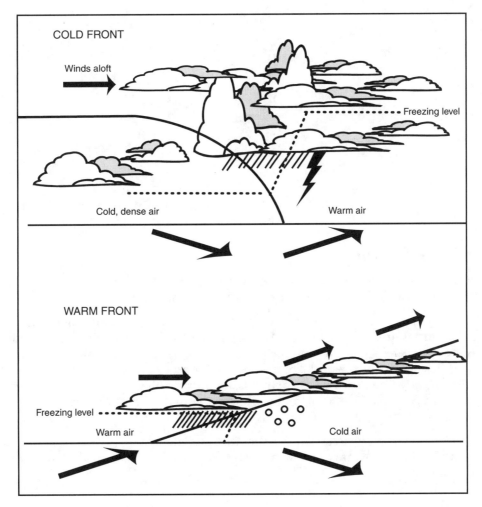

Cross-section of fronts.

Fronts on parade.

Frontal Attack

Air masses generate their own types of weather, but their interactions on a front can become thunderous and squally, or at least foggy and drizzly.

Along a front, whenever there are temperature contrasts, the atmosphere has a lot of energy just waiting to be released. That's called *potential energy*. All could be quiet, but as soon as there is some motion toward less-dense or more-dense air, the weather goes over the edge. An area where a temperature contrast exists is said to have *available potential energy,* and such areas are the flashpoints for big-time weather. The technical name is a *baroclinic zone.* (You might hear that term on the Weather Channel, but probably not on your local TV forecast.)

The next figure summarizes the weather that precedes and follows cold and warm fronts. Again, the nature of the weather is really just related to the degree of rising motions.

COLD FRONT

Weather	Before	During Passage	After
Winds	SSW	gusty, shifting	WNW
Temperature	warm	sudden drop	colder
Pressure	falling steadily	sharp rise	rising steadily
Precipitation	brief showers	heavy showers of rain or snow Thunder, hail or lightning.	decreasing showers then clearing
Visibility	fair to poor	poor, then improving	good
Dew point	high, remains steady	sharp drop	lowering

WARM FRONT

Weather	Before	During Passage	After
Winds	SSE	variable	SSW
Temperature	cool, cold	steady rise	warmer
Pressure	usually falling	leveling off	slight rise, then a fall
Precipitation	light to moderate rain, snow, sleet or drizzle	drizzle	usually none, could see showers or light rain
Visibility	poor	poor, but improving	fair
Dew point	steady	slow rise	rising, then steady

Cold- and warm-front weather.

There's a Storm a-Brewin'

Cold fronts bring the most violent conditions, which isn't surprising. After all, rising motions write the weather script, and lifting mechanisms are sharpest along a cold front. There, cold, heavy air is lifting warmer, lighter air—almost like a snow plow pushing aside a pile of fluffy, powdery snow. The warm air goes flying, and in the process, tall clouds form. The air is already unstable in the warmer air mass, and that added push is enough to get the storm rolling.

Weather-Speak

Potential energy is the potential to do work, or the potential to move. A deck of cards sitting on the edge of a table has the potential to fall, but its energy will only be released if it is pushed over the edge. Temperature contrasts represent potential energy in the atmosphere. When warm air masses mix with colder air masses, that potential energy becomes available for storm development, and is called **available potential energy**. Baroclinic zones are areas of temperature contrasts and available potential energy.

Thunderstorms and even tornadoes will form along cold fronts, generally in the warm air 50 to 100 miles ahead of the front. As a cold front approaches, the pressure falls rapidly because of all the lifting that's going on. The atmosphere is often hazy, steamy, and tropical. Winds freshen from the south and southwest, and then, through the haze, towering cumulus and cumulonimbus clouds form. Showers and thunderstorms develop, and if the lifting is really strong, tornadoes will form. The stormy weather is sharp, violent, but not necessarily long-lasting. Because the front is moving rapidly, the storm threat might only last for two or three hours.

Then, as the cold front passes, the barometer rises rapidly, the wind shifts into the northwest, the dew point lowers, and usually, the temperature drops. Typically, skies clear quickly because behind a cold front the air is subsiding, not rising. High pressure builds in from the west, and typically, the weather remains quiet for a few days.

It Looks Like Rain

In a warm front, the sequence of weather is different because the air is being lifted gently rather than sharply. Because the tropical air mass is less dense than the polar air it's replacing, the air rides up and over the colder air with a gradual slope. High, thin cirrus clouds appear in the colder air as much as 1,000 miles ahead of the warm front. The clouds form as the warm air comes into contact with the colder air mass and releases its moisture. The contact at 1,000 miles is at the very highest elevation within the atmosphere, so those cirrus clouds show up first. Those clouds will lower and thicken to cirrostratus, cirrocumulus, altostratus, altocumulus, and eventually, within 500 miles of the front, to nimbostratus. A steady, long-lasting rain develops. In the winter, the precipitation could begin as light snow.

As the warm front approaches and the depth of the warm air increases, snow will often change to sleet, freezing rain, and then to rain. Sometimes, the lifting is so gentle that only drizzle develops along the front. Fog often develops as the warmer air moves over a colder surface. In general, the precipitation is on the light side near a warm front, but as usual, there are exceptions. If the warming near the surface is very rapid, the atmosphere could turn unstable and thunderstorms could develop, but that class of weather is usually reserved for cold fronts.

As a warm front approaches, the barometer falls slowly but steadily. The wind can be from the north, but usually ranges from northeast to southeast. The temperature could be biting cold, but more typically it will just be on the cool side. A maritime polar air mass usually precedes a warm front with a maritime tropical air mass following. After the passage of the front, the pressure rises slowly or remains steady, the weather turns hazy, and the dew point climbs sharply. The rain ends, but as the tropical air takes hold, enough instability could occur to deliver isolated air-mass thunderstorms.

Stalled in Its Tracks

Stationary fronts deliver weather that is very much like warm fronts, with light precipitation falling in the maritime polar air and some clearing occurring in the tropical air mass.

Occluded fronts are similar to cold fronts, except the weather isn't as violent. The surface temperature contrast isn't as great with an occluded front, so the weather is less active. Typically, the occluded front divides maritime polar air from continental polar air, and the density difference is less than what is found between continental polar and maritime tropical air masses.

Storms on the Front

The weather within air masses is generally quiet, except when another opposing air mass comes along and challenges it. Then, fronts, with their ability to lift the air, generate a variety of weather. But these air-mass boundaries are not quite finished with us. Because of the density difference near fronts, medium- or synoptic-scale motions come into circulation. These atmospheric swirls can easily cover 500 to 1,000 miles. Half the United States can be enveloped by one of these systems. Because the air is rising and being drawn away, the pressure is relatively low, and these become typical low-pressure systems. They are technically called *frontal cyclones* because they spin counterclockwise and form along fronts. The common, everyday storm system is a frontal cyclone. The key source of energy here is that density difference across the front. Once these low-pressure areas form, they generate their own characteristic weather.

Weather-Speak

A **frontal cyclone** is a storm which forms on a front. In the Northern Hemisphere, it has a counterclockwise circulation, and it covers an area of several hundred miles, occasionally 1,000 miles.

Formation and Life Cycle

The following figure shows how these frontal cyclones kick in. Usually, two high-pressure systems are locked in place—one north of a stationary front, and the other south of the front. Because, in the Northern Hemisphere, the air moves clockwise around high-pressure systems, the wind is coming from the east just north of the front, and from the west just to the south of the front. Picture yourself holding a pencil between both of your hands. If one hand moves in one direction, and the other hand moves the other way, then that pencil will be set into motion. The air near the stationary front is just like that pencil. In the configuration of the next figure, the motion would be counterclockwise. A small, counterclockwise circulation forms, and it makes the front look wavy. These little waves form all the time, but only occasionally do they grow into a rip-roaring storm. Something else is needed.

Formation of frontal cyclone.

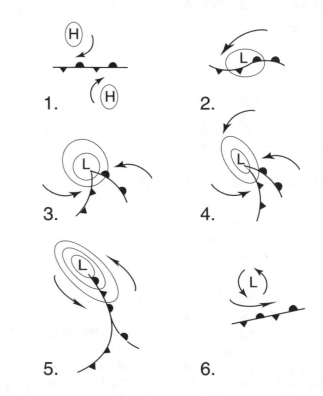

The upper atmosphere to the rescue! For a variety of reasons, the air above one of these waves could be diverging—drawn away. Strong wind differences at levels of 18,000 feet in the atmosphere can account for this divergence. The strong flow acts as an exhaust fan. When that exhaust takes place, the pressure is lowered near the ground, on the front, and in the vicinity of the wave. The pressure drops in that wave, and because of the greater pressure difference, its circulation increases. It then becomes a major low-pressure area—a major rain- or snow-maker.

The circulation causes the stationary front to move. A portion of it becomes a cold front, and another portion turns into a warm front. So, not only will the low-pressure system's upward motion help generate stormy skies, the fronts will deliver their own meteorological mix.

In the northeast quadrant of a frontal cyclone, the weather will be typical of what precedes a warm front—drizzly, rainy, foggy, sometimes icy or snowy. In the northwest quadrant, there is more of the same, except the air is colder and snow is most likely here—thanks to the north wind. In the southeast quadrant, the weather is typical of what follows a warm front and precedes a cold front. In the southwest quadrant, the weather is similar to that which occurs following a cold front passage. This distribution marks the mature stage of the storm.

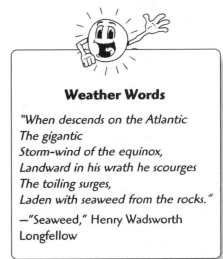

Weather Words

*"When descends on the Atlantic
The gigantic
Storm-wind of the equinox,
Landward in his wrath he scourges
The toiling surges,
Laden with seaweed from the rocks."*

—*"Seaweed,"* Henry Wadsworth Longfellow

Eventually, the cold front will catch up with the warm front—as you've learned, they always move faster. The temperature contrast across the frontal cyclone then weakens, losing some of that potential energy, so the storm eventually weakens. That is called the *occluded phase* because an occluded front forms.

Of Nor'easters and Sou'westers

These storms are special frontal cyclones—these are the big ones. They bring high winds, heavy precipitation, and locally severe thunderstorms and tornadoes.

Nor'easters are simply storms that are intense and deliver several days of heavy rain or snow along with strong northeast winds. That wind flow is what defines these storms. Because the circulation is counterclockwise around low-pressure systems, the areas west of the storm center will experience a northeast wind. The areas to the east will experience southwest winds, and for those locations, the same storm would be called a *sou'wester.*

Braving the Elements

A classic but severe frontal cyclone was the famous Blizzard of 1888. It hit the northeastern United States on March 12, 1888. The snowfall totaled 40 to 50 inches with drifts as high as 30 to 40 feet. There were 400 deaths resulting from this great blizzard.

These storms will generally form along fronts and move from the southwest to northeast. They frequently develop along fronts caught in the Gulf Stream waters off the East Coast, where a large temperature contrast prevails during the winter. The months of October through April represent prime time for these wild ones. The following figure shows the path of one of these meteorological marvels.

Nor'easters.

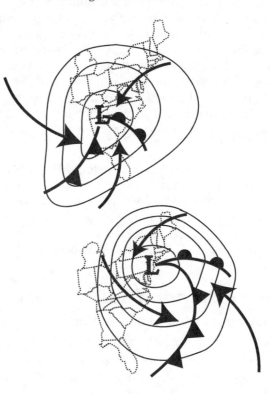

Telling What's Next

Much of the art of weather forecasting focuses on understanding the distribution of weather around these frontal cyclones and knowing when conditions will be just right for their formation.

Weather watchers study upper-air charts for clues about where divergence might be occurring. If those outflow areas occur over a stationary front, there's a good chance that one of those innocent waves will become unstable and turn into a full-fledged low-pressure area. It turns out that those same upper-wind patterns provide a clue about the path these storms will follow. That upper-wind current is known as the *jet stream,* and it reflects the general direction in which the weather flows. Often a frontal cyclone will move along the path of those winds at 18,000 feet and at a speed that is approximately half of the upper-level flow. A good cross-section of the atmosphere not only shows us whether a storm will form, but where it might be going.

The figure below shows a typical weather map for a fictitious December 24. The question on any December 24 is whether anyone will experience a white Christmas. The broad arrow shows the general flow of the jet stream. Based on the path, places like Chicago, Cleveland, and Buffalo will get snow in a big way. These locations will stay in the cold sector of the storm.

The speed and intensity of the storm will help determine how much snow will accumulate. But sorry, snow lovers in Washington, New York, and Boston—the warmer sector of the storm will be pushing through, and that means rain rather than snow on Christmas morning. But there's always New Year's Eve.

Weather-Speak

A **jet stream** is made up of relatively strong horizontal ribbons of wind found at the earth's tropopause, which is 6-10 miles above the ground.

This basic forecast technique was used routinely prior to the computer age; these days the forecast is automated. We'll have more on the new age of forecasting later. But there's really no substitute for looking out the window or at a weather map. It works!

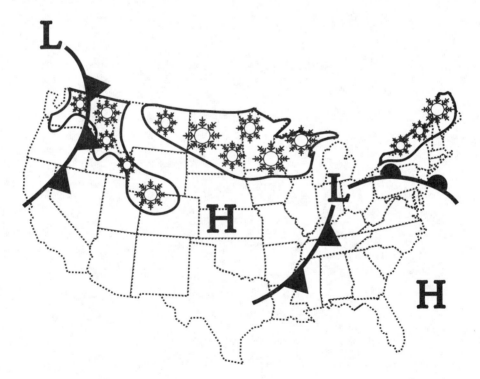

Snow for Christmas?

The Least You Need to Know

➤ Air masses are large bodies of air with uniform temperature and moisture characteristics.

➤ Each air mass brings about certain types of weather.

➤ When two contrasting air masses oppose each other, a front forms.

➤ Each type of front has certain characteristic weather.

➤ Fronts are zones where most of our storms develop.

Chapter 7

Hurricanes: The Greatest Storms on Earth

In This Chapter

➤ A look at tropical weather

➤ Development of hurricanes

➤ Predicting the unpredictable

➤ The hurricane threat

➤ Controlling the fury of hurricanes

Hurricanes are the most powerful storms on Earth. Whether called typhoons in the western Pacific or cyclones in the Indian Ocean, damage and destruction result wherever they strike land. These storms develop under different conditions than the everyday storm, and they're far less predictable.

Although hurricanes strike hardest in coastal areas, development and population growth along shore areas continues at a rapid rate. In the United States, there are 45 million permanent residents along the coast. During holidays, weekends, and in the summer, the population in some coastal areas increases ten- to a hundred-fold. Even though 80 to 90 percent of the population living in storm-prone areas have never experienced the core of a hurricane, a disaster, if not a catastrophe, is waiting to happen with every hurricane season. It's only a matter of time.

Weather Words

Hurricanes in the West, by Admiral Nares:

June—too soon;
July—stand by;
August—look out you must;
September—remember;
October—all over.

Weather-Wise

In July 1861, Cherrapunji, India, received 366 inches of rain—about 10 times the normal rainfall for an entire *year* in most of the world. In 1972, Hurricane Agnes flooded much of the eastern United States with an estimated 28 trillion gallons of water pouring out of the sky.

Weather-Speak

Latent heat is the heat that is absorbed or released during a substance's change of state, such as during evaporation or condensation.

It's Different in the Tropics

Most American meteorologists grew up in the mid-latitudes, and that's where they went to school. For many forecasters, tropical weather seems to come from another planet. It's far different from mid-latitude weather, and it is within these tropics that hurricanes are born.

The tropics are the area between the Tropic of Cancer and the Tropic of Capricorn—the latitude lines 23.5 degrees north and south of the equator. Within this zone, the excess heat and moisture contribute to tremendous potential instability. Often that instability will be capped by sinking motions at altitudes near 10,000 feet. Clouds form in the heat, but they aren't allowed to reach great heights because of that subsidence, that sinking air.

The weather stays under control. But if some mechanism removes that sinking trend and replaces it with rising currents, the weather goes absolutely wild. The process is similar to shaking a soda bottle and removing the cap. Those lifting mechanisms might simply be air running into a mountain range, or zones of convergence where winds at the surface run into each other, forcing the air to rise. And among the heavy lifters are those tropical low-pressure systems. The rising motions within these systems will cause torrential downpours.

Unlike frontal cyclones, tropical cyclones don't require temperature contrasts for development. There *aren't* any significant contrasts in the tropics; the temperature is relatively uniform. The standard forecasting techniques that hinge on those contrasts just don't work in the tropics. The big book of forecast methods was written for fronts and their associated weather. In the tropics, fronts do not exist, and a mid-latitude forecaster is often out of the game.

The source of energy for tropical weather is found in the tremendous heat release that occurs when clouds form. Heat is required to evaporate water off the ocean surface, and when that rising plume of water vapor goes back into its liquid phase during cloud formation, that absorbed heat is released. The heat has been stored and is called *latent heat*. A warm ocean surface is required to release enough latent heat for storm formation.

How It Happens

The hurricane story begins with a cluster of thunderstorms set off in the tropics, usually by some type of surface convergence. These initial squalls frequently develop in western Africa and move westward into the Atlantic. (The following figure shows a pattern of global winds that frequently provides for that initial convergence.) The organized area of convection then releases heat, which lowers the pressure. The lower pressure forces more air to converge, and as it comes together, it is forced to rise. This rising motion causes more huge thunderstorms that release more heat and reduce the pressure even more. That, in turn, allows more air to converge near the ground.

Hurricane formation.

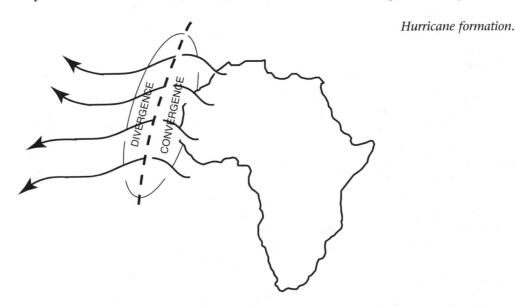

Remember the Coriolis force from Chapter 4? That's the force that makes the weather spin when air is put into motion. As more air rises, more air rushes toward the center, and the circulation becomes greater and greater.

There also has to be some mechanism for removing the air at high levels, which will ensure a steadily falling pressure through the net removal of the air. More air will leave than arrive. A high-pressure system aloft with diverging currents will do the job. Lots of tropical disturbances will form, but only a few will make a name for themselves. Usually, that high-level exhaust fan is missing with those storms that fail to make it. The figure on the next page shows how the entire pattern evolves.

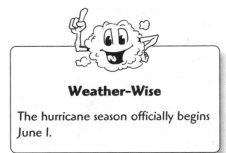

Weather-Wise

The hurricane season officially begins June 1.

Hurricane development.

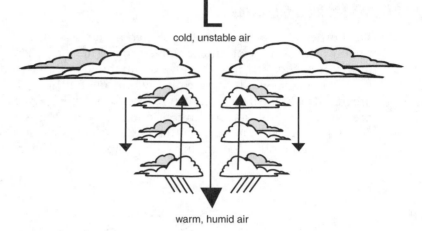

L

cold, unstable air

warm, humid air

When a disturbance forms with a well-defined circulation but winds under 39 mph, the system is called a *tropical depression*. When the wind reaches 39 to 73 mph, the system is called a *tropical storm*. When the wind exceeds 73 mph, the circulation is classified as a *hurricane*. In the western Pacific, hurricanes are called *typhoons*, and in the Indian Ocean, they are called *cyclones*, but in general, *tropical cyclones* refer to all organized tropical circulations.

These tropical cyclones have a unique structure (shown in the figure on the next page). A hurricane's circulation covers an area of about 300 to 700 miles. Moisture spirals into the center along *spiral rain bands*. The heaviest rain and the most violent weather will occur within these precipitation bands. The winds gradually increase toward the center of the hurricane, and the highest winds are found in the *eye wall,* where towering clouds extend up to 50,000 feet and higher. The most destructive portion of the hurricane occurs in the eye wall.

At the center is the relatively calm *eye,* where the wind may be about 10 to 15 mph. Air is subsiding into the eye, which is why the sky is clear. The rain will end, and the clouds will be broken. The eye itself is about 10 to 30 miles wide. Because tropical cyclones release tremendous amounts of heat, the center of the circulation is warmer than the surroundings, another characteristic that distinguishes these storms from frontal cyclones. Storms that form on fronts have a cold center.

Weather-Speak

When a system has winds under 39 mph, it's called a **tropical depression**. When the wind reaches 39 to 73 mph, the system is a **tropical storm**. When the wind exceeds 73 mph, the circulation is classified as a **hurricane**. In the western Pacific, hurricanes are called **typhoons**; in the Indian Ocean, they're called **cyclones**. A **tropical cyclone** generally refers to all organized tropical circulations.

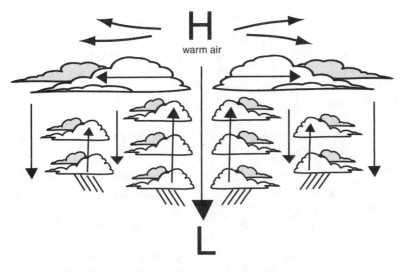

Hurricane structure.

These storms need energy, which limits the areas where they can develop. They have to form over the oceans, in locations where the water temperature is at least 79 degrees. If the water temperature is lower, the storm will actually lose energy to the ocean surface. That's why a hurricane weakens when it moves into colder water or over land areas: Its heat gets absorbed by the cooler land or water. The next figure shows the source regions and path for these storms.

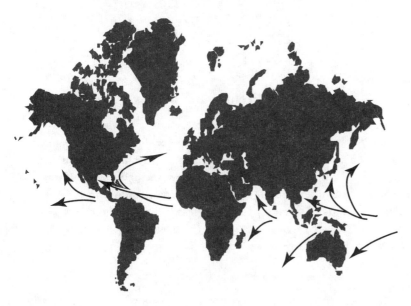

Source regions and path of hurricanes.

The Name Game

Prior to World War II, hurricanes were identified according to their latitude and longitude. That method became confusing, and during the war, the storms were given names such as Able, Baker, and Charlie. But the number of Ables and Bakers became so great that this naming scheme became confusing, too. So, in 1953, the National Weather Service began using female names. Later, in the 1970s, male names got into the mix—for Pacific storms in 1978 and Atlantic storms in 1979.

I am still waiting for Hurricane Mel, but the outlook for that is mostly cloudy. Lists of names are drawn up for a four-year rotation. Separate lists are drawn up for the Atlantic and Pacific. If a storm is responsible for noteworthy damage and destruction, the name is retired—something like a basketball jersey. But if the storm never does much, its name is repeated in four years. Tropical depressions do not receive names, but as soon as a system reaches tropical storm status, it earns a name. In the Gulf and Atlantic, about 10 named storms occur each year. In the Pacific, the alphabet could be exhausted—the wider oceanic area favors more development there.

Weather-Watch

A tropical storm watch *is* issued when tropical storm conditions are considered *possible* within 36 hours. That watch is elevated to a warning if those conditions are considered likely, usually within 24 hours. A hurricane watch and hurricane warning work the same way, with the watch issued when hurricane conditions are considered possible within 36 hours, and a warning issued when those conditions are *expected*.

Braving the Elements

Two Category-5 storms are known to have hit the United States, but only one has ever reached the mainland. In 1969, Hurricane Camille reached Category 5 status and slammed onto the mainland in Louisiana and Mississippi. The other Category 5 storm struck the Florida Keys on Labor Day 1935. It was called the Labor Day hurricane and stayed off the mainland, but technically hit the United States in the Keys. Hurricane Andrew in 1992 was borderline between Categories 4 and 5 when it pushed into Florida. Hurricane Hugo, which hit South Carolina in 1989, was a Category-4 storm. The Great 1938 Hurricane, which hit New England, was a strong Category-3 system.

Some hurricanes do reach super-storm status, and an intensity scale is used to classify the storms. It is called the Saffir-Simpson scale, after the people who devised the scheme. See the following figure for a general description of the different intensities.

Category	1	2	3	4	5
Pressure (mb)	>980	965-979	945-964	920-944	<920
Pressure (in)	>28.94	28.50-28.91	27.91-28.47	27.17-27.88	<27.17
Winds (mph)	74-95	96-110	111-130	131-155	>155
Winds (kph)	64-82	83-95	96-113	114-135	>135
Storm Surge (ft)	4-5	6-8	9-12	13-18	>18

Saffir Simpson Scale.

Hurricane Forecasting

Because hurricane dynamics are completely different than the typical storm, forecasting their next moves is quite an art. Frontal cyclones are embedded in a stream of air that determines their path and influences their intensity. That stream is absent in the tropics. Also, because tropical systems form in areas of weak temperature contrast, the standard forecast procedures go out the window. Additionally, heat as an element is poorly understood in the scheme of weather equations, and because hurricanes depend so heavily on that heat release, their behavior is often mysterious.

So, we may have a storm that has no apparent push and often spins like a top with no particular clear-cut path—an enormous heat engine that's just not well understood. As hurricanes move into northern latitudes they become more predictable, but that tremendous heat release persists and is always ready to throw us some curve balls.

One technique of forecasting simply involves persistence. Whatever path and trend the storm may be on, that is simply projected to continue for the next 12 to 24 hours. You've probably heard hurricane forecasts with the words, "Little change in path or intensity is expected during the next 24 hours."

Sometimes, climatology is used. What is the normal path that these storms take? Both persistence and climatology work well when the storm is in an area of a weak jet stream—like the tropics. But as the storm heads northward, the path can change

Weather-Wise

Because of their damaging histories, a number of hurricane names will never be used again: Agnes, Alicia, Allen, Andrew, Anita, Audrey, Betsy, Beulah, Bob, Bonnie, Camille, Carla, Carmen, Carol, Celia, Cesar, Charley, Cleo, Connie, David, Diana, Diane, Donna, Dora, Fifi, Flora, Fran, Frederic, Gilbert, Gloria, Gracie, Hattie, Hazel, Hilda, Hortense, Hugo, Inez, Ione, Janet, Joan, Klaus, Luis, Marilyn, Mitch, Opal, Roxanne.

erratically and unpredictably. Numerous computer-forecast methods have been developed using both dynamics and statistics, but one of the most reliable instruments for hurricane tracking is a simple barometer. A hurricane's path is nicely outlined by the pressure drop that occurs ahead of the center. These pressure drops can be mapped out, and where the falls are greatest is where the hurricane is heading. Unfortunately, this technique gives only a short-term warning—maybe six hours.

In a hurricane, the strongest winds are found within 50 miles of the center—that's where the most damage is likely to occur. Our ability to predict the position of a hurricane within 50 miles in a 24-hour period is not very great. There is less than a 50-50 chance that such a forecast will be accurate. So, because of the need for allowing enough time to prepare and perform evacuations, hurricane conditions are predicted far more often than they materialize.

The Triple Threat

Hurricanes are responsible for delivering, in a huge way, the three Ws: wind, water, and waves. Wind is often thought to be the real destructive element within a hurricane, even though the vast majority of damage and destruction will be related to water and waves. But the wind is not without its problems.

As the wind increases to hurricane intensity, the system seems to cross an important threshold. Damage becomes widespread, and because the force of the wind increases with the square of the velocity, a doubling of wind will cause a four-fold increase in the damage potential. But in addition to the normal hurricane winds, these storms frequently spawn tornadoes. Even after a storm moves inland and weakens, with winds dropping off, tornadoes can continue to spin for hours, even days. These tornadoes are not the huge, Midwest-variety, but they are strong enough to rip roofs off and uproot trees. Typically, the tornadoes form in the right-front quadrant of a hurricane. If the storm is heading northward, the tornadoes form in the northeast sector. In general, that sector contains the strongest wind.

Weather-Watch

Either pull your boat out of the water before the storm, or properly tie it down. If you are concerned about broken windows, use plywood rather than tape. Make sure you have a supply of batteries, canned food, and drinking water.

When a hurricane is moving northward, that northward trajectory combines with the northward flowing air on the storm's eastern side to enhance the strength of the wind. On the western side, the northward trajectory opposes the southward flowing air, so the net wind is lower. The figure on the next page shows how the wind is impacted by the storm path. In New England, one of the great concerns is for a hurricane making landfall in western portions of the region and moving onshore at a rapid forward speed. That combination is exactly what happened during the great hurricane of 1938, when 600 people were killed.

Torrential rains accompany hurricanes, and like the wind, can persist long after the storm has moved inland.

Some of the most destructive storms have delivered flash flooding. For example, Tropical Storm Claudette in 1979 brought 45 inches of rain to Alvin, Texas. Damage ran in the hundreds of millions of dollars. Hurricanes Connie and Diane teamed up to deliver about 20 inches of rain to New England in August 1955. The flooding created one of the greatest natural disasters known to that region with damage at $4.2 billion, adjusted to 1990s dollars. Two hundred people were killed. Then there was Hurricane Agnes in 1972, which moved onshore and lingered for days as a weakened but soaking-wet tropical storm. In terms of adjusted dollars, damage came to $6.4 billion, and the death toll reached 122.

Deadly right quadrant.

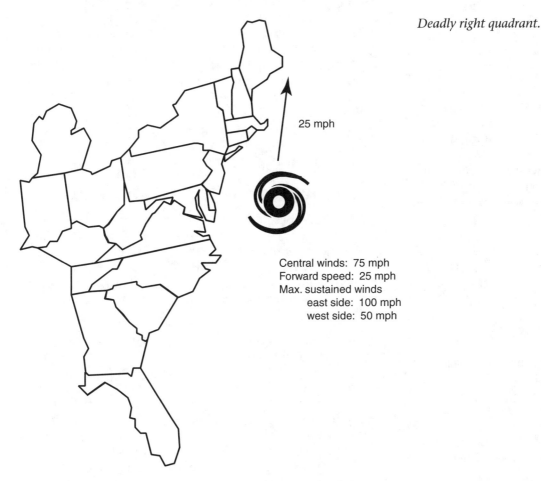

25 mph

Central winds: 75 mph
Forward speed: 25 mph
Max. sustained winds
      east side: 100 mph
      west side: 50 mph

In 1998, Hurricane Mitch became the most deadly storm to have struck the Atlantic basin since 1780. Its torrential rains set off mudslides in Nicaragua, Honduras and El Salvador. At least 9,000 people were killed. The only other hurricane that claimed more lives in the Atlantic basin was a storm that struck from Barbados to Martinique in October 1780. That storm claimed 22,000 lives.

The massive rains associated with these storms occur because of the huge mass of moisture tied up with these storms and the strong instability. If the terrain becomes rough with lots of hills, the air will be pushed upward and that will put the big squeeze on the atmosphere. Most inland areas fear the rains from hurricanes far more than the wind.

Weather-Watch

Just as with tornadoes, all doors and windows should be closed during hurricanes. Because no building is airtight, pressure differences between the inside and outside will not build up enough to cause explosive forces. An opened window could serve as entry for debris and water, and air rushing through could actually cause a roof to lift away.

Weather-Speak

A **storm surge** is a moving wall of water that races to the shore and crushes coastal areas. The eye's low pressure causes the sea beneath it to rise measurably, usually well above the high tide level. The strong winds force additional piling up of the water.

There are also the waves and surges of water that occur at the shore. The strong winds pile up the water along coastal areas that look into the wind. This creates a *surge*, which can measure 10 to 20 feet above the normal tide level. Additionally, waves of 20 or even 30 feet will combine with the surge. Also, the low pressure in the center of the storm will draw the water to even greater heights, as though it were drawn through a straw. When the storm arrives during a normal high tide, the situation is even worse. The Galveston Hurricane of 1900 took the lives of 6,000 people, most by the surging tide. Much of Hurricane Camille's damage in 1969 was related to a 25-foot storm tide when the storm moved into coastal Mississippi.

Another Big One Coming?

A season doesn't pass without the coastal areas of the United States being vulnerable to a major catastrophic hurricane, but a number of factors make these big hits relatively rare. The hurricanes don't cover a very large geographical area, and often, unless a hurricane's center comes within 50 miles of a particular location, damage is minimal.

In addition, a number of factors conspire to *enhance* the impact of a hurricane. If rain precedes a hurricane and the ground is saturated, flooding is more likely. Also, if the storm arrives during high tide, and if the tides are already higher than normal because of the positioning of the Moon and Sun, the storm surge will be much worse. In addition, if the dangerous right-hand sector of the storm barrels into a particular location, damage will be far more serious. The odds for all these factors coming together are slight—but they do happen, such as in New England during the 1938 hurricane.

This storm was not as intense as a Camille or Hugo, but it was responsible for the greatest disaster of the 20th century in New England. When it rapidly raced into that region with a forward speed of 50 to 60 mph, all the enhancements were in place.

Wind damage was extreme, flooding was widespread, and the storm surge inundated most of the Connecticut and Rhode Island shoreline. This 1938 hurricane has been the storm by which New Englanders have measured all others. Sustained winds (winds measured over a five-minute interval) reached as high as 126 mph, waves were 30 to 40 feet high, and the storm surge was as high as 17 feet.

But as rare as that storm might have been, ever since the Pilgrims came to New England, one or two 1938-type storms have occurred in that region every century. It will happen again and again. Likewise, all the 45 million permanent residents along the entire hurricane-prone coastline of the United States are at risk.

Weather-Wise

The eastern section of a hurricane always contains the heaviest squalls, greatest storm surge, and even tornadoes.

During the 1970s and '80s hurricanes weren't as frequent as they were from the 1940s to the 1960s. A false sense of security helped push coastal development into some very precarious locations, such as barrier islands. The greatest increase in population has been in the sunbelt area from Texas through the Carolinas, and Florida leads the United States in new residents. During the 1990s, hurricane frequency began to increase, and the opportunities for not just a disaster, but a catastrophe, are increasing.

Hurricane Andrew in 1992 signaled what lies ahead. Damage from that storm in southern Florida reached $20 billion with estimates up to $40 billion, and that was concentrated on a relatively small area around and just south of Miami. Hurricane Andrew is a warning of what will likely occur in the near future. It became the most costly natural disaster in U.S. history.

Although there is no well-defined cycle, the weather always balances in the long term. I call it the Law of Weather Averages, and it ensures that the past will always be repeated. In addition, if long-term climate changes are taking place with warmer ocean temperatures, then conditions could favor even more intense development—but that is a point of controversy which is a topic for another day. We'll get to the overheated debates about climate change a little later in Chapter 20.

Taming the Tiger

For decades, seeding experiments were performed on hurricanes with the hope of taming their fury. The project was called Stormfury and was a joint effort of the National Weather Service and the U.S. Navy. The concept was to diffuse the strong wind from the center of the hurricane. Silver iodide was released in different locations within the hurricane circulation, allowing for forced condensation and a forced heat release in zones other than the eye wall. The hope was for this procedure to deliver a less defined, single center of concentrated heat release and lowered pressure. The pressure field would become less organized and the wind field would become more confused. At least, that was the theory.

In 1963, when Hurricane Beulah was seeded, surface pressure in the eye began to rise, and the highest winds were no longer concentrated at the center. In 1969, Hurricane Debbie diminished in intensity after seeding, but the question always remained whether these changes would have taken place *without* the seeding. Also, the number of hurricanes that have been available for seeding have been relatively few. By 1990, because of mixed results, Project Stormfury was abandoned.

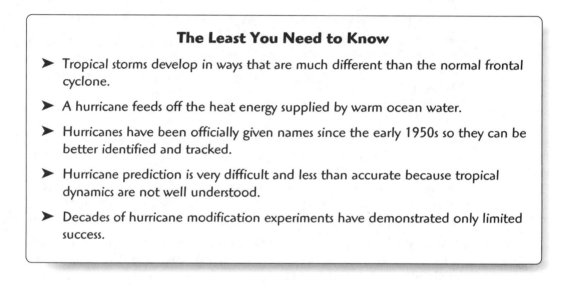

The Least You Need to Know

➤ Tropical storms develop in ways that are much different than the normal frontal cyclone.

➤ A hurricane feeds off the heat energy supplied by warm ocean water.

➤ Hurricanes have been officially given names since the early 1950s so they can be better identified and tracked.

➤ Hurricane prediction is very difficult and less than accurate because tropical dynamics are not well understood.

➤ Decades of hurricane modification experiments have demonstrated only limited success.

Chapter 8

Blowing Cold and Hot: The Big Ones

In This Chapter

➤ Looking at some big ones

➤ The storms that snowed us

➤ The Blizzard of 1888

➤ The mighty day in Galveston

➤ Hurricanes through the twentieth century

Our weather is always going to the extreme, and in this chapter we take a closer look at a few of the big storms that have made history. This will not only underscore the power of the weather but also bring together the principles we've looked at in previous chapters. We'll see how nature makes it happen. Of course, devastating storms are just too numerous to list, and all cyclopaths have their favorites. So this is just a partial list of some of my greatest hits; with some of these storms, I've even had some personal involvement.

Winter Gone South

A flake of snow may seem innocent enough, but there's nothing more disruptive than the combination of a few million of those flakes. An inch or two of snow in the wrong place at the wrong time can snarl traffic and bring a community to a standstill. A full-blown snowstorm with a foot or more of snow can tie up a region for days. The high winds and bitter-cold temperatures that often accompany snowstorms only add to the woes. Nearly every region of the United States has been hit by a paralyzing snowfall, even the Deep South.

Weather Words

*"No cloud above, no earth below—
A universe of sky and snow."*

—John Greenleaf Whittier

Weather-Wise

The weather does show plenty of bluster in Chicago, but is Chicago really the windiest city? Weather records suggest that it may be the Windy City more because of its politics. The average wind speed in Chicago is 10.4 mph, and while that's plenty of wind, other cities have significantly higher winds. Boston has an average wind speed of 12.5 mph. Other cities with higher winds include Buffalo, Cape Hatteras, Honolulu, and Milwaukee. One of the windiest cities in Dodge City, Kansas, with an average 14 mph.

In 1895, an unusual low-pressure system moved northward through the Gulf of Mexico. At the same time, a cold high-pressure area had dropped southward into the central Plains. The combination caused snow to break out in some very unlikely places. Snowfall amounts came to 8 inches in New Orleans, Galveston picked up 15 inches, Houston received 20 inches, and Pensacola received 3 inches. The pattern that caused the snowfall was classic, except it took shape about 1,000 miles farther south than normal. Another unusual snowfall occurred in more recent times, in January 1977, when snow was measured as far south as Miami.

Big-City Snows

While the southern snowfall experience is rare, the Midwest encounters just seem to go with the territory. One of the great ones occurred during the stormy, cold 1960s when, on January 26–27, 1967, Chicago picked up a record 19.8 inches in 24 hours. The Chicago total came to 23 inches. The snowfall rate was nearly one inch per hour for 24 hours—quite a heavy rate. That entire winter was rough in the Midwest, and Chicago's snow-removal cost for the season turned out to be 10 times higher than normal. In 1999, New Year's Weekend brought a similar snowfall to Chicago when a storm total of 21.6 inches fell.

Other "big city" blitzes include a snowstorm that moved into New York on the day after Christmas in 1947. The center of the storm pushed into eastern Long Island, and in New York City, the snow came down at a rate of two to three inches per hour during midday. Ten thousand cars were abandoned, and in Central Park, the snow measured 26.4 inches.

In Boston, where snowstorms are frequent visitors, the storm of February 6–8, 1978, turned out to be a record-setter. Snowfall came to 27.5 inches, and in addition, high winds caused extreme tides, which flooded coastal neighborhoods. Most of New England was shut down during that storm, which was preceded by very little warning. New computer models did indicate that a massive storm would move into the northeastern states, but in 1978, those computer projections weren't always used with confidence. On Sunday, February 5, the forecast called for some snow, related to a system moving eastward from the Great Lakes, but in the words of one official forecast that reached my ears, "We don't expect a *blizzard*." Snow began just before daybreak on February 6 in western New England, and it moved slowly eastward. Many commuters were on their way to work when their cars became trapped in the heavily falling snow.

Braving the Elements

March is named after the Roman god of war, and is famous for its blustery and stormy weather. Around the Ides of March—March 15—some of the biggest snowstorms of the past have occurred. In 1993, a huge snowstorm developed on March 12 and pounded New England on March 13. It was called "The Storm of the Century."

Storm of the Century?

A more recent mega-snowstorm in 1993 was thought to be one of the biggest winter storms of the twentieth century. It became known as the "storm of the century," although many veterans of winter weather thought that was just media hype. But it truly was one of the greatest storms in terms of both area of coverage and intensity. The storm brought harsh weather to the entire eastern portion of the country on that mid-March day.

Very heavy snow accumulated in the South, where Birmingham, Alabama, picked up a foot. Snow covered the ground from Mississippi to the Florida Panhandle. The heavy snow spread northward along the East Coast to Maine, and on Saturday, March 13, every airport in the eastern states was closed. Snowfall ranged up to four feet on Mount Mitchell, North Carolina. Atlanta, Georgia, picked up 3 inches; Chattanooga, Tennessee, picked up 21 inches. During the peak of the storm, about 30 percent of the entire country was hit by the rough weather.

Record low barometer readings were set all along the East Coast, and the storm spawned 27 tornadoes across central Florida. Very warm, humid air moved across central Florida, and that, combined with the energy of the storm, helped spawn the killer twisters. Winds were clocked at 99 mph on an oil platform off the Louisiana coast. Overall, the storm took 285 lives, mostly because of tornadoes. The storm became the costliest non-tropical storm in Florida's history. States of emergency were declared throughout the eastern portion of the country.

Weather-Speak

The National Weather Service says a **blizzard** is characterized by low temperatures, winds greater than 35 mph, and snow heavy enough to restrict visibility to less than a quarter-mile. In earlier days, the temperature had to be in the teens, but no longer. If blowing snow restricts visibility to below a quarter-mile, even after the snow stops falling, that's called a **ground blizzard**.

The Greatest One of All

While many might debate whether the 1993 storm was truly the biggest winter storm of the twentieth century, there can be no debate that one of the greatest storms in recorded weather history belongs to another century—the Blizzard of 1888. What a storm! We can only imagine the impact of four feet of snow when the main means of snow removal consisted of horse and buggy.

Actually, there were two Blizzards of '88. The first struck across the Plains from Montana to Texas and eastward to the Great Lakes. That storm hit on January 12–14. The temperature plunged as low as 53 below zero, and more than 200 people died. The second blizzard occurred during mid-March, focusing its energy on the northeast states from Washington, D.C., to New England.

This became the "granddaddy" of all "nor'easters," the East Coast storms that track slowly offshore. As discussed in Chapter 6, they actually arrive from the south, but because the wind comes out of the northeast direction, the storm becomes a nor'easter.

The next three figures show a sequence of weather systems that caused the great Eastern blizzard to occur. It is a classic weather pattern that leads to the development of every nor'easter, but in the case of the March 1888 storm, the weather went to extremes.

March 11, 1888 of the Blizzard of 1888.

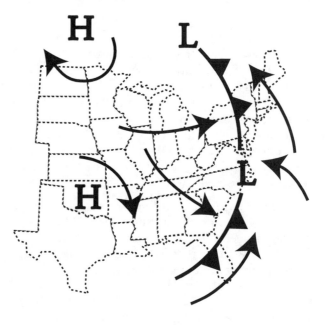

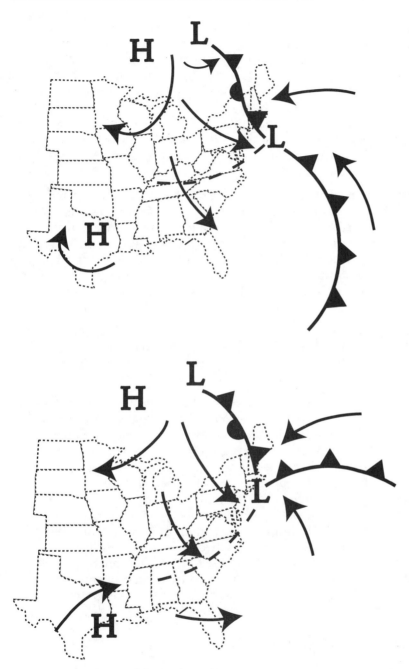

March 12, 1888 of the Blizzard of 1888.

March 13, 1888 of the Blizzard of 1888.

The storm had its original energy gather across the Midwest. An initial storm center, called a *primary center*, pushed into the Great Lakes on March 10. Another system was spinning in the Southern states, and it fired into a massive *secondary center* as the

103

energy from the primary system was transferred to it—a common chain of meteoro-logical events. One center of low pressure will move across the United States and eventually weaken, but enough spin remains to sweep eastward and tap into the temperature contrast found along the East Coast during the winter. Cold air masses sweep around the initial system and clash with the warm air along the coast and adjacent to the warm Gulf Stream waters. The temperature contrast represents that potential energy. The spin that translates from the primary center provides the vertical motion to unleash that energy. An East Coast storm is born. The process is called *cyclogenesis*, but because these storms can really explode, the process for extreme storms has been dubbed *bombogenesis*.

On March 11, the weather was relatively balmy in the Northeast, and a light rain was falling. All accounts of that winter show generally mild conditions, and crocuses were blossoming early. Everyone was looking forward to spring. As the secondary center pushed off the mid-Atlantic coast, its northeast wind tapped into a cold pool of air that was positioned over eastern Canada. That cold high-pressure system also helped to block the rapid motion of the storm. The storm became stationary near Block Island, where it spun like a top. Much of the rain turned to snow, and it snowed through the 14th.

In these situations, the winds in the upper levels of the atmosphere fail to push the storms along. Those high-level winds simply wrap themselves around the storm, and the system becomes caught in an atmospheric whirl-pool. The nor'easter can go out of control.

Weather-Speak

A **primary center** is the initial storm center. A **secondary center** forms from the primary center. **Cyclogenesis** is the development or intensification of a cyclone. **Bombogenesis** has been used to describe extreme cyclogenesis of an explosive nature.

Snowfall depths ranged up to 50 inches over a wide area from the nation's capital to New England. Communication systems were shut down and transportation was paralyzed. For a week, the northeastern states were cut off from the rest of the world. Snow drifts of 20 to 40 feet were common, and because the temperature plunged to near zero as winds shifted into the Northeast, slush turned to solid ice. Washington, New York City, Hartford, Albany, and Boston were completely paralyzed. Winds reached hurricane intensity and an estimated 400 lives were lost. Two hundred people were killed in New York City alone. Some survivors of the storm, called "Blizzard Men of 1888," held annual meetings in New York City until 1941.

Modern Winter of Deep Snows

On the subject of snowstorms, even though the 1990s were known for record world-wide warmth, the decade not only managed to deliver the 1993 "Storm of the Century," it also generated the snowiest season on record for much of the East. The 1995–96 season delivered a series of pounding nor'easters that pushed seasonal snow-fall totals up to 300 percent of normal.

The snowstorms arrived in November. During that month alone, nearly three feet of snow fell in places such as Syracuse and Binghamton, New York. On January 6–9, a storm delivered 30.7 inches of snow to Philadelphia, Pennsylvania, and 24.6 inches to the Washington-Dulles Airport. The following table shows the distribution of the snowfall in that storm. At the end of the season, 100 inches or more accumulated in places where the normal seasonal total is close to 40 inches. It certainly didn't seem like greenhouse warming during that season!

March 1993—Storm of the Century

City	Snow totals (inches)
Mount LeConte, TN	56.0
Mount Mitchell, NC	50.0 (14-foot drifts)
Snowshoe, WV	44.0
Syracuse, NY	43.0
Latrobe, PA	36.0 (10-foot drifts)
Lincoln, NH	35.0
Beckley, WV	30.0
Page County, VA	29.0
Albany, NY	27.0
Pittsburgh, PA	24.6
Mountain City, GA	24.0
Wilkes-Barre/Scranton, PA	21.4
Chattanooga, TN	20.0
Asheville, NC	19.0
Charleston, WV	18.9
Elkins, WV	18.8
Portland, ME	18.6
Birmingham, AL	17.0 (6-foot drifts)
Roanoke, VA	16.0
Williamsport, PA	15.9
Hartford, CT	14.8
Washington Dulles AP	14.1
Washington, D.C.	13.0
Boston, MA	12.8
Newark, NJ	12.7
Philadelphia, PA	12.0
Baltimore, MD	11.9
Bridgeport, CT	10.8
New York, NY	10.6
Providence, RI	10.2
Atlanta, GA	4.0

Galveston Storm Surge

Of course, snowstorms haven't been the only atmospheric heavyweights to come along. The warm season brings its own weather wonders, including hurricanes with their triple threat of wind, rain, and tidal surges. The twentieth century had just gotten underway when one of the greatest natural disasters in history took place. In 1900, Galveston, Texas, bore the brunt of a gigantic storm surge associated with a hurricane.

On Saturday, September 8, overcast skies and a light drizzle fell across the Texas Gulf coast. The wind increased and the surf started to pound. The barometer fell to a very low 29 inches. By midday, the pressure had fallen another half inch. The wind increased so much that weather instruments were knocked out of service. During the evening, the wind increased to over 80 mph, and a huge storm surge hit at 7:32 p.m. By midnight, the storm began to abate, but the damage had been done. Galveston Island had washed into the sea, and 6,000 people had been killed. In terms of loss of life, there hasn't been another disaster of that magnitude in U.S. history. At the time, Galveston's highest point was only five feet above sea level. Since then, the city has been rebuilt and the entire island raised 17 feet.

The Great New England Hurricane

Additional massive hurricanes such as the 1900 storm failed to reach the U.S. mainland for several decades, but again, another fierce blow was always lurking over the tropical horizon. In 1935, a Category-5 storm moved through the Florida Keys, but it stayed offshore. However, in 1938, good luck ran out and a super-storm crossed the coastline—this time along the East Coast. On September 21, 1938, New England experienced its greatest natural disaster ever. The death toll reached 600; about 30,000 people were injured, 93,000 were homeless, and 16,000 homes and businesses were destroyed. Property damage came to about four billion in 1990 dollars. Property damage was greater than the Great San Francisco Earthquake of 1906 and the Chicago Fire of 1871.

The storm began like so many that reach the East Coast—off the west coast of Africa. On September 16, it had reached a point 500 miles north of the Leeward Islands in the Caribbean. Prior to the storm, heavy rains had completely saturated the soil in the Northeast. Several inches of rain had fallen that month in New England, and a hurricane would only add more problems.

This system seemed innocent. It reached just east of Cape Hatteras around daybreak of September 21. The official forecast called for the storm to go harmlessly out to sea, but instead, a convergence of air along the East Coast forced the storm to move northward at an accelerating rate of 50 to 60 mph. By early afternoon, the storm center was crossing the Connecticut shoreline, and by evening, its center reached Canada. That strong northward trajectory, combined with the storm's

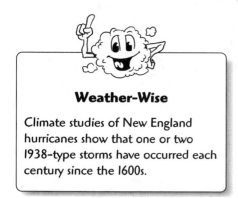

Weather-Wise

Climate studies of New England hurricanes show that one or two 1938-type storms have occurred each century since the 1600s.

circulation in its eastern sector, created a massive tidal surge in southern New England and Long Island. The storm came when the tide was high, too. Trains were derailed as waves poured over tracks, and many drowned in their automobiles. Wind gusts as high as 186 mph were clocked at Milton, Massachusetts. Sustained winds reached 121 mph. Waves were estimated to be 30 to 40 feet high. Carla Carlson in Guilford, Connecticut, was stalled in traffic, and she decided to read while the road was being cleared. While she was reading, another tree came down and hit her car, killing her. And the book she was reading? *Gone With the Wind.*

The Fabulous '50s and Super '60s

Once again, a lull in disastrous hurricanes took place, although an offshore storm just missed New England in 1944. The 1950s and 1960s became very active, with numerous big ones finding populated areas. In 1954, Hurricane Carol moved into New England with wind gusts to 130 mph. I remember that one: I watched the roof of my house just north of Boston blow away, piece by piece. The storm tide in Providence was nearly as great as the 1938 Hurricane. The year 1955 brought Hurricanes Connie and Diane into New England with a combined rainfall of more than 20 inches. The flooding became historic, and damage reached close to one billion in 1955 dollars. Every New England town was flooded. Rivers swept away homes and businesses. The death toll reached 82.

These same turbulent times brought Hurricane Donna in 1960. The storm delivered a one-two punch to southern Florida, first as it moved from the Atlantic into the Gulf of Mexico, and then back into the Atlantic. It was the first hurricane to cause hurricane-force winds from Florida to the mid-Atlantic states to New England. When the storm first crossed Florida, it was a powerful Category-4 storm.

Braving the Elements

Weather lore says, "October, all over," but during 1954, Hurricane Hazel didn't come along until mid–October. Two hurricanes, Connie and Diane, joined forces in October 1955. They struck within 10 days and caused historic flooding. Hurricane Andrew approached category 5 winds of 150 mph as it advanced on the southern Florida coast in 1992.

Southern Florida was hit hard again when Hurricane Betsy moved just south of Miami right after Labor Day in 1965. Winds reached over 100 mph. I have vivid memories of that storm, as well. I was in Miami that weekend, about to become engaged, visiting with my fiancé-to-be. The storm lurked off the East Coast from Saturday through Monday, sending occasional squalls into south Florida.

Nobody was sure where Betsy was going next. Some thought Cuba, but by about 2:00 p.m. Tuesday afternoon, there was little doubt. This time, the squall came, and it didn't abate. The wind roared, the rains pelted down, and the power went out. Through that night, the only flashes of light originated from short-circuited power transformers or lightning. By daybreak on Wednesday, the barometer seemed to steady. I went to the window and saw the sunrise through the eye of the storm as it passed across the Keys. I looked down and saw that our building, instead of being along Biscayne Bay, was *in* Biscayne Bay.

Soon after that unforgettable sunrise, the eye of the storm moved on, the winds picked up again, and the pounding continued until mid-afternoon, when finally the storm moved into the Gulf of Mexico. Unfortunately, the storm turned northward toward the Gulf Coast, intensified even more, and eventually ravaged the Louisiana coastline. Betsy became one of the most destructive storms in U.S. history, with over nine billion dollars in damage.

Weather-Watch

As you move into the eye of a hurricane, winds die down and the sky brightens. This does not mean the storm is over. It is just a brief lull. The worst part of the storm happens once the eye passes over.

Camille

The rip-roaring decades of the '50s and '60s were just winding down when another massive storm came along. This one became the only Category-5 storm to ever cross the U.S. mainland. The storm had a relatively compact structure, with hurricane-force winds extending out only 60 miles from the center, but Hurricane Camille delivered some of the strongest winds on record.

Once again, this storm developed off the west coast of Africa. The initial disturbance showed up on August 5, 1969. Over the next nine days, it pushed westward and steadily intensified. On August 14, it became "Camille." The storm moved into the Gulf of Mexico on the 16th, with winds reaching well over 130 mph. By the 17th, the storm was centered 250 miles south of Mobile, Alabama, and hurricane warnings began to fly along the Gulf Coast. Evacuations got underway. On that Sunday afternoon, reconnaissance aircraft reported surface winds reading an unheard-of 200 mph. At that point, the storm center was just 100 miles away from the mouth of the Mississippi River. At 10:30 p.m. on the 17th, the storm center made landfall on the Mississippi coast. Just as I watched my roof fly away in Hurricane Carol, bailed out my basement next to my grandfather during the floods of Connie and Diane, and became engaged during Hurricane Betsy, my first daughter was born during the time of Hurricane Camille's sweep into the United States.

When the storm came onshore in Mississippi, a 24-foot tidal surge occurred at Pass Christian. The surface pressure dropped to 26.61 inches. Southeastern Louisiana and Mississippi were swamped. The swath of destruction was complete along the

Mississippi coast up to three or four blocks inland. In the Biloxi area, 60 resort properties were damaged; one-half were destroyed. Again, damage topped $1 billion. Two-thirds of all telephones in the Gulf Coast of Mississippi were out of service. The tidal surge was also devastating in southeast Louisiana. The area from Empire southeastward was swept clean, and most structures were completely demolished—even those that survived Betsy just four years earlier.

Camille's winds rapidly diminished as the storm pushed inland, but its energy lingered, and its remnants contributed to as much as 25 inches of flash-flooding rains as far north as West Virginia and Virginia. Over 260 people who were caught up in Camille were killed.

Of Agnes, Gloria, and Hugo

With few exceptions, the 1970s and 1980s did not deliver mega-tropical storm action. But there were exceptions. June 1972 brought Hurricane Agnes to the mid-Atlantic region. It was only a Category-1 storm, but it was packed with moisture and energy. It moved inland on June 21 and stalled across interior Pennsylvania and New York. The rains came and stayed for four days. All rivers flooded, including the Susquehanna. The floods were monumental. Property damage reached over three billion. Over 300,000 people were left homeless; 5,800 businesses were wiped out. The flood waters took 118 lives, and the storm's estimated 28.1 trillion gallons of water was enough to fill a 67-square-mile lake with 2,000 feet of water.

Later, the 1980s delivered Hurricane Gloria to New England. It caused the single greatest power outage in Connecticut history when it moved onshore in September 1985, but overall, the storm's impact was minor compared to others. It could be called the "lunch hour" storm because it came during the early afternoon—if you took a long lunch, you'd have missed the whole storm.

One of the biggest headline-grabbers of the 1970s and '80s was Hurricane Hugo. Or was it "Huge-O?" Hugo really was enormous. Winds reached over 150 mph, and hurricane-force winds extended as far as 140 miles from the center. Tropical storm winds of 50 to 60 mph reached as far as 250 miles from the center. The storm developed off the African coast during September 1989. It became a super-storm as it slammed into Puerto Rico. The devastation in Puerto Rico led to riots and looting, which contributed to even more casualties.

After causing historic damage in Puerto Rico, the storm headed for South Carolina. Forecasters were hoping for and predicting a turn to the north, away from the coast, but that wasn't about to happen. On Sept. 21, the storm slammed into South Carolina.

The center moved onshore late that evening about 25 miles north of Charleston. Around Charleston, telephone service went dead just after 11:00 p.m. Tornadoes touched down as the storm pushed inland. The eye passed over the National Weather Service building at Charleston Air Force Base; immediately afterwards, its roof blew off. Just before midnight, winds in downtown Charleston were clocked at 100 mph with gusts to 119 mph. Windows were popping at hotels and century-old trees were up-rooted. Charleston was in ruins, and many people were without homes, food, or electricity for weeks. Hugo's storm tides in South Carolina came to 20 feet. The storm took 60 lives and caused seven billion dollars in damage—five billion dollars of damage occurred in South Carolina alone. Hugo was the most powerful hurricane to hit South Carolina since the mid-50s.

The Amazing Andrew

The most costly natural disaster in U.S. history took place on the morning of August 24, 1992, when Hurricane Andrew plowed a 25-mile-wide path of destruction through southern Florida, just south of downtown Miami. Even the National Weather Service lost its radar when the storm blew the installation off the roof of the government facility in Coral Gables. And Weather Service personnel were uncertain of the fate of their own homes and families—many of their homes were destroyed. The storm just rolled over everything in its path.

Overall, the 1992 hurricane season had been very quiet. By late August, the first hurricane of the season was still not in sight. On Friday the 21st, a suspicious system appeared east of the Bahamas, but forecasters at the National Hurricane Center were not especially impressed. Reporters were told that the threat was minimal. The circulation was surprisingly small. But it began to wind up rapidly on Saturday the 22nd, and at the same time, it was on a steady westward course of more than 20 mph. That speed is practically unheard of in the tropics, where hurricanes normally move at half that speed or less. But a high-pressure system north of Andrew was forcing the storm to take on a rapid and straight track—right at Miami. It would not veer, and on Sunday, the hurricane reached powerful proportions with winds of more than 150 mph.

I was getting ready for my evening weathercast that Sunday night, and took note of the observation from Miami. It certainly didn't seem like hurricane weather. The wind was out of the northeast but relatively gentle, and skies were partly cloudy. That was the classic calm before the storm. Yet, by daybreak Monday, most of the damage had already been done, and southern Dade County was unrecognizable. The storm rapidly reached its peak just after midnight on Sunday.

Damage reached catastrophic levels. Estimates ranged up to $40 billion. Because of the claims, eleven insurance companies became insolvent. One hundred and twenty-six thousand homes were damaged or destroyed, 353,000 people were displaced, and 100,000 of these never returned to Dade County. "Andrew" was a steamroller that had carved out a narrow zone of total destruction.

The storm bordered on Category 5 with wind gusts to 200 mph as it approached Miami. It became one of the great disasters of the twentieth century, and it sounded a warning signal for the next.

Weather-Wise

There are five categories of hurricane intensity. A storm of category 3 intensity (highest wind is 130–135 mph) is more than enough to cause destruction and historic damage.

The Least You Need to Know

➤ Strange and violent weather is as old as the atmosphere itself.

➤ A special set of circumstances have contributed to our historic storms.

➤ The hurricane storm surge is the most devastating feature of the storm.

➤ Hurricane intensity and frequency increased during the end of the twentieth century.

➤ More catastrophic storms are likely in the immediate future.

Chapter 9

El Niño: The Grown-Up Child

> ### In This Chapter
>
> ➤ Links between the atmosphere and oceans
>
> ➤ What are El Niño and La Niña?
>
> ➤ How El Niño contributes to extreme weather
>
> ➤ What the future may hold

I met Nick Muecci by accident when I got to JFK Airport on my way to California to cover the record El Niño of 1997–98. He recognized me from television, and couldn't wait to share how El Niño affected his life. His home was in Connecticut, but he was spending time in Marin County, just north of San Francisco, planning a permanent move. However, he felt so besieged by the unrelenting El Niño-related storms that he gave up, and opted instead to return to the "tranquil" Northeast. It was a strange year.

During the winter of 1998, the weather was more California-like in New England than in California itself. Sure, it was the West Coast's rainy season—but two feet of rain during the first nine days of February? That was a little too much!

New Kid on the Block?

My assignment to cover the 1998 El Niño came from my news director, who suggested the series be called "Mel Niño." In the early part of the winter, people referred to it as "El No-Show," because its impact in November and December seemed so minor. But the term *El Niño* comes from Spanish, meaning "the boy child" or "the Christ child."

The name was coined by fishermen in Ecuador and Peru. They noticed a warm ocean current periodically surfacing around Christmas, and El Niño seemed an appropriate name for it. El Niño has been going on for centuries, and probably much longer.

During the past 40 years, there have been 10 El Niños—meaning that on 10 occasions the water temperature reached above normal in the eastern Pacific because of an eastward drifting current of warm surface water. El Niño is no youngster.

Typically, the warm surface water prevents nutrient-rich waters from rising upward. When El Niño arrives, fish are less abundant off the west coast of South America. It has always been a time for those who fish to take a break, repair equipment, and spend more time with their families. Normally, El Niño will last for a few months, but sometimes the warm currents last longer, and economic ruin could come to the fishing industry. Weak events would have only a minor impact on fisheries, but major ones would be economically devastating.

Weather Words

"One of the brightest gems in the New England weather is the dazzling uncertainty of it."

—Mark Twain

Weather-Speak

El Niño is a name given to a periodical warming of equatorial ocean water. It disrupts weather and causes all kinds of havoc—from droughts to floods and landslides.

The Connection Between the Sea and the Atmosphere

So, how does something in the ocean influence the atmosphere? We already saw how hurricanes depend on the sea for energy, but there's more. The sea and air are really connected, each influenced by the other, with the same dynamics occurring in both. The sea and atmosphere are both fluids; they differ in terms of density. Sure, the sea is a thousand times more dense than the air, but that doesn't separate them. The sea and atmosphere come together at an interface.

Waves and surface currents are wind-generated. The atmosphere pushes the ocean surface along. But as the ocean moves, heat is redistributed and eventually tossed back into the atmosphere. The exchange of heat influences the pressure field in the atmosphere, which modifies the wind field. The figure on the next page shows how this exchange and feedback take place.

The heat exchange often occurs in storms when water evaporates from the surface. Hurricanes feed on that transfer, and most storms receive at least some energy from the process. The water vapor carries away the ocean heat and then, when condensation occurs, the borrowed heat is released into the atmosphere. In general, the oceans contribute more than two-thirds of the heat balance of the atmosphere in mid-latitudes. Without the oceans, our weather would be unearthly.

In the case of El Niño, the impact can be worldwide. The next figure shows the temperature departure from normal during El Niño periods. Strong El Niños can raise water temperatures by as much as 5 to 10 degrees in a huge area extending from the central Pacific to the west coast of South America—which the big El Niño that occurred in both 1983 and 1998 did. Other El Niño currents only elevate sea surface temperatures by two to four degrees, but even that can influence the atmosphere. The additional heat in the eastern Pacific feeds into the atmosphere. Tall cumulonimbus clouds appear, and the energy then delivers a strong jet stream that races northward from the tropics: a sub-tropical jet stream. It's always present, but it strengthens during El Niño years. The jet stream turns into the United States and even pushes through the Atlantic.

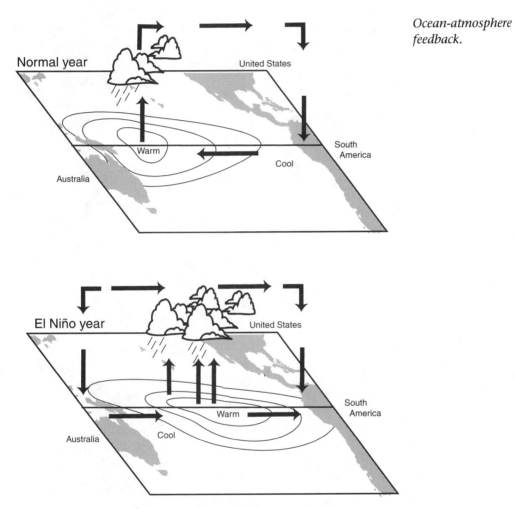

Ocean-atmosphere feedback.

At the same time, in response to that motion, a strong area of low pressure appears in the North Pacific. It, too, is always present, but during an El Niño, it shifts farther south. These shifting wind patterns dramatically alter the weather in the Northern Hemisphere. Floods, rains, and massive surf pound the West Coast. Floods and tornadoes rake the lower Midwest while balmy winters settle into the Northeast. At the same time, hurricanes are deflected from their normal paths. The figure at the bottom of the next page shows the changes that take place.

115

El Niño water temperature changes.

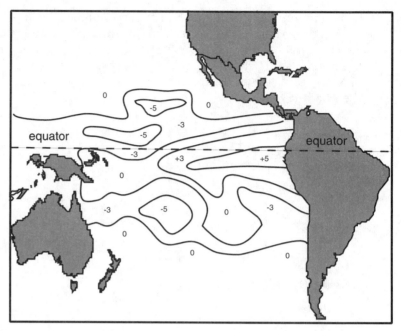

Atmospheric flow with El Niño.

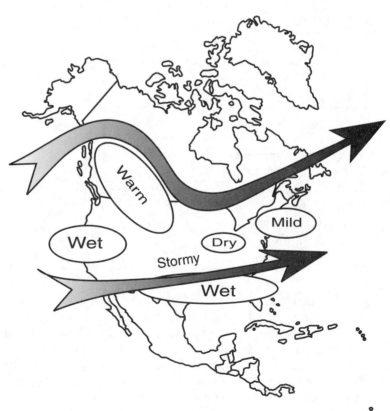

El Niño causes shifting wind patterns in the atmosphere, but other shifting wind patterns get El Niño going in the first place. El Niño is a perfect example of atmosphere-ocean feedback.

Here Comes the Kid

Normally, winds blow from the east in the tropics. These are called *trade winds*. But occasionally the pressure difference in the atmosphere across the Pacific will change. Higher pressure than normal builds across the western Pacific. Because the air flows from higher to lower pressure, the typical east-to-west flow will weaken and possibly even reverse. The air will move from high pressure to low, and in this case, from west to east.

Weather-Speak

There are two separate belts of steady winds found between latitudes 23.5 degrees, north and south. They marked popular sailing routes for commercial sailing vessels, and appropriately were called **trade winds.**

That atmospheric motion pushes the warm surface water eastward. It bumps into the west coast of South America and drifts southward as a warm current. Water temperatures off the coast will normally be in the mid 70s, but when El Niño arrives, the temperature jumps into the mid 80s. The water level rises in the eastern Pacific by as much as one foot. In the western Pacific, the water drops by a foot. Where the water level drops, the water is much cooler than normal; the surface water has been blown away. When El Niño is at its peak, strong high pressure will be present in the western Pacific with lower pressure to the east. At the same time, colder water will be in the western portion of the ocean with warmer water in the east.

Typically, after several months, El Niño begins to self-destruct. The warm sub-tropical high pressure in the western Pacific weakens as lower air temperatures develop from the exchange with the colder ocean surface. That west-east flow has no choice but to diminish. Also, like coffee in a cup, the water that piled up in the eastern portion of the Pacific basin sloshes back to the west. The warm surface water leaves the eastern Pacific and shifts west. The water temperature lowers off the coast of Peru and Ecuador. The pattern completely reverses. The technical name for this back-and-forth phenomenon is the El Niño Southern Oscillation (ENSO). The dynamics which lead to El Niño and its demise are shown in the top figure on the next page.

Both the 1982–83 and the 1997–98 ENSO events showed striking similarities. Both were extreme, with ocean surface temperatures differing from normal by 10 degrees or more. Each appeared during the spring when the easterly trades weakened. West of the International Date Line, winds shifted and came out of the west during May.

Within the next few weeks, the ocean began to respond to the wind shift with sea level rising a few inches at Christmas Island in the mid-Pacific. By autumn, sea level rises of up to a foot occurred as far east as Ecuador. Likewise, sea level dropped in the western Pacific. Coral reefs were exposed near many of the Pacific islands. By January, ENSO had peaked, and it seemed to show few signs of reversing. But, amazingly, by late spring and early summer, cold water appeared where great warmth had earlier prevailed. The change had occurred.

El Niño oscillation.

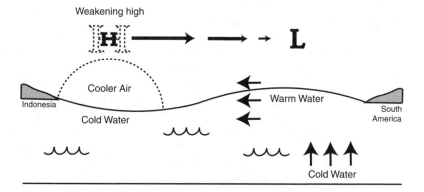

Child's Play

El Niño has always been associated with economic hardship along the west coast of South America—mainly because of its impact on marine life. Only recently has the warm current been shown to drastically alter world-wide weather. We'll get to the weather in just a minute, but first let's see what happens to the fish.

When the surface water piles up, the water subsides, sinking to greater depths. The water converges toward the coast and the surface becomes deformed. The water bulges up as well as moves downward, and that downward motion forces nutrients to sink to great depths, in a process called *continuity*. It's the "jelly sandwich" principle. If you sit on a jelly sandwich, the jelly will go out the sides. So, as you see in the next figure, if water is pushed to the coast, like a squished jelly sandwich, the warm water will not only bulge at the surface, but also sink.

Subsidence with El Niño.

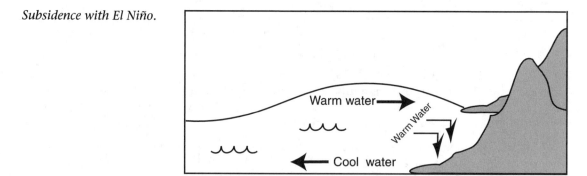

The sinking nutrients deprive many fish of their nourishment, resulting in heavy losses to the fishing industries in Ecuador and Peru. The anchovy harvest fails and sardines vanish. In addition, seabirds abandon their young and scatter over a vast area of ocean in search for food. In 1983, along the coast of Peru, 25 percent of that year's seal and sea lion adults died along with all the pups. At the same time, the warmer than normal water sent tropical fish northward into other latitudes. In 1998, prize marlin showed up in the Pacific Northwest. But at the same time, in 1998, sea lions on San Miguel Island, off California, starved because the water was too warm to support the fish they feed on. The warm water also damaged the coral reefs in the Galapagos Islands. The reefs also support marine life.

Global Weather Extremes

Strong El Niños always add enough energy to disrupt normal weather patterns. This usually features a cool Peru current that sweeps northward and generates a motion of water upward from great depths. As the current moves northward from the direction of the cold South Pole, it transports colder water. Also, because the Coriolis force (see Chapter 4) causes a deflection to the left in the Southern Hemisphere, water is drawn away from the west coast of South America. That causes the nutrient-rich water to rise in what is called *upwelling*. Marine life thrives. But during El Niño, the pattern is reversed and water flows southward rather than northward. The water sinks rather than rises. The shifting patterns of temperature during El Niño add heat into the atmosphere above the eastern Pacific, and from that point on, the weather begins to cook.

During 1997–98, El Niño raged. It was a classic. Let's take a closer look at the impact of that El Niño.

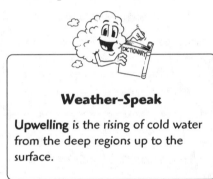

Weather-Speak

Upwelling is the rising of cold water from the deep regions up to the surface.

The Wet Coast

California always seems to bear the brunt of an El Niño winter, with rough seas, flooding, and mudslides. During these seasons, the southward shift of the polar jet stream brings a seemingly endless series of low-pressure systems that slam into the West Coast. The train of storms is not uncommon across the Pacific Northwest during each winter, but as the jet stream pushes southward, those storms plow into regions unaccustomed to such storm attacks. Also, the large temperature contrast set up by El Niño's warm water help contribute to larger storms.

In California during 1998, wave heights reached 30 feet, railroads were washed away, and major highways were washed out by flood waters and blocked by mudslides. Entire hillsides collapsed and turned into rivers of mud that swept away homes. Along the immediate coast, luxury homes crashed into the sea. In the first week of February alone, 22 inches of rain fell in San Marcos Pass, which is near Santa Barbara. In downtown Ventura, 12 inches came down. Three feet of snow fell in local mountains. The punishing onslaught of storms persisted well into early spring.

Also, earlier, in the fall of 1997, Hurricane Nora poured down on Yuma, Arizona, and Hurricane Pauline slammed into Acapulco, Mexico. The warm Pacific waters set the stage for super-strong hurricanes, including Hurricane Linda, which had winds of 190 mph and became the strongest storm on record for the eastern Pacific. Only by good fortune did that storm just miss hitting Southern California.

South America

In 1998, the extremely warm waters off Peru and Ecuador caused flooding rains in both countries. Hundreds of millions of dollars were lost, and the disaster led to social and political destabilization. The Ecuadorian president was replaced. During the height of El Niño, 22,000 people were evacuated from their homes.

Weather-Watch

When you receive a flood warning and are advised to evacuate, you should do so immediately. Move to a safe area.

In contrast to the storms that struck the west coast of South America, the east coast picture was vastly different. Brazil was hit very hard by a drought that affected 10 million people, and more than 50 percent of the crops were lost in the traditionally poorest region. Widespread looting occurred from famine-stricken people. Just as low pressure and rising atmospheric motions dominated along the west coast of South America, compensating sinking motions prevailed on the eastern coast. The resulting drought reached record proportions.

Western Pacific

While extreme rains punished the eastern Pacific region, Southeast Asia, Indonesia, Australia, and Japan experienced severe droughts. The drought led to great economic loss and hardship, and might have played a role in the Asian stock market plunge that eventually impacted the entire world. Fires spread throughout Indonesia and plumes of smoke fanned out across Southeast Asia. Pollution levels were extreme. In Japan, the lack of snow early in the winter created concern about sufficient snow in Nagano for the Olympic Winter Games. Eventually, the snow did fall, and then, too much.

The high-pressure area in the western Pacific that got El Niño rolling was exceptionally strong, especially early in the winter. This delivered sinking motions in the atmosphere that produced clear skies, stable air, and light winds—the perfect combination to generate hot, dry conditions and high levels of air pollution. Colder water eventually eroded that high-pressure area, but not before fires claimed over a million acres of forest in Indonesia alone.

June in January

One remarkable aspect of the 1998 El Niño was the complete lack of winter weather across most of the northern United States. The winter in the Northeast was the warmest on record. In Washington, D.C., cherry blossoms were blooming in January. In New England, crocuses were going strong by early February, and there was practically no snowfall in New York City. It was the "year of no winter" for the mid-Atlantic region. The strong, warm jet stream forced the normally cold jet stream far to the north, and the typical winter chill remained north of the U.S. border.

But winter weather wasn't totally absent—the winter patterns simply shifted to the north. Northern New England and Quebec were hit with the worst ice storm in that region's history. Ice storms occur when warm air streams over a cold surface. Southern New England to northern Georgia will occasionally be hit hard by freezing rain. A cold high-pressure area near the ground causes rain to freeze on contact with the surface. Normally, the precipitation will fall as snow in the deeper colder air of northern New England and Canada. But in 1998, the entire pattern moved northward and a heavy layer of ice accumulated during a powerful January storm across the north country. Ice brought down trees and power lines. Northern New England and Quebec were paralyzed. Millions of utility customers lost power for over a week, and that was during the winter. This became one of the greatest ice storms of all time.

Southern Floods and Tornadoes

Vicious storms ripped through the southern states. In December 1997, snow even fell in Guadalajara, Mexico, for the first time since 1881. During that month, Roswell, New Mexico, experienced its heaviest one-month snowfall since 1893. Accumulations came to 21 inches. From Texas to Florida, floods and tornadoes occurred with a punishing frequency. In one tornado outbreak, tornadoes around Kissimmee, Florida, killed more than 30 people.

The tropical jet stream that moved northward through Mexico and then eastward across the southern United States was responsible for the strong and damaging storms during the early winter. The temperature contrast and upward motion associated with the flow set the stage for the storms.

Ironically, the pattern in the South completely reversed as soon as El Niño weakened in the spring. Blistering heat and drought set in across Mexico, Texas, and Florida. Fires in Mexico obscured the atmosphere in Texas. The number of droughts and fires in Florida were unprecedented. The pattern had been broken and oscillated in the completely opposite direction.

Weather-Wise

El Niño was named after the Christ Child by local fishermen because it usually appeared during the Christmas season and departed before Easter. El Niño years are supposed to be minor hurricane years. As the El Niño diminishes, there should be an increase in storms which reach the East Coast of the United States.

Atlantic Hurricane Season

Although extremely intense hurricanes occurred in record numbers across the Pacific during 1997, the storm pattern was totally different in the Atlantic. Hurricanes had difficulty developing, and the storms that did form remained well offshore.

The El Niño-related tropical jet stream curved eastward across the Atlantic, and that effectively blocked any tropical storm that could be moving toward North or Central America. Also, that flow prevented the tropical storm circulation from taking much form. The tops of the clouds were sheared off by the flow before they could reach full development. In general, El Niño years tend to have few hurricanes threatening the east coast of the United States. During 1997, tropical storm activity was 30 percent below normal, and for the first time in the twentieth century, the month of August passed without a single tropical storm developing.

Weather-Speak

La Niña is the cold phase of the El Niño oscillation. The waters of the Pacific near the equator and off the west coast of South America are much colder than normal during the La Niña. La Niña is the cold water sibling of El Niño.

La Niña: The Kid's Sister

El Niño refers to the warm portion of ENSO, but it is an oscillation, and the temperature goes through natural reversals. The warm water surface will oscillate between the eastern and western portion of the Pacific. When the warm water shifts to the western Pacific, deeper, colder water reaches the surface in the eastern Pacific, and this cold portion of ENSO is called *La Niña*—"the girl."

Girl Power

An earlier figure showed how El Niño formed and weakened. La Niña occurs as soon as the western Pacific high-pressure system diminishes. That reduction in atmospheric pressure is hastened by the colder water that surfaces off the coast of Asia during El Niño. The high-pressure system gets El Niño rolling, but once it forms, the cold waters that surface in the west lead to its demise. Then as the high weakens, the normal east-to-west flow in the atmosphere resumes. Warm surface water is forced westward, and upwelling causes colder water to return to the eastern portion of the ocean. That is La Niña. A strong El Niño is frequently followed by a strong La Niña. It's nature's way of balancing the score, but there are no guarantees. Numerous factors contribute to global weather patterns. During the spring of 1998, the cold water of La Niña surfaced in a matter of days, and the weather patterns responded almost immediately.

Fire and Ice

Although record warm temperatures occurred across the northern states during the first four months of 1998, La Niña turned the pattern around very quickly. The polar air masses began pushing southward. Snow fell in northern New England during June, and storms occurred with great frequency across the Northeast. Rainfall amounts for

June were three times above the normal. Through July, most of the Northeast failed to experience a single heat wave, which is defined as a spell of 90 degree or higher temperatures for three or more days. Through June and most of July, the only encounter Albany, New York, had with 90-degree heat occurred at the end of March when El Niño still raged. It is no coincidence that a cool jet stream dips into the northern United States as soon as the tropical jet stream weakens. The resistance to the cold air breaks down as El Niño melts away. The winter of 1995–96 was the snowiest on record for many northern states. That occurred during a La Niña period. During the 1998 La Niña, record warmth did occur in early December from the Great Lakes to New England, but in California the cold was severe. A disastrous citrus freeze caused 600 million dollars of damage. In late December, the arctic blast moved into the Midwest with record snowfalls.

The fading of El Niño 1998 wasn't exactly followed by universal cooling, however. The weather did cool, but globally, June 1998 was still the warmest June on record—thanks to the blistering heat that was trapped across the southern portion of the United States and Mexico. Overall, thanks to El Niño of 1998, globally the year became the warmest on record.

Hundreds of thousands of wooded acres burned in Florida. Scores of homes and buildings were destroyed. Crop losses reached over $100 million. In Texas, temperatures reached 100 degrees or higher on a daily basis, with no rain in sight. Texas is famous for heat, but the unrelenting string of 100 degrees was of record proportions. During La Niña, there is a trend toward warmer weather than normal in the southern states, but other global factors might have contributed to the extreme nature of the 1998 heat wave. Some of those factors include changes in the global circulation patterns and even some astronomical changes, such as possible changes on the Sun.

Weather-Wise

Since 1950, El Niños have been around 31 percent of the time and La Niñas 24 percent of the time. That means that for 55 percent of the time, there's an El Niño or a La Niña stirring.

What's Next?

Generally, El Niño appears off the coast of South America every few years. The extreme 1982–83 El Niño claimed over 2,000 lives and resulted in losses of $13 billion. Several additional El Niño patterns developed during the next 15 years, but these were much weaker. After the string of weak to moderate ENSO occurrences, a record El Niño developed in 1997. Overall, El Niño patterns will continue to appear, but only occasionally should they have the amplitude of the types that surfaced in 1982 and 1997.

Weather relationships are more difficult to determine during weak or moderate El Niño years. The pattern is far less clear-cut when water temperatures are two or three degrees above normal, rather than when those temperatures are 5 to 10 degrees above. Meteorologists confidently predicted the impact of the 1997–98 event months in advance.

It was hard to miss that one. But the basic lack of understanding of all the interactions between the atmosphere and oceans will make future predictions far less reliable when those less-than-dramatic ENSO patterns come along.

The Least You Need to Know

➤ El Niño is a part of a natural oscillation that takes place in the Pacific Ocean.

➤ During El Niño, warm water piles up in the eastern Pacific.

➤ During La Niña, cold water surfaces in the same region.

➤ The shifting and development of these Pacific currents have a direct impact on the world-wide weather.

➤ The El Niño of 1998 was the strongest on record.

Part 2
The Weather and Us

Sometimes the atmosphere just isn't right—filled with smog and pollution. In some regions, the pollution level remains unhealthful, even after 30 years of legislative efforts to clear the air. Sure, there have been improvements, but definite problems linger, and the complete cleanup may take decades more. Pollution affects our physical and mental health, as well as the world's plants and animals. Paint peels before its time due to a smog-filled atmosphere. Respiratory diseases are very much affected by high air pollution.

The weather plays a key role in the mixing and dispersion of pollutants—cleansing the atmosphere—and if the weather is unfavorable for such mixing, watch out! Here, we'll look at the basic air pollutants and their effects, as well as the legal, political, and social aspects of pollution. How bad is our air quality? How much has it improved? And what about the ozone layer? The weather really can be hazardous to our health. Take a deep breath, and let's get started. On second thought, skip the deep breath.

Chapter 10

Warning: The Weather Can Be Hazardous to Your Health

In This Chapter

➤ Looking at the relationship between weather and health

➤ The roles of heat and cold

➤ Catching cold along with those allergies

➤ Feeling blue

Since the beginning of time, the weather has played a key role in the physical and social well-being of people and their environment. We are immersed in a sea of air, and the behavior of the atmosphere is a major factor in how good we feel. Hippocrates, who is called the "father of medicine," wrote his famous work, "On Airs, Waters, and Places," which opens with the words:

> *Whoever wishes to investigate medicine properly, should proceed thus: in the first place to consider the seasons of the year, and what effects each of them produce (for they are not all alike, but differ much in themselves and in their changes). Then the winds, the hot and the cold, especially such as are common to all countries, and then such as are peculiar to each locality.*

More than 2,000 years later, those words seem just as appropriate for an opening to any chapter on weather and health.

Weather Words

"The common feelings of every man will convince him, if he will attend to them, of the superior advantages health derives from a pure and temperate atmosphere."

—Virgil, "Georgics," Book I

Weather-Watch

You must be careful to protect older people against hypothermia because they are more susceptible in less extreme temperatures. Their temperature regulation mechanism is less efficient. Also, as you age, the perception of cold is less.

Weather Words

"Keep cold, young orchard. Goodbye and keep cold. Dread fifty above more than fifty below."

—Robert Frost

Weather and Health

Finding a direct link between weather and health has never been easy; they're two relatively inexact sciences. The variables that influence one's health are nearly infinite, and each person responds to them in an infinite variety of ways. Thousands of documents can be found in the literature that try to explain some linkage.

In the early 1990s, I even contributed to a study attempting to show how the mood of arthritis patients is affected by weather changes. Patients were asked to circle facial images which best reflected their own feelings of well-being. The images ranged from a full frown to an ear-to-ear grin. We then tried to correlate the reaction to the numerous weather variables such as wind speed, wind direction, amount of cloudiness, temperature, relative humidity, pressure, and pressure change. Another study that I was involved with focused on the relationship of the breathing capacity of emphysema patients to the same set of weather variables, as well as air pollutants. Both studies showed a link, especially when weather changes and air quality are included, but each person's response seemed to be different. There are common threads, but the pattern comes out differently for each individual. It isn't clear-cut.

In addition, the weather can influence our health in surprisingly indirect ways. For example, according to weather lore, "A snow year is a rich year," or the flipside, "A green Christmas makes a fat churchyard." What? Since when are snow and a cold winter good for us? They are good for several reasons.

The health benefits of a rough winter center around the observation that mild winters lead to fickle springs. The weather always balances the score. Exceptionally cold weather will eventually follow a warm spell—just in time for spring, and all will be well with the world. But a mild winter will lead to an early blossoming of trees and flowers. If the weather decides to reverse the warm pattern during the spring, watch out. Frost and freeze will set in. The early blossoms could freeze on the vine. Crop failures and food shortages will occur. People can become sick and die—and the churchyard starts growing fat.

When you're talking about crop failures, weather extremes of any kind—too much heat, too much cold, too much rain, or too little rain—will impact productivity. Some more direct ways the weather impacts your health include aggravation of arthritis or other connective-tissue diseases, colds, allergies, and, yes, your mood. There are unnatural changes in the atmosphere, including air pollution, that also affect your well-being. We'll get to that in a few moments; first, let's talk about those natural fluctuations that can become a real pain.

My Aching Back

You might want to include your knee, your elbow, or your wrist as well. Let's face it, we're under a lot of pressure—10 to 20 tons of it! Normally, the pressure inside our bodies will push outward and balance the crushing pressure of the atmosphere. But if something is out of joint with our bodies the normal balance is upset, and the atmosphere starts feeling pretty heavy. It hurts. People who've had an operation or broken bones seem to be far more sensitive to those pressure changes. If any aspect of the body is disturbed, it seems more sensitive to weather changes.

In the case of those with connective-tissue problems, such as arthritis, falling atmospheric pressure along with increasing humidity seems to enhance the pain. High humidity or low pressure alone doesn't seem to be nearly as troublesome as the combination of lower pressure and increased humidity. Of course, those are the conditions that precede storms, and as the wisdom of the ages says, "A coming storm our shooting corns presage/Our aches will throb, our hollow tooth will rage."

If You Can't Stand the Heat...

Of all the meteorological disasters that descend on this planet, excessive heat claims the most lives. In the United States, an average of 200 lives are lost each year to heat waves, and in some years, the death toll exceeds 1,000 or more. During the 1930s, the heat was legend, and from 1930 to 1936 there were at least 15,000 deaths—and those were just the direct casualties. Nobody really knows how many additional deaths were hastened through heart failure because of the added strain of coping with the heat. The elderly and sick are most susceptible to those long, hot summers. In July 1901 alone, over 9,500 deaths were attributed to the heat. No other disaster takes so many lives.

Weather-Wise

In 1988, excessive heat combined with a drought in the United States to deliver economic losses of more than $20 billion. Nearly the entire population of the United States was impacted by the hot, dry weather. Ten years later, the 1998 drought in the lower Midwest challenged the impact of the 1988 one.

Weather-Speak

Sensible perspiration is visible on the skin. **Insensible perspiration** evaporates before it becomes visible.

129

Excessive heat attacks the normal cooling system of our bodies. Our natural built-in thermostat, called the hypothalamus gland, rests behind the ear. As soon as it senses that the blood temperature is above 98.6 degrees, it sends out a signal causing an increased blood flow. The blood vessels dilate so that blood can circulate more rapidly, and it is brought closer to the skin surface. There, the excess heat is vented into the air, as long as the air temperature is lower than the body temperature. Heat flows from a region of higher temperature to a lower one.

At the same time, water circulates near the skin and evaporates as insensible perspiration—insensible because the water evaporates before it is even sensed on the skin.

If the hypothalamus still detects overheating, the millions of tiny sweat glands near our skin surface are called into action. Water is given off—we sweat—and the subsequent evaporation allows for additional cooling. Our bodies have quite a central air conditioning system. About 90 percent of the heat shed from our bodies is accomplished through perspiration—both *insensible* and *sensible.*

If too much humidity is present in the atmosphere, less perspiration can be given off, and the cooling system begins to break down. The humidity only worsens the effects of the heat, and that's when people get sick. In addition, when we sweat we lose salt within our bodies, which can lead to a chemical imbalance—further enhancing the impact of the heat.

The process that unfolds from an overstressed body air conditioning system is called *heat syndrome,* and it takes on many different forms. The following table shows the different effects, at different levels, brought on by heat syndrome. It also suggests what can be done at the different stages. The numbered list on the next page gives some tips about what can be done to avoid heat stress. Much of that involves common sense, but sometimes those options are not available, especially to those who are elderly, sick, or living alone. These already-weakened bodies are put to an even greater strain. It is always important to look after neighbors who are sick or old during these summer heat waves.

Weather-Wise

Heat is nothing new to the United States. In 1917, the summer was especially hot, and in Death Valley, California, the temperature reached over 120 degrees on 43 straight days!

Weather-Speak

Heat syndrome is a severe disturbance of the human thermoregulatory system. It ranges from heat stress to heat stroke.

Heat Syndrome

Heat Index or Apparent Temperature	Heat-Related Syndrome
130+	Heatstroke or sunstroke imminent
105-130	Sunstroke, heat cramps or heat exhaustion likely
90-105	Sunstroke, heat cramps and heat exhaustion possible
80-90	Fatigue possible

Prevention of Heat Stress

1. Acclimate your body to the heat by spending increased amounts of time outdoors (this can take 4-7 days, on average).

2. Drink at least 4-8 ounces of fluid every 15-20 minutes (thirst IS NOT a good indicator of dehydration).

3. Alternate work and rest cycles to prevent overexposure to heat (be sure to relocate to a cool environment for the rest periods).

4. Avoid alcoholic beverages.

5. Eat light, preferably cold meals (fatty foods are harder to digest in hot weather).

6. Wear lightweight, light-colored clothing.

Catching the Common Cold

That old rhinovirus. It just seems to be ageless, although new drugs are always coming along to treat the common head cold. Why do we even call it a cold? Well, because it seems to be related to drafts and chilly weather. But it really isn't the cold by itself that causes that runny nose, cough, and stuffiness.

During the winter, we're indoors more of the time with the windows closed, and there's less air circulation in our offices and homes. It's the perfect setup for a germ hotel—the germs check in, but they don't check out! The indoor party season is in full swing too, when handshakes and kisses are liberally exchanged. It's an affectionate time of year, when infections are easily passed along. The hands are probably the greatest transmitters of common respiratory infections.

Also, while indoors during the winter, we are exposed to humidity levels which are desert-dry. The figure on the following page shows what happens when outside air is brought indoors during the winter.

Weather-Wise

About 50 percent of the body's heat escapes through the head so you should wear a hat in cold weather.

Lowered indoor humidity in winter.

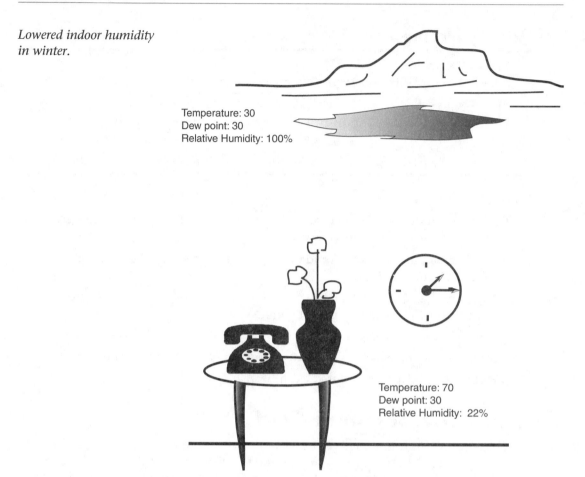

Temperature: 30
Dew point: 30
Relative Humidity: 100%

Temperature: 70
Dew point: 30
Relative Humidity: 22%

Outside, the humidity could be reasonable, but because of the low temperatures, the water content is also low. Then, when that air gets indoors and is heated to around 70 degrees, the humidity plunges. The air has a much greater capacity to hold water vapor at a higher temperature—but the moisture just isn't there. Inside, the humidity could be 10 percent or even less. Our indoor environment becomes as dry as the Sahara. The extreme dryness puts a strain on the respiratory system, and infection can more easily occur. A humidifier will help add moisture to the air; even placing pans of water near radiators will help. But don't add *too* much moisture to the air; mold and mildew will result.

The early winter seems to be the more likely time for catching a cold than late in the season. After a healthy summer, our white blood counts are lowered. Without infections, our bodies had no need to put up their defenses and produce more infection-fighting white blood cells. But early in the winter, those defenses are low enough that we're more susceptible to having infection develop. By late winter, our blood counts have increased and our immune systems are more capable of dealing with invasions of viruses.

Also, during the late fall and early winter, the weather undergoes dramatic changes that additionally stress our bodies. We have difficulty dealing with change. But as the winter moves along, we adjust to the weather changes—we acclimatize.

So, cold weather doesn't, by itself, cause colds during the winter. The factors which lead to infections are numerous. Going outside without a hat is not the reason one catches a cold, although a hat is very important.

Those Nasty Allergies

The weather and seasonal changes in our environment play a huge role in setting off allergic reactions in those who are sensitive. People with asthma will be affected by dust, molds, and pollens, along with dramatic weather changes. Hay fever is not generated by hay, nor is it a fever—it's a sensitivity to ragweed pollen. That pollen reaches its peak in late summer—around the hay season. These pollens are present in highest concentrations across the Midwest, and the typical response includes sneezing, coughing, and itchy eyes. The figure on the following page shows the distribution of ragweed pollens across the United States. These pollens blossom best under good growing conditions; if your tomato plants are doing well, ragweed will also flourish. The days with the highest concentrations of pollen are dry and breezy. Late August and early September are the prime times for the buildup of these pollens.

Tree and grass pollens also become problems during the spring. Normally, trees blossom at a staggered pace, with maples and oaks pollinating first and pines pollinating last. People with sensitivity will experience varying levels of response depending on their particular pollen problem. Sometimes the weather is chilly during the early spring and the early trees fail to pollinate until the warmer temperatures arrive. During these late springs, many trees pollinate at the same time, and the pollen level becomes extreme.

Weather-Wise

Is there an optimal relative humidity? Whenever the humidity drops below 30 percent, dry lips and respiratory discomfort become possible. Static electricity becomes a nuisance, as well as a hazard to your home computer's electronics. Above 60 percent, the additional moisture causes a buildup of molds and mildew. Indoor humidity should be regulated to average between 30 and 60 percent.

Weather-Watch

Indoor air pollution can become a serious problem during the winter months. Carbon monoxide is released from malfunctioning heating systems, causing suffocation. Indoors, carbon monoxide poisoning kills 1,500 Americans each year and sends 10,000 or more to the hospital. If the heating system is running properly, combustion is carried out to its completion, and carbon dioxide, not carbon monoxide, will be generated.

Ragweed pollen in the United States.

Unlike ragweed pollen, which can be carried great distances and redistributed, spring pollens tend to be more localized. Most of the pollen from an oak or ash tree in the yard will likely stay in the neighborhood. Spring pollen levels can fluctuate widely and tend to be site-specific.

Weather Words

A quote from Montaigne (Cotton's Translation) is:

"The minds of men do in the weather share,
Dark or serene as the day's foul or fair."

Although dry, breezy weather favors the transport of pollens, a rainy growing season is not necessarily a friend to allergy sufferers. Moist weather might keep those pollens close to the ground, but at the same time, it will help generate molds that can cause severe allergic reactions. Those with sensitivity to allergens tend to be sensitive to molds, too. As I mentioned earlier, while increasing the indoor relative humidity is important during the winter, humidifiers can add enough moisture to create mold and mildew. Allergy sufferers sometimes just can't win!

Air pollution will only worsen the naturally generated pollens and molds—but that's a topic for the next chapter.

SAD and Other Moods

There is little doubt that the weather has an impact on our moods. Long stretches of cloudy, rainy weather have always seemed capable of bringing on the blues, and recently, the relationship between dark weather and dark moods has found a basis in scientific work. It's called SAD—Seasonal Affective Disorder. This condition is a problem for 35 million Americans, and it relates to reduced sunlight. Sunlight stimulates hormones that make people feel better.

The symptoms of SAD include depression, fatigue, increased appetite and weight gain, irritability, and a general difficulty coping with life. These most often appear at the beginning of the fall and continue into early spring. The cause is related to hormonal changes that are linked to changes in light. The pineal gland releases the hormone *melatonin* in greater quantities when light is reduced. Its peak production occurs between 2 and 3 a.m., and winter months seem to enhance the process. Although a room may be well lit, there usually isn't enough light to counteract the dullness of the environment and the level of melatonin. The release of increased levels of this hormone adversely affects our moods, and of course, some people have a greater sensitivity to increased melatonin production.

Diagnosis of SAD can be difficult because other factors in a person's life may complicate the picture. Professional treatment should be sought, and often the remedy includes light therapy or phototherapy. Some examples of treatment include sitting in a strong light, equivalent to at least ten 100-watt bulbs. A computerized system of lighting a bedroom can also be used, so that an artificial day is generated—including an artificial dawn, sunrise, and then, full light. In addition, visor caps, equipped with lights that shine into the eyes, have been used. But regardless of these efforts, some patients still don't respond.

You can control a mild case of wintertime blues by keeping drapes and blinds open, sitting near windows, and keeping the lights on during overcast days. Getting outside as much as possible helps too. Sometimes all it takes to avoid that cabin fever is a daily stroll to the mailbox. You might also consider scheduling a vacation during the winter rather than the summer—perhaps to a warm and sunny location.

Weather-Wise

Light therapy may help seasonal depression. On dark days, you should stay in brightly lit rooms, and you also can buy full-spectrum fluorescent lights for light treatment.

Weather-Speak

Melatonin is a hormone produced by the pineal gland, a cone-shaped structure in the brain. An increase in melatonin is related to seasonal depression.

Weather-Wise

Are you looking for a sunny climate? In the Atacama desert of Chile, only 0.2 inches of rain falls over a 50-year period. Closer to home, Yuma, Arizona, has an average of 4,055 hours of sunshine each year—only 401 hours of cloudiness.

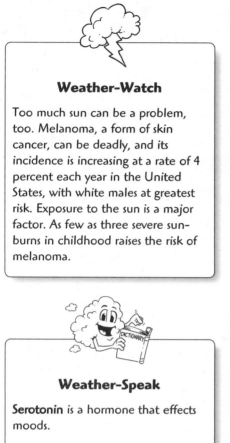

Weather-Watch

Too much sun can be a problem, too. Melanoma, a form of skin cancer, can be deadly, and its incidence is increasing at a rate of 4 percent each year in the United States, with white males at greatest risk. Exposure to the sun is a major factor. As few as three severe sunburns in childhood raises the risk of melanoma.

Weather-Speak

Serotonin is a hormone that effects moods.

SAD is not the only behavioral change related to the weather. Hot, dry, downslope winds, such as Santa Ana winds in California, chinooks along the eastern slopes of the Rockies, and foehns along the Alps, are suspected of causing both psychological and physiological reactions. When the air moves downslope, the moisture content is constant from top to bottom, and often, that content is low. On the upslope side, rising motions help release the moisture in the form of clouds and precipitation. But then, as the air pushes downslope with depleted moisture, the temperature rises. That process lowers the humidity even more. Those affected by the hot, dry winds have reduced concentration and increased irritability, which can lead to more accidents, crimes, and suicides.

Some of these mood swings may be related to ions in the atmosphere. Atmospheric ions are charged gases. Some have positive charges, and others have negative charges. These ions play a role in cloud electrification, and some studies show that they may also influence behavior. About 20,000 positive ions and 16,000 negative ions are found for every cubic inch of atmosphere. An excess of positive ions may cause changes in the production of *serotonin,* a chemical that our bodies produce that can impact moods. Those positive ions increase when hot, dry winds blow. But overall, the relationship between ions and moods is not universally accepted.

All these naturally occurring health influences are only enhanced when there's air pollution. In the next chapter we'll add that into the atmospheric mix.

The Least You Need to Know

➤ The weather has a far-reaching impact on our physical and mental health.

➤ Heat is the greatest atmospheric killer.

➤ During the winter, extreme indoor dryness can lead to infection and colds.

➤ Cold germs are passed along through contact with others.

➤ Outdoor light has an important impact on mood and behavior.

➤ During the winter months, try to keep yourself surrounded by as much light as possible.

Chapter 11

Air Pollution

In This Chapter

➤ The major air pollutants

➤ Sources of air pollution

➤ Health and environmental effects of air pollution

➤ The smoggy urban sky

Air pollution is nothing new. Ever since the discovery of fire, less-than-desirable substances have been vented into the air. One of the first air-pollution regulations dates back to the fourteenth century, when King Edward I banned the burning of sea coal in lime kilns. Our own air-pollution regulations have their roots in British Common Law. But regardless of those efforts, air pollution continues to be a serious local and world-wide problem. In this chapter, we take a look at some of the most common pollutants, their sources, and their effects on our health and environment.

The Main Players

What is this thing called air pollution? A standard definition goes like this: It is the pressure within the air of one or more substances that are harmful to human health, welfare, animal or plant life, or property. In the past, the definition has included mainly outdoor pollutants, although in recent years a strong case can be made for the indoor variety, too.

A number of pollutants fall within this definition, but a half-dozen major ones never seem to go away. These are called *primary pollutants,* because they come directly from various sources. Then there are *secondary pollutants,* which are by-products of chemical interactions of the primary pollutants within the atmosphere.

In addition to the pollutants that affect local air quality, other pollutants seem to have a global impact. Hardly a day passes without some news story about these agents of suspected global change. We'll save these global-change pollutants for Chapter 19. For now, let's focus on the air we breathe.

Here's the Dirt

Although air pollution might be thought of as unwanted gases present in the atmosphere, two of the five primary pollutants are really solid substances called particulates. Soot has always been a sure indicator of a polluted atmosphere, but other than soiling and a negative psychological effect, soot can't settle into your lungs and cause serious respiratory disease. Thick, black smoke coming out of a stack is ugly, but it's the particles we *can't* see that really cause the damage. Those particles are called *suspended particulates*. Also, particulate lead can have a poisonous effect when absorbed by our bodies, and it is treated as a separate pollutant.

Suspended particulates come from any incomplete burning and can consist of a variety of substances. The most harmful type of particulate is so small that it's microscopic. Called PM-10, its diameter is less than 10 one-millionths of a meter. The "PM" comes from particulate matter.

These particulates are harmful for several reasons. When inhaled, they can damage the interior of the lung; they can also be poisonous. In addition, these particulates can carry other pollutants into the lung. Sometimes gases will cling to their surfaces in a process called *adsorption,* and those gases will get a free ride into your lungs. In addition, the suspended particulates can serve as surfaces for harmful chemical reactions in the lungs.

These particles are mainly products of combustion, although the grinding and crushing of ores can cause emissions of fine dusts. The major sources include industrial

Weather Words

"—this most excellent canopy, the air...appears no other thing to me but a foul and pestilent congregation of vapours."

—William Shakespeare

Weather-Speak

Primary pollutants are directly emitted whereas **secondary pollutants** are formed by chemical reactions of the primary pollutants in the lower atmosphere. **Suspended particulates** are solids or liquids that have a very small diameter and are suspended in exhaust gases. They can be discharged into the atmosphere.

processes, power plants that are both coal- and oil-fired, residential heating, and transportation. But coal burning is the greatest source.

The following table shows estimates of U.S. particulate emissions from various sources. Only 13 percent of the total is generated by transportation. But industrial sources account for nearly three times as much: 37 percent. Interestingly, fires account for just about as much particulate emissions as transportation. That amount is matched by combustion from sources, which include the generation of all heat and electricity.

National U.S. Emission Estimates - 1990 (Million metric tons/year)			
SOURCE	PARTICULATES	SULFUR OXIDES	CARBON MONOXIDE
Transportation			
-Highway	1.3	0.6	30.3
-Aircraft	0.1	0.0	1.1
-Rail & Sea	0.0	0.3	1.9
-Off-Highway equipment	0.1	0.1	4.4
SUBTOTAL	1.5	1.0	37.7
Stationary Fuel Combustion			
-Electric Utilities	0.4	14.2	0.3
-Industrial Furnaces	0.3	2.3	0.7
-Commercial	0.0	0.4	0.1
-Residential	1.0	0.3	6.4
SUBTOTAL	1.7	17.2	7.5
Industrial Processes	2.8	3.1	4.7
Solid Waste Disposal	0.3	0.0	1.7
Miscellaneous			
-Forest Fires	1.1	0.0	8.1
-Other Burning	0.1	0.0	0.6
-Misc. Organic Solvents	0.0	0.0	0.0
SUBTOTAL	1.2	0.0	8.7
TOTAL	7.5	21.3	60.3

(Data from U.S. Environmental Protection Agency)

Pollution emissions.

Pollution Emissions

When coal was king, power plants and homes accounted for a much greater contribution. The switch to oil and nuclear power has lowered those concentrations, but it hasn't been without its own problems. In addition to health-related problems, particles can damage materials through corrosion and erosion, as well as soiling. Particles can also impact the weather, through changes in visibility, and even in enhancing precipitation. Studies around major urban areas show an increase in precipitation and in thunderstorms with hail downwind from downtown areas. The weather modification is localized but definite, and may be related to an increase in the large condensation nuclei that the particulates provide.

Braving the Elements

In one community, La Porte, Indiana, observations of heavy precipitation were suspected of being bogus and a result of an overzealous weather observer. But even after the observer retired, the observations of heavier precipitation continued. It turns out that La Porte is downwind from downtown Chicago. The enhancement of precipitation is confined to the immediate downwind area, and certainly not of global change extent.

Weather-Wise

Lead is not automatically present in gasoline. It was an additive used to prevent engine knocking, something that's not a serious problem with today's gasolines.

Lead particulates are a brutal primary pollutant. However, their presence in our atmosphere has diminished sharply during the past 25 years. Since 1975, the concentration of lead has decreased by more than 90 percent, which can be directly linked to the elimination of lead from gasoline. The table on the next page shows that huge drop.

Particulates are measured by a vacuum-cleaner–type of device called a hi-volume sampler. Air is drawn across a filter paper, and after 24 hours of drawing in air, the paper is analyzed for both concentration and type of particulate matter.

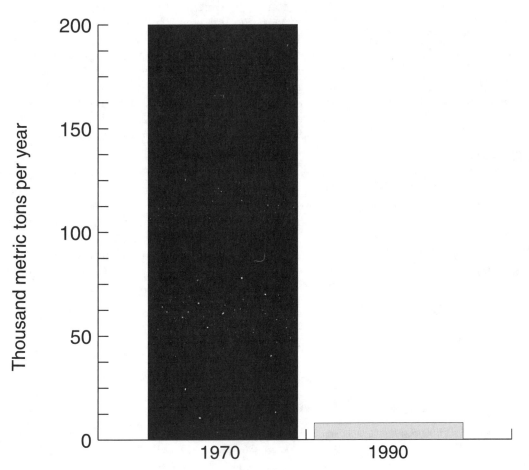

LEAD EMISSIONS
U.S. Environmental Protection Agency

Change of lead emissions.

It's a Gas

Another primary group of pollutants consists of the sulfur oxides (SOx), and the major contributor is SO_2, sulfur dioxide. This is generated whenever sulfur is burned, most often where fuel with a high sulfur content is used. Coal can have very high sulfur concentrations, as can some oil. Overall, coal and oil are the major sources for sulfur oxide pollution.

Ever since the industrial revolution, sulfur dioxide has been linked to numerous health and environmental problems. In London, the combination of smoke and fog gave birth to a new term, *smog*. Sulfur oxides and particulates were the chief ingredients of the London smog. Whenever the weather was uncooperative, the pollutants would build, and hundreds or even thousands of deaths would occur. Even in the United States, severe air-pollution episodes were common through the 1960s—until legislation began to make a difference. Most often, the problem was directly linked to that London-type smog of sulfur oxides and particulates. Coal was really the burning issue—sulfur dioxide and particulates are bad enough, but in combination, they become a deadly duo.

Weather-Speak

You can have two possible responses to pollutants. One is an **acute response**, which is immediate and occurs from a sudden increase in the concentration of a pollutant. This is reversible—unless you die. A **chronic response** may not be realized for years; it's the result of a longer term at a lower dose, and is irreversible.

The table on the next page shows the various sources of sulfur oxides. The vast majority of this pollution comes from the generation of heat and electricity. These stationary sources account for about 80 percent of all sulfur oxides. Transportation's contribution is minor, about 5 percent. The rest comes from industry, but without question, the burning of coal and oil makes sulfur oxides possible.

Braving the Elements

In 1952, 4,000 deaths were attributed to a three-day London smog outbreak. During the 1960s, New York City had some serious air-quality problems, and deadly episodes also occurred in some of the small industrial towns, such as Donora, Pennsylvania, in 1948, when 7,000 people were sickened and 20 killed by a four-day attack of air pollution.

Sulfur dioxide clogs the respiratory tract. Those who have a tendency toward bronchitis or suffer from asthma or emphysema will be most directly impacted by the pollution. The very young, the very old, and the sick have the highest mortality rates during periods of sharp increase in sulfur oxides.

There are a couple schools of thought concerning the effect of sulfur dioxide and pollutants in general. One theory claims that below a certain threshold, there is no impact. This is called the *threshold effect*. Another theory says that regardless of concentration, some damage is done by the pollutant. The effect may be small, but it is there and potentially irreversible. This is called the *linear effect*.

National U.S. Emission Estimates - 1990
(Million metric tons/year)

SOURCE	PARTICULATES	SULFUR OXIDES	CARBON MONOXIDE
Transportation			
-Highway	1.3	0.6	30.3
-Aircraft	0.1	0.0	1.1
-Rail & Sea	0.0	0.3	1.9
-Off-Highway equipment	0.1	0.1	4.4
SUBTOTAL	1.5	1.0	37.7
Stationary Fuel Combustion			
-Electric Utilities	0.4	14.2	0.3
-Industrial Furnaces	0.3	2.3	0.7
-Commercial	0.0	0.4	0.1
-Residential	1.0	0.3	6.4
SUBTOTAL	1.7	17.2	7.5
Industrial Processes	2.8	3.1	4.7
Solid Waste Disposal	0.3	0.0	1.7
Miscellaneous			
-Forest Fires	1.1	0.0	8.1
-Other Burning	0.1	0.0	0.6
-Misc. Organic Solvents	0.0	0.0	0.0
SUBTOTAL	1.2	0.0	8.7
TOTAL	7.5	21.3	60.3

(Data from U.S. Environmental Protection Agency)

Pollution emissions.

Sulfur dioxide is soluble and absorbed by the upper respiratory tract. That absorption can result in *bronchoconstriction* (less air gets into the lower lung for exchange with the bloodstream). A person can experience shortness of breath, wheezing, and coughing. The pollutant can set off an asthma attack, and long-term exposure can lead to heart problems. Those who have some pre-existing heart or respiratory problems will suffer the most.

Also, because sulfur dioxide is soluble, it can react with the moisture lining the lungs and undergo an acid reaction. The sulfur dioxide and water become sulfuric acid, a corrosive substance that can cause additional damage.

143

Interestingly, sulfur dioxide seems far less harmful alone than when combined with particulates. The particulates seem to direct the sulfur dioxide into a deeper portion of the lung and provide a surface for the acid reaction. In the early days of pollution studies, volunteers were exposed to sulfur dioxide alone, and little effect was observed. But when suspended particles were put into the mix, breathing problems began to appear. In the real world, the sources that generate sulfur oxides are the same as the ones that cause particulates. Neither really stands alone.

Weather-Speak

Chlorosis is the condition where plants do not develop enough chlorophyll. **Plasmolysis** is tissue collapse.

In addition to their impact on our lungs, sulfur oxides cause damage to vegetation and material. One effect on plants is called *chlorosis,* or the loss of chlorophyll, the plant's food factory. Another is *plasmolysis,* or tissue collapse. Again, sulfur dioxide combined with other substances does the most damage. Because of its solubility, sulfur dioxide becomes a major contributor to acid precipitation or acid deposition. Leaves are bleached and show a spotted pattern of damage. Tree growth is stunted, and vegetation can even die. Patterns of damage show up clearly in the countryside, downwind from big fossil-fuel burning power plants. Damage to vegetation occurs at concentrations lower than what's harmful to people.

A Silent Killer

Although industry has taken the heat for pollution so far, we'll now look at some pollutants that develop from sources much closer to home—our cars. The first is carbon monoxide (CO).

This gas is colorless, odorless, and tasteless. There's no way to know when it's around, except we may not feel so well. The gas is generated through the incomplete combustion of carbon-based fuels. In the combustion process, the carbon combines with oxygen. If the burning were efficient and complete, carbon dioxide (CO_2) would be given off, not CO.

Unlike other pollutants, carbon monoxide is not directly harmful to plants or materials. It *is* harmful to people and animals, which depend on oxygen, because carbon monoxide substitutes for oxygen in the blood. Hemoglobin is the chemical carrier of oxygen through our bloodstream. When we inhale, oxygen goes into our lungs and is transferred to our blood by way of hemoglobin. But that hemoglobin has a much greater affinity for carbon monoxide, and if air contains both carbon monoxide and oxygen, the hemoglobin is more likely to grab the carbon monoxide. Actually, because of the different pressures between the gases, hemoglobin is 210 times more attracted to carbon monoxide than oxygen. Our bodies need that oxygen, and without it, we can suffocate. A carbon-monoxide-filled atmosphere chokes off the supply of oxygen. Carbon monoxide poisoning can begin at concentrations of 20 to 50 parts per million (ppm). Cigarette smoke contains 400 to 450 ppm. In a busy intersection, concentrations are about 100 ppm.

The response from carbon monoxide is often thought to be acute: sharp, immediate, but reversible if death doesn't occur. A person exposed to 10 or 20 ppm of CO over the course of a day might have a headache and feel uncomfortable. As the concentrations climb into the hundreds of parts per million, suffocation becomes possible, but the quick removal of a person from the polluted air will allow a return to normal. The excess carbon monoxide will be expelled through the lungs. Still, chronic responses are likely. After all, a heart must work harder if a person is even modestly deprived of oxygen. Those long-term, chronic responses are always more difficult to pin down. But a toll-booth operator who smokes is definitely asking the body to take more abuse than it should.

National U.S. Emission Estimates - 1990
(Million metric tons/year)

SOURCE	PARTICULATES	SULFUR OXIDES	CARBON MONOXIDE
Transportation			
-Highway	1.3	0.6	30.3
-Aircraft	0.1	0.0	1.1
-Rail & Sea	0.0	0.3	1.9
-Off-Highway equipment	0.1	0.1	4.4
SUBTOTAL	1.5	1.0	37.7
Stationary Fuel Combustion			
-Electric Utilities	0.4	14.2	0.3
-Industrial Furnaces	0.3	2.3	0.7
-Commercial	0.0	0.4	0.1
-Residential	1.0	0.3	6.4
SUBTOTAL	1.7	17.2	7.5
Industrial Processes	2.8	3.1	4.7
Solid Waste Disposal	0.3	0.0	1.7
Miscellaneous			
-Forest Fires	1.1	0.0	8.1
-Other Burning	0.1	0.0	0.6
-Misc. Organic Solvents	0.0	0.0	0.0
SUBTOTAL	1.2	0.0	8.7
TOTAL	7.5	21.3	60.3

(Data from U.S. Environmental Protection Agency)

Pollution emissions.

The main source of carbon monoxide isn't a sooty smokestack, it's your car. Certainly, other sources exist, but the table on the preceding page shows how transportation is responsible for most of our carbon monoxide. Fossil fuels are simply not efficiently burned. The carbon in the fuel combines with oxygen in the burning process—but not completely. Carbon monoxide, rather than carbon dioxide, comes out of the exhaust. About half of all carbon monoxide comes from highway vehicles, even in an age when strict controls have been instituted.

After transportation, the remaining carbon-monoxide emissions seem to be fairly well distributed through industry and power generation. Interestingly enough, forest fires account for 13 percent of all national carbon-monoxide emissions. Wood burning is a big producer, and those with wood or coal stoves should make sure they are properly vented. Improperly vented fireplaces can be health hazards, too.

Out of the Blue

Once again, transportation takes a big hit here, but unlike with carbon monoxide, stationary sources shoulder equal responsibility. In our study of the other primary pollutants, they appeared because of the chemical composition of the fuel. Fuels are burned, and particles, along with sulfur oxides and carbon monoxide, are emitted because of the presence of solid matter, sulfur and carbon. But nitrogen oxides are different: They just come from thin air. How is that possible?

Seventy-eight percent of the atmosphere is made up of nitrogen. Another 21 percent consists of oxygen. So, 99 percent of the atmosphere is nitrogen and oxygen. Whenever fuel is burned, air is drawn in to provide the necessary oxygen. Once the fuel is fired up, plenty of heat is given off. That forces the nitrogen and oxygen in the air to combine and form nitrogen oxides—of which nitrogen dioxide (NO_2) and nitric oxide (NO) are the main products. Ironically, the more efficient burning gives off the most heat and causes the most nitrogen oxides. An efficient engine could deliver less carbon monoxide, but it will also produce more nitrogen oxides.

Nitrogen oxides absorb enough light so that an atmosphere filled with them gives off a brownish haze. That discoloration of the air can be seen frequently over urban areas.

Weather-Wise

Transportation and utilities account for nearly 80 percent of all nitrogen oxide emissions, and each share an equal responsibility.

White light, which consists of all the colors of the rainbow, has a blue-green area that is absorbed by nitrogen oxides, so without that blue-green color, the sky has that brownish look. But discoloration is a minor effect of too much nitrogen oxide. The gas itself can be toxic, and can combine with other gases for even more poisonous mixtures.

By themselves, nitrogen oxides are damaging to plants, animals, and people. Just a few parts per million of nitrogen dioxide can damage leafy plants. Somewhat higher levels of 10–30 ppm can cause difficulty in breathing and contribute to bronchitis and pneumonia.

Nitrogen oxides also become major contributors to acid precipitation. Just as sulfur oxides can be absorbed by water to yield corrosive acids such as sulfuric acid, nitrogen oxide can combine with water to form nitric acid. The following table shows the various sources for nitrogen oxides.

National U.S. Emission Estimates - 1990 (Million metric tons/year)		
SOURCE	NITROGEN OXIDES	VOC's
Transportation		
-Highway	5.6	5.1
-Aircraft	0.1	0.2
-Rail & Sea	0.7	0.6
-Off-Highway equipment	1.1	0.5
SUBTOTAL	7.5	6.4
Stationary Fuel Combustion		
-Electric Utilities	7.3	0.0
-Industrial Furnaces	3.3	0.1
-Commercial	0.2	0.0
-Residential	0.4	0.7
SUBTOTAL	11.2	0.8
Industrial Processes	0.6	8.1
Solid Waste Disposal	0.1	0.6
Miscellaneous		
-Forest Fires	0.3	1.1
-Other Burning	0.0	0.1
-Misc. Organic Solvents	0.0	1.5
SUBTOTAL	0.3	2.7
TOTAL	19.7	18.6
(Data from U.S. Environmental Protection Agency)		

Trends of VOC and Nitrogen Oxides.

Nitrogen oxides' combination with water is not the only troublesome chemical combination. These gases can combine with hydrocarbons and other volatile organic compounds (VOCs) to deliver photochemical smog. Let's first talk about the VOCs.

VOCs

These volatile organic compounds consist of assorted substances, some of which are carcinogenic. Many are hydrocarbons, consisting of a combination of hydrogen and carbon. These hydrocarbons come from unburned fuel. If fuel is burned properly, the hydrogen will combine with oxygen to deliver steam, and the carbon will yield carbon dioxide. But if the burning is incomplete, assorted hydrocarbons will be emitted.

Other VOCs take on the name of aldehydes, ketones, and chlorinated solvents. The next table shows the different sources for these VOCs, and again, transportation becomes a major source, along with industry. The combination accounts for about 80 percent of all emission.

National U.S. Emission Estimates - 1990 (Million metric tons/year)		
SOURCE	NITROGEN OXIDES	VOC's
Transportation		
-Highway	5.6	5.1
-Aircraft	0.1	0.2
-Rail & Sea	0.7	0.6
-Off-Highway equipment	1.1	0.5
SUBTOTAL	7.5	6.4
Stationary Fuel Combustion		
-Electric Utilities	7.3	0.0
-Industrial Furnaces	3.3	0.1
-Commercial	0.2	0.0
-Residential	0.4	0.7
SUBTOTAL	11.2	0.8
Industrial Processes	0.6	8.1
Solid Waste Disposal	0.1	0.6
Miscellaneous		
-Forest Fires	0.3	1.1
-Other Burning	0.0	0.1
-Misc. Organic Solvents	0.0	1.5
SUBTOTAL	0.3	2.7
TOTAL	19.7	18.6
(Data from U.S. Environmental Protection Agency)		

Trends of VOC and Nitrogen Oxides.

Ironically, more efficient burning can reduce VOCs, but that will increase nitrogen oxides. It is this combination of VOCs and nitrogen oxides that creates smog. So, the decrease of one ingredient doesn't guarantee that the problem will disappear, especially when the other ingredient increases. After decades of legislation, the smog problem continues.

Photochemical Smog

In London, smog might have initially been defined as that mixture of smoke and fog which contains sulfur oxides and particulates. But there has been an Americanization of that chemical stew, and it's called photochemical smog, or Los Angeles–type smog. It's different than the smog of days gone by; this variety is a chemical mix that is cooked by sunshine. And what better location for this variety of smog than sunny southern California?

The initial ingredients consist of nitrogen oxides and the volatile organic compounds, mainly hydrocarbons. The final product delivers a mix that is so complex it defies definition. Many of the constituents contain oxygen and are called oxidants. The major product of this chemistry turns out to be ozone. This becomes the "bad" ozone—the ozone we breathe, not the protecting ozone found in the upper reaches of the atmosphere. We'll get to the "good" ozone in Chapter 13.

Ozone is a modified oxygen molecule. Neutral, regular oxygen consists of two oxygen atoms (O_2). But ozone contains three oxygen atoms. How does that happen? There are numerous ways for that to occur. In the lower atmosphere when nitrogen dioxide (NO_2) is acted upon by sunlight's ultraviolet radiation, it splits into nitric oxide (NO) and a single oxygen atom (O). That single O can combine with O_2 to give ozone, O_3. Then, if all goes well, the O_3 will absorb radiation, combine with the nitric oxide and break down to O_2 and nitrogen dioxide. A very nice cycle occurs and the ozone really never builds up.

But when hydrocarbons are present, they latch onto the available nitric oxides, NO, and they are no longer available to help break down the ozone. The ozone level increases along with the complex oxidants that result from the nitric oxides' involvement with the hydrocarbons. It really is a highly polluted chemical stew that we call Los Angeles–type smog, or more technically, peroxyacetyl nitrate. The elements within the mixture can't be measured completely, and only the ozone level is given as a short-hand way of getting the message across. All the products

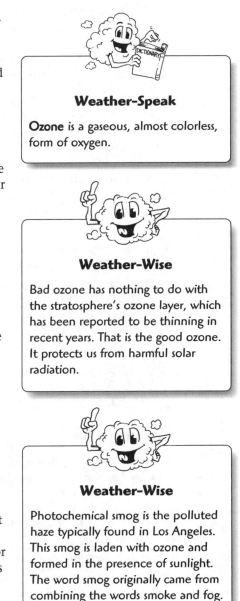

Weather-Speak

Ozone is a gaseous, almost colorless, form of oxygen.

Weather-Wise

Bad ozone has nothing to do with the stratosphere's ozone layer, which has been reported to be thinning in recent years. That is the good ozone. It protects us from harmful solar radiation.

Weather-Wise

Photochemical smog is the polluted haze typically found in Los Angeles. This smog is laden with ozone and formed in the presence of sunlight. The word smog originally came from combining the words smoke and fog.

are oxidants and extremely damaging, but ozone is the only one that is routinely monitored by weather experts. This is definitely the bad ozone, and its chemical cousins aren't any better.

These oxidants can cause irritation of the eyes, nose, or throat at levels as slight as 0.1 ppm, and at 0.2 ppm, severe coughing can take place. Levels of at least 0.1 ppm are reached on a regular basis in urban areas during the summer when the sun is strongest. Ozone is not soluble in water, so it can sink into the deep lung. Long-term exposures at low levels will take a toll, too. The lung will lose its elasticity, and emphysema can develop. Lungs will age much faster in an atmosphere that regularly contains ozone, even at low levels. Again, that long-term chronic response is difficult to follow.

In addition to its impact on our health, ozone is very damaging to materials and vegetation. It causes cracking of synthetic rubber, like your tires, and deterioration of clothing and paint. Nylon stockings worn in Los Angeles have a much better chance of developing runs. Leaves will discolor and show damage at ozone levels that are even less than those that cause health problems in people. Concentration as slight as .05 ppm can seriously damage crops and plants. Some estimates place ozone damage to crops at one billion dollars annually in the United States. The pollutant may also be a factor in causing forest fires by killing off trees, thus reducing the cool, moist leafy canopy of a forest.

Amazingly, too, this poisonous gas has not been substantially controlled in all the years of air pollution regulations. The table on the next page shows the trend of those volatile organic compounds and nitrogen oxides, the basic ingredients for this smog. While there has been a slight decrease in the VOC emissions, nitrogen oxides continue at their peak levels. The chief source of both happens to be transportation. So bright, warm, heavily traveled areas will experience the highest concentrations of smog.

Weather-Wise

Ozone is a product of hydrocarbons and nitrogen oxides, gases generated mainly by automobiles. In strong sun, these gases break down to form ozone. Ozone is chemically similar to oxygen, except ozone has an extra molecule that causes damage to lung tissue.

Places such as southern California and the Southwest have been havens for those trying to seek relief from fickle northern climates. But these same places, with their bright skies, experience high levels of ultraviolet radiation—the energy that causes the smog process to unfold. So, as traffic increases with the influx of new residents, pollution levels increase. The bright, clear atmosphere that attracts many helps trigger the severe pollution problems. The air isn't so bright and clear anymore.

Los Angeles isn't the only location with a severe smog problem. Even the breezy, stormy Northeast has its days. Places such as Connecticut are among the major ozone producers in the nation. Geography and meteorology play roles in the process, but the dependency on the automobile for travel is really the ultimate source.

National U.S. Emission Estimates - 1990
(Million metric tons/year)

SOURCE	NITROGEN OXIDES	VOC's
Transportation		
-Highway	5.6	5.1
-Aircraft	0.1	0.2
-Rail & Sea	0.7	0.6
-Off-Highway equipment	1.1	0.5
SUBTOTAL	7.5	6.4
Stationary Fuel Combustion		
-Electric Utilities	7.3	0.0
-Industrial Furnaces	3.3	0.1
-Commercial	0.2	0.0
-Residential	0.4	0.7
SUBTOTAL	11.2	0.8
Industrial Processes	0.6	8.1
Solid Waste Disposal	0.1	0.6
Miscellaneous		
-Forest Fires	0.3	1.1
-Other Burning	0.0	0.1
-Misc. Organic Solvents	0.0	1.5
SUBTOTAL	0.3	2.7
TOTAL	19.7	18.6

(Data from U.S. Environmental Protection Agency)

Trends of VOC and Nitrogen Oxides.

The figure on the following page shows a typical sequence of chemical changes that take place each day. Automobiles emit the nitric oxide (NO), and its concentration peaks at about 8 a.m. when traffic is heaviest. Then it drops sharply as it coverts to nitrogen dioxide and eventually gets tied up with the hydrocarbons. Nitrogen dioxide increases for a little while, but by mid-morning it drops as it absorbs ultraviolet radiation and goes to nitric oxide and a single oxygen atom (O). Then, just as NO_2 drops, ozone (O_3) moves up, reaching a peak during mid-afternoon. Then, as the sunshine diminishes, the ozone level quickly drops.

Smog formation.

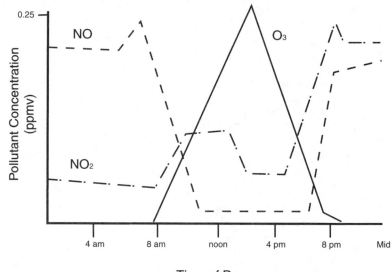

St. Louis, Missouri - 1962

Time of Day

(Data from U.S. Environmental Protection Agency)

So, numerous pollutants contribute to our modern-day atmosphere. Amazingly, our own automobile has become one of the chief sources of pollution, with photochemical smog dominating some unlikely locations. There is no doubt that air pollution is taking a toll on our health.

The Least You Need to Know

➤ Carbon monoxide, particulates, sulfur dioxide, volatile organic compounds, nitrogen oxides, and ozone are the main pollutants.

➤ Each pollutant has a major source and an effect on our health and environment.

➤ Power plants and the automobile contribute to much of our air pollution.

➤ Photochemical smog forms through a complex chemical reaction of sunlight with nitrogen oxides and hydrocarbons.

➤ An acute response to pollution is immediately observed, but unless death occurs, it is reversible.

➤ A chronic response is less easily detected and long term, and its effects are irreversible.

Chapter 12

Control of Pollution

In This Chapter

➤ A look at environmental law

➤ The mechanics of control

➤ If the wind isn't right

➤ Paying for air pollution control

Now that we know the major players in the pollution problem, what do we do about it? In this chapter, we'll look at the methods of control and environmental engineering. We'll examine the fundamental issues of control: What can be done, and what are the laws? We'll discuss the natural processes, mainly the weather, that help shape a polluted environment. Finally, we'll look at the question of whether we can afford to control air pollution, even if we have the legislation and the tools. The political and socioeconomic dynamics of pollution control can be more difficult than the physical and engineering mechanics of maintaining a clean environment.

Politics of Control

Ever since humans started burning things, either to get rid of them or to warm themselves, somebody else has been looking at the smoky results and getting steamed. The legal foundation of air pollution control goes back to the beginning of conflict itself.

It's a Nuisance

The legal basis for all environmental regulations is found in the nuisance provision of ancient Common Law. *Nuisance* is a word that's carefully defined. First, there is a *private nuisance*, which involves a party who has been shown to be directly injured or harmed. In addition, the pollution has to be shown to be unnecessary. A private nuisance isn't easily proven.

Although we now understand the harmful effects of pollutants, that hasn't always been the case. Even now, there are uncertainties about long-term harm, so proving direct injury is a challenge. Also, even if you can prove a direct, harmful impact, how do you prove it was unnecessary? Sure, if your neighbor burns trash in his incinerator right under your dining-room window every Friday night, and you can prove that your difficulty in breathing is directly related to the dinnertime attack, then you might win your case.

But normally, the situation isn't so clear-cut. A local industry or power plant might not intentionally cause poor air quality. Its pollution may be necessary for its operation and, therefore, for the economic well-being of the community.

These days we know more about the effects of pollution, as well as the availability of known alternatives. As a result, class-action suits have been filed claiming a private nuisance. But overall, the private nuisance road is pitted with hazards.

Most environmental control has evolved out of the public-nuisance provisions. The state has the power to develop and enforce laws for the public good. Today's air pollution regulations are based on this principle. Politics are very much a part of the process, and the regulations are only as strong as the state's willingness and ability to enforce them. Fines or prison sentences can be imposed on violators.

Weather-Watch

There is a greater incidence of bronchitis in areas of severe air pollution. If you have chronic lung disease and work around heavy air pollution, try to limit your exposure. Perhaps you could even change jobs.

Weather Words

"Smoke and blood is the mix of steel."

—Carl Sandburg

The Regulations

The very early air pollution laws were passed within particular communities and concerned the color and density of smoke emitted from stacks. Smoke ordinances first appeared in Chicago and Cincinnati and, around the turn of the century, began to show up in other communities. A special chart determined the level of smoke. The chart showed the smoke with its different shades of gray and black. At a particular coded level, violations would be set. Enforcement wasn't based on any chemical analysis of the smoke, just how it looked. These laws were strictly local. No national air-pollution legislation appeared until the 1950s.

The first federal legislation appeared in 1955 when the Air Pollution Control Act was passed. During the 1950s, it became apparent that air pollution wasn't simply a local problem. More was being learned about the Los Angeles–type smog, which comes from transportation (see Chapter 11). Still, the 1955 act only provided funds for federal research and technical assistance; there was no effort to establish or impose national standards or federal enforcement. Air pollution remained a local issue.

Although there are advantages to managing environmental issues at the local level, the conflicts inherent in local politics and economics are infinite and eternal. Also, air pollution doesn't respect the boundaries of a particular community or state. Air pollution is a national, even international, problem. So, it was only a matter of time before more significant federal regulations were passed.

The first of a series of Clean Air Acts was passed in 1963. These acts began to address the interstate nature of air pollution by giving the federal government authority to at least study the problem. But this act wasn't especially far-reaching, and local communities remained in charge of their own regulations.

In 1965, however, the Motor Vehicle Air Pollution Act was passed, establishing national automobile emission regulations for the first time. Then the Air Quality Act of 1967 was passed, providing funds for additional federal research and designating air-quality control regions to help establish air-pollution limits or criteria. It also was set up to look at the costs and effectiveness of available engineering control techniques. That paved the way for the most sweeping air pollution regulations of the century—the National Environmental Policy Act and the Clean Air Act amendments of 1970.

Braving the Elements

I was caught up by these regulations in the late 1960s, when the secretary of Health, Education, and Welfare awarded grants and scholarships to students interested in becoming air-pollution control administrators or air-pollution control engineers. Laws were being written, but there was no trained work force to implement them. A crash-training program was set up. I chose the administrative track and, during my senior year, eight hours a day, five days a week, I was introduced to every aspect of air-pollution control and management. From day one, I learned that there were no easy solutions.

The legislation established the federal Environmental Protection Agency (EPA), which then led to the development of state agencies. The EPA provided technical assistance, along with matching funds for the establishment of local agencies. The states were required to come up with a state implementation plan (SIP) to show how the federal regulations would be met.

National Air Quality Standards (NAAQS) were set for the major pollutants. *Primary standards* were set for health, with *secondary standards* for vegetation and general environmental welfare. But it was still left to the states to manage the control program. States could be fined, and major funds, such as federal highway funds, could be withheld if an adequate plan was not implemented. Stiff fines and penalties of up to $25,000 per day and a year in prison were authorized for industries that failed to meet the regulations. Aggressive national emission standards were set for automobiles.

Additional amendments to the 1970 legislation came along in 1977 and 1990. Each revised some of the previous specific regulations. In some cases, the standards proved to be too strict and unattainable. But overall, each amended version strengthened and broadened the previous version.

How Are We Doing?

The following figure shows the air-quality standard set up by the Clean Air Act. For the most part, these standards have been achieved, but there are glaring exceptions. Carbon-monoxide levels regularly exceed the standard in very busy intersections, for example.

Air-quality standards.

National Ambient Air Quality Standards

Carbon Monoxide (CO)
8-hour Average 9 ppm (10 mg/m3)
1-hour Average 35 ppm (40 mg/m3)

Nitrogen Dioxide (NO_2)
Annual Arithmetic Mean 0.053 ppm (100 µg/m3)

Ozone (O3)
1-hour Average 0.12 ppm (235 µg/m3)
8-hour Average 0.08 ppm (157 µg/m3)

Lead (Pb)
Quarterly Average 1.5 µg/m3

Particulate < 10 micrometers (PM-10)
Annual Arithmetic Mean 50 µg/m3 P
24-hour Average 150 µg/m3

Particulate < 2.5 micrometers (PM-2.5)
Annual Arithmetic Mean 15 µg/m3
24-hour Average 65 µg/m3

Sulfur Dioxide (SO_2)
Annual Arithmetic Mean 0.03 ppm (80 µg/m3)
24-hour Average 0.14 ppm (365 µg/m3)
3-hour Average 0.50 ppm (1300 µg/m3)

The biggest problem has turned out to be ozone (see Chapter 11). After three decades of progressively stiffening federal regulations, photochemical smog is still a serious problem. Many states violate the standard, especially during the summer, and in 1998, the standard was tightened even more. Instead of .12 ppm for a one-hour concentration, the standard was changed to .08 ppm in an eight-hour period. The hot summer of 1998 delivered some of the highest numbers of violations of the ozone standard in years. Both weather and politics were responsible.

Overall, however, many of the other basic pollutants have much lower concentrations since the passage of the first amendments in 1970. The figure below shows the drop in emission rates for the major pollutants. The changes are impressive, but nitrogen oxides and volatile organic compounds continue unabated. And that explains our continuing photochemical smog problem.

During the 1990s, the amendments were expanded to include chemicals of global concern—pollutants that influence the chemical composition of the upper atmosphere and worldwide climate. But those deserve a chapter for themselves, Chapter 13.

Weather-Wise

In the 1970s and 1980s, research showed that chlorofluorocarbon gases (CFCs), which are used as aerosol propellants and components of refrigerants such as Freon, were eroding the ozone layer. The United States banned CFC aerosols in 1978.

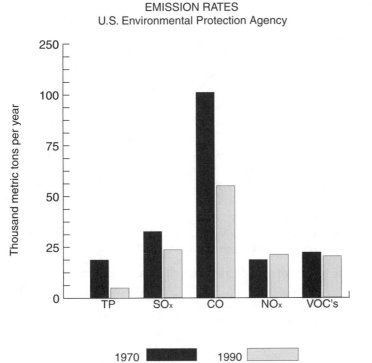

EMISSION RATES
U.S. Environmental Protection Agency

Change of emission rates.

Engineering Techniques

Now that we understand the problem and have the legislative means for controlling it, how is it done? The mechanics of control are far easier than the politics—provided we're willing to pay. And payment doesn't mean just in dollars—it could mean a major change in lifestyle, such as traveling by bicycle instead of car, or more realistically, carpooling and better public transportation. These are effective alternatives, but they're not very popular in America—and the automotive industry is *very* reluctant to allow significant changes. So, let's take a look at just the basics.

Change of Fuels

The most direct method of pollution control involves simply changing the fuel. High-sulfur coal was responsible for the great smog outbreaks of the early twentieth century. Sulfur oxides and particulates reached dangerous levels in many industrial areas. But during the 1960s and 1970s, a switch to low-sulfur oil, natural gas, and nuclear power brought the levels of that form of smog down to relatively low concentrations. Although complex control devices are available, the fuel switch in power plants accounts for most of the improvement. Sulfur-oxide pollution and particulate pollution are problems of the past, thanks to the change in fuels. Of course, change can introduce new problems. Natural-gas combustion can increase the levels of nitrogen oxides, and nuclear power opens a whole Pandora's box.

Getting the Dirt Out

Particles come in assorted sizes and shapes, and a number of control systems have been designed for removing them from the stream of gases that go up the smokestack. The type of device depends on the type of particle and its size. Soluble particles can be drained out of an effluent by washing with *scrubbers*. Sometimes, the particles will simply settle out before being emitted, in what are called *settling chambers*. Sometimes, the gas is pushed through filters or cloth collectors. Other devices are even more sophisticated. The gas might be whipped around in a circular path, so that centrifugal force separates the particles. Those devices are called *cyclones* or *centrifugal separators*. And then there are devices that deliver an electrical charge to the particles. An opposite charge is placed on a metal plate, and, because opposites attract, the particles will collect on the plate. Then, the plate is cleaned off. That device is called an *electrostatic precipitator*.

Of course, once the particles have been removed, the problem becomes how to dispose of the sludge. The toxicity of the material and its impact on the environment become new considerations.

Weather-Speak

Adsorption is the process by which molecules coming from a gaseous phase are retained by the surface of a substance. **Absorption** is the process by which gas is dissolved into a substance.

Degassing

Just as particles can be removed through various methods, gases can be taken out in a variety of ways. Did you ever notice how charcoal removes odors from a refrigerator? Sometimes gases will adhere to the surface of particular porous materials (charcoal is a perfect example). The gas isn't taken in, it just sticks to the surface. This process is called *adsorption,* and it's effective for filtering out volatile organic compounds (VOCs) such as benzyne, ethanol, and other hydrocarbons. The gas is run through chambers filled with this material, and the pollutants are taken out.

In contrast to adsorption, there is *absorption,* where the gas is dissolved in a liquid and scrubbed or washed. The pollutants react with the liquid, and the by-products are separated. These scrubbers are used for a variety of gases, including sulfur dioxide, and the techniques can become complex. The next figure shows a schematic of a scrubber for sulfur-dioxide removal. Limestone is used to react with the sulfur dioxide. The material collected includes sulfur and sulfuric acid, which could be resold for other uses.

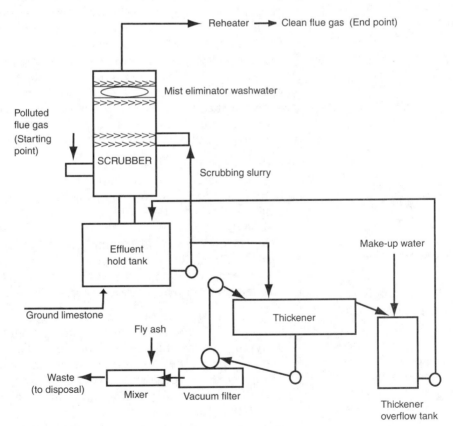

Sulfur dioxide removal.

159

The Infernal Combustion Engine

As you know from the last chapter, one of the greatest polluters on Earth is the automobile. Although we have seen great strides in the clean-up of some basic pollutants such as sulfur oxides and particulates, we still have a serious problem with respect to volatile organic compounds, nitrogen oxides, and carbon monoxides—all of which are related to transportation, particularly the automobile and the internal combustion engine. For example, in the United States, two-thirds of all carbon-monoxide emissions come from mobile sources. A third of all volatile organic compounds, such as hydrocarbons, come from transportation. Nearly half of all nitrogen oxides come from transportation.

There are four basic mechanisms of the internal combustion engine: the intake stroke, the compression stroke, the power stroke, and the exhaust stroke. During the intake stroke, fuel and air are brought into the cylinder. That mixture is compressed in the compression stroke. At that point the spark plug will fire and ignite the air-fuel mix. As that mixture burns, it expands rapidly, causing the cylinder to move downward and giving a power stroke, making the car move. Then the cylinder begins to compress again, and that stroke exhausts the gases out the rear of the car. The whole process begins all over again. The nature of the pollutants emitted depends on the type of fuel used and the air-fuel mix.

If the air-fuel mix is *lean*, there is a good deal of air and less fuel. The combustion temperature will be relatively high, which will favor the complete burning of the gases, and hydrocarbons will convert to water vapor and carbon dioxide. However, if the mix is not so lean, but richer with more fuel, the temperature will be lower. Instead of completely burning the hydrocarbons with the oxygen, you end up with unburned hydrocarbons and carbon monoxide instead of carbon dioxide.

So, wouldn't the natural conclusion be to have a very lean mix of air and fuel? The problem with that is the high temperature of efficient combustion. The oxygen and nitrogen in the air combine, resulting in a lot of nitrogen oxides. You may reduce the carbon-monoxide pollution in having a transformation to carbon dioxide, but on the other hand, you're going to end up with more nitrogen oxides. Any hydrocarbons that don't burn can now combine with nitrogen oxides under strong sunlight to deliver photochemical smog.

Weather-Wise

When sulfur dioxide is released into the air and combines with atmospheric moisture, it causes sulfuric acid to form. Rain that contains sulfuric acid is called acid rain and causes metals to corrode and damages forests and crops. Other acid reactions in the atmosphere include nitrogen oxides, and even carbon dioxide.

Weather-Wise

The state vehicle inspection programs set minimum air pollution standards high so only the highly polluting vehicles do not pass. These inspection stations are usually operated by private contractors but are under state supervision and issue inspection stickers. Cars that fail must repair their problems and be reinspected.

That's one of the main dilemmas of the internal combustion engine. We may be able to reduce through the combustion process some of the gases, but only at the expense of others.

There are control devices that can eliminate some of the pollutants from the internal combustion engine, most notably the *catalytic converter*. It raises the temperature of gases that will be exhausted, so there will be further burning of the hydrocarbons. As a result, we end up with more water vapor and carbon dioxide, rather than unburned hydrocarbons and carbon monoxide. The catalytic converter helps; however, we're still left with the problem of nitrogen oxides. The more efficient the burning remains, the greater the nitrogen oxide problem becomes.

As a result, although some pollutants have been reduced in our environment over the years, those related to automobiles have remained high. Also, another problem is the simple number of vehicles on the roads. In fact, it turns out that on a worldwide basis, the growth rate for automobiles is far greater than the overall population. During the past 40 years, the number of motor vehicles in the world has risen by a factor of ten. In comparison, the growth of the world population has just doubled.

Weathering the Pollution

If atmospheric conditions are favorable, our environment would be able to tolerate a vast amount of air pollution. There are two ways that the pollution is dispersed in the atmosphere. The first is through horizontal flow—the wind—and the other is through vertical, upward motion. If the smoke coming out of the stack is blown horizontally, it can be diffused, and if it is lifted up to great heights, it can also be diffused and dispersed.

Horizontal Dispersal

Here, we are just talking about the wind. Windier locations can tolerate more pollution than other areas with lighter winds. Valleys are often protected from the wind, and pollution has a better chance of collecting there. Coastal areas experience fresh breezes, and would be better suited for development, such as housing and manufacturing. Mountain tops tend to be windier, but they're not really practical locations for a power plant.

Also, certain weather situations deliver more wind than others. Wind is a function of pressure differences. In the center of high-pressure systems, the pressure differential is negligible. The sky is sunny and the wind is calm. Regions that experience frequent, slow-moving, high-pressure systems will experience less dispersion. Also, the Sun is shining in these high-pressure systems, so photochemical smog has a better chance to cook. There are more reasons high-pressure systems are troublesome, which we'll talk about next.

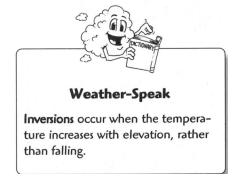

Weather-Speak

Inversions occur when the temperature increases with elevation, rather than falling.

Vertical Mixing

If the atmosphere is unstable, with cold air overlying warmer air, the heavy, cold air overturns, and there's a whole lotta shakin' going on. The cold air sinks, the warm air rises, and the pollution becomes diluted. Sure, there might be a thunderstorm or tornado, but the air pollution goes away. However, if the atmosphere has the opposite configuration with warm air overlying cold surface air, the mixing is limited because light, less dense air is resting on colder, heavier air. All is well with the world, until a cloud of smoke comes along. When smoke gets caught up in such an atmosphere, it really can't rise. The configuration is called an *inversion*—the normal decrease of temperature with elevation is inverted. These inversions are big troublemakers for air quality. High-pressure systems are notorious for delivering these inversions—valley regions, too.

In high-pressure systems, the wind is light and skies are clear. During the night, heat escapes rapidly from the surface. A nocturnal inversion develops, with cold air collecting near the ground and warmer air above. The following figure shows the development of the inversion. If the wind were stronger and the atmosphere well mixed, the ground-level cooling would be less because less heat would radiate out. But with little wind, the heat can escape without interruption. A cloudy sky will also maintain more of the surface warmth. But clear skies and light winds develop in the center of all high-pressure systems, and, there, pollution becomes trapped. Valley regions simply enhance the development of these inversions by limiting the horizontal flow, or horizontal mixing.

Inversion development.

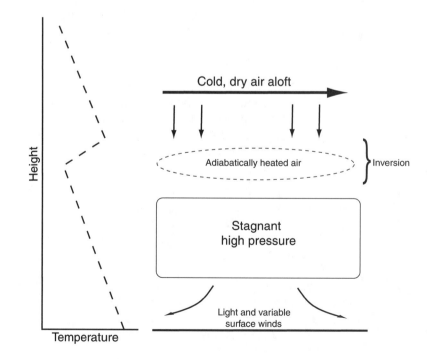

162

Those Dirty Highs

In general, those high-pressure systems become real headaches, because they not only restrict the horizontal mixing, but the vertical mixing too. Also, with high-pressure systems, the atmosphere is already delivering sinking motions. Those sinking motions produce the high-pressure system in the first place, and can dynamically prevent additional rising motions. And we're not finished. The sinking, or subsidence, that takes place causes an additional warming above the ground by forcing the air molecules to push closer together. The air is squished and warmed at levels of 5,000 feet and higher in the atmosphere. That warming helps generate and maintain an inversion, called a *subsidence inversion.*

Under normal circumstances, nocturnal or valley inversions will disappear during the day because of the warming of the ground by the Sun. But if a real warm layer persists above the ground because of a subsidence inversion, forget about it. The pollution buildup becomes extreme. Strong, warm, high-pressure systems will deliver the ingredients for these such episodes. And if the high pressure is stagnant and sticks around for a few days, you might need gas masks. The following figure shows the frequency of stagnant high-pressure systems in different parts of the country.

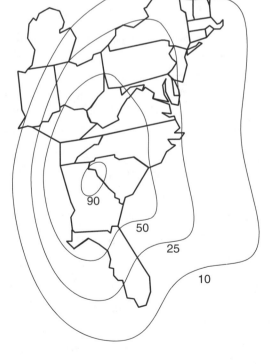

Periods of four or more consecutive days

Frequency of stagnant highs.

The Ohio Valley has a very high frequency for these systems, and one of the big problems with California and the Southwest is that a large high-pressure system plants itself overhead for weeks, even months. The air becomes very stable, and sunny. The photochemical smog builds to dangerous levels. If New York and New Jersey experienced the same climate as California's, the air would be completely intolerable. Frequent storms and gusty winds keep the atmosphere mixed. It is ironic that the weather system that delivers the calmest, sunniest weather becomes the system that generates the most pollution. Sometimes very good can be very bad.

Economics of Control—Can We Afford It?

That, of course, is the $100,000 question. A company that has to install million-dollar electrostatic precipitators may have a serious economic problem with pollution control. But in general, the overall costs of not controlling air pollution are far greater than the collective costs of engineering control.

Tangible cost estimates of pollution-related damage in an uncontrolled environment can reach $30 billion each year. We're talking about direct medical costs, cleaning bills, damage to vegetation and materials. These are the tangibles—costs that can be measured—but there are the intangibles, too.

How do you put a price on human life? What does a shortened life span cost? What about the psychological damage of living and working in a polluted environment? What about the chronic, long-term health problems that can't be readily measured and priced?

Still, setting aside the intangibles, air-pollution control is a very good buy. The estimated cost of conforming with the Clean Air Act provisions comes to about $3 billion annually—just one-tenth of the estimated tangible costs of doing nothing.

The problem, of course, is the concentration of costs within specific industries. Creative techniques of distributing that cost could go a very long way in maintaining our standard of living while having good and healthy air to breath. We can have our cars and breathe at the same time. What a concept!

The Least You Need to Know

➤ The legal foundation for air pollution control can be found in the private and public nuisance provisions of the Common Law.

➤ Engineering methods exist for efficient control of pollutants.

➤ One of the most basic forms of control simply involves a change in fuel.

➤ Temperature inversions and high-pressure systems become areas of poor air quality.

➤ Compared to the costs of an uncontrolled environment, the costs for air pollution control seem slight.

Chapter 13

Ozone—The Good and the Bad

> ## In This Chapter
>
> ➤ Here comes the Sun
>
> ➤ The layered look of the atmosphere
>
> ➤ Caught in the ozone
>
> ➤ Changes of the ozone layer

In the previous two chapters, we gave ozone plenty of bad ink. It is an irritant, even a toxic gas. It contributes to serious lung problems and damages materials, crops, and vegetation. But as bad as ozone may be, we still can't live without it. The ozone that collects at nose-level is bad ozone, but the ozone that forms in the upper atmosphere is *good* ozone. It protects the earth from the harmful radiation that comes from the Sun. Without that protection, the Earth wouldn't be habitable.

There isn't a lot of ozone. In the region of maximum ozone formation, there are just 12 ozone molecules for every million air molecules. But that's enough to shield the potentially cancer-causing radiation from reaching the Earth's surface. That concentration of good ozone is also enough to prevent excessive heating of the earth's atmosphere.

Old Sol

Our amazing weather engine is completely driven by the energy that comes from the Sun. The Sun is the nearest star to Earth—a mere 93 million miles from us. It is a massive nuclear reactor where hydrogen atoms fuse together and form helium. This fusion reaction releases mega-amounts of energy, which is transmitted in the form of assorted waves in their various colors. The energy manifests itself in the form of tremendous heat. The center of the Sun, its *core*, has a temperature of 15 million degrees. It cools down near the surface to just a few thousand degrees, but that's hot enough, and the energy travels through space to be intercepted by Earth and its atmosphere.

Atomic-Powered Fireball

The Sun doesn't constantly emit the same amount of energy; although there is a parameter called the *solar constant*, even that happens to be a variable. Huge bursts of energy shoot off in flares, and these solar storms transmit charged particles into the earth's atmosphere. Because the center of the earth has an iron core, its rotation sets up a magnetic field, and that field directs those charged particles toward the poles. In the high atmosphere, above the polar regions, those charged particles react with some of the gases within the atmosphere, and that sets the stage for brilliant flashes of light called the aurora borealis in the Northern Hemisphere, and the aurora australis in the Southern Hemisphere. The northern lights (aurora borealis) are not normally seen south of the northern border states of the United States, although when the solar storm is especially large, the aurora can be seen even in southern states. The stream of charged particles that comes from the Sun makes up the solar wind.

In addition to delivering these violent bursts of energy, the Sun's turbulence leads to relatively cooler spots on its surface, called *sunspots*. They aren't exactly cool, but their temperature of a few thousand degrees is less than surrounding regions. During high sunspot periods, the Sun seems to experience more stress, and there appears to be a cyclic pattern to the sunspots. They seem to reach a maximum about every 11 years. The maxima, too, seem to follow a pattern where the 11-year peaks become greater and greater over a period of 80 to 90 years.

Because the earth's weather derives its life force from the Sun, many have tried to link these changes on the Sun to changes in weather. Some researchers show how these solar fluctuations can bring about major climate changes, even the warming observed through the twentieth century. We'll get to that in the next chapter, when we explore climate.

Weather-Watch

Excessive exposure to the Sun's ultraviolet rays (UV) causes sunburn. The ozone layer, which screens out much of the harmful UV rays, has become thinner. Ozone holes have developed. The likeliness of sunburn as well as the incidence of skin cancer increases with the thinning of the ozone layer.

Weather Words

"Give me the splendid silent Sun with all his beams full-dazzling!"
—Walt Whitman

But even when the Sun is quiet, its radiation becomes important in regulating the earth's atmosphere. The radiation travels in an assortment of waves coming out of the Sun. The waves are just like the waves on a string or rope when it's shaken. The *wavelength* is the distance from peak to peak. Most of the wavelengths coming from the Sun are quite small, about a millionth of a meter, or a micrometer.

The following figure shows the entire spectrum of emitted energy, and the percentage of radiation found coming from the Sun at different wavelengths. Those waves with wavelengths of about 0.4 to 0.5 micrometers deliver a blue color. Those in the 0.6 to 0.7 range tend toward red and orange. When all the colors are grouped together, from wavelengths of 0.4 to 0.7 micrometers, the emitted light is white. So, visible light is really composed of all the colors of the rainbow, and as visible light moves through various materials, some of those colors can be separated, like in a prism. Even a raindrop can separate the light waves, which is why we have rainbows.

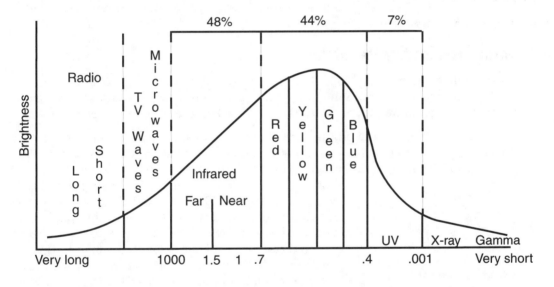

Spectrum of light.

Crazy with the Heat

Much of the radiation that comes from the Sun is in the shorter wavelengths, and that is called *ultraviolet* (UV) radiation. The longer wave radiation is called *infrared* (IR) radiation. Heat itself is IR radiation. UV radiation may be energy, and it may *generate* heat, but it is not heat. As molecules absorb the UV radiation, they move around, and that motion generates collisions and heat. So, the atmosphere, or the earth, will absorb UV radiation and become hot. The heat then radiates out as infrared.

The entire greenhouse concept rests on this principle. In a greenhouse, glass is invisible to incoming ultraviolet radiation. The sunlight just sweeps through the glass. But after the UV radiation is absorbed by the plants in the greenhouse, heat is given off, and glass isn't invisible to those IR beams. So the heat is trapped within the greenhouse. It becomes hot, allowing flowers to bloom even during the winter. In the atmosphere, gases such as carbon dioxide act the same as glass, and although they allow the UV radiation to check in, they don't allow the IR radiation to check out.

The stability of the sun-earth-atmosphere system depends on a balance between the amount of heat that comes in and the amount that goes out. If that balance is upset, major changes in weather become immediately apparent.

Weather-Watch

You may be more susceptible to sun damage if you take certain medications, such as antibiotics, antihistamines, antidepressants, diuretics, estrogen, and sedatives.

Atmospheric Structure

Understanding natural ozone formation begins with an understanding of atmospheric structure and the behavior of sunlight as it moves toward the earth's surface. The figure on the next page shows the structure, which is based on the variation of temperature.

Amazingly, the temperature profile zigzags, going up in some regions and decreasing in others. Let's take a ride on a ray of sunlight as it enters the top of the atmosphere. At the very top, air molecules are tough to find, but any oxygen absorbs some of the Sun's short-wave, ultraviolet radiation. The absorption of UV radiation at levels of 300 or 400 miles above the surface creates a higher temperature. That relatively warmer layer is called the *thermosphere*. However, the number of oxygen molecules available is slight; the oxygen that is present will do the initial absorption, and the temperature becomes lower at the bottom of the thermosphere.

The air density becomes great enough that absorption can resume at levels below 90 km, or 60 miles. The temperature begins to increase once again. The layer through which that absorption increases is called the *mesosphere*, and the boundary between that layer and the thermosphere is called the *mesopause*. At the mesopause, a definite shift in the temperature profile appears. Once again, oxygen molecules absorb the UV radiation, and as the sunlight continues to descend, it is absorbed more and more, down to a level of 50 km, or about 30 miles. The air is still ultra-thin, even at that level. The pressure is just one-thousandth the pressure at ground

Weather-Speak

The **troposphere** is the bottom layer of the atmosphere, extending from sea level to 7 miles high. The **stratosphere** is the layer next to the troposphere and is 30 miles high. The **mesosphere** is the layer above the stratosphere and is about 50 miles deep. The **mesopause** separates the mesosphere from the thermosphere. The **thermosphere** extends up for about 400 miles.

level. But as thin as the air is, enough oxygen molecules are present to increase the temperature dramatically. This layer where mega-absorption gets underway is called the mesosphere.

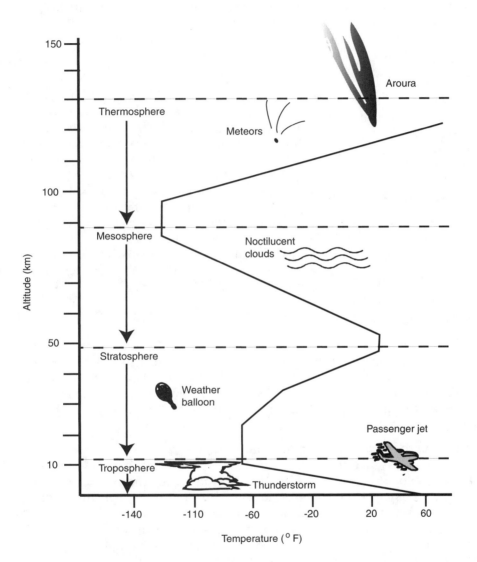

The atmospheric structure.

Absorption continues through the next layer, the stratosphere, but in decreasing amounts as the light continues its descent. Again, there is a finite amount of oxygen present for the absorption, and once that has occurred, the process begins to diminish. The next layer, the *stratosphere*, is closer to the earth's surface temperature.

The entire absorption process through the mesosphere and into the stratosphere generates ozone. The ozone reaches its maximum concentration at 25 km, even though the highest temperature occurs at 50 km. The radiation is more intense at 50 km, so the temperature can be warmer, but fewer oxygen molecules will deliver less ozone. Ozone production is made possible by the absorption of that radiation. We'll get to the mechanics of that formation in just a little while, in the next section.

As the radiation continues to move downward, it will eventually hit the earth's surface, and again, heat will be generated. The heat will be given off in the form of that long-wave, infrared radiation. If you happen to be outdoors soaking up the Sun, you too will be emitting IR radiation. The release of heat close to the surface allows the earth to be on the warm side, and that warmth heats the lower portion of the lowest atmospheric layer, the *troposphere*. At the top of the troposphere the pressure is about one-tenth the value at ground level, and it is within the troposphere that all our weather takes place. Seldom will clouds be able to penetrate the stable stratosphere where the temperature increases with height, the standard temperature inversion. The stable layer puts a lid on cloud heights, although there is mixing between the troposphere and stratosphere during violent storms.

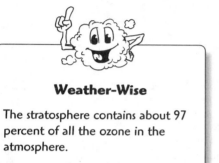

Weather-Wise

The stratosphere contains about 97 percent of all the ozone in the atmosphere.

The Good Ozone

In the high atmosphere, oxygen (O_2) is zapped by UV radiation and becomes atomic oxygen (O). One oxygen molecule breaks apart and becomes two single atomic oxygen molecules. Then O can combine with O_2 to deliver O_3, which is ozone. But we aren't finished. The ozone is zapped, too, by UV radiation, and that breaks up the O_3 into a molecule of regular oxygen and one of atomic oxygen. Then, of course, the O and O_2 can combine to reform ozone.

The figure on the next page shows the chemical process, a neat example of equilibrium. Ozone breaks up into molecules that are then available to form ozone again. But the absorption of ultraviolet radiation is key to the entire process; thanks to the chemistry, many of the incoming UV rays are absorbed in the high atmosphere, so we are protected from the harmful radiation. The greatest absorption takes place between 25 and 50 km. The ozone that forms during the initial absorption reaches its peak concentration at around 25 kilometers—the famous ozone layer. All that energy absorption creates the warmth found in the stratosphere.

Unfortunately, UV radiation isn't the only means by which ozone can be broken down. Other gases will react with it, and some, such as chlorine, are devastating. One chlorine atom removes 100,000 ozone molecules, and that brings us to the ozone hole.

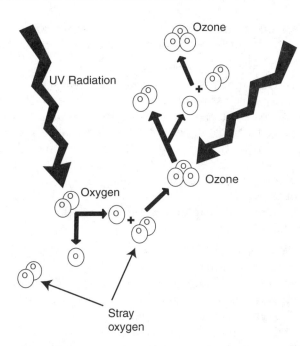

Formation of good ozone.

Ozone Hole—Here Today, Gone Tomorrow?

Is there really a hole in the atmosphere? Well, not exactly. Because ozone is an oxidant, it readily combines with other chemicals; some more effectively than others. Under the right conditions, the ozone in the stratosphere can be depleted, but as long as oxygen is present, the ozone can regenerate. The absence of ozone is not necessarily permanent. Actually, it turns out to be seasonal.

Cold temperatures during the Antarctic winter help form ice-laden clouds in the stratosphere. In fact, the stratosphere around the South Pole comes right down to the surface during the Southern Hemisphere winter in July and August. The chemical destruction of ozone is assisted by this ice. At the same time, strong west-to-east winds circle the Antarctic, choking off the supply of air from more northern latitudes. The atmosphere isn't well mixed. Because of those meteorological conditions, gases that contribute to the reduction of ozone can really go to town. By October and November, the depletion of ozone reaches a maximum.

During December, however, which begins summer in the Southern Hemisphere, the stratosphere

Weather-Speak

The **ozone hole** is the area in the stratosphere where the ozone is depleted. The ozone hole is a seasonal thing. It reaches its peak during the Antarctic spring, in October and November. It fills by December and January.

warms and that diminishes the reactions, and at the same time, those strong west-to-east winds diminish. The atmosphere becomes better mixed and ozone is replenished.

It's likely that an ozone hole has been appearing in the Southern Hemisphere for ages, although it's only been detected since the 1970s. At that time, two scientists, F. Sherwood Rowland and Mario J. Molina, warned that increasing levels of chlorofluorocarbons (CFCs) would steadily decrease the ozone concentrations in the atmosphere. In 1995, Rowland and Molina received a Nobel Prize for their research. Freon is the common name for those CFCs, and during the first part of the century it seemed that this particular chemical could do absolutely no harm. It has many desirable properties: It's a good propellant for use in hair spray and deodorant and a good coolant that can be used in refrigerators and air conditioners. Also, it is not poisonous. In addition, CFCs are inert in the lower atmosphere—they can't combine with anything else. It seems to be a win-win-win chemical.

The problem arises when these CFCs hit the stratosphere where UV radiation is strong. No longer are these chemicals inactive. Chlorine is stripped off the CFCs and becomes an effective partner for ozone, combining to create chlorine monoxide (CLO) and oxygen. In addition, chlorine monoxide can combine with atomic oxygen (O) to deliver a single chlorine atom and oxygen. Less atomic oxygen means less ozone formation, and that chlorine can take out more ozone. Eventually, chlorine and chlorine monoxide can be removed, but the average lifetime of a CFC molecule in the stratosphere is 100 years. So the damage is potentially huge, with 100,000 ozone molecules wiped out by a single chlorine atom.

Another powerful ozone destroyer is nitrogen. The United States never went forward with the development of supersonic stratospheric jets because of the fear of releasing nitrogen oxides, but the response to the CFC problem has been slower.

During the 1980s, special aircraft were sent into the high atmosphere to sample the ozone concentration. The airplanes were part of a project called NOZE—National Ozone Expedition. Also, satellites named Total Ozone Mapping Satellites (TOMS) were called into action. The experiments showed a far greater depletion than earlier projected, and during the 1990s, the results led to the goal of eliminating CFC releases by the year 2000. Originally, the goal for a 50-percent reduction by the year 2000 was set by the Montreal Protocol of 1987. But that was accelerated in 1996 when observations showed an alarming decrease in ozone along with a sharpening increase of chlorine. The protocol also limited the amount of bromine that could be released. Bromine destroys 10 times as much ozone as chlorine.

Weather-Wise

In 1987, the Montreal Protocol was established. It was a treaty developed by 46 countries to reduce CFC production on a scheduled basis.

Dramatic evidence of the power and beauty of the skies.

Cirrus clouds.

Stratus clouds.

Cumulus clouds.

Thick storm clouds over Texas.

Flooding in southeastern Arizona due to 1983's El Niño.

Hurricane Andrew in action in South Florida, 1992.

Tornado damage in Saragosa, Texas, May 1987.

A home flooded off its foundation in Oregon City, 1994.

A view from above of a swirling hurricane . . .

. . . and a view from the ground as a hurricane strikes the coast of Florida.

Auntie Em! Auntie Em!—A tornado touches down.

Electrical power.

Changes in Ozone

More than 12 billion pounds of CFCs have been pumped into the lower atmosphere, but the big question remains: How much ozone is really being destroyed? The chemistry is impressive enough, but what's really happening?

Generally, estimates of worldwide ozone depletion are in the range of 1 to 6 percent each decade. That is significant, because a 1-percent reduction is thought to be able to cause a 2- to 5-percent increase in skin cancer. Also, the increased UV radiation that reaches the earth's surface can affect plants and animals. Yet there are uncertainties in the quantitative link between what comes out of an aerosol can and how much ozone will be destroyed. For one, the Sun's output is constantly changing, and fluctuations there impact the release of charged particles and radiation. So, ozone formation and destruction will naturally fluctuate.

Then there is the meteorology. The top of the troposphere is quite cold, with temperatures of about 80 degrees below zero. Yet, because of the ozone layer, the top of the stratosphere has a temperature of 20 degrees above zero. A 100-degree warming takes place through the stratosphere. This strong temperature inversion, where the temperature increases with elevation, creates tremendous stability. It isn't easy for tropospheric air to float up through the stratosphere. Just look at what happens to those tall cumulonimbus clouds. Upward motions can reach 15 or 20 mph or more; yet, when the updraft hits the bottom of the stratosphere, it just spreads horizontally rather than continuing vertically. The clouds are flattened and form an anvil top. If strong updrafts can't poke through the stratosphere, how can the wisp of Freon that comes out of a spray can, or the Freon that diffuses from a refrigerating system?

Weather-Watch

The National Weather Service and the U.S. EPA (Environmental Protection Agency) have developed a UV index to use in weather reports. This helps you evaluate the level of danger from sun exposure on any day the level is issued. Minimal danger is a 0–2 UV index number. Low is 3–4. Moderate is 5–6. High is 7–8. Very high is 9–10+.

Certainly, not all of the 12 billion pounds of CFCs released are going to make it. In addition, as we saw, ozone depletion is a seasonal thing, much of it confined to the Antarctic atmosphere. Measurements around the Northern Hemisphere have found elevated concentrations of chlorine and chlorine monoxide within the stratosphere, but there has yet to be detected a dramatic seasonal drop as is observed in the Southern Hemisphere. The temperature in the stratosphere over the Arctic may not be cold enough to form ice clouds, which appear important in the ozone destruction process.

To add to the uncertainties, increased levels of UV radiation have not been detected in the troposphere of mid-latitudes, where most people live and breathe. Perhaps ground-level smog is reacting with that UV. Could the bad ozone have a good side?

Still, the present state of knowledge shows that stratospheric ozone has been decreasing at a good clip. At the South Pole, a huge area—approximately 22 million square kilometers—has an average seasonal depletion of 50 percent with some local spots going down to zero ozone. And there is plenty of chlorine and chlorine monoxide present to indicate CFCs as the source.

Finally, possibly because of CFC restrictions imposed by the Montreal Protocol, the ozone hole stabilized in the late 1990s. Balloon soundings at the South Pole in 1997 showed ozone reaching a minimum of 112 radiation units, called Dobson units, on October 8. That is similar to the minimum readings of the previous few years. Large changes in the magnitude of the ozone hole are not occurring. Also, satellite observations show the extent of the ozone hole in 1997 to be the same as 1996 and 1995.

The problem is complex, but there is definitely light at the end of the ozone tunnel—and not necessarily UV light.

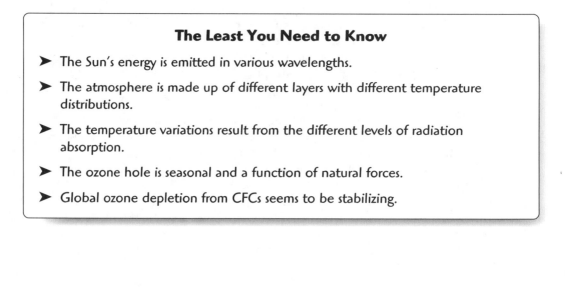

The Least You Need to Know

➤ The Sun's energy is emitted in various wavelengths.

➤ The atmosphere is made up of different layers with different temperature distributions.

➤ The temperature variations result from the different levels of radiation absorption.

➤ The ozone hole is seasonal and a function of natural forces.

➤ Global ozone depletion from CFCs seems to be stabilizing.

Part 3
Climate and Global Change

So, what is really going on with this weather? In recent years the weather has been going to extremes. The hottest years on record have occurred during the 1990s. Yet, record snow has managed to fall during the same period. Some say that the climate is warming, and that the landscape around us will dramatically change during the twenty-first century. Others say we're just looking at normal weather fluctuations, not a long-term, human-induced climate change. The debate is heated, and it has become politicized, too. We'll try to sort the whole thing out.

In these chapters you'll learn about climate, and look at the climate of some of the fastest-growing regions around the United States. By knowing some basic meteorology, we can understand the climate of any particular location. History tells us that climate change really goes with the territory. Places that were once tropical are now frozen over. Those ancient climates really do deliver clues about our future. Glacier-front property, anyone?

Chapter 14

Well-Seasoned

> **In This Chapter**
>
> ➤ How the seasons happen
>
> ➤ Solar radiation, the source of it all
>
> ➤ Balancing the global budgets
>
> ➤ The role of oceans, land and topography

Climatology might seem a little boring. The weather is dynamic, ever-changing, destructive, exciting, and sometimes beautiful. But climate? It is just an average of weather conditions of a particular location—something that changes, but only glacially. But climate is no longer viewed as something staid and steady. Climatology has become the hottest topic of all, and we begin our exploration of climate with a look at the thing that makes it all possible—the earth in its orbit. We start with the seasons.

The Earth in Motion

I'm always amazed when I remember the earth is moving at all. But it's *revolving* around the Sun at 80,000 mph, and *rotating* around its axis once a day. If you feel a little dizzy at the end of the day, now you know why!

The figure on the following page shows the gyrations of the earth. The earth's rotation causes day and night. That same rotation delivers a spin to the atmosphere. We call it the Coriolis force (see Chapter 4), and it's the reason for our weather systems spinning in a clockwise or counterclockwise direction.

The earth's gyrations.

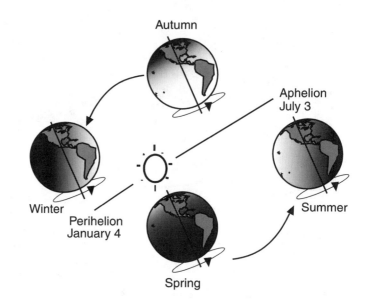

The other component of motion is revolution, which allows the days to fade into years. In days of old, the earth was thought to be stationary, with the entire universe revolving around it. But Copernicus came along in the sixteenth century, and the picture changed. You really can't blame the ancients for getting it inside-out. After all, can you sense that we're moving at 80,000 mph? Because the atmosphere is attached to the earth through gravity, just as we are, we really can't feel the air rushing past us. We have no sense of that motion.

In any case, the earth's orbit is not an exact, neat circle. It follows an elliptical path. The distance between the Sun and the earth averages 93 million miles, or about 150 million kilometers.

Weather-Speak

The two principal motions of the earth are **revolution** and **rotation.** Revolution is the movement of the earth in its orbit around the Sun. Rotation is the spinning of the earth around its axis.

But as the previous figure shows, the path brings the earth closer to the Sun during different times of year. The closest approach is the *perihelion*, and the farthest is the *aphelion*. During perihelion, the earth is about 3 million miles closer to the Sun than during the aphelion. Amazingly, we are closer to the Sun on January 4 and farther during the hot summer on July 3. I guess distance to the Sun has precious little to do with our seasons because the earth's orbit seems to have it backward. Although our climate in the Northern Hemisphere would be even more extreme if perihelion and aphelion were in phase with the seasons.

The key to our seasons can be found in the tilt of the earth on its axis.

The Seasons

As the days of the year move along, the Sun's elevation changes. During the noon hour, the Sun is more directly overhead during the summer than in winter. At any particular time of day, the Sun is lower (closer to the southern horizon) in the sky during winter rather than summer. The next figure shows that shift. When the Sun is more directly overhead, its energy will be more focused, more direct, and stronger. If the angle is greater—if the Sun is lower on the horizon—it must pass through more atmosphere before reaching the earth. There is now a better chance for the sunlight to be absorbed, reflected, and scattered. Rays directed toward the earth at just a 30-degree angle from the vertical will move through twice as much atmosphere than when arriving directly overhead. The following figure shows that, too.

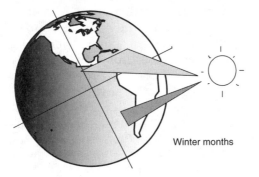

The shift in the Sun's elevation.

Winter months

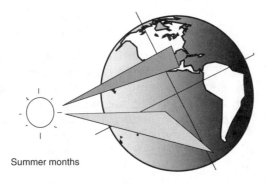

Summer months

Obviously, the different parts of the world experience different sun angles, different intensities of light, and potentially different climates. But the clincher for the seasons is the tilt of the earth's axis. The earth's axis is tilted at 23.5 degrees from the vertical, as you saw in the previous figure. This tilt is not constant, and there is some long-term wobbling of about 1.5 degrees. But for the sake of argument, let's just imagine that the tilt is fixed in one particular direction of 23.5 degrees.

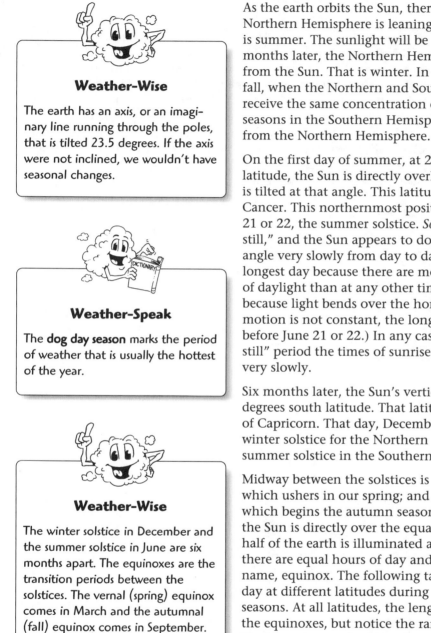

As the earth orbits the Sun, there will be times when the Northern Hemisphere is leaning toward the Sun. That is summer. The sunlight will be most direct. Then, six months later, the Northern Hemisphere is pointed away from the Sun. That is winter. In between are spring and fall, when the Northern and Southern Hemispheres receive the same concentration of solar radiation. The seasons in the Southern Hemisphere are just opposite from the Northern Hemisphere.

On the first day of summer, at 23.5 degrees north latitude, the Sun is directly overhead, because the earth is tilted at that angle. This latitude is called the Tropic of Cancer. This northernmost position will occur on June 21 or 22, the summer solstice. *Solstice* means to "stand still," and the Sun appears to do just that, changing its angle very slowly from day to day. It's also called the longest day because there are more hours and minutes of daylight than at any other time of year. (Actually, because light bends over the horizon, and the earth's motion is not constant, the longest day will happen before June 21 or 22.) In any case, during the "standstill" period the times of sunrise and sunset will change very slowly.

Six months later, the Sun's vertical rays are striking 23.5 degrees south latitude. That latitude is called the Tropic of Capricorn. That day, December 21 or 22, marks the winter solstice for the Northern Hemisphere and the summer solstice in the Southern Hemisphere.

Midway between the solstices is the *vernal equinox,* which ushers in our spring; and the *autumnal equinox,* which begins the autumn season. During these periods, the Sun is directly over the equator, and because exactly half of the earth is illuminated at any particular time, there are equal hours of day and night—hence the name, equinox. The following table gives the length of day at different latitudes during the start of the different seasons. At all latitudes, the length of day is 12 hours at the equinoxes, but notice the range during the solstices. The biggest range between seasons is in the northern latitudes. No wonder these become the zones for air masses, fronts, and frequent storms.

Length of Day in the Northern Hemisphere

Latitude (in degrees)	Spring Equinox	Summer Solstice	Fall Equinox	Winter Solstice
90	12 hrs.	6 months	12 hrs.	0 hrs.
80	12 hrs.	4 months	12 hrs.	0 hrs.
70	12 hrs.	2 months	12 hrs.	0 hrs.
60	12 hrs.	18.4 hrs.	12 hrs.	0 hrs.
50	12 hrs.	16.3 hrs.	12 hrs.	7.7 hrs.
40	12 hrs.	14.9 hrs.	12 hrs.	9.1 hrs.
30	12 hrs.	13.9 hrs.	12 hrs.	10.1 hrs.
20	12 hrs.	13.2 hrs.	12 hrs.	10.8 hrs.
10	12 hrs.	12.6 hrs.	12 hrs.	11.4 hrs.
0	12 hrs.	12 hrs.	12 hrs.	12 hrs.

Although the equinoxes and solstices define the seasons, in practice, the seasons tend to run ahead of the astronomy. Snow can fall in mid-latitudes by late November and early December, and summer heat can appear by late May. Meteorologists have their own definition of the seasons, with summer being the months of June, July, and August. Fall becomes September, October, and November. Winter consists of December, January, and February. And spring is made up of March, April, and May.

Sun Matters

When we looked at the structure of the atmosphere in the previous chapter, we saw how the absorption of UV radiation is related to the different layers and to the formation of ozone. We glossed over the behavior of the Sun in the lower atmosphere, the troposphere. But now, as we look into climate and weather, we can't treat the Sun so lightly. It's time to explore the behavior of the Sun in the lowest 10 miles of the atmosphere—where we live, breathe, and get rained on.

Scattering, Reflection, and Absorption

Only about half of the earth-bound radiation manages to make it to the surface. The other half is scattered, reflected, or absorbed. Light that is

Weather-Wise

You can easily calculate your local sun angle at noon of the first day of each season. Subtract the Sun's position from your latitude, and subtract that difference from 90 degrees. For example, if the Sun is at 23.5 degrees north latitude the first day of summer and you live at 43.5 degrees north latitude, the difference would be 20 degrees. Ninety degrees – 20 degrees = 70 degrees, the elevation of the Sun outside your window at noon.

scattered still brightens the sky because the light is diffused and spread in different directions. Gas molecules and very small particles are good scattering agents, but blue light is preferentially scattered by these small molecules. So, when the Sun is high in the sky, the blue light is scattered in different directions and the sky appears blue. At sunrise or sunset, the sunlight is angling in through a thicker atmosphere, and the blue light scatters before any light reaches our eyes. Blue light is scattered the most because it consists of the shortest wavelengths. What remains are the reds and oranges that characterize sunrise and sunset.

Weather-Watch

Protect your eyes from the ultraviolet radiation of the Sun by wearing sunglasses that block these UV rays. This type of radiation will even filter through an overcast sky.

Reflection is similar to scattering, except the light that bounces off materials does so at an angle determined by the angle of incoming radiation. The incoming angle equals the outgoing one. Light doesn't just scatter in all directions, it bounces in a very definite way. Overall, 30 percent of the solar radiation that arrives on the top of the atmosphere is reflected back to space before being absorbed. Some materials reflect light better than others. The following table gives the reflectivity of different surfaces). That reflectivity is called the *albedo*. Notice the albedo of clouds; the earth appears bright when observed from outer space largely because of this.

Albedo of Surfaces

Object	Albedo
Moon	7%
Forest	3%-10%
Water	10% on average
Dry, plowed field	5%-20%
Grassy field	10%-30%
Mars	17%
Earth	30%
Sand	15%-45%
Ice	30%-40%
Venus	78%
Clouds (thin)	30%-50%
Clouds (thick)	60%-90%
Fresh snow	75%-95%

Radiation Budget

The amount of radiation received from the Sun is exactly balanced by the energy that returns to space. Incoming equals outgoing. If that weren't the case, the earth and its atmosphere would continually heat up or cool down. Our environment would be unstable, and eventually, threaten life. But, like so many aspects of nature, there is balance—although a rather complex one.

Let's suppose that 100 units of radiation are arriving at the top of the atmosphere. Thanks to particles and molecules, about 30 units reflect directly back to space. Of the 70 units that come down, 19 are absorbed by the atmosphere and 51 by the earth's surface. Because of the absorption in the atmosphere, heat is generated and given off in the form of long-wave radiation. Some of the emitted heat radiation from the atmosphere is also directed toward the earth's surface. In addition, some atmospheric gases, such as water vapor and carbon dioxide, capture some of the long-wave radiation given off by the earth, and that heat, too, can be redirected toward the earth.

It gets confusing, but the following figure breaks it all down. Notice how we start with just 100 units but refer to a greater number of units near the surface of the earth. That's because the energy bounces around in the atmosphere and is re-radiated back to the earth. So, the earth appears to be dealing with more than 100 units. Yet, in each component of reflection and scattering, the amount of energy entering is exactly balanced by the amount that leaves.

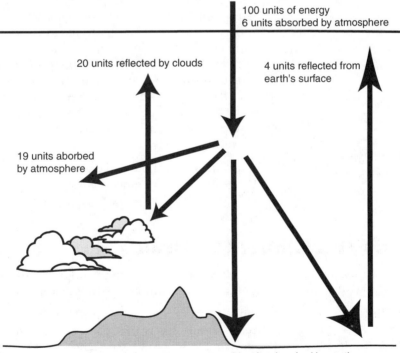

Changes in units of radiation.

As the preceding figure shows, the gases in the atmosphere play an important role in absorbing the heat that escapes from the earth's surface. If it weren't for that absorption, the earth would be about 60 degrees colder. Instead of the average world temperature being around 60 degrees, it would be near zero. So, those gases, called *greenhouse gases,* make life possible. The gases allow the short-wave radiation to reach the earth's surface, but then those gases maintain some of the warmth that radiates out. The greenhouse effect is a good thing. Interestingly, carbon dioxide only makes up .035 percent of the entire atmosphere. The main greenhouse gas is naturally occurring water vapor, which makes up about 0.1 to 0.2 percent of the atmosphere. Even if the same quantities of carbon dioxide and water vapor were present, water vapor would still absorb more radiation because chemically it's a much more effective absorber.

Overall, water vapor absorbs five times as much heat radiation as all the other gases combined. But as relatively slight as the impact of carbon dioxide may be, climate researchers have built a strong case for it being a major agent of climate change. We'll return to this later—but because I can't wait, let's just say that the theory projects only a slight increase in temperature from carbon-dioxide absorption alone. But that slight increase is enough to increase the water vapor content of the atmosphere through increased evaporation. With the water vapor, we start cooking. And as we heat up more, there is more evaporation, which leads to more water vapor and more heating. It's called positive feedback.

But wait! What about the clouds that form? Couldn't they put a lid on the heating by reflecting incoming radiation? Now, we have the start of a very overheated debate.

Weather-Speak

Greenhouse gases are the gases in the atmosphere, especially water vapor and carbon dioxide, that give it the capacity to retain heat.

Weather-Wise

The greenhouse effect was named after the effect of glass in a florist's greenhouse. It was thought to keep the air warm, trapping infrared energy.

Balancing the Global Heat Budget

Although an interesting balance exists between incoming and outgoing radiation, heat does tend to collect in differing amounts around the earth's surface.

Because the Sun's direct radiation is concentrated between 23.5 north latitude and 23.5 south latitude, the tropical latitudes should receive a surplus of heat—more comes in than goes out. In contrast, the polar regions should experience a net deficit of heat. Just as the rich get richer, the hot should get hotter and the cold, colder. Sure, there's a global balance of radiation energy, but there are some serious geographical differences in heating. If there was no check on these differences, it would be an even crazier planet.

Fortunately, the atmosphere-ocean system does a neat job redistributing the tropical warmth so that an almost-steady state exists. The difference is what we call *weather*. Unequal heating over the surface of the earth creates global-scale winds, thanks to pressure differences that occur due to the imbalance. The winds carry excess heat to areas of need. At the same time, the winds help create ocean currents that provide additional heat distribution. And finally, the contrasts lead to storms, which grab heat energy from the ocean surface and deposit it in higher latitudes in the form of rain or snow.

Local Heat Budgets

In addition to the latitudinal differences that require balance, local differences exist in the level of heating. And again, those differences set up winds that take care of the imbalance.

Ocean and Land Heating

Oceans heat up and cool more slowly than land surfaces for a couple of reasons. Water molecules tend to bind together very strongly. A change in temperature is really a function of the change in molecular motions and collisions. But water molecules, in their stickiness, don't move very quickly. Once they get going, they don't slow down so quickly, either. It takes a lot of energy to raise the temperature of a volume of water. The energy required to make that change is called the *heat capacity,* and water has one of the highest heat capacities of all common substances. So, the binding forces of water would be enough to account for differences in temperature between land and sea—but there's more.

The oceans are in constant motion. The water is well-mixed. During the day, the Sun warms the surface of the water, but waves and currents cause colder water from lower depths to rise and mix with the surface water. So, the warming will be moderated. Likewise, the cooling or loss of heat that takes place at the surface when the sunlight is gone is also moderated. This process unfolds as day goes into night and summer goes into winter.

Land surfaces don't have the high heat capacity or mixing that happens in the oceans. During the daytime, the land heats up faster than the sea, and at night, it cools faster. The same kind of unequal heating occurs between the seasons.

This process has a huge impact on local climatology. Unequal heating sets up unequal pressures, and the pressure gradients cause wind. Once again, the wind tries to balance the differences.

Coastal communities benefit from the balancing during the summer with refreshing *sea breezes* that take the edge off the heat. During the day, lower pressure develops over land areas because of the

Weather-Speak

Heat capacity is the amount of heat required to raise the temperature of a substance.

increased heating. The warm air rises, and then cooler maritime breezes sweep onshore to replace the rising air. Overall, the coasts are more comfortable than inland locations in the summer.

But snow-lovers who live on the coast are often very disappointed during the winter. The coastal areas are warmer than inland areas because the sea doesn't lose its heat as quickly as the land masses. Storms come along, but snow is much harder to find along the immediate shore during the winter than just a few miles inland. In New England or New York, for example, annual snowfall can range from 20 inches near the shore to 120 inches 50 miles inland. (Elevation plays a role here, too.)

Temperature differences between land and sea are also important in the development of coastal storms, especially during the winter. Off the East Coast, the warm Gulf Stream current can provide 70-degree temperatures even in the dead of winter. When arctic or polar air masses sweep toward the coast, with temperatures that are close to zero, the contrast becomes more than the atmosphere can handle. The slightest disturbance sends the atmosphere into a spin, and vicious storms develop. Once again, the atmosphere attempts to balance the heat budget by going into motion and reducing the temperature contrast. Nor'easters are products of the land-sea temperature differences. As soon as summer fades into fall, nor'easters are common along the East Coast.

Weather-Speak

A **sea breeze** develops from the ocean, but the same kind of breeze that develops on the shore of a large lake is called a **lake breeze**.

Monsoons

In Arabic, "mausim" means season, and from that term comes *monsoon*, which refers to a seasonal wind difference. The seasonal differences in heating between land and sea largely account for the monsoon circulations, although global winds and topography are also important in enhancing the impact of the circulation.

The basic monsoon is like a giant land and sea breeze. During the summer, low pressure develops over the warmer land and high pressure over the ocean. In places like the Indian Ocean and Southeast Asia, the differences become great enough that a strong flow of moisture is directed onshore, setting the stage for the rainy season, where as much as 1,000 inches of rain can fall in a few short months.

Weather-Speak

Monsoon is the term commonly used in reference to torrential rains, but it actually describes the wind that brings this weather. This wind reverses direction between winter and summer and usually causes dry winters and wet summers. The wind blows from the land to the sea in winter and from the sea to the land in summer.

The excessive rain is also enhanced by topography, which provides a lift to those breezes moving inland. Moisture is a basic ingredient for precipitation, but as we know, air must also rise for tall clouds to form and raindrops to develop. So, the sea breeze provides the moisture, and tall mountains, such as the Himalayas, provide a solid lift. In addition, seasonal shifts in the global wind patterns provide convergence, which lifts the air even more. We'll look at that a little later in Chapter 16, but Asia is where all these rainmakers come together during the summer.

In contrast, during the winter higher pressure develops over the land, so a flow develops from land to sea. The air becomes dry, especially where the air is now moving downslope rather than up. No more rain—although some locations, such as Vietnam, receive rain during the winter monsoon as the north or northeast flow runs into mountains after moving through the Gulf of Tonkin. The following figure shows the monsoonal shifts in wind across Asia.

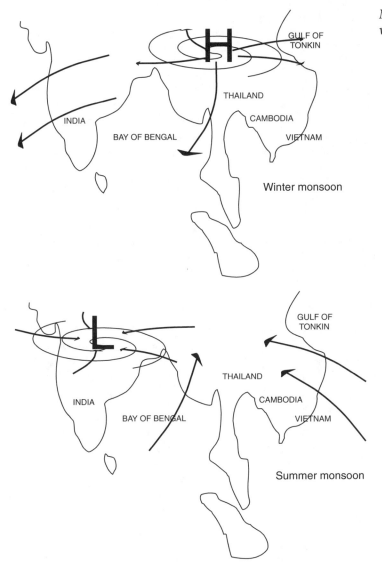

Monsoonal shifts in Asian wind patterns.

187

Similar seasonal wind shifts occur in the United States to a much lesser degree. During the summer, southwest winds come up from the Gulf of Mexico, the tropical Pacific, and the Bay of Campeche. These provide moisture, which is lifted by the Rockies, and locally heavy downpours can develop on the High Plains and even the Southwest desert. If a front comes along and provides additional lift, the skies can really open up. The desert blooms.

Ups and Downs

On the subject of heat distribution, some of the coldest temperatures on Earth have been measured in tropical or near-tropical latitudes. In Hawaii (20 degrees N), the temperature plummeted to 14 degrees on January 2, 1961. In Australia (36 degrees S), the temperature bottomed out at 8 degrees below zero on July 22, 1949. In Moscow, North Africa (February 11, 1935), the temperature reached 11 degrees below zero. Shouldn't it be warmer near the equator? Yes—but only at sea level.

In these chilly tropical zones, elevation plays a role, and mountainous areas will have a huge temperature differential. In the lower atmosphere, the temperature decreases by about four degrees every 1,000 feet of elevation. Theoretically, the top of a 20,000-foot mountain could be 80 degrees colder than the base—even in the tropics—but it doesn't happen that way. The mountain absorbs incoming radiation and heat is given off to the air near the surface, so it isn't as cold as it could be.

Still, many mountains can support snow even in the middle of the summer and in relatively mild tropical zones. Also, the effect of unequal heating sets the stage for winds that again try to balance that local heat budget. During the day, the mountain slopes receive radiation and warm more than the air well off the slope. That lowers the density of the air along the slope so it moves upward along the mountain. This rising motion can lead to clouds and even showers. It's called a *valley breeze,* and the dynamics are similar to a sea breeze.

At night, the surface cools more rapidly than the surrounding air, so the air is heavier on the mountain slope, and it drains into the valley. That's called a *mountain breeze.* The cold air collects at the base of the valley, where fog and frost appear.

Valley breezes are most dominant during the summer, when the heating of the mountain slopes is greatest. During the winter, mountain breezes dominate.

Weather-Wise

Sea breezes are strongest in the afternoon, as are valley breezes.

The Least You Need to Know

➤ Seasons are generated by the orientation of the earth and its path around the Sun.

➤ The Sun's radiation is reflected, scattered, and absorbed.

➤ The earth is a great balancer of its budgets, and in the process, weather and climate are made.

➤ Differences in ocean and land heating are responsible for major weather events.

➤ The monsoon is like a giant sea breeze.

Chapter 15

Staying in Circulation

In This Chapter

➤ What do we see—on the average?

➤ The doldrums

➤ The horse latitudes

➤ Polar front

➤ What sets up the global pattern?

➤ Ocean circulations

Because of the Sun, the tilt and motion of the earth, topography, and the distribution of land and sea, huge heat imbalances exist around the globe. In meteorology, unbalanced budgets are unacceptable, and the atmosphere goes all-out to even the score. Storms form, sea breezes appear, mountain winds develop, and monsoons appear. Those heat-balancing circulations are localized, but effective in making the weather happen.

Now, in addition to the local gyrations, there are motions that appear on a far bigger scale, a global scale. The large-scale circulations ensure that the tropics do not grow hotter while the polar regions become colder. These, superimposed on the smaller-scale circulation, are responsible for our weather, and weather averaged over a period of time becomes climate. These large-scale motions are called the *general circulation,* because it represents an average of all motions.

What Do We See—On the Average?

Although day-to-day changes occur, on the average, global wind patterns show some consistency. The following figure shows the average wind flow at ground level. In the tropics, the wind comes from the east. These are called the trade winds. Northeast trade winds appear in the Northern Hemisphere, and southeast trade winds are present in the Southern Hemisphere.

Average surface wind.

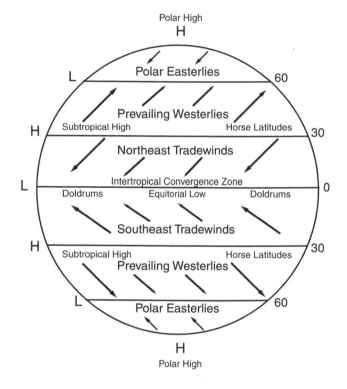

In the mid-latitudes, between 30 degrees and 60 degrees north or south latitude, the wind is mostly from the west. These are called the *prevailing westerlies*. They come from slightly south of west in the Northern Hemisphere, and north of west in the Southern Hemisphere. Then, north of 60 degrees north and south of 60 degrees south, the winds come from the east, and these are called *polar easterlies*.

Although the surface winds differ at various latitudes, the winds in the upper levels of the troposphere are more uniform. From about 15,000 feet and up, the wind generally is from the west, although that changes from season to season, especially in the tropics where the flow

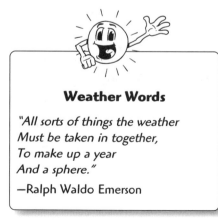

Weather Words

"All sorts of things the weather Must be taken in together, To make up a year And a sphere."

—Ralph Waldo Emerson

is weak and the winds can shift to the east during the summer months. These prevailing westerlies in both the Northern and Southern Hemispheres are responsible for pushing weather systems along from west to east.

The Doldrums

Across the equator, the northeast trades of the Northern Hemisphere meet up against the southeast trades of the Southern Hemisphere. In this so-called Inter-tropical Convergence Zone (ITCZ), the converging air streams force the atmosphere to lift upward. And of course, where the air rises, rain pours down. The tropical rainforests are found along this ITCZ, and it shifts northward during the warmer months. It's a favorite place for organized squalls that grow into hurricanes.

Before hurricanes can form, the ITCZ must have moved far enough north to find enough Coriolis force to instigate a rotation. Because the earth is round, the air at the equator moves across the earth's surface with only a slight change in the earth's radius. A 5-degree latitude shift of air across the equator does not experience a significant change in radius. But that same 5-degree shift at a more northern latitude will occur with a large enough change in the earth's radius to account for a larger Coriolis force. And once that force sets in, the atmosphere spins. Theoretically, the magnitude of the Coriolis force is zero at the equator, and that's why hurricanes don't form there. Later in the summer, the ITCZ reaches its northernmost latitude, where enough spin can be delivered to create a hurricane.

The migration of the ITCZ northward also plays a role in the development of the heavy precipitation during the monsoon season.

Because rain occurs regularly along the convergence zone, the zone has been called the doldrums—but I think it's pretty exciting. Generally, the zone of rising air has a lower pressure—so more air is removed than brought in.

The Horse Latitudes

Farther north and south, around 30 degrees north and 30 degrees south, the surface wind diverges, so air must sink to replace it. That sinking creates high pressure, sunny skies, dry air, and tons of evaporation. Many of the world's deserts are found at this latitude. The divergence causes very light winds. The high-pressure system is centered here. In days of old, explorers heading for the New World ran into calms within this zone. The ships wouldn't move, so they tossed everything they could spare overboard to lighten the load, including their horses. So, the region became known as the *horse latitudes*.

The high-pressure systems that appear at the divergence area take on different local names. In the eastern Atlantic, the high-pressure system is called the Azores High because it's often centered near the Azores. In the western Atlantic, it's called the Bermuda High. Its arrival and strengthening is frequently associated with heat waves in the eastern United States. In general, all these high-pressure areas are known as the subtropical high-pressure systems. The massive hot, dry spells along the West Coast are always linked to the Pacific version of the subtropical high. In the next figure you can see the different types of weather generated around the United States by these high-pressure systems.

*Weather generated by
high-pressure systems.*

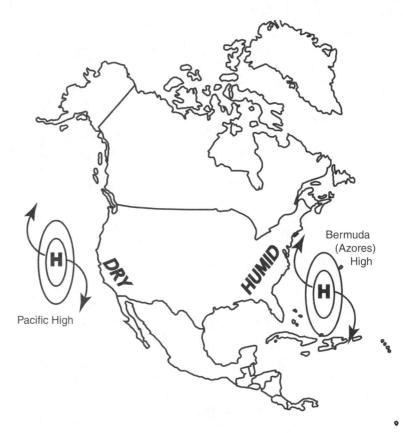

Polar Front

Near 60 degrees north and south latitudes, the atmosphere converges once again. That convergence creates rising motion, and once aloft, the air fans out. The zone becomes one of low pressure, and because it's a region where more moderate westerlies run up against the cold polar easterlies, the temperature contrast is huge. Fronts form on the convergence boundary, and the temperature contrast itself causes more circulation. Vigorous storms develop along these polar fronts. The fronts will dip southward and bring frequent bouts of stormy weather to mid-latitudes. Much of the precipitation that occurs in the United States, Canada, and Europe is associated with the polar front. One front with numerous dips and rises and a few breaks can wrap around the entire Northern or Southern Hemisphere, as shown in the following figure.

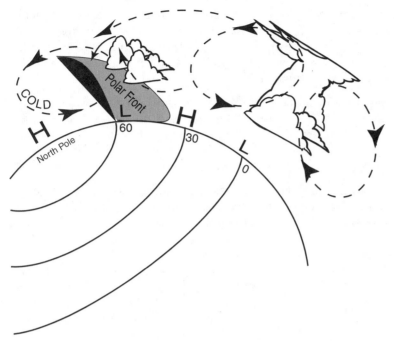

A single massive, polar front.

Wow. I bet your head is almost spinning. We've just explained a lot about the nature of weather that we see around the world. If the past couple of pages made sense, you're on your way to being a major weather guru!

What Sets Up the Global Pattern?

Knowledge of the general circulation helps to explain much of what we see as average weather, or climate. But a big question that remains concerns the origin of that circulation.

Once again, it's a matter of the earth and its atmosphere trying to correct imbalances in heat and moisture. Because of geography, the equatorial region receives more solar radiation than it can give back, causing a surplus of heat. On the other hand, the polar regions are in darkness six months of the year, and the earth gives off more heat than it receives across this region. So part of the globe gets more heat than it needs, and the other part doesn't get enough. If the situation remained unchecked, the equatorial zones would become unbearably hot while the poles would become brutally cold—as if they weren't cold enough!

Because of the excessive heat in the tropical areas, the evaporation rate is quite high, and around 30 degrees north and south latitude where precipitation is sparse, there is more evaporation than precipitation. At the equator and at 60 degrees north and south latitudes, there is more precipitation than evaporation. The upward motions are strong enough to unleash heavy precipitation. The evaporation rate may be high near the equator, but the precipitation rate is even higher. So, again, there appear to be some imbalances. The equator receives more precipitation than can be accounted for by its own level of evaporation. Water vapor must be brought in from someplace else to account for all the rain. Any attempt by the atmosphere to even the heat imbalance must also account for the moisture imbalance.

Many theories have been advanced to explain the big picture. They involve the development of circulation cells that are driven by the heat imbalances. Let's take a closer look at a few of these theories.

Unicell

In this theory, there is a single cell forced by the strong heating at the equator (see the following figure). The air rises at the equator because of the heating, and then it spreads out north and south. It then sinks at the poles.

The single-cell theory of general circulation.

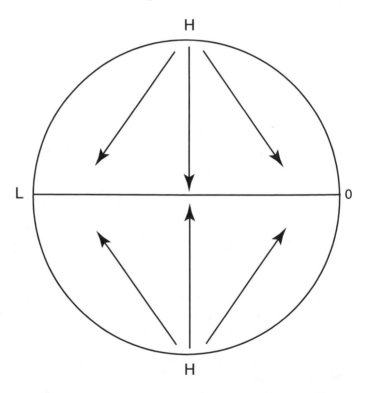

The unicell concept removes the excess heat at the equator and carries it to the poles, but does it really account for the observed winds? Not really. The winds would push back toward the equator along the surface. And the Coriolis force would act on the flow, turning it to the right in the Northern Hemisphere, and to the left in the Southern Hemisphere. That would create east winds at all latitudes. The westerlies at mid-latitudes are completely unaccounted for, even though an energy balance would be possible.

Also, there may be some unrealistic winds in the upper levels of the atmosphere at the poles because of the conservation of momentum. At the equator, the atmosphere spins around a large radius. Then, as the air reaches the poles, the radius is much smaller. The momentum is conserved just as a skater's momentum is conserved when she makes her circle of spin smaller by pulling in her arms, causing her to spin faster and faster. So, as air with a huge equatorial radius of spin arrives around the poles, its spin—its wind—would likely be unrealistically high.

Tri-Cell

Because of the problems associated with the single-cell theory, it was at one time replaced by a three-cell or tri-cell concept. The following figure shows the motion.

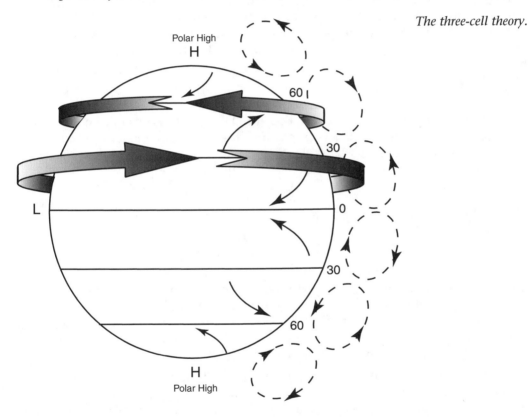

The three-cell theory.

It's a neat theory, and almost meets all the needs. The heat rises at the equator. It spreads north and south, but then sinks at 30 degrees latitude. The sinking motions create the high-pressure areas found at that latitude. Also, the air spreads north and south along the surface from 30 degrees to 60 degrees and toward the equator. Coriolis will turn the air to the right in the Northern Hemisphere, and the left in the Southern Hemisphere. That shift creates westerlies in mid-latitudes and easterlies in the tropics. The air also sinks at the poles and spreads southward. Again the Coriolis force acts on

197

it and shifts it so that easterlies develop around the poles. As these move away from the poles and head toward the westerlies, convergence takes place at around 60 degrees latitude and the air rises.

On the surface, this triple-cell process seems to take care of most of the budget-balancing needs and accounts for the observed winds. Also, the excess water vapor at 30 degrees north and south is brought equator-ward where there is a water-vapor deficit. All seems right with the world—and for decades, this was the theory of choice for describing the mechanisms of the general circulation.

But there's a problem. Notice what would happen to the winds in the upper troposphere, especially in mid-latitudes. The top part of the cell shows the flow going from 60 degrees to 30 degrees. If that were the case, the Coriolis force would act on that flow, and it would shift and blow out of the east. The upper winds would be from the east, and weather systems would generally move from east to west rather than west to east. Something is definitely wrong with this picture. The tri-cell idea gets unraveled here.

Bi-Cell

Okay, the single-cell concept is way off, the tri-cell is close, but not close enough, so how about a two-cell theory? That's exactly how the general-circulation concept evolved. Sensitive instruments came along, too, and helped support a two-cell idea. Here's what happens: Once again, the air rises at the equator and spreads north and south in the upper atmosphere, as shown in the figure on the next page.

Interestingly, some of the air heading to the poles is then diverted, thanks to the Coriolis force, and converges at 30 degrees latitude. That high-level convergence forces the air to sink at 30 degrees. The atmosphere behaves like a squashed throw rug. It moves vertically where it was pushed together. Only a portion of the air is caught up at 30 degrees latitude; the remainder makes it to the poles. The air that sinks at 30 degrees hits the surface and spreads toward the poles and the equator. Thanks to Coriolis, the air is deflected, and that delivers the westerlies in mid-latitudes, and the easterlies in the tropics. The northward-flowing air converges with air that's heading southward from the poles. The convergence occurs at around 60 degrees latitude. There the air rises, and we have that polar front and heavy precipitation.

Two distinctive cells take shape—one in the tropics and the other in the polar regions. In mid-latitudes, there really is no closed cell. All winds appear to be explained by this theory, including the westerlies in the upper atmosphere around mid-latitudes. The flow is from 30 degrees latitude to 60 degrees. The right-directed turning in the Northern Hemisphere, and the left-directed turning in the Southern Hemisphere, provides westerlies aloft for both hemispheres in these mid-latitudes. Both the heat and water budgets are balanced with this explanation of the general circulation.

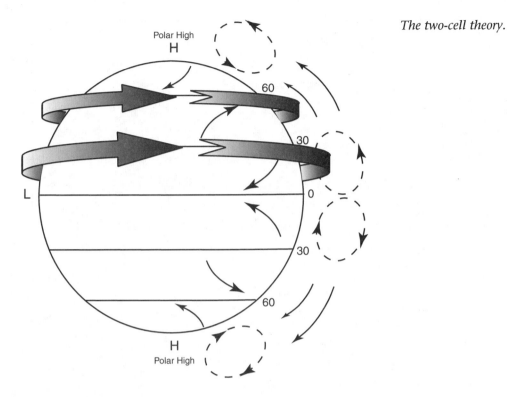

The two-cell theory.

Ocean Circulations

The atmosphere and oceans are very much linked. The global impact of El Niño shows how dependent the atmosphere is on the behavior of ocean currents. But those currents really have at their origin the variation of wind within the atmosphere. The global wind patterns of the general circulation go pretty far in explaining many of the currents observed on the ocean surface.

For the most part, the subtropical high-pressure circulations cover much of the ocean surface. The flow around these circulations is clockwise in the Northern Hemisphere and counterclockwise in the Southern Hemisphere. The air drags on the ocean surface, and the water is forced to move in a similar fashion. The high-pressure circulations force similar circulations on the ocean surface. These ocean circulations are called *gyres*. The figure on the following page shows the major surface currents on the oceans. All of these can be explained by understanding the behavior of the overlying air.

On the southern edge of the gyre, the water is flowing from east to west, and that pretty much describes the equatorial current. During warm El Niño episodes, that high-pressure system shifts westward in the Pacific. The pressure becomes higher in the western Pacific, and that forces a reversal of the wind which forces a reversal of the west-moving current in the Pacific. The current now moves toward the east, the warm surface water piles up in the eastern Pacific, and there is El Niño.

199

Major surface current on the oceans.

Off the East Coast, the northward-moving Gulf Stream is a dominant feature. That current moves swiftly to the northeast from the coast of Florida to just off North Carolina, and then it disperses in the North Atlantic. The initial motion for the current is again delivered by the subtropical high-pressure system, which forces a northward flow of air along the East Coast. The exact dynamics of the Gulf Stream become complex, but they are linked to the same concept of momentum conservation. The flow speeds as it heads northward, but disperses as it moves across the North Atlantic and then to the south in the eastern Atlantic where the flow forms the Azores current.

The Coriolis force also acts on the ocean currents, and there is a right-directed drift to the surface water in the Northern Hemisphere. Near the fast-moving Gulf Stream the right-directed motion forces warm surface water to pile up to the east of the current, while colder water is exposed to its west. A strong temperature differential is set up. That will then send feedback into the atmosphere and set the stage for large storms to form off the East Coast, especially during the winter.

The Gulf Stream phenomenon is found in the western Pacific, too. The Japanese current has many of the characteristics of the Gulf Stream. Actually, because of the turning of the earth and its shape, an intensification of currents occurs on the western borders of all oceans.

200

Meanwhile, off the West Coast, the current normally drifts from north to south, thanks again to the Pacific high-pressure system. The chilly north Pacific current leads to the California current and is strongest when the high-pressure system reaches its northernmost position. That, of course, is during the summertime. So, strangely, the air temperature along the coast of northern California can be nearly as chilly in July as in January. But a slight shift of that high-pressure system to the east can bring about blistering heat. The early autumn is prime time for some of that big West Coast warmth.

In the North Atlantic, a chilly Labrador current develops because of the southward moving air associated with the general circulation.

Although the surface wind forces surface currents, these currents are also acted on by the Coriolis force and vertical circulations appear. For example, off the west coast of South America, a northward-moving Peruvian current will be forced somewhat to the left, away from the coast. Water will be transported away from the coast, and that forces water to rise from lower depths along the coast. That upwelling brings colder, nutrient-rich water closer to the surface. Marine life thrives along with the fishing industries of Peru and Chile. But during El Niño, that Peruvian current is reversed, and warm nutrient-poor water accumulates off the South American coast. The sinking water suppresses the surfacing of those nutrients, and marine life suffers, along with the economies of the South American countries.

Another region of sinking water occurs in the middle of the Atlantic. It occurs at the center of the gyre where the Coriolis force creates a convergence of water. The water comes together, and then it sinks. The nutrients are again suppressed. This region is called the Sargasso Sea.

Braving the Elements

The study and description of the Gulf Stream is one of Benjamin Franklin's many accomplishments. While he was serving as deputy postmaster general for the American colonies in London, he noticed that mail delivered to America often took longer than when sent to London. In 1768, Franklin discussed this with his cousin, Timothy Folger, a Nantucket ship captain. Folger pointed out the existence of the strong Gulf Stream current, and together, they mapped its location. The first Gulf Stream chart was printed in 1769.

The Least You Need to Know

➤ Well-defined wind patterns are found at different latitudes.

➤ Converging and diverging winds mark specific climates and weather.

➤ The general circulation is an average wind pattern around the globe and is brought about by the atmosphere's attempt to balance its budgets.

➤ Major surface ocean currents are forced by the general circulation of wind.

Chapter 16

Climatology

In This Chapter

➤ Climate factors

➤ Figuring out Continent X

➤ Classification of climates

➤ Distribution of world climates

➤ Weather records

We're now ready to look at world climate. Actually, there is very little more to learn about what makes climate happen. We just need to apply the basic principles that we already know—the earth's motion, the general circulation, ocean-land influences, and topography. That's all there is, and the rest falls into place. So, let's start off with some fun—How about a quiz?

Guess This Climate

Take a look at the figure on the following page. It's a make-believe island located between 10 and 15 degrees north latitude. The zigzags in its center represent mountains that divide the island into two distinct regions or zones: 1 and 2.

Okay, overall, is the climate on the island warm or cold? That's easy. Now, try this one: Which side is more likely to support rain-forest growth?

We know that this island is found in tropical latitudes where the Sun is bright and strong, so the climate will be a warm one—both in zones 1 and 2. But which side of the island receives most of the precipitation? The general circulation shows that the prevailing wind is from the east. The eastern portion of the island, then, is directly influenced by the flow of moisture coming from the ocean. As the moist tropical air runs into the mountains, it's lifted upward, which ensures rain, and plenty of it.

The tropical atmosphere has a high potential for precipitation; you just need some mechanism to unleash it. Normally, a stable inversion layer is found above the surface. It's similar to the cap on a shaken-up soda bottle. When the cap is removed, look out! The slightest rising motion will lift that cap away. As the air rises upslope, there goes the cap, and the deluge begins. So, zone 1, on the eastern side of the island, is very wet, especially along the mountain slopes.

Island climate zones.

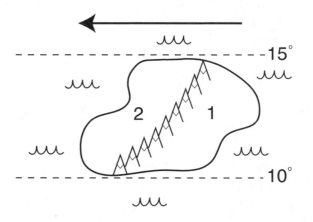

In contrast, the western portion, zone 2, is much drier. The air flow is still from the east because of the trades, but here the flow is subsiding rather than rising. The sinking air warms, with depleted quantities of water vapor. The weather tends to be sunnier, drier, and less belligerent than on the island's eastern end.

If you were to buy a condo, I'd get one on the western side of our tropical paradise. If you prefer the lush life of a rain forest, select the eastern side. Just make sure the roof doesn't leak.

Now Try to Guess This Climate, Too

Okay, we're climate experts, already making investments based on our knowledge. So let's crank up the level of difficulty a bit.

Consider the next figure. This land mass has four distinct zones and should look familiar, but just pretend you never saw it before. We'll begin by figuring out the prevailing wind flow. Because this land mass is located mostly between 30 and 50 degrees north latitude, the wind generally comes from the west. At the same time, we know this land is in mid-latitudes, where storms are numerous, and variations from the average flow occur frequently. Also, because each zone covers so much territory, the temperature varies.

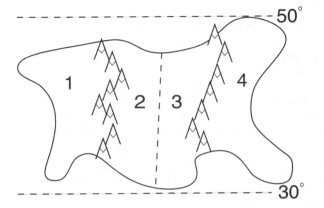

Climate zones of continent X.

Zone 1

Let's go from west to east, along the prevailing wind direction. Zone 1 receives that typical moisture-laden flow directly from the ocean, especially in the northern portion. The lift provided by the mountains enhances the chances for precipitation. So, the northern half of zone 1 tends to be wet. The polar front mixes things up, too, which contributes rising motions for additional precipitation. The temperature is on the chilly side, because of latitude, but the maritime influence moderates winter temperatures.

The west wind diminishes at 30 degrees latitude, where that subtropical high-pressure system resides, so the climate in the southern portion of zone 1 is quite different: warmer and drier. Instead of a moist wet wind coming onshore, the breeze is fickle, and the high pressure delivers sunny skies and subsiding air currents. It's a bright, warm place much of the year—a great place to retire! But the same high pressure can deliver blistering heat at times and provide plenty of stability, so photochemical smog could become a problem, depending on how many people retire here.

Although precipitation is limited across the lower portion of this zone, the skies can open up at times. During the winter, the subtropical high-pressure system drops southward and those westerlies arrive. Very heavy downpours develop, especially in the mountains. The rainy season arrives.

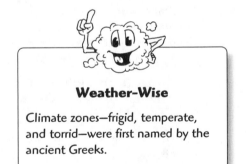

Weather-Wise

Climate zones—frigid, temperate, and torrid—were first named by the ancient Greeks.

Zone 2

This particular zone could potentially be especially dry. The west wind loses much of its moisture along the western slopes of the mountain range, subsiding air settles into this zone, and the sinking and compression can deliver desert-like conditions.

The lower portion of zone 2 gets hot, dry weather. Also, the latitude favors that subtropical high-pressure system and its subsidence. Only cactus thrives here. Air pollution thrives here, too, if there are enough cars. The sunny, stable atmosphere is ideal for the build-up of photochemical smog.

The northern portion of zone 2 is also dry, but not as dry as southern areas. It's colder, too, with a higher humidity. But most importantly, the polar front swings by with its vertical motion, and any limited moisture is squeezed out. In addition, because of the development of low-pressure systems, the wind occasionally comes from the east. It flows upslope, making possible some heavy precipitation. Tremendous temperature changes are generated in this region when the wind shifts from west to east. The rising motion associated with the east wind causes the atmosphere to expand and cool. The sinking motion associated with the west wind causes compression and warming. The passage of the polar front can bring up sharp temperature swings, too.

In some cases, upslope motion is possible even in the southern portion of zone 2. The water masses on the southern side of the area cause that giant, seasonal sea breeze to occur in the summer. A monsoon-like flow is possible, but overall, not enough to change the character of the desert landscape for long.

Zone 3

This region has quite a variety of weather. The northern portion is once again cold. Its proximity to the polar front again sets the stage for precipitation, even though the weather tends to be dry because of the dry west wind. But that cold, subtropical high-pressure system is very strong over the oceans, and it reorganizes over the ocean, east of the land mass. Because the circulation around the high-pressure system is clockwise, surface winds occasionally come from the south throughout all of zone 3. That south wind transports moisture into what could be a very parched region. At the same time, that warm south wind contrasts sharply with cold air associated with the polar front, producing more energy than the atmosphere can handle. Vicious storms develop, including tornadoes. That region, especially the central and northern portion, has the potential of being the tornado capital of the world.

The southern portion is active, too, because of the influx of tropical moisture. But fronts don't always make it that far south. The weather has its quiet days, but it has some wild moments, too.

The subtropical high-pressure system could center itself over a good portion of zone 3. Also, at times, the moist south wind just doesn't show up. Those would be periods of drought.

Zone 4

Like zone 3, this zone gets it all, and its proximity to the ocean provides additional weather action. The mountain range isn't as impressive as the western mountain range, but it's enough to cause at least some impact on the weather. The large ocean high-pressure system becomes a source of south winds that transport moisture into all latitudes within this zone. The southern portion is extremely warm and humid—the southernmost areas take on tropical characteristics.

Meanwhile, northern portions are slammed by the polar front, and precipitation is abundant throughout the year. The relatively mild ocean during the winter provides a large temperature contrast with continental air masses and coastal storms often develop, delivering heavy snow and even blizzard conditions.

The polar fronts reach into the southern portion of the zone during the winter, but in summer, the fronts are confined to the north. Hurricanes and tropical storms are coastal threats during the summer because of the classic northward turn storms take around the ocean high-pressure system. Although droughts are possible, the proximity and interaction with the ocean makes them less frequent than in zone 3. The northern part of the zone features frequent weather changes, and the weather can be quite harsh. The warm southern portion is a great haven for retirees, but high levels of humidity might be rough on those with heart or respiratory problems. But you could play golf there year-round!

Weather-Watch

After a jet flight of several hours between time zones, a person may suffer from jet-lag. This is a fatigue caused by throwing off your body clock. Try to avoid alcohol and smoking for several hours before and also during the flight to lessen the effects.

Can You Name Continent X?

I'm sure you've figured it out. We have just described and explained the major climate zones of the United States. Applying a few basic principles about the factors that determine climate, we can figure it all out. Sure, local variations complicate the picture, but the same principles apply. You can understand the European climate, the Asian climate—even the climate on Mars—just by keeping the basics in mind.

Of course, our technique is a little too qualitative and relative. What does "hot" really mean? How do we really define a "dry" climate? A real scientific system for defining climates has to go beyond our description. It should be specific and quantitative. Even if a "hot" climate is defined by a specific temperature, the system is not absolute. Different people feel "hot" at different temperatures.

One objective climate scheme tries to get around some of the difficulties by defining climate zones according to the vegetation that grows there and the range of temperature and moisture it requires. (Plants are easier to deal with than people.) The system is called the *Koppen classification scheme*, and we'll take a closer look at it next.

Climate Classification

One of the most basic schemes for climate classification was put together early in the twentieth century by a Russian-born German scientist, Waldimir Koppen. The boundaries of the different zones are based mainly on the nature of each area's vegetation, which is supported by the different weather variables. The Koppen classification centers around five basic groups: A, B, C, D, E:

A. These are tropical climates with a year-round average temperature in excess of 18 degrees C, or 64 degrees F.

B. These are dry climates where evaporation exceeds precipitation, and there is a constant water deficiency.

C. These are mid-latitude climates with tolerable winters. The average temperature of the coldest month is below 64 degrees, but above –3 degrees C, or 27 degrees F. This is sometimes called the *temperate zone*.

D. These are mid-latitude climates with harsh winters. The average temperature of the coldest month is below 27 degrees. Here, the warmest month still exceeds 10 degrees C, or 50 degrees F. This zone is often called the *polar snow forest*.

E. This is a polar climate where the temperature of the warmest month averages less than 50 degrees F. Here the ground is frozen much of the year. This is called the *tundra zone*.

There are also subheadings: f, w, m, S, W, s, T, F. It might seem complicated, but these headings have very specific limits.

Tropical Moist Climates (A)

This category includes those tropical climates that are wet year-round (f), those with a dry winter (w), and those with a dry season but enough rain in the rainy season to support rain forests (m). The Af climate is a rain-forest climate, the As is a savanna climate, and the Am is a monsoon climate.

In general, the weather in these climates is dynamic, with heavy amounts of rain, yet horizontal and annual temperature contrasts are slight. Temperature differences are reflected in topographic variations, but even with the influence of the sea, fronts are weather systems that will rarely reach the tropics. Even between winter and summer, the temperature doesn't change by more than 6 degrees F.

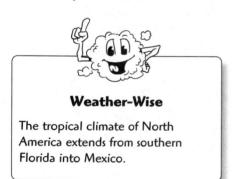

Weather-Wise

The tropical climate of North America extends from southern Florida into Mexico.

Yet rainfall is huge, frequently 100 inches or more annually. While the horizontal temperature change is slight, the vertical-temperature gradient is large because of all the heating near the ground. The intense surface warmth sets up a turbulent, unstable air mass with the potential of explosive, localized storms. The slightest vertical motion unleashes the instability. The ITCZ, that Inter-Tropical Convergence Zone, or even topographic lifting causes very heavy downpours.

The monsoon climate is interesting. Here, a seasonal variation in wind direction generates enough precipitation during the rainy season to produce rain-forest growth. The following figure shows the dynamics of the Indian monsoon.

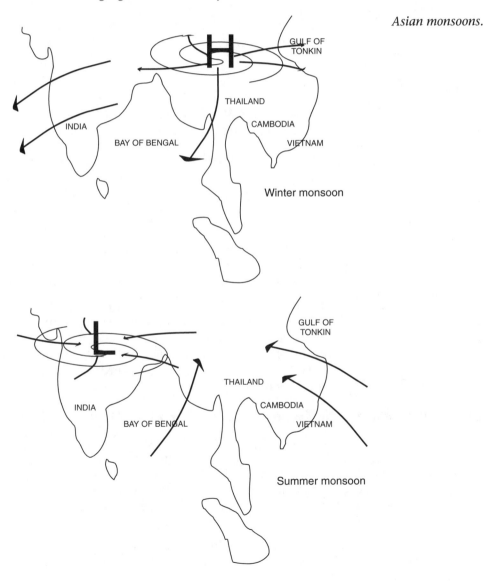

Asian monsoons.

During the winter, the wind comes out of the northeast, moves down-slope, and the weather is dry. But during the summer, a giant sea breeze pushes moist air onshore. In addition, a major shift in global winds enhances that sea breeze circulation.

During the summer, the ITCZ shifts northward. As it does, the southeast trades of the Southern Hemisphere reach across the equator. At the same time, Coriolis force turns the southeast trades to the right, creating a southwest wind. Those southwest winds enhance the sea breeze, and a strong, moist, unstable air mass moves inland. That moisture-laden air then runs upslope, and the skies open up. Also, the ITCZ is a place for convergence that provides its own lift. No wonder Cherrapunji, in northern India, receives an average of 425 inches of rain each year—most of that between April and October. In1861, Cherrapunji received a world record of 1,042 inches of rain. In July 1861 alone, 366 inches fell. In a mid-latitude, moderate climate, rainfall averages between 40 and 50 inches.

Dry Climates (B)

This climate generally occurs between 20 and 30 degrees latitude. The subtropical high-pressure system resides here, and the rate of evaporation exceeds precipitation. That feature is key. Limited precipitation may occur, but the high temperature causes strong evaporation, and everything dries out. If the temperature were lower, that limited precipitation could support thick vegetation, but the high temperature wipes out that possibility. About one-quarter of all land masses in the world have a B-type climate.

Weather-Wise

Deserts have the most arid climate, and rainfall can be as low as one to two inches per year. However, there is plant life adapted to the desert, such as cacti.

Dry climates also occur outside the tropics, in mid-latitudes where continental air masses dominate and where down-slope motion has dried out the atmosphere.

The two general dry climate types are the arid (BW) and the semi-arid (BS). The arid is the true desert; the semi-arid is found in the central portion of continents, such as the plains of North America or the steppes of central Asia. These two zones are divided further into groupings that describe the annual temperature variations.

Mid-Latitude, Moist Subtropical Climates (C)

This climate is characterized by abundant precipitation and chilly but not harsh winters. This type can generally be found between 25 degrees and 40 degrees, on the eastern and western portion of the continents. Most of the C-type has precipitation evenly distributed throughout the year, and the classification becomes Cf. The polar front generates numerous opportunities for rain. Also, along the coast, sharp temperature contrasts set off large storms, especially during winter.

Other locations will have a dry summer (Cs) or dry winter (Cw). The American West Coast experiences drier summers because of the northward drift of the subtropical high-pressure system. The Mediterranean also experiences a dry summer (Cs) for the same reason. Cw climates are tougher to find, but occur in places like northern India and China, where seasonal winds in the winter move down slope.

In addition to subheadings for dry summers or dry winters, there are sub-subheadings for a long, hot summers (a); long but moderate summers (b); and short, cool summers (c). Most of the eastern United States comes under the Cfa heading: wet all year, with a long, hot summer.

Moist Continental Climates (D)

These are similar to the C-type climate, except they are farther north and colder. Sometimes this is referred to as the polar snow-forest climate. Winters are severe and summers can be hot. The criteria for the coldest winter month to average below 27 degrees F is accompanied by long-lasting snow cover during the winter, which is why Koppen used that as a boundary of the climate. The types of vegetation that dominate are conifers and birches—the *boreal forests*. Boreal is also used to describe the D-type climate. In addition, conifer forests are known as taiga, so this is also called the taiga climate.

In general, huge annual temperature variations occur here—mainly because of the continental nature of the climate. The northern portion of the United States, Europe, Asia, and much of Canada falls into the D category.

Weather-Speak

A **boreal forest**, also known as taiga, is made up of conifers and birches.

Weather-Wise

Moist continental climates (D) have more severe winters than moist subtropical climates (C) and are usually north of the moist subtropical climates.

Polar Climates (E)

Here the winters are severe, and even in the warmest month the average temperature is 50 degrees or lower. There are two types: polar tundra (ET), where some vegetation growth can be found; and (EF), which is basically polar ice cap.

Even in the tundra region, much of the ground stays frozen, except near the surface in summer. The permanently frozen state is called *permafrost*. Mosses, lichens, and small trees make up the tundra vegetation that manages to grow during the very short summer.

Overall the polar climate is extremely dry; the cold temperatures prevent the climate from turning into a desert. The cold temperatures also cause higher humidity, and any precipitation has trouble evaporating. The lack of precipitation is related to the general circulation, which sinks at the very high latitudes.

There is another group (H) that's similar to polar, except it is caused by elevation, not latitude. This highland group (H) is found in the Rockies, Alps, Himalayas, and Andes.

Mapping It All Out

Okay, you've got it down. Now take a look at a world map of climate types (see the following figure). Based on what you now know, you can come up with a solid explanation for each and every zone that is depicted. There certainly are a lot of climates, but it all makes sense.

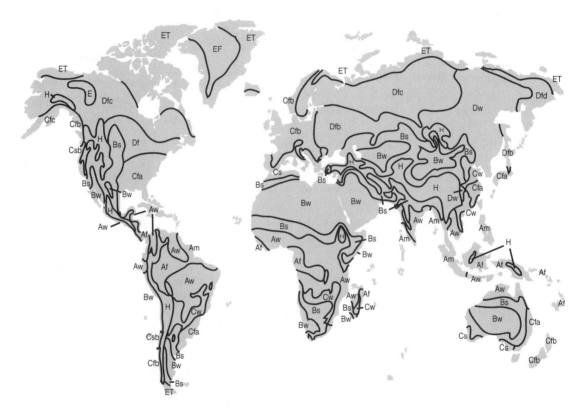

World climate.

Going to Extremes

Although climate represents the average weather, the weather within these climate zones can always go to extremes. The following three tables show the hottest, coldest, and wettest spots on Earth, based on weather records.

Hot Spots

Place	Continent	High (degrees F)	Date
El Azizia, Libya	Africa	138	Sept. 13, 1922
Death Valley, CA	North America	134	July 10, 1913
Tirat Tsvi, Israel	Asia	129	June 21, 1942
Cloncurry, Queensland	Australia	128	Jan. 16, 1889
Seville, Spain	Europe	120	Aug. 4, 1881
Rivadavia, Argentina	South America	108	Dec. 11, 1905
Tuguegarao, Philippines	Oceania	104	Apr. 29, 1912
Vanda Station, Scott Coast	Antarctica	59	Jan. 5, 1974

Cold Spots

Place	Continent	Low (degrees F)	Date
Vostok	Antarctica	-129	Jul. 21, 1983
Oimekon, Russia	Asia	-90	Feb. 6, 1933
Verkhoyansk, Russia	Asia	-90	Feb. 7, 1892
Northice	Greenland	-87	Jan. 9, 1954
Snag, Yukon, Canada	North America	-81.4	Feb. 3, 1947
Ust'Shchugor, Russia	Europe	-67	January ?
Sarmiento, Argentina	South America	-27	June 1, 1907
Ifrane, Morocco	Africa	-11	Feb. 11, 1935
Charlotte Pass, NSW	Australia	-9.4	June 29, 1994
Haleakala Summit, Maui, HI	Oceania	14	Jan. 2, 1961

Wettest Spots

Place	Continent	Highest Average Rainfall (inches)	Years of Record
Lloro, Colombia	South America	523.6	29
Mawsynram, India	Asia	467.4	38
Mt. Waialeale, Kauai, HI	Oceania	460	30
Debundecha, Cameroon	Africa	405	32
Quibdo, Colombia	South America	354	16
Bellenden Ker, Queensland	Australia	340	9
Henderson Lake, British Colombia	North America	256	14
Crkvica, Bosnia-Herzegovina	Europe	183	22

Notice that the record highest temperatures have occurred around 30 degrees latitude. Any surprises? Here the world's deserts are found, and scorching sun will send temperatures to great heights. The sinking motions associated with the subtropical high-pressure system put a fire under the thermometer.

It's no surprise either that the coldest temperature readings happen in far northern latitudes, or on top of mountains. But precipitation records show a more complex pattern. The heaviest annual precipitation occurs in the monsoon region of India. Yet, because of a hurricane, Alvin, Texas, holds the U.S. record for the most amount of rainfall in a 24-hour period, 43 inches. Holt, Missouri, and Unionville, Maryland, hold records because of vicious localized thunderstorms. The snowfall records in the Rockies are a function of lifting and cold temperatures associated with upslope motions.

So, some very basic elements determine climate. The direction of the wind, the topography, the latitude, the distribution of land and water all give a particular climate its distinct characteristics. You don't have to be a rocket meteorologist to figure out climate.

In the next chapter, we'll be looking for that ideal climate, if in fact it really exists.

The Least You Need to Know

➤ Numerous but understandable factors determine climate.

➤ When we know the basic climate variables, we can understand any climate.

➤ Classification schemes of climate are based on vegetation.

➤ Because of climate factors, the weather can go to great extremes.

Chapter 17

Are You Planning to Move?

In This Chapter

➤ Searching for the ideal climate

➤ Degree days: heating and cooling

➤ Comfort factors: wind chill and heat

➤ Evaluating the climates of selected areas

Ideal Climate

Is there such a thing as an ideal climate? In Part 2, we looked at the effects of weather on our health. We saw that changes in temperature and humidity can put a real strain on our bodies. The impact of heat and humidity can exacerbate respiratory and heart problems. The cold takes its toll, too. Air pollution is now a serious problem in places that were once considered ideal. There are psychological effects of too little sunshine, or maybe the boredom of weather that just doesn't change. An even-tempered climate with slight day-to-day change may be less physically stressful, but can someone from the stormy north happily adjust to the change? The adjustment itself requires time and patience. Acclimatization doesn't always come easily.

In the 30 or so years that I have been providing weather forecasts to the public, the most frequently asked questions focus on the quest for the ideal climate. But ideal is a relative thing.

Economics of Relocation

If you're considering a new job or if you're retiring, economics will be one of your prime concerns. If you relocate, you certainly want to consider the cost of living, and some of those costs will be related to heating and cooling needs. If you head south, you might save on your heating costs, but what about your air conditioning expenses? Meteorologists and fuel companies have come up with an index, called the "degree day," that can assist in your evaluation. This is calculated by computing the difference between 65 degrees and the average temperature of the day. Here's the story on degree-days:

Fuel companies assume that when the average temperature of a day falls below 65 degrees F, many thermostats will turn on. A greater departure from 65 degrees requires more heating and fuel consumption. The daily average comes simply by adding the day's maximum and minimum temperatures and dividing by two. For example, if the high temperature was 70 degrees and the low 50, the average would be 60 degrees. Then the average is subtracted from 65, and the difference represents the number of degree days. So, in our example, the number of degree days would come to 65–60, or 5. For that particular day, there were five degree days.

Weather-Wise

The degree-day totals for a given year are used as indicators of heating or air-conditioning needs. When the average temperature of a day is below 65 degrees, you get heating degree-days. When the average temperature of a day is above 65 degrees, you get cooling degree-days.

Those 5 degree days are added to the previous day's total, to keep a cumulative running total. The heating degree-day count begins on July 1, and it ends on the following June 30. A fuel dealer will watch your fuel consumption over a period of time and relate that to the number of degree days that accumulate. Each home will be different, but the dealer assumes you'll consume the same amount of fuel oil in a period with the same number of degree days.

Thousands of heating degree days will accumulate during the July to June heating season. The system is quite simplified. Some degree-day calculations account for sunshine and wind speed, but the standard degree-day system recorded by meteorologists and climatologists only utilizes the simple average temperature. The following table lists the heating degree days, along with an assortment of other parameters for selected cities.

Heating Degree Days for Selected Cities

City	Record High	Record Low	Days with Precip.	Snowfall (inches)	Total Precip. (inches)	Heating Degree Days
Houston, TX	107	5	101	T	46.9	1,568
Atlanta, GA	105	–9	106	2	49.8	2,941
Phoenix, AZ	122	16	37	T	7.3	1,442
Denver, CO	105	–29	89	63	15.4	5,937
Orlando, FL	102	19	115	T	47.7	652
Salt Lake City, UT	107	–30	92	63	15.6	5,752
Las Vegas, NV	117	8	27	1	4.0	2,420

City	Record High	Record Low	Days with Precip.	Snowfall (inches)	Total Precip. (inches)	Heating Degree Days
Raleigh-Durham, NC	105	–9	110	8	42.0	3,502
Fresno, CA	115	17	44	T	10.6	2,513
Cincinnati, OH	109	–25	127	23	40.9	5,140

Since the l950s, a new degree-day has been factored into the climate mix. Because of the population growth in the South and Southwest, air conditioning has become a necessity. Without it, most northerners would never head south. Overall, energy demands on utilities are far greater during summer rather than winter. So, a cooling degree-day has been developed to gauge the demand for air conditioning.

The calculation for the cooling degree-day is just like the heating degree-day, except the temperature differential above rather than below 65 is considered. If the average temperature is 70 degrees, then five cooling degree-days would accumulate. If the average were 85 degrees, 20 cooling degree-days would be added. Annual cooling degree days are also shown in the preceding table.

Like the heating degree-day, the cooling degree-day is an oversimplification of energy needs. Wind, sunshine, and humidity are not included. The dew-point temperature is key in our comfort level, but that is not included. Still, the cooling degree-day does provide an index of relative warmth.

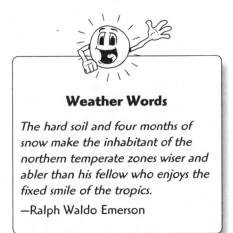

Weather Words

The hard soil and four months of snow make the inhabitant of the northern temperate zones wiser and abler than his fellow who enjoys the fixed smile of the tropics.

—Ralph Waldo Emerson

A Dew-Point Reminder

Temperature and humidity together have a lot to do with comfort and health. The two factors are used to come up with a heat-stress index. But the dew point is a useful, simplified index of comfort. The humidity could be 100 percent in the morning, but as the afternoon heat takes hold, the humidity could drop to 40 percent. But it's so hot in the afternoon! The relative humidity matters little.

The dew point is a measure of water vapor in the air. In previous chapters, we made quite a point of the dew point. If you're looking for the ideal climate, it really is important to check out the normal dew-point reading. For northern folk, the weather begins to feel uncomfortable as the dew point reaches the 60s. As the dew point climbs into the low 70s, it's too steamy for most—time to get the air conditioner going. By the time the dew point reaches the mid to upper 70s, you don't feel like moving, especially as the sun beats down and the temperature reaches the 80s and higher. If you have heart and respiratory problems, think twice before relocating to a region where the dew point is frequently in the 70s. Of course, if you have air conditioning and take it

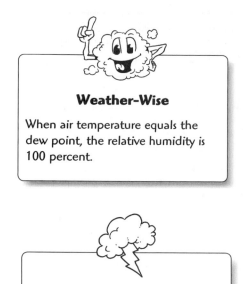

Weather-Wise

When air temperature equals the dew point, the relative humidity is 100 percent.

Weather-Watch

A person must acclimatize on moving to a new place, and each person is affected differently. It is a combination of physical and mental well-being that determines a person's "ideal climate."

easy, you'll be fine, but for a number of retirees, adjustments will be needed to successfully manage a tropically moist climate.

Whenever the dew point falls into the 50s or lower, the weather will generally be comfortable—except, of course, if the temperature is too hot or too cold. In the desert southwest, the dew point can drop into the 30s and 40s. That's okay, except when the thermometer climbs to oven-like levels. Also, in cold climates, the dew point is frequently low, but the temperature is also low. Who cares if the dew point is 20 degrees when the temperature is only 32 degrees? That low temperature might be the single-most reason for your relocation in the first place.

Bring on the Chill

Although the dew point is an important comfort variable, it doesn't stand alone. The wind can be a problem, too. It isn't always a gentle breeze, and when the temperature is low, the wind intensifies the cold. An index called the *wind chill* was developed to describe the effective skin temperature based on the wind speed.

When the wind blows across the skin, it does two things. First, the motion of the air helps conduct heat away from our bodies. Second, the wind speeds up the evaporation rate, and as any perspiration evaporates, the vapor pulls more heat away. Remember latent heat? That's the heat stored in vapor as it transforms from the liquid phase. If you apply rubbing alcohol to your wrist, your wrist will feel cool—not because the alcohol is cool, but because the evaporation rate of alcohol is high and it extracts heat as it vaporizes.

The following figure shows the effective wind chill for various combinations of temperature and wind. For example, if the wind speed is 10 mph and the temperature is 35 degrees, the effective temperature is 22 degrees. When the wind chill dips to 20 below, frostbite can occur in a matter of minutes. You need gloves and a hat in such severely low wind-chill readings. Clothes should be kept dry too, because water conducts additional heat away from the body.

Hypothermia is a condition where the body temperature falls so low that a mental and physical collapse becomes possible. When the internal body temperature drops below 79 degrees, collapse and death occur. Amazingly, most cases of hypothermia occur between air temperatures of 32 and 50 degrees. The entire process is hastened with wind and wet clothing. Damp air always feels colder because water is a good heat conductor. And it's chillier still if the wind is blowing.

	Air Temperature (°F)																		
Wind Speed (mph)	45	40	35	30	25	20	15	10	5	0	-5	-10	-15	-20	-25	-30	-35	-40	-45
4	45	40	35	30	25	20	15	10	5	0	-5	-10	-15	-20	-25	-30	-35	-40	-45
5	43	37	32	27	22	16	11	6	0	-5	-10	-15	-21	-26	-31	-36	-42	-47	-52
10	34	28	22	16	10	3	-3	-9	-15	-22	-27	-34	-40	-46	-52	-58	-64	-71	-77
15	29	23	16	9	2	-5	-11	-18	-25	-31	-38	-45	-51	-58	-64	-71	-78	-85	-92
20	26	19	12	4	-3	-10	-17	-24	-31	-39	-46	-53	-60	-67	-74	-81	-88	-95	-103
25	23	26	8	1	-7	-15	-22	-29	-36	-44	-51	-59	-66	-74	-81	-88	-96	-103	-110
30	21	13	6	-2	-10	-18	-25	-33	-41	-49	-58	-64	-71	-79	-86	-93	-101	-109	-116
35	20	12	4	-4	-12	-20	-27	-35	-43	-52	-58	-64	-72	-82	-89	-97	-107	-113	-120

Wind chill

Climates of Selected Areas

When I was once in the Caribbean, a waiter who described himself as a "Yankee Doodle Pakistani" critiqued items on the menu as "yummy-yummy" or "yucky-yucky." I guess you could use the same classification system to describe the climate in various places. But most climates fall somewhere between yummy-yummy and yucky-yucky. The "ideal" climate is elusive, but as a public service, I thought it would be good to evaluate the climates of some metropolitan regions that are experiencing the fastest population growth. More and more people call these areas home, so just in case you're planning a move, check out this climate rundown to find out whether you should pack your warm jacket or put it in your moving sale.

Houston, Texas

The Houston/Galveston region is hot. The average high temperature during the summer is in the low 90s. The dew point reaches well into the 70s, with daily high temperatures averaging 94 degrees during July and August. That combination of temperature and dew point frequently brings the heat-stress index to 105 and higher in the summertime. Of course air conditioning has made the living much easier during the hot summers. But if you experience heat-related problems, you should think twice before relocating to a region with such extreme heat.

Weather-Speak

When the winds are high and the air is below freezing, exposed skin may freeze. This is called **frostbite.**

Rainfall is abundant and spread evenly throughout the year, but during the summer, tropical disturbances can cause extreme downpours. One of the great disasters in U.S. history occurred during the famous Galveston flood, when a hurricane caused a storm surge that claimed 6,000 lives in 1900 (see Chapter 8). After that historic flood, Galveston Island was raised several feet above sea level, but those massive Gulf of Mexico hurricanes still occur.

On the positive side, typical wintertime highs are in the 60s, with lows in the 40s. Heating degree days are only a fraction of the 5,000 or so degree-days that occur up north. You'll save on your heating bills, but air conditioning is a way of life.

Atlanta, Georgia

Warm temperatures draw people to the Atlanta area, but the summers can be scorchers. The heat isn't as extreme as in Houston, but the normal high temperature is in the mid 80s during July and August, and the dew point averages close to 70 degrees. Still, the heat is manageable. Atlanta's elevation of nearly 1,000 feet helps moderate summer temperatures, and 100-degree heat is rare. Also, for those who like a chill, the winters can cool down. The average high temperature in the winter is in the low 50s with normal lows in the low 30s. That's chilly enough to get out the warm jackets, but compared to more northern latitudes, that's balmy! Freezing temperatures can occur as soon as early November, but the average frost-free period is 233 days. Snow does fall in Atlanta—average annual snowfall is about 1.5 inches—but a snowfall of 4 inches or more only happens once every 5 years or so. The region around Atlanta can be hit hard with winter ice storms about once every 2 years. Severe ice storms occur about once in 10 years.

Overall, precipitation is evenly distributed throughout the year, but October is the driest month, with rainfall being half of what is found during the wettest month, March. Thunderstorms can become quite severe during the spring, and some spawn tornadoes.

If you are tired of tough winters, still want a little seasonal variation, and don't mind some hot and humid spells during the summer, Atlanta might be the place for you.

Phoenix, Arizona

If you like your weather sunny, Phoenix is for you. Overall, there is an enormous 86-percent chance of sunshine for Phoenix. The minimum occurs in January with 77 percent, but the maximum is 94 percent, in July. All that bright sun is due to the desert climate's extremely dry conditions. The midday relative humidity is generally below 30 percent, and it can drop to 10 percent or less. A combination of high pressure and down-slope motions contributes to the dry conditions. Those same parameters provide for plenty of heat, too. During the summer, you can expect temperatures each day to exceed 90 degrees. Actually, the average high temperature is greater than 100 degrees during June, July, and August.

The extreme heat can be too much to handle, even if the dew point is low. Some folks with respiratory problems have settled here, but the dryness and intense heat can also cause unexpected physical stress.

In addition, as more people settle in the region, air pollution becomes an increasing concern. Phoenix is located in a valley, in an area of very stable air. The pollutants do not disperse very well, and the bright sun becomes an agent for delivering photochemical smog. So, the sun might draw many to the region, but that same sunshine combined with the influx of population has created a smog problem.

Phoenix does get rainfall, but the average number of days with measurable rain per month ranges from one to five, depending on the time of year. Fall and spring are the driest seasons. During the summer, the monsoon-like circulation from the Gulf of Mexico and the west coast of Mexico can deliver localized but heavy showers. During the winter, an occasional storm might arrive from the Pacific. Total annual rainfall is generally less than two months' worth in the storm-tossed Northeast.

The winters are mild, with daily temperatures averaging in the mid 60s with lows near 40. Nighttime temperatures frequently drop below freezing during the winter, but the days are very pleasant. Those bright, mild winter days definitely have their appeal.

Denver, Colorado

Denver's climate is interesting. There is plenty of variability, and heavy snow can fall as early as October, but in mid-winter there might hardly be a trace of it. The Denver region is very much influenced by the Rocky Mountains. If the wind is moving down-slope, the weather is mild and dry. If it comes up-slope, look out!

Because of prevailing west-to-east winds, and because Denver is situated on the eastern slopes of the Rockies, the weather is generally dry and relatively mild. Any extreme weather, hot or cold, is usually short-lived. On the average, the temperature reaches 100 degrees in only one year in five, although temperatures in the 90s may be experienced about 35 days of the year.

Generally, because Denver is shielded from the Pacific by the Rockies and because it's far to the west of the Gulf of Mexico, moisture is limited. The climate leans in the direction of low humidity, low precipitation, and plenty of sunshine.

Total precipitation for the year only averages 14.6 inches—one-third of what occurs in many northern areas. If there is a stormy season, it occurs during the spring, but the wettest month is May, when Denver averages 2.4 inches of precipitation.

Denver does have its cold days, and snow can fall any time from September to May. In January, the normal high is 43 degrees; the normal low is 16 degrees. Plan on investing in a snow shovel—an average five feet of snow falls each year, more than the seasonal snowfall in Boston. That's plenty of snow for a dry climate, but many of the storms that come along during the winter are snowmakers. Also, the snow does melt, or evaporate, quickly in Denver. As soon as the west wind returns, the snow can vanish before your very eyes.

Generally, Denver's climate is close to ideal for many people. There are enough stormy days to keep the weather interesting. The winters are manageable and the summers are dry. Overall, the weather will stay out of your way. The region has become popular with those who have respiratory diseases such as asthma.

However, Denver's location favors the build-up of air pollution. Because of the shielding of the Rockies, light winds allow for inversions during the many clear nights. These occur when heat radiates out from the surface, leaving a cold layer near the ground and a warmer layer above (Chapters 11 and 12). The warmer air is less dense than the underlying cold air. The atmosphere does not overturn. The air is stable, pollutants build up and smog becomes a problem. Ironically, those with respiratory problems might have sought out Denver's dry climate, but the presence of an expanding population has made the once-pristine atmosphere less than ideal.

Orlando, Florida

Anyone for Disney World? If you enjoy playing golf through the year and can handle some oppressive summer humidity, then Orlando is for you. During the summer, the average high temperature is 90 degrees and the dew point is 70 degrees or higher—a very taxing combination. Because Orlando gets breezes from the Atlantic or the Gulf, the summer heat is moderated somewhat. Also, frequent showers can put a lid on the thermometer. Despite the summer heat and humidity, the temperature in Orlando has never reached 100 degrees.

Thunderstorms occur almost daily during the summer rainy season. From June through September, monthly rainfall comes to seven or eight inches. But during the winter, only two to three inches fall each month. Hurricanes are rare, but at least some fringe rain or wind from weakened tropical storms occurs nearly every late summer or fall.

The winters are delightful, and may be reason enough to move. Only 8 to 10 days each month average mostly cloudy skies, and measurable precipitation occurs on just 6 days each winter month. The weather is free of rain at least 80 percent of the time. The average wintertime high temperature is a comfortable 71 degrees, and the low is a cool but comfortable 50 degrees. On rare occasions the nighttime temperature will drop to freezing, but the temperature will recover quickly during the day. There is nothing Mickey Mouse about these winters!

Salt Lake City, Utah

If you want to avoid snow and winter cold, Salt Lake City may not be the place for you. The region has enjoyed impressive population growth, so the weather must have some redeeming value—and it does—but plan on a real winter.

The climate is semi-arid, with a total precipitation of just over 15 inches for the entire year. Generally, less than two inches of precipitation occur in each month. Summer is the driest period, when monthly average precipitation turns out to be less than one inch. During the summer, the weather is hot and dry with daily average high temperatures in the low 90s. But the dew point is in the 50s or lower, so the heat is more tolerable than in other locations where the dew point reaches 70 or higher. Because of the dry air, the temperature at night can sink into the relatively cool low 50s—definitely pleasant.

During the winter, the normal high temperature is close to 40, with the low near 20. That's just about as cold as most northern cities. Although total annual precipitation is not heavy, plenty of snow manages to fall; the season average is 58 inches. Most of the time, there is no snow; only 1 inch or more on an average of four days of each winter month, but when it snows, it can snow in a big way. Still, the weather has a cold side, with about 6,000 heating degree days accumulating during the season, matching the numbers in Chicago or New York.

Las Vegas, Nevada

Many people have rolled the dice on Las Vegas's climate, and the odds are high that your outdoor activities will seldom be washed out. In the summer, an average of less than one day each month delivers measurable rainfall, and even the winter delivers an average of only three days each month with precipitation—seldom in the form of snow. Total precipitation for the entire year is under four inches, which is the normal total for a single month in the Northeast.

Las Vegas is located in a desert valley, so precipitation of any form is scattered through the year. If there is a humid season, it occurs for about two weeks during the summer. Scattered thunderstorms, some severe, will occur during this relatively brief period. The humidity keeps the minimum temperatures on the very warm side, and many find these couple weeks the most miserable of the year. Most of the time in the summer it's just hot and dry—and I mean *hot*. The average high temperature during July is about 104 degrees; the minimum is 75 degrees. And unlike Salt Lake City, temperatures don't cool down much at night. During the humid spell, the temperature at night hovers around a sticky 80 degrees.

Las Vegas winters are cool and pleasant, however, with daytime temperatures in the 50s and low 60s, and overnight readings just above freezing. The most popular seasons are spring and fall, with April and October daytime temperatures reaching near 80 degrees and falling to around 50 at night. During the course of the year, heating degree days are half or fewer than the degree-day numbers in northeastern cities.

Raleigh-Durham, North Carolina

The Raleigh area is just east of the mountain ridges on the Piedmont Plateau, and its climate is influenced by these ridges as well as by the Atlantic coastal plain to the east. The summers can be quite warm and humid, with daytime high temperatures averaging between 85 and 90 degrees. The summer temperature reaches 90 degrees or higher on an average of one every three days. Still, because of the mountains, the nighttime temperatures fall to near or below 70 degrees.

The mountains help block cold wintertime air masses. Daily average winter temperatures reach the low 50s and drop to near 30 at night. That is jacket-chilly, but definitely tolerable. Snowfall averages seven inches each season—hardly anything according to northern standards. Snow occurs each year, but heavy snowfalls are rare.

Precipitation is evenly distributed throughout the year, with the heaviest amounts occurring in summer thunderstorms. During July, 11 days will, on the average, have some thunder. Rainfall occurs approximately 30 percent of the time through the year.

The brightest weather of the year occurs during the fall with an average of 13 clear days each month, and only 7 days each month with precipitation. Many consider the fall to be the best time of year.

The Raleigh-Durham area has plenty of summer, some winter, and enough rain to keep your umbrella handy. But the summers, the winters, and the stormy spells do not regularly go to great extremes.

Fresno, California

Another dry region that has experienced strong population growth is the San Joaquin Valley around Fresno. This area is nestled between the Sierra Nevada mountains to the east and the coastal range to the west. The valley climate is dry: Just under l0 inches of rain falls during the year, with the majority falling from November to April. Hardly any rain falls during July and August. On the average, only 40 days each year have measurable rain, and snow is very rare. Fog is common during the winter months and can persist for up to two weeks.

Summers are warm, with daily highs close to l00 degrees and sometimes over ll0 degrees. The dew points are only in the 50s, so the summer heat is more tolerable than in other areas, but plan on running the air conditioner. The relative humidity drops to l0 percent during summer afternoons.

Winters are pleasant, but heavy frost occurs each year. The first frost of the season occurs in late November; the last in early April. Normal daily high temperatures in the mid 50s make for an easygoing winter.

The limited number of storms, pleasant winter temperatures, and abundant sunshine are reason enough to consider Fresno. But because of its valley location, smog and air pollution can become a problem, as it has in many California locations.

Cincinnati, Ohio

I'm sure the climate wasn't a major attraction for those who have made Cincinnati one of the fastest-growing metropolitan areas, but Cincinnati is becoming home to more and more people, and just in case you become one of them, have we got climate information for you!

Generally, Cincinnati has a *continental climate*, which means wide variations in temperature through the year. During the summer, the Bermuda high-pressure system delivers its southwest flow of very warm, humid weather. But during the winter, blasts of polar air send the thermometer the other way. The clash of air masses makes Cincinnati very meteorologically active. Severe thunderstorms occur during the warm months. Also, the city is located along the Ohio River, and major floods occur about once every third year. (A major flood is one in which the river runs at least five feet above flood stage.)

Although the winters are chilly, snowfall is not excessive. On the average, only six days each year will deliver an inch or more of snow. Total seasonal snowfall comes to about 18 inches. The normal winter high temperature is about 40 degrees, and the normal low is in the mid 20s.

The summers are very warm, with daytime temperatures in the upper 80s and lows in the 60s. Nearly half of July has 90-degree temperatures.

Total precipitation comes to approximately 40 inches, which is fairly evenly distributed through the year, but the driest spells occur in the fall. Through the year, precipitation occurs on 35 percent of the days.

Weather Words

Charles Dickens said in his *American Notes* in 1842, "Cincinnati is a beautiful city; cheerful, thriving, and animated."

Overall, you'll need an umbrella and some winter clothes, but don't worry too much about snow. Air conditioning in the summer is a must.

An ideal climate is a relative thing. Heating and air conditioning needs are important. Some like it hot, and others just can't wait for snow to fall. In the next few chapters, we'll be looking at whether these climates are really changing.

The Least You Need to Know

➤ There's no ideal climate for everyone.

➤ If you are relocating, consider all the weather angles of an area before you make the move there.

➤ Wind chill and dew point are two indexes that weathercasters use to evaluate comfort levels.

➤ Sunny, bright cities can also be highly polluted.

Chapter 18

Climates Are Made to Be Broken

In This Chapter

➤ Dating ancient climates

➤ The age of the earth

➤ Are climates really changing?

➤ The climate changes of the past two million years

➤ The warmth of the twentieth century

The earth and its atmosphere have been in circulation for billions of years. And how do we know? Well, there are some elements that decay in predictable ways, and by examining a sample of soil or a fossil for those elements, we can get an idea of that sample's age. But to really understand this, we first need to take a detour into the concept of radiation and radioactive decay. And once we know the sample's age, we can then figure out the nature of the climate that made it possible, and we get a picture of ancient climates.

Aging with a Glow

Maybe the entire Earth doesn't exactly glow in the dark, but some elements do. It is the study of the process that opens doors to the past.

The Atomic Clock Is Ticking

All living and non-living materials, all elements, consist of small building blocks called *atoms*. These contain mostly empty space, but also contain a central core, or *nucleus*, surrounded by negatively charged elements called *electrons*. The nucleus consists of numerous subatomic elements, the main players being *neutrons*, which are neutrally charged, and *protons*, which are positively charged. Most of the mass of an atom is contained within the nucleus, and the total number of neutrons plus protons is called the *atomic mass number*. The number of protons, alone, is the *atomic number*.

Now, some atoms of the same element differ from each other in the number of neutrons. They have the same number of protons and electrons, the atomic number is the same, but the atomic mass number is different. Atoms that have the same number of protons but different numbers of neutrons are called *isotopes*.

Some isotopes are stable and don't break down into other isotopes or elements, but others are very unstable. In these unstable atoms, change is always happening.

Weather Words

"Let the great world spin forever down the ringing grooves of change."

—Alfred, Lord Tennyson

Two forces seem to be at work within an atom: the *nuclear binding force,* which keeps the atom together, and the *electrical force,* which wants to break the structure apart. Because "like" charges repel one another, it is surprising that a nucleus consisting of all these protons can manage to stay together. You would think that the electrical forces would cause the protons to repel one another and that would be it for life and our world.

But amazingly, the nuclear binding forces normally prevent this electrical force from taking over. The neutrons act as some of this cement, but if an atom is too large, the outer protons don't benefit as much as the ones closer to the center. The binding force diminishes with distance from the center, so some elements become unstable and lose protons. That loss leads to additional changes, until eventually a stable atom forms. The process of decay from a highly energized, unstable state to a stable element is called *radioactive decay.*

Weather-Speak

Radioactive decay is the process by which the atomic nuclei break apart and form other, more stable elements. **Half-life** is the time it takes for the decay of one-half of the atoms of a radioactive substance. The half-life of carbon-14 is about 5730 years. The half-life of uranium-238 (a uranium-bearing rock) is 4.51 billion years. The half-life of uranium-235 is 713 million years.

The decay is predictable and takes a certain set time to occur; the *half-life* is the time it takes for half the original unstable material to decay. For example, radium-226, radium with an atomic mass number of 226, will take 1,620 years to decrease by one-half. In another 1,620 years, radium will go down by one-half again. So in 3,240 years, one-quarter of the original radium will remain.

Carbon Dating

The earth's atmosphere is constantly bombarded with high-energy particles from outer space. These are called *cosmic rays*. When these rays arrive in the upper atmosphere, they charge the atoms present and cause a scattering of protons and neutrons. The protons link back up with electrons and form hydrogen, but the neutrally charged neutrons stay single for a longer period. Some will reach into the lower atmosphere and combine with nitrogen—after all, 78 percent of the atmosphere consists of nitrogen.

Nitrogen contains seven protons and seven neutrons. When another neutron smashes into it, one of the protons is dislodged. The new atom contains six protons and eight neutrons. That is a brand new element called carbon-14. Regular, stable carbon is carbon-12. It has six protons, like carbon-14, but just six neutrons. Carbon-14 is an unstable isotope of carbon. It doesn't remain in that state forever, and it will go back into nitrogen. The half-life of the return to nitrogen is about 5,760 years.

Because plants take in carbon dioxide, and animals eat plants, all living things contain carbon. Both carbon-12 and carbon-14 will form carbon dioxide. So, everything that has been alive will contain some carbon-14. And as carbon-14 decays, more will form—as long as the plant or animal is alive. In living things there is about one carbon-14 atom for every 100 billion carbon-12 atoms. But once the plant or animal dies, that's it. No additional carbon-14 will form. The percentage of carbon-14 that remains will decrease according to its half-life. If the half-life of carbon-14 is 5,760 years, and if only half remains in a particular formerly alive skeleton, then those bones are assumed to be 5,760 years old. If only one-quarter remains, then those old bones are even older—11,520 years old.

Of course uncertainties do exist. Changes on the Sun and in the earth's magnetic field, which draws in the charged solar elements, influence the cosmic-ray bombardment. That influences the generation of carbon-14. Also, carbon dioxide levels in the atmosphere fluctuate with temperature—more is released from the ocean during warm periods, and less during cold periods. So, the base ratio of one carbon-14 atom to 100 billion carbon-12 atoms is not necessarily fixed. As a result, simple carbon dating can become complex.

Generally, this form of carbon dating is good for samples up to 50,000 years old with an uncertainty of approximately 15 percent.

Weather-Wise

In 1946, chemist Willard Frank Libby introduced the radioactive carbon-14 method of dating ancient objects. In 1960 he won the Nobel Prize for Chemistry for his invention of radio-carbon dating.

Weather-Speak

Carbon dating is the process used to date formerly living plants and animals by measuring the radioactivity of the remaining carbon-14 isotopes. **Uranium dating** can be used for both very old, as well as non-living things. Isotopes of uranium will decay in predictable ways, and the remaining isotopes give clues of the sample's age.

Uranium Dating

In addition to carbon dating, there is uranium dating. Uranium-238 decays into lead-206. Uranium-235 eventually decays into lead-207. This form of dating is good for non-living things such as rocks. Also, larger periods can be studied because the half-life of Uranium-238 is about 4.5 billion years. All lead-206 or lead-207 comes from decayed uranium. So, in a sample of rock, if there is an equal amount of lead-206 as uranium-238, then the sample is 4.5 billion years old. That is how the age of the earth or moon is determined. The following table shows the half-life of the radioactive isotope commonly used for dating. In addition to uranium and carbon, potassium is used. That works well for potassium-rich rocks such as mica and feldspar.

Half-Life of Common Isotopes Used for Dating

Radioactive Parent	Half-Life (years)	Stable Daughter Product	Minerals and Rocks Commonly Dated
Uranium-238	4510 million	Lead-206	Zircon; uraninite; pitchblende
Uranium-235	713 million	Lead-207	Zircon; uraninite; pitchblende
Potassium-40	1300 million	Argon-40	Muscovite; biotite; hornblende; glauconite; sanidine; whole volcanic rock
Rubidium-87	47,000 million	Strontium-87	Muscovite; biotite; lepidolite; glauconite; microcline; whole metamorphic rock

Weather-Wise

The geological time scale is divided into three eras—Cenozoic (recent life), Mesozoic (middle life), and Paleozoic (ancient life). The eras are subdivided into periods. The time before the Paleozoic is called Precambrian.

Just as with carbon, complications exist with uranium. If a rock undergoes metamorphism because of pressure or heat, the clock is reset. But cross-checking with nearby samples helps increase the accuracy.

It's a Very Old Earth

Based on radioactive dating, scientists have been able to come up with a timeline of the earth divided into different eras, periods, and epochs. The figure on the next page shows the geologic time scale.

The three eras consist of Paleozoic (ancient life), Mesozoic (middle life), and Cenozoic (recent life). Preceding the Paleozoic is the Precambrian (hidden life). The Precambrian goes from 570 million years ago to about

4.5 billion years ago when the earth is thought to have formed. That represents 85 percent of Earth's history, and a period which is so little understood. The appearance of abundant life 570 million years ago begins the Paleozoic area.

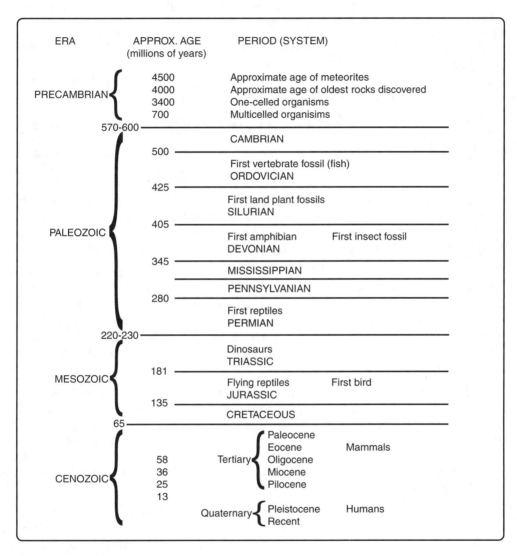

Geologic time scale.

The eras, periods, and epochs are defined by the different forms of life as well as geologic features. In addition, climate has set the stage for these divisions. For example, in the *Carboniferous Period,* about 300 million years ago, warm and moist climate conditions accounted for the lush vegetation and dense swamp forests. These

Weather-Speak

The **Carboniferous Period** includes the Mississippian and the Pennsylvanian Periods under the Paleozoic Era. There was lush vegetation and dense swampy forests, caused by a moist and warm climate.

swamps became the source for coal beds that are now found around the world. The warmth and humidity contributed to giant insects, too, including massive cockroaches and dragon flies with nearly three-foot wingspans!

Appendix B summarizes the different goings-on during Earth's checkered and rocky history. The type of life provides clues about climate while the radioactive dating lets us know when the life and climate occurred.

Evidence of Climate Change

As you know, Earth is an ancient place, and materials collected from the far corners of the earth indicate that climate has changed for hundreds of millions of years. In the early days of the earth, there wasn't even an atmosphere as we know it. Simple microorganisms and plants were able to take in carbon dioxide that was probably vented from volcanoes and convert that to oxygen. Eventually, the atmosphere took shape, and weather came about. But the weather has gone through many extremes.

Changes that have occurred from the past few hundred years up to the past 2,000 years can be found in historical documents; George Washington, for example, kept a weather diary until the day before he died. Fossils, pollens, coal beds, and sand dunes also provide clues of past climates. The study of tree rings, called *dendrochronology*, is also helpful. Layers of wood form beneath the bark of a tree, and these show a greater thickness when precipitation and temperature increase. Each year of the tree's growth is represented by one of those rings.

In addition, cores of deep sea sediment show shells of old organisms that were once at the surface. The type of organism provides clues to the temperature. Also, these cores contain certain chemicals in particular ratios that can exist only in particular climate conditions. Oxygen comes in different forms. The oxygen we know and breathe contains eight neutrons and eight protons. We're talking about oxygen-16. But another heavier form of oxygen contains two more neutrons, so its atomic weight is then 18. That's called oxygen-18.

There is only about one oxygen-18 molecule for every thousand oxygen-16 molecules. During cold periods, oceans will be drawn down when ice forms and takes up some of the water. At the same time, there is a greater amount of oxygen-18. So examining the ratio of oxygen-18 and oxygen-16 contained in the shells of ancient organisms within the core samples gives scientists an idea of changes that have occurred. If the proportion of oxygen-18 to oxygen-16 is higher in one sample than another, we know the sample was from a colder period. So, the record of change can be found.

The Last Two Million Years

The following figure shows a generalized temperature profile of the past two million years. There have been plenty of ups and downs, and each change profoundly influenced the nature of life. Analysis of fossil remains along with oxygen-18 measurements helped provide the data for the profile. The cold periods have been times of glacial advances, while the warmer spells have been interglacial periods. During the glacial advances, more snow would fall than would melt. The snow piled up, layer upon layer. Then, under pressure, it would spread to the south and carve out new landscapes.

Notice that during the last 500,000 years, there have been five periods of major glaciation. Generally, the past two million years have been cold with long periods of glaciation, and the interglacial periods have been relatively brief. Consequently, many scientists feel that regardless of the warmth in recent years, we are really in an extremely cold period, and the warming is only a passing thing. The last two million years in Earth's history have been cold, and the glaciers will try to return.

Overall, glacial periods run about 10 degrees colder than the interglacials. That is not a huge change. Climate prognosticators predict a two- to five-degree increase due to human activities by the year 2100. Considering the slight change involved with natural processes, that increase, if true, will be very significant.

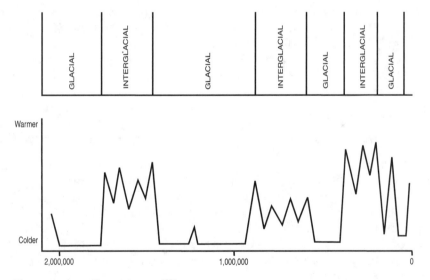

Temperature of past two million years.

The Last 500,000 Years

Close analysis of deep-sea cores with oxygen dating reveals quite a variation of sea-surface temperatures during the past half-million years. The average sea-surface temperature is a good clue of sea-level air temperature. The following figure shows the variation. Numerous glacial advances and recessions are indicated by all the fluctuations.

Variation of sea-surface temperatures.

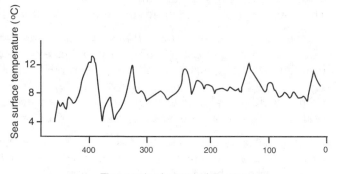

Thousands of years before present

The last very warm interglacial with sea-level temperatures in the low 60s occurred about 120,000 years ago. Then the temperature dropped, and the earth entered its most recent glacial age—broken by several glacial advances and retreats. The last major advance began 23,000 years ago and ended 10,000 years ago. The warmest period of the past 10,000 years occurred around 5,000 years ago with a temperature of 61 degrees. Our current sea-level temperature is 59 degrees—very close to the warm period of ancient times. That warm period has been called the "climatic optimum." If the climate predictions prove correct, human activities will be responsible for a worldwide temperature that will exceed that climatic optimum by the end of the twenty-first century.

These changes in climate have had a profound effect on life. During the last ice age, 10,000 to 23,000 years ago, the first people arrived in North America. At the time, two giant ice sheets covered North America—one from Alaska to the Pacific Northwest, and the other from the Arctic south to the eastern slopes of the Rockies and eastward to New England and New York. The ice was as much as two feet thick, and because it drew so much water from the oceans, sea level was 350 feet lower at the peak of the ice age. The lowered sea level exposed a plain between Siberia and Alaska. This created a land bridge across the Bering Sea, allowing the passage of people from Asia to America for the first time.

The early settlers were big-game hunters, going after huge mastodons, ancestors of our elephants. They also hunted species such as saber-toothed cats and wooly rhinoceroses, but these, too, have become extinct due to over-hunting or climate warming about 10,000 years ago. The following figure shows the ice sheets and migration patterns that were present during that period.

Ice sheets and migration patterns.

By about 7,000 years ago, the ice sheets were gone, and climatic changes took place. The region between the Rockies and Cascades dried up and formed the Great Basin. The Great Salt Lake shrank—at one time it was 1,200 feet deeper than it is now. Spruce trees, which thrive in cold weather, retreated. Mastodons and other large animals could not adapt to the warm and dry conditions and became extinct.

Climate of the Last 3,000 Years

In the figure on the following page, you can see the fluctuation of temperature during the past 3,000 years. Again, change dominates the pattern. The warm period around A.D. 1000 is striking, along with the cold spell that lasted from about 1400 to 1850, a period so cold it was called the "Little Ice Age." Since the middle of the nineteenth century, the temperature has been generally increasing. That increase is occurring in an overall cold period, but it is happening.

The warmth of the eleventh century, about 1,000 years ago, allowed vineyards to flourish in England. The summers were warm and dry. During that period, the first Europeans set foot in North America. Led by Eric the Red, the Vikings settled in Greenland, which might very well have shown some "green" in those days. The son of Eric, Leif Erikson, led an expedition that is thought to have settled in Newfoundland. But the colony was abandoned when the Little Ice Age arrived around 1400.

Fluctuation of temperature during the past 3,000 years.

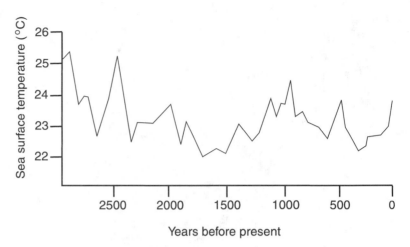

Years before present

Weather-Wise

The fifteenth through nineteenth centuries were part of the famous "Little Ice Age." Although the winters were colder than modern winters, the actual average temperature difference from today was no more than a few degrees.

Weather-Wise

The Anasazi people in the western United States had an economy centered around corn farming and built cliff dwellings. Those dwellings were abandoned by 1300.

Actually, by as early as A.D. 1200, the weather showed increased fluctuations. In western Europe, floods and droughts occurred. Some winters were extremely cold, while others were extremely warm. During the fourteenth century, major famines occurred. By the fifteenth century, the cooling trend became very well-defined and that had a global impact. Glaciers began to expand; winters were long and hard while summers were short. The vineyards in England disappeared and farming became very difficult in northern latitudes.

The accounts of weather during the colonial period are legend, with major harbors freezing and snow that was several feet deep. The year 1816 became known as the "year of no summer." Frost and freeze occurred during every month in New England. Snow fell as far south as Connecticut during June. Famine and crop failure were widespread. The westward migration occurred at that time. But those with "Ohio Fever" found the weather in Ohio to be just as harsh. In Europe, a poor wheat crop accompanied other crop losses, and famine was common.

The Climate of the Twentieth Century

The figure on the next page shows the fluctuation of average temperatures through the twentieth century. After the Little Ice Age, the weather seemed determined to make up for lost ground. The temperature began to rise in the late 1800s. During the first four decades of the twentieth century, the temperature increased a total of 0.5 degree C or 1 degree F. Then, from the 1940s to the 1960s, a definite cooling occurred. People were writing ice-age disaster novels at that time. But since the late 1970s, the temperature has warmed to its highest levels of the century—and close to the highest levels of the past 10,000 years.

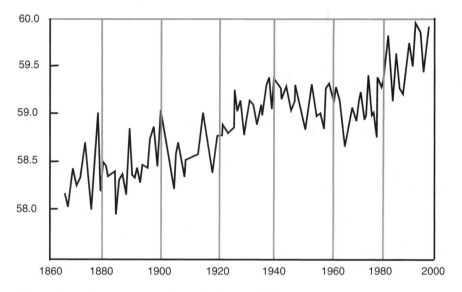

Fluctuation of temperature through the twentieth century.

The next matter for us to explore is the causes of all these changes. Stay tuned.

The Least You Need to Know

➤ Radioactivity is used to date ancient climates.

➤ Climates have changed frequently and dramatically during the geologic past.

➤ Our current position within geologic time places us in an overall cold period, although we are currently warming.

➤ The colonial period, up to the late 1800s, was extremely cold with great hardship.

➤ The twentieth century has delivered some of the warmest temperatures of the past several thousands of years.

LIGHTS-
CAMERA...

Chapter 19

Making the Change Happen

In This Chapter

➤ Factors for climate change

➤ The importance of the sun

➤ The role of Earth changes in climate

➤ The importance of the greenhouse effect for life

➤ Greenhouse contribution to twentieth-century climate change

---

Theories on glaciation and climate change are almost too numerous to list. Every climatologist and geophysicist has a favorite, or even a list of favorites. If weather forecasting is tough, climate prediction is even tougher. The variables are numerous. The Sun, the earth and its position with respect to the Sun, and those greenhouse gases all contribute to the climate that we experience. And this is just a partial list.

What's the Problem with Understanding Climate Change?

The atmosphere is complicated, and as we know, its behavior is closely linked to changes taking place within the ocean as well as on the earth. The interactions are almost infinite, and none are that well understood. Constant feedback mechanisms come into action. For example, if a greenhouse gas such as carbon dioxide increases, a warming may occur. That warming creates more evaporation, which puts more water vapor into the air. Water vapor is an even more powerful heat absorber. So the atmosphere heats up even more, and that causes more evaporation, which traps even more heat. This is a positive feedback, and it would lead to a runaway warming of the atmosphere.

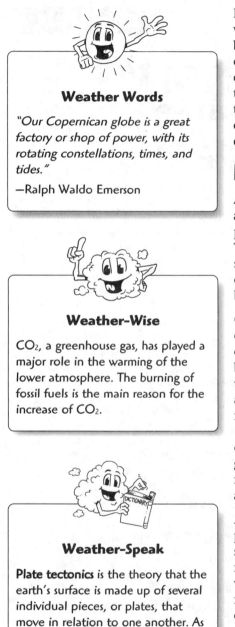

Weather Words

"Our Copernican globe is a great factory or shop of power, with its rotating constellations, times, and tides."

—Ralph Waldo Emerson

Weather-Wise

CO_2, a greenhouse gas, has played a major role in the warming of the lower atmosphere. The burning of fossil fuels is the main reason for the increase of CO_2.

Weather-Speak

Plate tectonics is the theory that the earth's surface is made up of several individual pieces, or plates, that move in relation to one another. As the plates move, the continents also move. The theory of continental drift has been absorbed by the theory of plate tectonics.

But there are also negative feedbacks. The increased water vapor could lead to more clouds, which would block incoming radiation, and that would serve as a check on the runaway warming. And this is only one complicated example. In addition, we don't understand the processes of evaporation and condensation enough to even develop a confident judgment. The theories on climate change are open to plenty of criticism and debate.

Plate Tectonics: Get My Drift?

Amazingly, fossils and land features give evidence of ice-age conditions existing some 250 million years ago in present-day Africa, Australia, South America, and India. These equatorial locations were once cold enough to support glaciers. Likewise, there is evidence of tropical climates in now-frozen Antarctica. There had to be some big changes in weather.

One theory that would account for these rare and extreme climate upheavals is centered on the idea of continental drift, now called *plate tectonics*. The earth beneath our feet is in motion. The concept is based on the principle that the earth's continents are shifting around on these crustal plates. The concept was first put forward by a German meteorologist, Alfred Wegener, in 1912. He proposed that a super continent, Pangea, once existed (see the figure on the next page). The theory goes that about 200 million years ago, this supercontinent began to break and the pieces drifted apart. Eventually, the continents drifted to their current positions.

Although the earth is rock-solid, the extremely high pressures and temperatures that develop beneath the surface cause the layers to turn plastic-like, and some melting occurs. Then the crust begins to move as convective currents develop from below—just like the motion of water being heated on the stove. These currents come up toward the surface, spread out or diverge, and this exerts pressure on the plates to drift apart. They actually drift apart an average of two inches per year. In other regions, plates may converge, while in others, they may slip past each other.

Pangea—the super continent.

Evidence of these drifting plates can be seen in how South America and Africa once fit together, as shown in the following figure. The concept of plate tectonics goes a long way in describing changes that occurred 200 million years ago. Tropical climates of today could easily have been positioned in a colder latitude during the distant past. Also, the position and shape of ancient continental masses would influence ocean currents, and that would impact climate.

Shifting continental masses.

It sounds interesting, still, there is much more to the climate change story. After all, plate tectonics is something that takes millions of years to occur in a big way. It might explain the ice-age conditions of 200 million years ago, but what about the many glacial advances and recessions that have occurred on smaller time scales, such as during the Pleistocene epoch, during the past 2 million years?

Changes in Earth's Orbit

Around 1930, a Serbian scientist named Milatin Milankovitch came up with a unique way of explaining climate changes within a time frame of 10,000 to 100,000 years. The sun is responsible for the energy received by the earth, but the earth's position with respect to the sun is constantly changing, and Milankovitch proposed that these changes correspond to major climate shifts. His theory was initially accepted, but later rejected. But because of recent examination of deep-sea cores, his theory is being embraced once again.

Eccentricity of Earth's Orbit

Although the earth moves around the Sun, it doesn't carve out an exact circular path. The path is like a squished circle, or an ellipse, which causes the earth to be closer to the Sun at some times of the year than others. If the path were circular, there would be no difference in distance throughout the year. The *eccentricity* is a function of that elliptic shape. During periods of low eccentricity, the path is more circular, and the differences of solar energy received at the top of the atmosphere are smaller than during periods of high eccentricity.

For example, currently the earth is closest to the Sun in January and farthest in July. But that difference in distance is relatively slight—a few million miles—and the path is one of lower eccentricity. The difference in energy received between the far point and the close point is just 3 percent. But when the eccentricity is high, the difference is as much as 20 percent, and that can have a strong impact on climate.

The change from a highly elliptical orbit to a circular one, and back to elliptical again, takes about 100,000 years. Interestingly, ice sheets during the Pleistocene epoch have peaked about every 100,000 years. At the moment, the earth is heading in the direction of maximum eccentricity—heading toward a time when a 20 percent reduction of incoming solar radiation will occur. In other words, we're heading for a major ice sheet advance. But it will not reach that full elliptic shape for another 40,000 years. The next figure shows the orbital variation.

Weather-Speak

Eccentricity relates to the shape of the earth's orbit as it revolves around the Sun. More elliptically-shaped orbits will have a higher eccentricity than circular-shaped orbits.

Orbital variations of Earth.

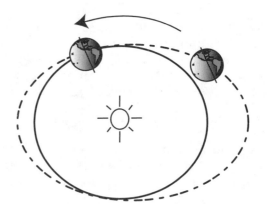

The Wobbling Earth

The earth doesn't just revolve around the Sun, it also rotates on its axis. That rotation causes day and night, and according to Milankovitch, might impact climate. Here's the idea: Just as a spinning top wobbles, so too does the earth. Right now, the earth has wobbled in such a way that its axis is pointed toward the North Star, Polaris. By about A.D. 14,000, it will be pointing toward Vega, which will be the new North Star. Then, in another 12,000 years or so, it will be pointing toward Polaris again. The tilted angle of the earth's axis hasn't changed in this case, it just points in different directions as the earth wobbles.

This wobbling process is called *precession*, and is currently responsible for the earth being closer to the Sun in January. In the year 14,000, we'll be closer to the Sun in July. Northern Hemisphere winters will be much more severe. The following figure shows the precession.

Precession of Earth.

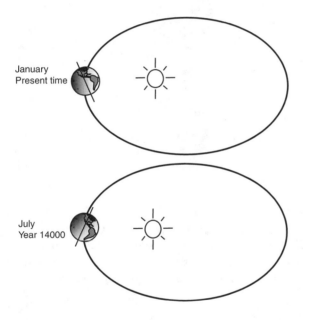

The Tilted Earth

Besides wobbling and being eccentric, the earth is tilted. The leaning tower of the earth's axis shifts between 22.5 degrees and 24.5 degrees. That is called Earth's *obliqueness,* or obliquity. This obliquity is now 23.5 degrees, as shown in the figure on the following page. When this tilt is less, seasonal variations are less, and the theory holds that glaciers will have a better chance for expanding. The summers will be cooler. But when the

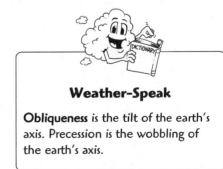

Weather-Speak

Obliqueness is the tilt of the earth's axis. Precession is the wobbling of the earth's axis.

obliquity reaches 24.5 degrees, the contrast between summer and winter will be large. The warmer summers will allow for more melting of the northern snow packs. A complete cycle from low obliquity to high and back to low again takes about 41,000 years.

Earth's tilt or obliqueness.

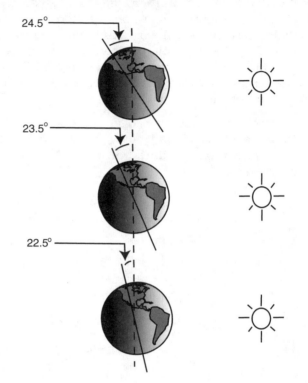

While the huge glacial ice sheets appear every 100,000 years, smaller ice advances appear in intervals of 41,000 years and 23,000 years. The timing of these "shorter-term" events matches up with the timing of the tilt and wobble. These are interesting correlations with a scientific basis, but the complexity of the climate-change problem remains huge, and there could be numerous other factors forcing change.

Changes in Solar Output

While the Milankovitch concept is based on Earth's position with respect to the Sun, a large school of climate-change thinking focuses on fluctuation of solar output. The old assumption that the amount of solar energy emitted is constant seems to have withered. The solar constant really isn't constant at all.

The Sun is very active. It is a gas, and it is in constant motion and turmoil. During especially active periods, an assortment of solar features appears. There are cloud-like structures draped or arched over the Sun surface called *prominences*. Then there are *solar flares,* bursts of high-energy particles away from the Sun. On Earth, these can disrupt communication systems, and cause the northern or southern lights, aurora borealis and aurora australis, respectively.

Also, during these highly energized times, *sunspots* appear, which are relatively cooler regions on the solar surface that appear as little blotches. You can observe sunspots by projecting the Sun's image onto a screen (see the following figure). By the way, sunspots aren't exactly cool; they are just 1,000 to 2,000 degrees cooler than the surroundings, which range from 10,000 degrees to 1 million degrees.

Sunspots have been observed for hundreds of years, and Galileo himself did extensive studies on them. Over the centuries, observations have shown that the number of sunspots on the solar disk varies according to an approximate 11-year cycle. Every 11 years or so, the Sun seems to have a bad case of acne, and sunspots break out all over. Then, midway in the cycle, many of the blotches clear up.

Weather-Speak

Sunspots are cooler, relatively dark areas found on the surface of the Sun. They are associated with solar disturbances, such as solar flares.

Viewing sunspots.

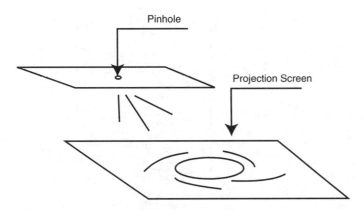

Because the Sun is a big deal in the scheme of meteorology, people have tried for decades to correlate sunspot activity with weather and climate change. But the problem has always been explaining how solar activity influences the weather. It should, but by how much? The scientific, objective link has not been identified. Still, some interesting correlations have been found.

Weather-Watch

Never look directly at the Sun to find sunspots. The direct contact with radiation will seriously damage your eyes.

The next figure shows the variations of sunspots since the 1600s. Notice the minimum between 1645 and about 1715. This was discovered by a British astronomer, E. W. Maunder, and it is called the *Maunder minimum*. It turns out that this was a very cold period around the entire world. This was the coldest period of the Little Ice Age (which we discussed in the previous chapter). Other striking minima occurred early and again late in the 1800s. Those were cold periods, too. The Year of No Summer occurred in 1816, and very snowy winters were part of the 1880s. The Blizzard of 1888 took place during that minimum.

Sunspot variations.

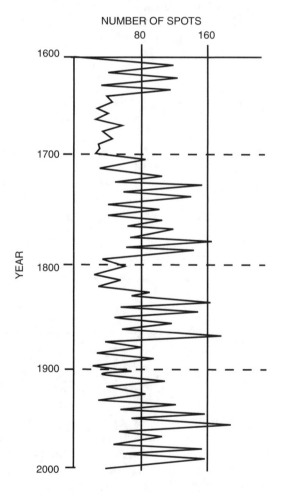

In addition to the simple 11-year sunspot cycle, there seems to be a longer 22-year magnetic cycle. The Sun's magnetic field reverses every 11 years, and returns to its original orientation every 22 years. The shifts occur during the sunspot maxima, when sunspots are at a peak. Some researchers have tried to correlate a 20-year drought cycle in the central part of the United States with the 22-year magnetic cycle.

This is getting complicated, but suffice it to say that the energy output of the Sun changes during high sunspot activity. The Sun is actually brighter during these periods. This has been known since the 1970s, when satellites were first used to study the Sun directly, outside Earth's obscuring atmosphere. Although sunspots are cooler regions, they occur when the Sun is more energetic, so overall, the Sun is brighter and emitting more energy during sunspot periods. Because the earth receives more energy, the weather should be influenced in the warmer direction. During extended periods of high or low sunspot activity, climate could undergo change.

But not everyone is convinced. The energy output changes by a fraction of a percent during the solar cycle, and that may not be enough to directly impact world temperature. Yet, other computer models suggest a change of as little as 0.5 percent over a century will generate a 1 degree F change in average temperature. That is approximately the change in temperature that has occurred during the twentieth century.

Along those lines, when solar output is graphed along with average temperature, something interesting shows up, as you can see in the following figure. Notice how the fluctuations of temperature fit a pattern of solar activity. Could the Sun be the reason for the climate change of the twentieth century? We'll revisit this climate change in Chapter 20.

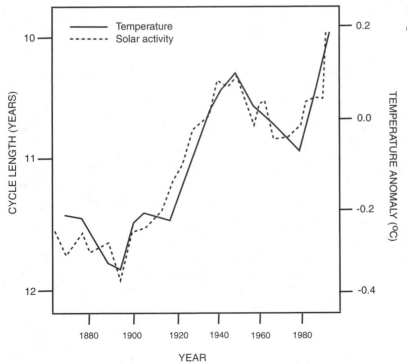

Temperature variation and changes of solar output.

Volcanism

There seems to be little doubt that volcanoes have had an important impact on global weather. Although the changes brought on by a single eruption may be temporary, periods of high volcanic activity around the world could impact climate, or at least serve as a trigger for change.

Braving the Elements

During the summer of 1816, the "Year Without a Summer," Mary Shelley was often confined to the house because of incessant rain. She and her companions—her husband poet Percy Shelley, and their friends Lord Byron and Dr. John Polidori, passed the time away by writing ghost stories. Mary, also inspired by a dream, penned the famous tale *Frankenstein*.

In 1815, Mount Tambora in Indonesia erupted and sent ash and gases into the high atmosphere. In 1816, the Year of No Summer occurred. Was that a coincidence? Then, in 1882, Krakatoa exploded, and it may not be a coincidence that the 1880s were quite cold, with the biggest blizzard of all time in the northeastern United States occurring at the end of that decade.

Then, in the early 1990s, one of the most powerful eruptions of the twentieth century took place in the Philippines. Mount Pinatubo, 55 miles north of Manila, began to erupt on June 9, 1991. Over 400 people were killed as lava poured down the mountainside and ash buried nearby towns. Rainstorms only worsened the situation. U.S. military bases were damaged. Following the eruption, the average world temperature dropped by 1 degree F, and the average Northern Hemisphere temperature fell by 1.5 degrees. The winter of 1992–93 turned out to be a snowy one, with the famous "Storm of the Century" occurring in March 1993. This cool-down took place at a time when the climate was in a generally very warm phase, and that made it remarkable.

These volcanic eruptions have some features in common. They were very powerful and managed to send ash and gas well into the stratosphere. In addition, they were all big sulfur emitters. The sulfur combines with water vapor to form sulfuric acid particles, and because they are sent into the stable stratosphere, they can float around for months. Their presence forms a haze in the stratosphere and reflects incoming sunlight. The reduced levels of sunlight could be responsible for the drop in global temperature.

But not all big sulfurous eruptions have been linked to world-wide temperature drops. In April 1982, El Chichon erupted in Mexico, one of the biggest sulfur spewers of the twentieth century. This volcano was followed by some record cold in the United States during December 1983, but record warmth also occurred in Europe during the same month. The picture was mixed, and did not cause an expected 1 degree drop in global temperature.

The failure of El Chichon to bring about the unified cooling might be related to the occurrence of a strong El Niño in 1982–83. That could have created a warm enough component to offset the volcano. All of this goes to show how complex the climate thing can become. There are many players in the game and they are not all moving the ball in the same direction.

And just to underscore the complexity, remember the Maunder minimum, when the sunspot number was low? That was in the 1700s, the deep dark depths of the Little Ice Age. Well, ice-core analysis from Greenland and Antarctica shows a high level of sulfur particles and acid-ice during that same period. That would go along with increased volcanism. So, sunspot minima may not stand alone as the cause for cooling during that time. A large eruption did occur during this cold period, and it was associated with the Laki volcano in southern Iceland. The volcano erupted during April 1783. It erupted for eight months, giving off an estimated $4^{1}/_{2}$ cubic miles of lava. Famine and the deaths of nearly 10,000 people followed. An English naturalist of that time, Gilbert White, described the summer sky of 1783: "A peculiar haze, or smokey fog unlike anything known within the memory of men."

One last note about volcanism: The eruption must be sulfurous and powerful enough to send gases into the stratosphere in order for global weather changes to occur. Mount St. Helens in Washington erupted on May 18, 1980, and even though some local cooling seemed to occur, there was little or no global impact. This is because Mount St. Helens erupted with mostly ash, and ash can settle out of the atmosphere relatively quickly.

Carbon Dioxide and the Greenhouse Effect

In Chapter 14, we looked at heat budgets and introduced the greenhouse effect. A figure in that chapter showed the different gases that absorb and trap long-wave heat radiation that is given off the earth's surface. Gases such as water vapor, carbon dioxide, and methane may be invisible to incoming short-wave radiation from the Sun, but after that radiation is absorbed by the earth, the picture changes. The absorption creates heat, which is given off as long-wave radiation. The greenhouse

Weather-Wise

In 1896, Svante Arrhenius, a Swedish chemist, first raised the issue of global warming and the greenhouse effect. He realized that burning coal would increase the carbon dioxide in the air and lead to an increase in the temperature of the earth.

gases are no longer willing to let those long waves go, and the heat is trapped in the lower atmosphere. The following figure shows the greenhouse effect in full action. Those gases behave just like a glass roof of a greenhouse.

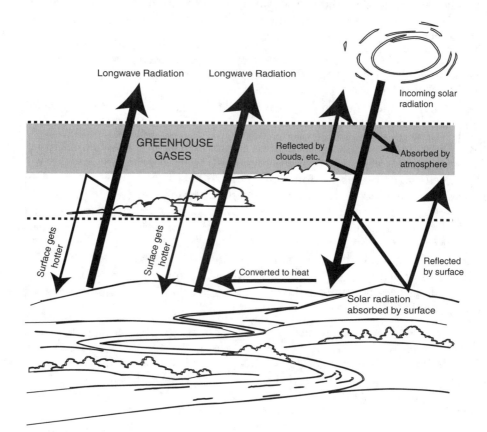

The Greenhouse Effect.

Without greenhouse gases, the earth's average temperature would be about 60 degrees lower than it is currently. The average world temperature would range from 0 to 5 degrees above zero. That would be fierce, and we could forget about life as we know it. So, the greenhouse effect is a very good and necessary part of our environment.

Because of the importance of the greenhouse effect, many scientists expect modifications to the greenhouse process will cause dramatic weather changes. If carbon dioxide levels fluctuate, then even climate could change. The figure on the next page shows the change of carbon dioxide through the ages graphed against the change of temperature. Pretty impressive, isn't it? You'd think we had a slam-dunk here. The temperature goes up, and so do the levels of carbon dioxide. It's one of those impressive correlations that does have some underlying scientific link going for it. The dramatic increase in carbon-dioxide levels shown in recent years is tied to fossil-fuel burning.

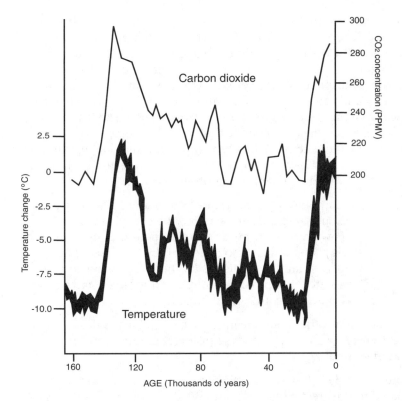

Variation of carbon dioxide and temperature.

There is really no controversy about the presence and importance of the greenhouse effect, but the exact nature of climate change brought about by specific changes in greenhouse gases is up for grabs. That's the basis of the great climate debate going on today.

First and foremost, the atmospheric engine has so many variables that it's impossible to find exactly the right set that will deliver the observed response at all times. There probably is no magic climate bullet, but rather, during any given day or century, the earth is being peppered by an array of forces, each with its own assortment of components that play in an infinite number of directions.

For example, just staying with the greenhouse gases, one could argue that carbon dioxide, which consists of only .03 percent of the atmosphere, is far less effective a greenhouse gas than water vapor, which is about 10 times more abundant and absorbs 5 times as much radiation as all greenhouse gases combined. But the entire concept of carbon-dioxide warming hinges on a positive-feedback concept, whereby a slight increase in temperature brought about by increased carbon dioxide causes more evaporation, which places more water vapor into the atmosphere—and that does much of the work.

Still, will the increased water vapor cause more clouds, which will have a negative effect on warming by reflecting incoming radiation?

251

And going back to the impressive correlation that we saw in the previous figure, could the change in carbon dioxide levels result from the increase in temperature, rather than the other way around? The oceans turn out to be a great reservoir of carbon dioxide, and if the temperature of the water increases, it will be easier for carbon dioxide to escape into the atmosphere. At higher temperatures, the gases in the water move around more rapidly and can escape into the atmosphere. So, maybe something other than carbon dioxide changes created the temperature change, and it was this temperature change that forced the carbon dioxide fluctuation. Also, once the carbon dioxide increased, it could have enhanced the temperature change that was already happening for other reasons.

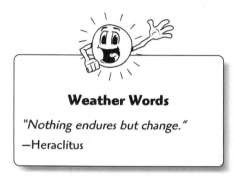

Weather Words

"Nothing endures but change."

—Heraclitus

Carbon dioxide and water vapor aren't the only greenhouse gases. Methane is very powerful: One flatulent cow gives off as much as a half-pound of methane each day. Methane is also generated by the breakdown of plant materials. This gas has been increasing at a rate of 1 percent each year, and it's a far more effective greenhouse gas than carbon dioxide.

Laughing gas, nitrous oxide, is another good greenhouse gas, and it has been increasing at a rate of 1 percent every four years. And let's not forget chlorofluorocarbons, which also can serve as greenhouse gases.

And we've only explored the tip of the receding glacier. In the next chapter we'll sort out the arguments related to the great climate debate. We'll be objective—try not to take sides, at least not at first.

But for now, let's just say that there are no easy answers or solutions. The Sun plays a key role, and the earth's positioning is important, too. Natural earth processes are important as well. No single feature has yet been isolated to prove without doubt that it is "Climate Changer Number One." We're looking at a composite of influences that act on different scales and in different time frames.

The Least You Need to Know

➤ Numerous factors contribute to climate change.

➤ Continental drift can bring about change in the time frame of 100,000 to a million years.

➤ Changes in earth's orbit and axis of rotation can bring about change in the range of 1,000 to 100,000 years.

➤ Fluctuation in solar energy may be responsible for changes in the time frame of 10 to 1,000 years.

➤ Volcanism causes important short-term changes.

➤ The greenhouse effect is alive and well but the subject of a complex debate.

Chapter 20

The Greenhouse Wars

In This Chapter

➤ The warring factions in the greenhouse debate

➤ Limits to our knowledge

➤ Possible impacts of greenhouse warming

➤ Determination of climate change

➤ Courses for action

By now you must be able to appreciate the complexity of the climate-change issue. It's likely that human activity plays a role in changing climates, but to what degree and to what consequence? Unfortunately, the question has become politicized, and the policymakers who need to sort out the truth from the inconsistencies don't always get an unbiased, objective view. Let's try to make some sense out of the whole issue.

The Players

In one of the greatest debates of all time, two distinct factions are pitted against each other. On one side are the scientists who believe with as much objectivity as possible that we are heading for a series of truly great catastrophes because of greenhouse emissions. Their interpretation of data has convinced many policymakers that the time to act is now, if not yesterday.

Because of the concern, in 1988 the United Nations established the Intergovernmental Panel on Climate Change (IPCC). Through the *IPCC*, more than 2,000 scientists from over 150 countries have assessed the information and have looked into the environmental and economic effects of the observed and projected change. Through the

1990s, the IPCC issued a series of climate assessments, and officially concluded that "the balance of evidence suggests that there is a discernible human influence on global climate." The panel concluded that world climate has warmed an average of 1 degree F, and another 2- to 6.5-degree warming is expected during the next 100 years. The rate of warming is claimed to be greater than anything of the past 10,000 years.

On the other side, too, are some very sincere scientists who have a more cautious view of human intervention in climate change. These scientists might seem outnumbered if you follow the headlines and news reports, but useful scientific principles have never been democratically derived. This group claims we should keep an open mind because all the facts aren't in, and most importantly, we really can't predict what we don't understand. Opinion polls shouldn't drive science, but rather information and reasoning.

This group feels that the jury is still out, and they have data to back up their viewpoint. The group consists of scientists from a variety of universities, some of whom are accused of being biased because their financial support comes from coal and oil companies. But that is a political jab, not a scientific one, so let's stick with the science.

Weather-Speak

The **IPCC,** or the Intergovernmental Panel on Climate Change, was established by the United Nations in 1988. It is composed of many of the world's leading atmospheric scientists.

Have We Really Warmed?

The scientists in this debate can't even agree on whether our climate has significantly warmed since the end of the nineteenth century. If there is no agreement there, then we really do have problems. The figure on the next page shows the temperature trend based on IPCC data. Since the pre-industrial era, carbon dioxide concentrations have increased 30 percent, methane has doubled, and nitrous oxide has increased 15 percent. These greenhouse gases are thought to have trapped enough heat to contribute significantly to that temperature change. At the same time, 11 of the warmest years of the twentieth century have occurred since 1980. As we noted earlier, overall, global average temperature has increased 1 degree F during the twentieth century.

Amazingly, even if the IPCC data seem to support a warming pattern, many other scientists have data that dispute it. On one hand, we have reports of 12 of the warmest years occurring since 1980, and on the other, some data will show that this period has actually been cooling. How confusing is that?

Satellites have monitored temperatures in the troposphere since 1979. The figure on page 256 shows this trend. Although there have been plenty of ups and downs, the world-wide average temperature has slightly decreased from 1979. Yet, the trend from ground-based stations is just the opposite. How can that be?

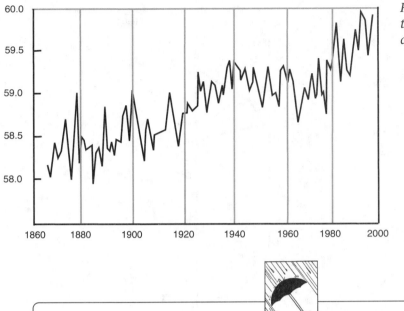

Fluctuation of temperatures through the twentieth century.

Braving the Elements

A new study shows that carbon dioxide, that greenhouse gas, seems to be sinking into the ground across North America. It seems that the carbon dioxide level should increase from west to east across North America, because of the west to east flow in the atmosphere. That flow should cause carbon dioxide to accumulate in eastern areas. But, instead, the study shows the carbon dioxide decreasing. There seems to be enhanced absorption by the ground, perhaps because of the increase in plants and vegetation on abandoned farm land.

The satellite data shows what occurs through the lower troposphere, not just at the ground. The two data sets are not the same. You would think that the two sets of data would be in phase, but there are some strange differences. In the figure on page 257 you can see the temperature trend for satellite and ground-based stations at different latitudes. In mid-latitudes, where most scientists live and where the data is abundant, the temperature trend is upward for both satellite and ground stations. But for the rest of the world, the differences are striking and large. Near the equator, the negative satellite trend is the mirror image of the positive ground-station trend. Maybe the satellite data is misleading.

*Temperature trends from
satellite observations.*

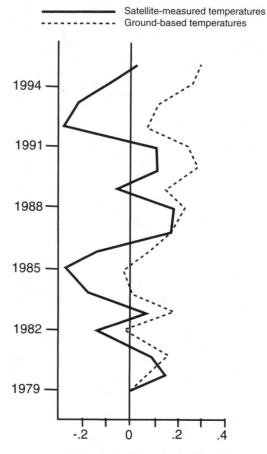

Temperature Departures (°C)

Criticism of the satellite data focuses on its short record. Fifteen years of data might simply not be enough to conclude anything, especially if short-term events such as volcano eruptions and strong El Niño oscillations take place within the period. For example, Mount Pinatubo's eruption in 1991 sent a huge volume of sulfur particles and aerosols into the high atmosphere, creating a cooling that might be more striking on the satellite data than on ground-based data.

But other factors could account for the discrepancies. Much of the greenhouse warming is derived from water-vapor absorption, not carbon-dioxide absorption. The assumption has been that a slight increase in temperature from carbon-dioxide absorption will force more water to evaporate into the atmosphere, and that water-vapor absorption really does the work. But we really don't have a good handle on how water vapor behaves. It could be unevenly distributed in the lowest layers of the atmosphere. So the satellite trends wouldn't be affected as much by the positive feedback of the water vapor.

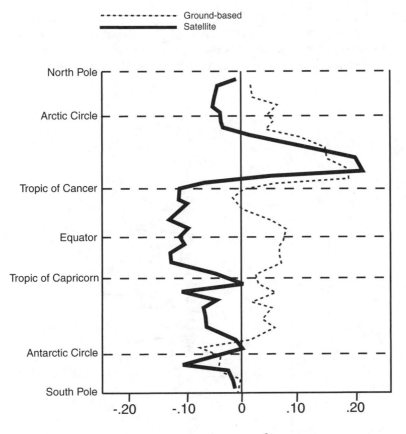

Temperature trends at different latitudes.

The surface data could also be misleading. This information comes from weather stations set up for weather purposes, not climate purposes. For the most part, they were set up where people live and work—in, or at least adjacent to, populated areas, where the weather is warmer by several degrees. Overall, urban warming—the *urban heat island* effect—is enough to influence snowfall patterns as well as the intensity of precipitation and thunderstorms; locations downwind of urban areas receive more thunderstorms than those on the opposite side of the city. This demonstrates a striking human influence on climate, but it's a localized change, and the feeling of some IPCC critics is that the local climate data used to show a warming has been contaminated by this urban heat island effect. The world-wide temperature isn't as warm as it might seem from the given data set.

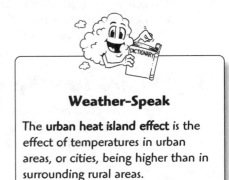

Weather-Speak

The **urban heat island effect** is the effect of temperatures in urban areas, or cities, being higher than in surrounding rural areas.

257

The following figure shows a temperature trend derived from ground-based stations in the United States after filtering out the urban heat island effect. Look at that! It shows that the warmest part of the twentieth century has really been around 1940, and since then, the temperature has been following a negative trend. A similar trend has been shown in Europe, too.

Temperature variations outside urban areas in the United States.

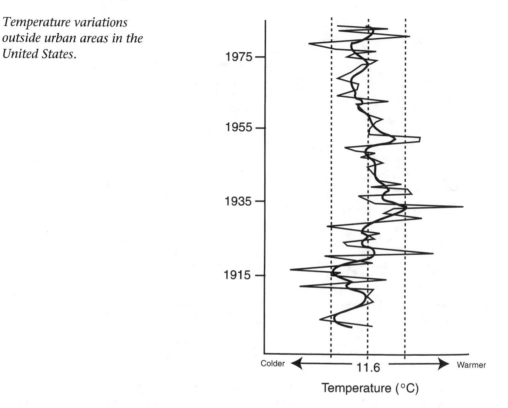

So, are we warming? That is the conventional wisdom. But there is data showing the possibility of world-wide temperatures actually lowering. Critics of the IPCC claim that standard instruments may not be properly placed to indicate global climate change. At the same time, satellite data seems to counter the basic impression that warming is happening.

So, Where Are We Going?

If there isn't even an agreement on whether the world is warming, how can there be agreement on anything else, including future trends? As heated—no pun intended—as the argument might be on past temperature patterns, future temperature patterns are even more hotly disputed.

The panel of international scientists concludes that the forced warming by greenhouse gases will cause a global surface temperature increase of 1.8 to 6.3 degrees F by 2100.

The warming is based on the projected increase of greenhouse gases and their heat-trapping abilities. For example, during the 1990s, world-wide emissions of carbon dioxide delivered 6 gigatons of carbons (Gtc) per year. That's six billion tons. By 2025, world emissions are projected to range from 8 to 15 Gtc per year.

That's quite a range, and the uncertainty is based on world demographics, economics, policy, and technological advances. By 2100, the uncertainties expand and the projected range goes from 5 to 36 Gtc per year. A frequently used projection has the carbon-dioxide level more than doubling the pre-industrial concentration by 2100. That early carbon-dioxide concentration was 280 parts per million (ppm). It's expected to be around 700 ppm by 2100. During the 1940s, the carbon-dioxide level exceeded anything that was present for at least 160,000 years. By the year 2100, the projected concentration will exceed anything of the past 50 million years.

What does such an increase mean in terms of climate change? Don't forget that carbon dioxide is almost a trace gas in the atmosphere with a concentration of .035 percent. So what if it doubles?

Weather-Watch

Some scientists warn that the enhanced, human-induced greenhouse effect could cause global temperature changes of a few degrees—this could melt ice caps, raise sea levels, flood coastlines, and alter the shape of continents.

Plenty, says the IPCC. Land areas will warm more than ocean areas, and northern latitudes will warm more effectively than areas near the equator. Also, the nights will be more affected than daylight hours because the normal nightly heat loss will be reduced by the blanket of greenhouse gases. This doubling of carbon dioxide is expected to cause an increase in U.S. temperature of 5–10 degrees F. If the levels were to increase four-fold, the estimated increase in U.S. temperature would range from 15 to 20 degrees.

The projected warming is based on computer models that take into account the many variables that make the atmosphere click. Computers solve basic equations, and those solutions are compared to history to see if the models have properly accounted for past trends. The models are adjusted based on the climate testing of the past, and then geared up to predict the climate for the next 20, 50, or 100 years. It sounds straightforward enough, but these models always attract criticism.

First and foremost, our understanding of the atmosphere is hampered in some very fundamental areas. While we know why it rains, the entire process of condensation, cloud formation, and precipitation is not adequately understood. There are enough holes in our knowledge that small errors that show up in the predictive time frame of hours or days are certainly magnified over months, years, and decades. Also, the impact of the precipitation process on heating is very complex. How effective is water vapor in the overall heating of the atmosphere? Sure, it's an effective greenhouse gas, but do clouds form and shade out incoming radiation? That would force a cooling.

Also, is the water vapor mainly confined to the lower atmosphere, and how effectively does rainfall deplete the amount of water vapor present? How much rainfall will really occur? And what about pollutants like sulfates and aerosols? These can shade the earth and reflect incoming radiation.

The computer models predict a warming twice as great as what has been observed since the late 1800s. Could the actual temperature have been lower because of these pollutants? And if these pollutants are so important, how much will they be reduced in coming decades?

These are examples of the limits to our knowledge, but there are additional difficulties with the engineering of the computer models themselves. As sophisticated as computers have become, they're still not powerful enough to deal with all the scales of atmospheric motions. Weather fronts and lows and highs can be tackled, even if the knowledge of the processes is somewhat flawed. But scales involved with thunderstorms down to small turbulent twists and turns can only be included collectively. In the computer models, the thunderstorms are clustered together and a parameter is placed into the equations to account for their contribution. Individual thunderstorms just can't be handled separately.

Also, because the calculations are carried out over decades and centuries, the data points can't be too numerous. Currently, the spacing of each data point is 300 kilometers, or about 260 miles. There would just be too many calculations to come in much tighter. The computer run would take too much time. A decade would come and go before the computer finished its forecast!

More powerful machines in the future will reduce some of the mechanical problems of climate projection, but that still leaves us with lapses in understanding the overall climate process and the contribution of small-scale but important elements. Let's face it. If computers have problems predicting tomorrow's weather, they certainly will draw skepticism when they try to project 100 years into the future.

And there are additional, natural changes taking place in the environment, such as changes of incoming radiation from the Sun. There is the unknown of atmospheric and ocean interactions.

So, given all the uncertainties and limitations, any long-range climate projection is bound to generate plenty of heat.

What If We Really Do Warm Up?

If we can't agree on where we've been or where we're going, don't expect much agreement here, either. Many are convinced that a doubling of carbon dioxide by 2100 will have dire consequences. Others conclude that the projected temperature change would actually be beneficial.

The Negatives of Greenhouse Warming

Scientists with the IPCC predict serious consequences from the steady increase of greenhouse gases. The change will impact health in a number of ways. The increased temperature will cause additional heat waves. The heat wave of July 1995 caused the deaths of 465 people in Chicago alone. The estimate is that heat waves of this magnitude will be six times more frequent in 2100 than they are currently. The heat-stress index will increase, along with the temperature. This effective temperature derived from the humidity and the air temperature itself averages close to 85 degrees in Washington D.C. during July. The doubling of carbon dioxide is thought to be capable of sending that index up to 95 degrees. Anything over 90 indicates very oppressive weather. Heat-stress related mortality would increase.

With this increased warmth, diseases that thrive in warm climates will spread throughout the world. Malaria, yellow fever, encephalitis, and cholera will expand because of the increased range of disease-carrying organisms like mosquitoes. The warming could cause 50 to 80 million more cases of malaria each year by 2100. The warmth will help generate new breeding sites for pests.

Braving the Elements

A recent study indicates that the 1878 yellow fever epidemic in the southern United States may have been caused by the strong 1877–78 El Niño episode. Yellow fever is caused by a virus transmitted by a mosquito bite, and the mosquito population increased because of above-normal precipitation in the several months preceding the epidemic and abnormally warm conditions from late spring through summer. The rain and warmth are El Niño–related. The death toll reached 20,000 people.

In addition, the IPCC looks for a steady increase in sea level, which will make coastal areas more vulnerable to storms. By 2100, sea level is expected to increase from 6 to 37 inches. The rise in sea level is assumed to come from melting glaciers and the expansion of water itself due to heating. A 20-inch increase of sea-level would double the global population at risk of storm surges. Many low-lying areas would be inundated, even without a storm. Parts of the Maldives, Egypt, and Bangladesh would be under water. In the United States, 5,000 square miles of dry land and an additional 4,000 square miles of wetlands would be completely inundated. Much of southern Florida would flood. The Everglades has an elevation of just 12 inches above sea level. Salt water would move into the area and adversely affect the ecology. Serious economic losses would be experienced by those living along most coastal regions.

In addition to coastal flooding, inland flooding would be more widespread because of a projected trend toward heavier rainfall. It is thought that the additional warmth would feed more energy into weather systems. Storms would be bigger and more menacing. During 1993, the damage from the Mississippi River flood reached from $15 to $20 billion. Flood damage in the Pacific Northwest during the 1996–97 winter came to $3 billion. The Ohio River flood of 1997 caused $1 billion in damage. The IPCC concludes that these disasters will become even more frequent in the future.

Then there is the problem of too little rain. In regions that are normally dry, the increased warmth would create increased evaporation, which would affect agriculture, water supplies, and water quality. Water scarcity is thought to be a real problem in the future for much of the western United States, and an even worse problem for Middle Eastern and African countries. This would lead to world-wide food shortages, especially with the growth of population. Overall, the IPCC does not expect food shortages uniformly across the world, but rather, selective areas, such as developing countries, would be more affected.

Also, changes in the overall ecology could be dramatic. For example, the anticipated climate change is thought to be able to shift some North American forest species as much as 300 miles to the north. The entire climate would be making that 300-mile shift. The climate of the mid-Atlantic states would retreat northward into New England. The famous sugar maples of New England would also shift northward; that species could not survive in a warmer climate and would be lost to New England by the end of the twenty-first century.

Forest damage from fire, insects, and disease could also increase. Wetlands would decrease and change dramatically. Waterfowl could diminish. Also, all the glaciers of Glacier National Park are projected to disappear by 2030. The consequences of climate change appear to be incredibly far-reaching. Life as we know it would be adversely affected. And all with just a simple doubling of carbon dioxide by the year 2100.

But There Are Positives

As with everything else related to climate, there is an alternative view. In fact, a case has been made that greenhouse warming would be a positive, not a negative. For example, because the projected warming would impact nighttime temperatures more than daytime readings, and winter temperatures more than summer, longer frost-free growing seasons would be expected. Crop yields would actually increase, while daytime heat-stress would not necessarily increase significantly because the added warmth would occur mostly at night.

In addition, the increased level of carbon dioxide would provide more fertilization to the biosphere. Plants use carbon dioxide for growth, so forests would thrive! Also, more oxygen would return to the atmosphere. We could be breathing more easily. During the last ice age 18,000

Weather-Wise

Rising temperatures could have positive effects on some agriculture, which thrive during warm periods.

years ago, carbon-dioxide levels were about half of the current levels, and plants were on the verge of extinction.

Remember, too, that the assumption of increased floods due to global warming and droughts is far from a sure thing. Even the IPCC has said, "An enhanced greenhouse effect may lead to changes in the hydrologic cycle, such as increased evaporation, drought and precipitation," but it adds, "our ability to determine the current state of the global hydrological cycle, let alone changes in it, is hampered by inadequate spatial coverage, incomplete records, poor data quality, and short record lengths."

According to the IPCC, global precipitation increased about 1 percent during the twentieth century, the increase being mainly over land areas in the Northern Hemisphere. Rainfall has decreased in the tropics and subtropics. The overall increase in precipitation could again be a positive for crop yields, and even the IPCC projects a 20 to 30 percent increase in crop yields across North America by 2100.

The conventional assumption today is that the increased temperatures will lead to more coastal flooding because of ice-cap meltdowns and the thermal expansion of water. But even here, there is disagreement and uncertainty. For example, if the temperature warms, there will be increased evaporation from the oceans, and increased snowfall in the polar areas. The weather would always be cold enough for snow in Antarctica. So, a warming could actually lower sea level! The ice caps would expand. How do you like that?

During the twentieth century, sea level increased about seven inches. But nobody can say for sure if that increase is from a warming trend. The IPCC itself concludes that, "In total, based on models and observations, the combined range of uncertainty regarding the contributions of thermal expansion, glaciers, ice sheets, and land water storage to past sea level change is about −19 cm to +35 cm." In other words, global warming might have had a negative impact of 19 cm on sea level change during the twentieth century. The warming kept sea level down! The rise in sea level may have been caused by changes in geology rather than climatology.

So What Should We Do?

Compelling arguments can be made for global warming, but is the change just a natural bounce from the bitter cold of the little ice age, or is it something caused by human activities? The answers are simply not known. Changes in solar output may explain some of the observed warming, but even the warming itself is in dispute. Then there are the computer models limited by both technology and knowledge. And then there are the arguments that a modest warming would generally be favorable. For every pair of climatologists, there seems to be three arguments. Much more must be learned about the climate system.

But because of the complexities of the atmosphere, that knowledge isn't necessarily at hand. We may never have the answer, and those who urge an aggressive environmental approach argue that if we don't immediately act, it may be too late in the future.

Carbon dioxide is active in the atmosphere 50 to 200 years. The greenhouse gases now in the atmosphere will contribute to warming for decades, even if carbon dioxide emissions are immediately cut off.

Inaction will only worsen the situation. Growth of developing nations will feed increasing levels of greenhouse gases into the atmosphere. The IPCC pointed out that a worldwide reduction of carbon-dioxide emissions of more than 60 percent from 1990 emissions would be required just to keep the carbon-dioxide concentration of 350 ppm constant. Stabilizing the concentration at 500 ppm would require an emission reduction of 50 percent. Critics claim that such reductions would have disastrous economic consequences.

A measured control policy that can be modified along the way by open-minded policymakers might be the best path to follow. Knowledge will certainly increase during the coming years, and advances in technology could help define practical alternatives. If we find the control policy is too aggressive, we should be able to retreat. Likewise, if the policy is not aggressive enough, we should leave ourselves ways to crank it up.

And it's never idiotic to ask questions of those who are making these decisions.

The Least You Need to Know

➤ The climate change debate is heated and complex.

➤ Numerous factors, other than the burning of fossil fuels, can contribute to global warming.

➤ The amount of warming since the nineteenth century is up for debate.

➤ Dire prospects are projected by many scientists if greenhouse gas emissions are not checked.

➤ Current technology and knowledge can't predict with certainty and precision the impact of greenhouse gases on the climate.

Part 4
Now for the Real Forecast

The ultimate objective in any science is to predict. I'm constantly told by consultants that television viewers would much prefer being shown the forecast rather than the meteorology. They may have more confidence in the prediction if they feel the forecaster understands the meteorology, but really, every news director I've worked under has said, "Mel, just tell them what it's going to do." Most television weathercasts are about three minutes in length, and that's a big chunk of a commercial-filled thirty-minute newscast.

You're about to learn how to tell it all in three minutes or less. Actually, you'll learn how to find out for yourself. Weather forecasting is the ultimate challenge in meteorology. And now that we have the basics down, forecasting should be a breeze—although, at times, a turbulent and fickle one.

Chapter 21

Measuring the Atmosphere

In This Chapter

➤ Measuring and recording the temperature

➤ Checking out the pressure

➤ Observing the humidity

➤ Setting up the instruments

➤ Upper air data collection

➤ Sending the data around the world

A good prediction must begin with a set of observations. The atmosphere needs to be measured, weighed, and analyzed before we can begin to make a forecast. We've already checked out the basic weather variables in Chapter 3 and looked at how they can be measured. So, this is going to be a partial review, but we'll take a more detailed look at how weather data is collected and transmitted from one part of the world to another.

The Take on Temperature

The temperature is measured with a thermometer. No kidding! Galileo Galilei (1564–1642) is often credited with being the first to come up with this instrument. But the discovery is not without controversy. More than 2,000 years ago, Hero of Alexander designed a temperature measuring device. Galileo's contemporaries Sanctorius Sanctorius and Cornelius Drebbel also did work on thermometers. The standard version consists of a liquid enclosed in a glass. The liquid usually consists of mercury or alcohol, which expands and rises in the tube when the temperature increases, and contracts and drops when the temperature decreases.

Braving the Elements

Before Pope John Paul II visited St. Louis in January 1999, a group of nuns were given the responsibility of praying for sunshine for his two-day stay. The prayers began before his arrival, and as the arrival day approached, the official weather forecast did call for rain on the second day of the visit. But the rain never materialized. Instead, sunshine helped send temperatures up to a balmy un-Januarylike 60 degrees.

But what about temperature scales—Fahrenheit, Celsius, and all that? It's all relative. In the early 1700s in his hometown of Leipzig, Germany, G. Daniel Fahrenheit defined the *zero-point* as the lowest point the column would fall when the thermometer was immersed in a mixture of ice, water, and salt. He then assigned the number 32 to the level that the column reaches when ice melts, and that automatically made 212 degrees the point at which water boils. Now, Fahrenheit could have defined the zero-point and assigned the freezing point an infinite number of ways. The intervals are completely arbitrary. You could define the zero point to be the lowest point on the column ever reached in your hometown and go from there.

The Fahrenheit (F) scale suffers from bad press, and most countries have abandoned it—but it is a detailed scale, and one that is familiar to many. The Celsius scale is most commonly used around the world because it is a metric scale. Swedish astronomer Anders Celsius came up with this scale in the eighteenth century. On the Celsius scale, ice melts at zero degrees and water boils at 100 degrees. Because there are one hundred divisions between melting and boiling, this scale is also referred to as the centigrade scale.

In any case, because there are 180 degrees between melting and boiling on the *Fahrenheit* scale, each *Celsius* degree is $180 \div 100$ or 1.8 times larger than a Fahrenheit degree. That's why the Fahrenheit scale is more detailed. An increase of 1 degree C is equivalent to an increase of 1.8 degrees F. The conversion from degrees F to degrees C is given by a formula: degrees $F = \frac{9}{5}$ degrees $C + 32$. So, 20 degrees C would come to $\frac{9}{5}(20) + 32$, or 68 degrees F. A quick, although not precise, conversion would be to double the Celsius reading and add 32. It at least puts you in the ballpark. So, if you happen to be an American in Paris and hear that the temperature is 25

Weather-Watch

Don't put thermometers directly into the sun. The temperature reading will not be accurate. The thermometer will simply indicate radiation absorption, not air temperature.

degrees C, double it and add 32 to get the Fahrenheit equivalent (50 + 32, or 82 degrees). It's really
78 degrees, but at least you'll know how to dress
without getting out a calculator.

The most scientific temperature scale is the Kelvin
(K) scale, which also has 100 divisions between the
freezing and boiling points of water, but the zero-
point is defined as the point where all molecular
motion comes to a grinding halt. That is the absolutely coldest temperature possible, and it is called
absolute zero. British scientist Lord Kelvin defined
this scale in the nineteenth century. Here, ice melts
at 273 degrees and water boils at 373 degrees. The
temperature could never be negative on this scale,
and because of that, it's used in all mathematical
calculations where the temperature is a variable.
The first figure on the following page shows the
three scales: Fahrenheit, Celsius, and Kelvin.

In addition to standard liquid-in-glass thermometers, air temperature can be measured in more
hi-tech ways. Electrical thermometers are very
accurate. They work on the principle of the
electrical resistance of a wire often made of
platinum or nickel. The resistance increases with
increasing temperature. A meter will measure the
resistance and that reading will be set to correspond to the temperature. Along these lines,
thermistors, which are made of ceramic materials,
are used in remote sensing. These run on the same
principle of electrical resistance.

On the subject of remote sensing, satellites use
infrared instruments, which record the strength of
long-wave radiation emitted through the atmosphere. That strength is also proportional to the
temperature. We'll get to satellite measurements
later in Chapter 22.

Another popular instrument is a *thermograph,*
which measures and records the temperature on a
revolving drum (see the bottom figure on the
following page). A metal strip consisting of two
different pieces of metal provides the mechanism
for this instrument. The two metals are usually iron
and brass. One expands more than the other when

Weather-Speak

Fahrenheit (F) is a temperature scale
based on 32 degrees as the freezing
point of water and 212 degrees as the
boiling point of water at sea level.
Celsius is a temperature scale based
on 0 degrees as the freezing point of
water and 100 degrees as the boiling
point of water at sea level. **Kelvin (K)**,
also called the absolute scale, is a
temperature scale that has intervals
equivalent to the Celsius scale, but
begins at absolute zero.

Weather-Speak

Absolute zero is the point where all
molecular motion is presumed to
cease. It is the coldest possible
temperature: –273 degrees C or
–459 degrees F or 0 K.

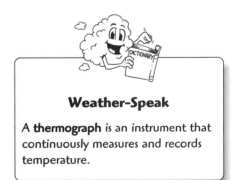

Weather-Speak

A **thermograph** is an instrument that
continuously measures and records
temperature.

269

the temperature increases, so the strip bends in one direction. Then when the temperature drops, the strip moves the other way. This bimetallic thermometer is used in thermostats. In thermographs, the motion of the strip moves an arm up or down, and a pen at the end of the arm records its position on graph paper. The paper is put on a clock-driven rotating drum so that the change of temperature with time can be seen.

Temperature scales.

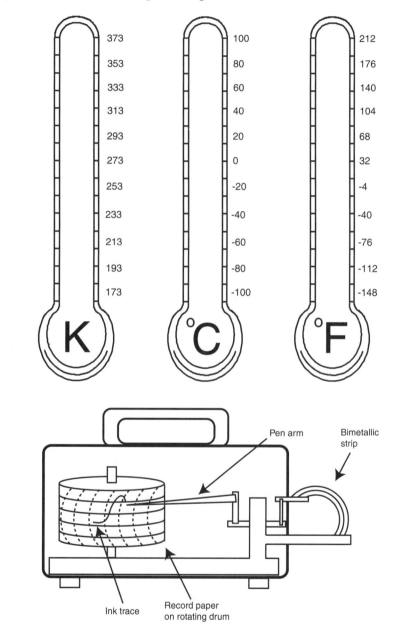

Thermograph—temperature trace.

Last but not least, some thermometers measure the maximum and minimum temperature of the day. The maximum thermometer looks like a fever thermometer—it goes up but doesn't come down, unless it is shaken. When the minimum thermometer column goes down, it drags a barbell-shaped marker along with it. But that marker goes one way—it can't go up when the temperature increases. Its position marks the lowest temperature. The minimum temperature is reset by turning the thermometer upside down until the barbell marker hits the top of the liquid column.

Is the Pressure Getting to You?

The seventeenth century was quite an age of discovery. Evangelista Torricelli, a student of Galileo, invented the first mercurial barometer. It consisted of a glass tube open at one end and closed at the other. The open end was covered and immersed into an opened container of mercury. The cover was removed, and the mercury moved up the tube, about 30 inches above the container. That height represents atmospheric pressure. The weight of the atmosphere on the surface of the mercury exerts a pressure which is then transmitted through the fluid, forcing it to rise. The greater the weight, the higher the rise. The barometric pressure seldom goes above 31 inches or drops below 29 inches. Normal sea-level pressure is 29.92 inches.

But the "inch" is really not a unit of pressure, or force per area. It is a unit of length. So, a metric unit has been defined to describe normal atmospheric pressure, called a "bar," and the instrument becomes a "barometer." Actually, normal average sea-level pressure is 1.01325 bars or 1013.25 millibars (mb). The millibar is a commonly used unit of pressure.

During the same Galileo-Toricelli era, French scientist and philosopher Blaise Pascal discovered that air pressure decreases with height, and that pressure changes at ground level at any one place can be related to daily weather changes. In his honor, the newest unit of pressure has become the hectopascal (Hpa). The pascal (Pa) is one-hundredth of a millibar. The hectopascal is one hundred pascals and is the same as the millibar. So, 1000 mb and 1000 Hpa are the same.

A two-and-a-half-foot tube is kind of awkward to keep around the house, and the need for a smaller and more practical device led to the development of the aneroid (without liquid) barometer. Instead of the expanding and shrinking of a mercury column, an expanding and contracting metal chamber does the work. Much of the air has been evacuated from the chamber, so slight changes in pressure around it cause it to respond by shrinking if the pressure increases or expanding if the pressure decreases. The metal chamber is attached to a pointer that indicates the pressure—the basic design of most barometers, including the home variety. A barograph (shown in the

Weather-Wise

The type of barometer that you are probably most familiar with, the kind you see in stores and give as presents, is the aneroid barometer. As a rule, falling pressure means deteriorating weather and rising pressure means fair or improving weather.

figure below) allows the pressure to be recorded on a rotating drum so that a time series analysis of pressure can be made. This works similar to a thermograph.

By the way, altimeters work just like barometers. Because the pressure decreases with height, these instruments are marked off in meters or feet rather than millibars or inches. The pressure drop with elevation is proportional to the change in height.

Barograph—trace of atmospheric pressure.

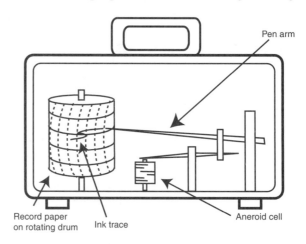

Pen arm

Record paper on rotating drum

Ink trace

Aneroid cell

The Wind in the Willows

When the atmospheric pressure varies between the horizontal points, the wind blows. As the English poet Christina Rossetti once wrote, "Who has seen the wind, neither I nor you." But that hasn't stopped us from measuring it. A wind vane is almost as old as the beginning of time. A simple pennant or flag will point in the direction from which the wind is coming. On airport runways, a cone-shaped bag opened at each end extends horizontally and points in the direction of the wind. This simple wind vane is called a windsock. Pilots can tell the wind direction as they land.

By the way, and very importantly, the wind direction is never the direction the wind is going, but rather, the direction from which the wind is coming. A northeast wind is coming from the northeast; a south, or southerly, wind blows from the south.

Okay, what about wind speed? Again, back in the seventeenth century, English physicist Robert Hooke came up with a device consisting of a plate that moved proportionally to the wind speed. The plate swung out farther in a stronger wind. That became known as a *pressure plate anemometer*.

In more recent times, rotating cups mounted on a shaft have been used for measuring wind speeds (see the

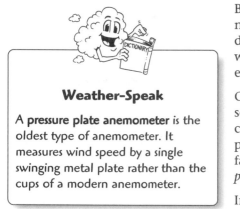

Weather-Speak

A **pressure plate anemometer** is the oldest type of anemometer. It measures wind speed by a single swinging metal plate rather than the cups of a modern anemometer.

figure below). This cup anemometer records the wind speed as the cups spin. Those rotating cups might turn some gears or generate an electrical current. The greater current indicates higher wind speeds.

Some anemometers, called *aerovanes,* look like airplane propellers. The device swings into the wind, and then the propeller blades rotate with the increasing wind speed.

Of course, something that easily beats an old rusty anemometer is the traditional Beaufort scale, which relates wind speeds to the motion of objects such as trees or water. Anemometers become inaccurate because of their constant exposure.

> **Weather-Wise**
>
> An anemometer measures wind speed, while a weather vane or wind vane measures wind direction.

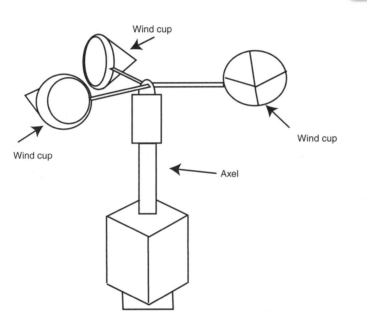

Anenometer—wind speed instrument.

It's Not the Heat, It's the Humidity

The most common instrument for measuring relative humidity is the *sling psychrometer.* It consists of two thermometers mounted next to each other. One thermometer has a wet wick attached to its bulb, and the other is dry. The wick is moistened with water at air temperature. The two thermometers are attached to a handle which is swung around. Water evaporates off the moist wick, causing a lowering of temperature on that bulb—called, for obvious reasons, the wet bulb.

Eventually, no additional water will be able to evaporate into the air. The temperature stops going downward, and that reading is called the wet bulb temperature. This is

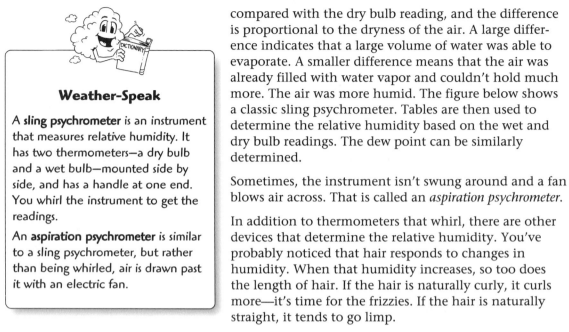

Weather-Speak

A **sling psychrometer** is an instrument that measures relative humidity. It has two thermometers—a dry bulb and a wet bulb—mounted side by side, and has a handle at one end. You whirl the instrument to get the readings.

An **aspiration psychrometer** is similar to a sling psychrometer, but rather than being whirled, air is drawn past it with an electric fan.

compared with the dry bulb reading, and the difference is proportional to the dryness of the air. A large difference indicates that a large volume of water was able to evaporate. A smaller difference means that the air was already filled with water vapor and couldn't hold much more. The air was more humid. The figure below shows a classic sling psychrometer. Tables are then used to determine the relative humidity based on the wet and dry bulb readings. The dew point can be similarly determined.

Sometimes, the instrument isn't swung around and a fan blows air across. That is called an *aspiration psychrometer*.

In addition to thermometers that whirl, there are other devices that determine the relative humidity. You've probably noticed that hair responds to changes in humidity. When that humidity increases, so too does the length of hair. If the hair is naturally curly, it curls more—it's time for the frizzies. If the hair is naturally straight, it tends to go limp.

Sling psychrometer—measuring the humidity.

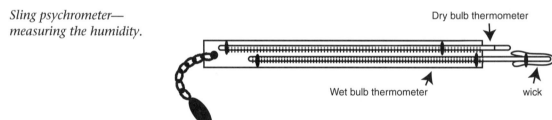

The relationship between hair length and humidity is used in an instrument called a hair hygrometer. Strands of naturally blonde hair or horse hair with oils removed are attached to a system of levers. These amplify the change in hair length, and then cause a dial to move. Sometimes the dial becomes an arm on a rotating drum, and a record of the humidity can be determined. The hair hygrometer is not as accurate as a sling psychrometer and it requires considerable calibration, especially when there are large variations in humidity.

More modern instruments are electrical and are based on the principle that electrical resistance changes for some materials when exposed to differences in moisture. One type of electric hygrometer uses carbon coating on a flat plate. The current depends on how much moisture is present on the plate. Other devices use a lithium chloride solution from which water is evaporated by the passage of an electrical current.

Measuring the Rain

Rain gauges are thought to be the most ancient weather instruments, and they're believed to have been used in India more than 2,000 years ago. A *rain gauge* is really just a cylinder that catches rain. If an inch collects in the cylinder, it means an inch of rain has fallen. It's that simple. Most standard rain gauges have a wide funnel leading into the cylinder, and are calibrated so that one-tenth of an inch of rain measures one inch when it collects inside. The funnel is 10 times the cross-sectional area of the tube. Rainfall as low as .01 inches can be measured with this instrument. Anything under .01 inches is considered a trace. This standard rain gauge is shown in the figure below.

In the more modern era, a common rain gauge is called the tipping bucket type. A bucket doesn't really tip; a pair of small receiving funnels alternate in the collection of the rain. When one fills up with water, it tips and spills out, and the other comes into place to do the collecting. These little funnels tip each time rainfall amounts to .01 inches. The tip triggers a signal that is transmitted and recorded.

Weather-Speak

A **rain gauge** is an instrument that measures the amount of rainfall at a given time interval.

Rain gauge—rainfall measurements.

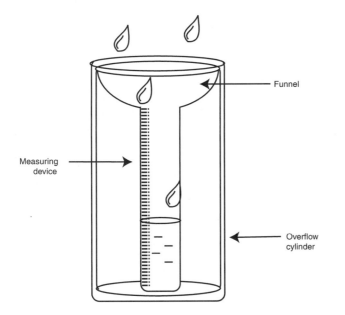

Funnel

Measuring device

Overflow cylinder

Of course, these rain gauges have a problem when the temperature drops below freezing, so the standard versions are heated for the occasion.

What about snowfall? When snow falls on these heated rain gauges, it melts and a water equivalent is determined. The recorded precipitation is always expressed in terms of rainfall or melted snow. The snow depth doesn't count—unless of course you have to shovel it! Sometimes a foot of snow amounts to just a half-inch of water, other times it amounts to three inches of water. It really depends on the water equivalent of the snow, and that varies widely.

On the average, 10 inches of snow is equivalent to one inch of rain, but that's only an average. If a rain gauge measures one inch of water during a snowstorm, an observer can't automatically assume that 10 inches of snow has fallen. The snow depth can only be determined the old-fashioned way—by measuring it.

That depth is determined by taking an average of three or more representative spots. A ruler is stuck into the snow and its depth is recorded. Because of blowing and drifting, the determination of three or more representative locations is not always easy. You would think that there would be a better way, but there really isn't.

Placing the Instruments

Now that we have a set of weather instruments, where do we place them for the most accurate and most representative readings?

First of all, thermometers must never be placed in the sun. It might be fun to put a thermometer out onto a tennis court during the summer to see how hot the players might be. But as long as that thermometer remains in the sun, it will continue recording a higher and higher temperature. The energy from the sun, the radiant energy, will make that liquid expand and expand.

In order to shade thermometers from the sun, special instrument shelters are used to house thermometers, as well as other weather instruments. The shelter is painted white to reflect the sun, and it has louvered sides so that air circulates through its interior. The housing is placed a standard five feet above a grassy surface. However, out of necessity, the shelter is often located on top of a building with other surfaces: tar, gravel, or concrete. The shelters also protect the instruments from rain and snow. Humidity instruments are normally placed in these shelters.

Anemometers are installed well above buildings and away from obstructions. Ideally, the instrument tries to indicate the wind as it flows freely above the surface, and these instruments are placed about 10 meters, or 33 feet, above the surface.

Barometers can be placed conveniently indoors because the outdoor and indoor pressures should be the same, unless some dramatic changes are taking place, such as with an approaching tornado.

Upper Air Observations

So far, we've looked at how weather is observed near the ground, but the atmosphere is like a layer cake. We must examine all the layers before we can determine a complete picture. The lowest layer is important because it's where we live, but what happens at ground level is really a result of the integrated behavior at all the different levels. So before we can put together a good forecast, we must figure out what is going on above the ground.

In the early days of upper air observations, kites were sent upward with instruments attached. In one of the earliest attempts to record high-level readings, eighteenth-century physician John Jeffries went up in a balloon and took weather instruments along with him. On November 30, 1784, he made the balloon voyage, which lasted an hour and 21 minutes. He took numerous readings of the pressure and temperature. Thomas Jefferson wrote about the meteorological utility of balloons in April 1784, when he said that balloons would be useful in "throwing new lights on the thermometer, barometer, hygrometer, rain, snow, hail, wind, and other phenomena of which the atmosphere is the theatre." During this century, balloons are still used daily, but they are self-contained with remote sensing instruments.

The simplest balloon is called a pilot balloon, and it is filled with gas. After being released, it's tracked with a telescope-like device called a *theodolite*. At equal intervals, such as once a minute, the balloon's position is noted in terms of its vertical and horizontal angles. These can be put into a formula to determine wind speed and direction.

Other balloons carry a special instrument package called a *radiosonde,* which measures the pressure, temperature, and humidity at the different heights. The balloon is tracked, often with radar, and the wind can be determined, just as it is with a pilot balloon. At the same time, the data is transmitted back to the tracking station at given intervals. For example, every few millibars of ascent, the switch goes on and data is sent. The balloon's position is known and its pressure given, and the strength of the returning signal is proportional to the temperature and humidity.

Even during the era of space-age technology, these balloon observations remain the mainstay of upper-air weather observations. They are taken twice each day, at 12-hour intervals. The stations across land are spaced from 200 to 500 miles apart. Consequently, a dense collection of upper-air observations is not routinely available. The balloons provide data through the troposphere, up to about 19 miles where they normally pop. The

Weather-Wise

John Jeffries is considered to be America's first weather-person, and in his honor, his birthday, February 5, is called Weather-Person's Day. He kept a weather diary during the colonial period. As a physician, he served the British during the Revolutionary War.

Weather-Speak

A **radiosonde** is a balloon-borne instrument that measures and transmits meteorological data of temperature, pressure, and humidity. A theodolite is an instrument used to track a radiosonde.

instrument package falls to the ground and used again if it's returned to the National Weather Service. The package contains a message asking that it be returned if found.

Above 19 miles, radar and rockets are used to determine weather conditions. The rocket drops an instrument package, and it's tracked by radar. Also, infrared sensors are being used to examine the temperature as well as the motion of the atmosphere. These are called radiometers, and they can detect sharp changes in temperature that also correspond to sharp changes in wind. Water vapor is also a good emitter of infrared radiation, and its variation can be measured with these radiometers. That variation can often be linked to turbulence. Such instruments are helpful in aviation to help pilots determine when they are moving into rough air. (In the next chapter, we'll take a look at some of the advances in remote sensing from radar and satellites.)

Putting the Data Together

Although languages may differ from one country to another, the weather recognizes no national border. The United Nations set up an agency called the World Meteorological Organization (WMO) to see that the weather information is collected and transmitted with uniformity from one part of the world to another. The WMO consists of 130 nations, and each is required to collect data at certain times and transmit the information in a universal code. The times for collection are based on Universal Time (UT), or *Greenwich Mean Time (GMT),* which is the local time at the Greenwich Observatory in England. The radiosonde data is collected at 1200 GMT (noon at Greenwich), and 0000 GMT (midnight). Local times depend on the longitude of other locations. Every 15 degrees of longitude away from Greenwich is another hour different. Greenwich is used as a standard because it's located at zero degrees longitude, the prime meridian.

Weather-Speak

GMT—Greenwich Mean Time—is the local time in Greenwich, England, and is measured on the prime meridian (0 degrees longitude). Meteorological and navigational clocks are set to GMT so there will be uniformity in reporting the time of data observation and collection.

After an observation is taken, it's immediately transmitted by teletype, radio, or satellite. The data is collected at several world-wide centers and then processed and retransmitted to the multitude of users. At these centers, such as in Washington D.C., the data is analyzed and put into super computers that draw charts and project future patterns.

The data is transmitted in a special code and plotted in a particular format on weather maps. Appendix B shows the coding system and the model for plotting the data.

The Least You Need to Know

➤ Weather data is collected in a variety of ways.

➤ The temperature is never measured in the sun.

➤ The weather conditions are observed both at ground level and at levels above the surface.

➤ Some observing devices have changed little over the past few centuries.

➤ World-wide data is collected at specific times and is transmitted in a universal code.

Chapter 22

Radar and Satellites

In This Chapter

➤ A look at weather technology

➤ Conventional and Doppler radar operations

➤ History and use of satellites

➤ Automated surface observations

➤ New and improved forecasts

Although there really is no substitute for a personal look at the weather by an observer, those eyes can't be everywhere. Weather goes on across the entire world, over vast bodies of water and across sparsely settled lands. It's important to know if a storm is brewing in these distant areas, and in the computer age, that data becomes vital input. A day doesn't go by without us realizing that the slightest disturbance, even that generated by the proverbial flapping of a butterfly's wings could impact the weather in some distant place. Energy is transmitted through all scales, and it cascades like falling dominoes. The advances in technology of the second half of the twentieth century brought meteorology from the Balloon Age into the Space Age.

Radar—Scanning the Skies

The first radar (radio detection and ranging) device was developed in 1935 by a team of British scientists led by Robert Watson-Watt. Beams of radiation are sent out from the device, reflect off something, and return as an *echo*. It didn't take long for this instrument to be adopted by meteorologists who wanted to detect both the location and the intensity of precipitation.

The emitted radiation is in the microwave range. The pulses, or waves, are sent out at the speed of light. The distance between crests is the *wavelength*, and the *frequency* is the number of waves that go by every second. The *period* is the time interval between the passage of the crests. The following figure shows the different wave parameters.

The speed of the wave is constant—it is the speed of light, 186,000 miles per second. In mathematical terms, the frequency multiplied by the wavelength is equal to the speed of light. If the wavelength decreases, the frequency must increase, so the speed of the wave stays fixed at the speed of light. The frequency is controlled by the generator of the signal, and it can be adjusted. As it is regulated, the wavelength will also adjust.

A classic wave.

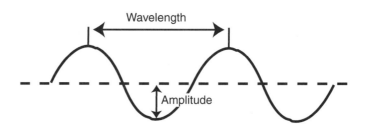

Now, if the outgoing wavelength is very small compared to what's in the air, it will be scattered by everything it encounters. If the wavelength is too large, the beam will only be reflected and scattered by the largest of objects. So, it's important to use the right wavelength for what you're monitoring. If the radar is focusing on aircraft or buildings, a much larger wavelength is needed than if it were to focus on raindrops.

Radar was first used in the military, to keep an eye out for large objects (like German bombers). The principle and nature of military and meteorological radar systems are the same. Only the target is different. Meteorologists modified radar signals for their own use so the raindrops would serve as the reflecting and scattering surfaces. The required wavelength needed for detection must be small enough to bounce off that size object, but also large enough not to be completely reflected and absorbed by a good number of small drops.

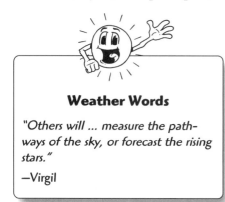

A radar beam's bounce back to the receiver detects both the presence of precipitation and its distance. The strength of the echo is indicative of the intensity of the precipitation, and it can be color-coded. On television, the bright red echoes on radar displays show the heaviest precipitation, the yellows and oranges include moderate to heavy activity, and the greens show lighter activity. All of this is called *reflectivity*. Because the time elapsed between transmitting the signal and receiving the echo is known, and because the signal speed is fixed by the speed of light, the distance to that precipitation can be determined.

In general, weather radar not only provides a horizontal scan of precipitation distribution, it also shows the vertical distribution of moisture—from which cloud elevation can be measured. The radar can be tilted up and down, as well as in a horizontal circle. This vertical scan is very helpful in determining thunderstorm intensity because severe storms have high cloud tops. Cumulonimbus clouds are mountainous, and when their tops exceed 30,000 feet, you know the weather's going to be interesting. Beyond cloud tops of 40,000 feet, the weather becomes severe, with damaging winds and torrential downpours. Beyond 50,000 feet, the weather becomes absolutely violent. Tornadoes are most frequently spawned in these tall thunderstorm clouds. Radar operators also look for hook-shaped echoes, which often show up during tornadoes. These actually appear as hooks on the radar screen.

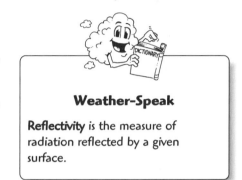

Weather-Speak

Reflectivity is the measure of radiation reflected by a given surface.

Weather radar does have its limitations. Because of the problem related to beam wavelength and raindrop size, lighter precipitation may not be detected. If it is, other clutter will show up on the screen. Also, near the antenna, buildings and hills can block the signal. This ground clutter is always a problem, although radars now have clutter-suppression devices. Sometimes precipitation is falling but evaporating before reaching the ground. The echo will look impressive, but nothing is happening at ground level. This is common during the winter, when a dry layer prevails in the lowest layers of the atmosphere and prevents the onset of precipitation. Rain or snow might look like it's falling for hours before it's actually observed on the ground. Eventually, after two or three hours, the moisture will usually penetrate the dry layer.

Speaking of snow, radar has more trouble detecting it than rain. That's because snow doesn't reflect well, and when it does show up strongly, there's usually rain or sleet mixed with it. Sleet, frozen droplets or ice pellets, is very reflective, and when the winter radar screen shows pockets of red, there's usually sleet. In addition, the radar beam sometimes gives false echoes if atmospheric conditions force the signal to bend toward the ground. This happens when a temperature inversion exists, causing the radar screen to be filled with clutter. This is called *anomalous propagation*. Sometimes, too, a strong storm outside the normal range of the radar will cause an echo that mixes with the regular signal. The radar becomes confused. So, radar may allow for valuable observations of the atmosphere, but sometimes the picture is foggy.

Doppler—The New Generation

Although the standard radar provided useful information, its displays were often confusing, and never went far enough in detecting severe weather. The last version of the conventional radar was produced in 1957. By the late 1980s, spare parts for this antique were becoming harder to find—mainly available in the former Soviet Union. It was time for some new technology, and in 1988 a new version was put into official operation, part of a National Weather Service multimillion-dollar modernization effort known as *NEXRAD*, Next Generation Weather Radar, or the WSR-88 (Weather Surveillance Radar-1988).

The *Doppler effect* was first applied to the apparent shifting frequencies of, say, a train whistle as it approaches and then passes. When the sound is approaching, the waves are pushed together more than when the source moves away. That makes sense (see the figure on page 286). When the waves are pushed together, the wave length is shorter and the frequency is higher. As a train approaches, the higher frequency of its whistle is heard as a higher pitch. Then, where the waves are stretched, the wavelength is longer, and the frequency is less. So, as a train departs, its whistle will sound at a lower pitch. That's the *Doppler shift.*

The Doppler shift works with light waves as well as sound waves. For example, astronomers have concluded that the universe is expanding because of the shift to longer wavelengths, or red shift, by distant galaxies. That shift indicates that these galaxies are moving away from the earth.

When microwaves are used, the Doppler shift will indicate whether raindrops are moving away from the radar or toward it. That motion is called *radial velocity.* Doppler radars not only detect precipitation, they also tell us something about how the air is behaving. Also, the Doppler radar is more sensitive than the old 1957 conventional version, and its reflectivity is more exacting. Many levels of precipitation can be detected. In severe weather, winds tend to shift dramatically. For example, in one location, the flow will appear to be away from the radar, and adjacent to that will be a flow that is directed away. These outgoing or incoming motions are color-coded on the Doppler radar so when a sharp change in direction takes place, the colors contrast sharply. That contrast indicates that a severe storm is present, even a tornado. That wind difference is called

Weather-Speak

NEXRAD stands for Next Generation Weather Radar, and is the National Weather Service's new Doppler radar network installed in the 1990s. Doppler radar detects precipitation and measures the speed of falling precipitation, like conventional radar. But Doppler also measures the speed at which precipitation is moving horizontally toward or away from the radar.

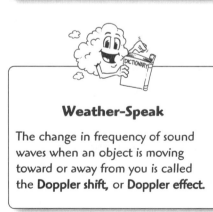

Weather-Speak

The change in frequency of sound waves when an object is moving toward or away from you is called the **Doppler shift,** or **Doppler effect.**

wind shear. You can demonstrate this easily by putting a pen between your two hands. Move your left hand in one direction, and your right hand in the other. What happens to the pen? It will rotate. That rotation can be detected on the radar screen by looking at the color shift of the radial velocity. A strong shift is a tip-off that some severe weather is happening.

In violent thunderstorms, the individual storm cells are part of a larger rotating cloud mass. That is called a *mesocyclone*, and this rotation shows up nicely on the Doppler radar screen, thanks to the shifting frequencies. Approximately half of all mesocyclones are associated with tornadoes. And when tornadoes do appear, strong wind shears show up within the mesocyclone itself. There's a special tornado signature that appears as those shifting colors, called a *tornado vortex signature* (TVS). The tornado-detection capability of Doppler works best within 50 miles of the antenna.

In the old conventional radar days, tornado warnings were only issued when a tornado was spotted on the ground. Today, tornado and severe thunderstorm warnings are given as soon as the signatures appear on the screen. The warning can be issued as much as 20 minutes before a tornado touchdown. That isn't huge, but it's far better than a warning after the fact, which was common in former times. Now the alarm can go off and provide enough time to seek shelter. It's important to realize that Doppler doesn't show the actual velocity of the air—only the velocity away or toward the radar. If the motion is perpendicular to the outgoing beams, that motion won't be detected. A double-Doppler system would be helpful here, but even a single Doppler can provide a wealth of useful data.

During the 1990s, over 150 NEXRAD sites were established across the United States and its island territories. The National Weather Service, Department of Defense, and the Federal Aviation Administration participated in the effort. In addition to providing detailed reflectivity, NEXRAD provides rainfall accumulations for one and three hours, as well as storm totals. Specially designed algorithms allow for these displays as well as hourly rainfall rates, and vertically integrated liquid water, which is the total amount of water from the ground up to the top of the atmosphere. That's a lot of information.

Weather-Speak

Wind shear is the rate of change of wind direction or speed, especially when it is a sudden variation. It can be dangerous to aircraft when landing or taking off.

Weather-Speak

A **mesocyclone** is the intense rotating region of air containing a severe thunderstorm. **Tornado vortex signature** (TVS), is the image of tornadic wind shear found on a Doppler radar screen. It shows up inside a mesocyclone.

The Doppler effect.

Satellites—A Far-Out Look

If a picture is worth a thousand words, then weather satellites have proven their worth time and time again. After all, more than 70 percent of the earth is covered by oceans. Before satellite information became available, storms could go undetected for days before being reported. Ships always provided useful data, but satellites now fill huge gaps. Also, the newer satellites serve as powerful clearinghouses for vast amounts of data—not just photographs, although that's how it all got started.

A picture of the first weather satellite, TIROS 1, launched on April 1, 1960, is shown in the figure on the next page. TIROS (Television and Infrared Observation Satellite) was equipped with TV cameras and radiometers, which measured the infrared radiation given off by the earth and atmosphere. That radiation indicates something about temperature because higher temperatures will emit longer wavelengths of energy. But the cloud pictures were essentially snapshots, and pretty basic. While the photographs revealed the location of storms and indicate atmospheric wind and circulation, the general strength of a rain-bearing system couldn't be well determined. There were few shades of gray. What the camera saw is what you got. Also, the early satellites were rotated to maintain stability and for 75 percent of the time, the rotation pointed the camera away from the earth. Pictures could only be taken for six hours each day.

TIROS orbited the earth at an average height of 400 miles, and it made a complete circuit in 100 minutes. Because of the angle of its orbit, it could take pictures both north and south of the equator. Regardless of the limitations, thousands of pictures were transmitted back to Earth by TIROS 1, which operated for 79 days.

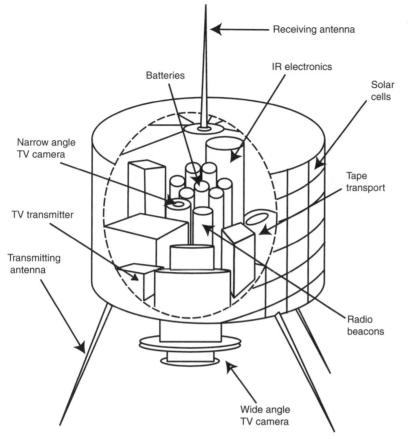

TIROS 1: First weather satellite.

Receiving antenna

IR electronics

Batteries

Solar cells

Narrow angle TV camera

Tape transport

TV transmitter

Transmitting antenna

Radio beacons

Wide angle TV camera

Nine versions of TIROS were launched between 1960 and 1965. Then toward the end of the TIROS era came a new and improved version called Nimbus. Infrared cameras now allowed for more than just visible photography. Clouds could be examined and recorded in detail and at night.

The infrared photography measures the strength of radiation being emitted by a cloud top. Warmer clouds give off more energy. Warmer clouds are the lower ones; colder, higher clouds give off less energy. The system is programmed to show this difference in reverse. The taller clouds appear brighter than the lower, warmer ones. Presumably, the taller clouds are thicker and evidence of more precipitation, but that's not always the case. A veil of high, thin cirrus clouds appear very brightly on the infrared image. With straight visible images, brighter clouds indicate thicker clouds because of the increased reflectivity from a thicker mass of moisture.

Another problem with infrared imagery is that it can't differentiate between a very low cloud and the surface of the earth when both are at the same temperature. Often the weather appears to be crystal clear on the infrared imagery, but the visible image is completely different. A weather forecaster really needs those visual images, along with the advanced infrared pictures. The infrared provides for nighttime viewing of clouds, and delineates the clouds into numerous shades. The infrared photographs can be computer-enhanced to show the range of clouds present, and that becomes helpful in locating the heaviest precipitation and most violent weather within a storm, but those pictures can't stand alone.

During the 1960s, satellites were launched into both equatorial and polar orbits. The polar-orbiting satellites are at an altitude of just 530 miles, and they go around once every 100 minutes. The orbits shift westward by 15 degrees after each pass, and that shift allows them to photograph the entire Earth twice each day. Because of their low altitude, they can show great detail, down to a resolution of about 0.5 miles. Satellites that orbit around the equator are at a much higher altitude of 22,300 miles, so they can photograph a wider region—but the resolution decreases and they can't detect objects under 2.5 miles across.

Weather-Wise

The main role of many of the early weather satellites was simply to look at the weather and to give us cloud pictures.

Soon after the Nimbus versions were launched, a whole new generation of satellites was put into operation. The first was launched in 1966, 22,300 miles up and directly over the equator. The satellite orbited the earth at the same speed at which the earth rotated, so it appears to remain fixed over a particular point. These were aptly called *geostationary satellites*, or *GOES*. The high altitude is necessitated by the requirement of a speed of revolution to match the earth's rotation, and that distance results in a loss of resolution.

Weather-Speak

GOES, or geostationary satellites, orbit the earth but remain in a fixed place because they revolve around the earth at the same rate as the earth rotates.

Still, GOES imagery has become the mainstay of modern meteorology. Over the decades, new and improved versions of GOES have been launched. These satellites provide continuous coverage of cloudiness over the same region of the earth's surface. The satellite transmits the data as quickly as the picture is taken. Cloud movies or loops can be put together, and the development of storms can be monitored. The GOES system takes both visible and infrared images.

The Modern Era

Satellites are capable of providing a wealth of information. Around the earth, there are five geostationary orbiting satellites giving considerable coverage of the earth and its atmosphere. The United States has GOES East, positioned over 75 degrees W longitude, and GOES West at 135 W longitude. Japan has a Geostationary Meteorology Satellite (GMS) that covers portions of Asia and the Pacific. Over Europe, there is the METEOSAT, which observes Europe, parts of the Atlantic, Mediterranean, and Africa.

India has INSAT, which watches over Asia and the Indian Ocean. Polar-orbiting satellites are also very important in providing detailed imagery of surface conditions. For example, infrared sensors on these satellites show areas of deforestation.

Because of the infrared sensing, temperature profiles of the atmosphere are now possible. These sensors help determine the pattern of global climate change. Also, because moisture emits infrared radiation, water vapor can be monitored. Water-vapor imagery is especially helpful in examining the flow of moisture into a developing storm. Also, areas of dry-air intrusion can indicate sinking motions, which inhibit storm development. In addition, laser instruments are used to detect wind motions.

The satellites also serve as platforms for collecting and disseminating a wide variety of data from ground-based observational platforms. Buoys on the ocean surface, along with other automated devices, transmit the data to the satellite, which then relays that to land-based receiving stations. Wave heights, sea-surface temperatures, and seismic information can be sent around the world from remote locations along with standard weather data. Satellites now monitor the stratosphere and provide valuable data on ozone concentrations.

Weather-Speak

ASOS is an Automated Surface Observing System. Over 850 of these systems are being installed in the United States to serve as the nation's primary surface weather observing network.

The array of remote sensing devices, used separately and in conjunction with satellites, is dazzling. Across the United States, over 800 *Automated Surface Observing Stations (ASOS)* were installed during the 1990s. The ASOS program is a joint effort of several federal agencies, including the National Weather Service. The number of automated stations doubles the number of full-time surface weather observing sites. A much greater network of data is available. ASOS even provides computer-generated voice observations directly to aircraft in the vicinity of airports. Such messages are even available from automatic buoys placed out on the ocean. Of course, there's no substitute for human observers. For example, ASOS doesn't measure snow depth, it provides cloud information just up to 12,000 feet, and thunderstorms can't be directly determined. But it does provide a wealth of data over a vast area across a very dense network.

Putting It All Together

Now, this is a chore! The National Weather Service has a high-speed computer work station that tries to do just that. Here comes another acronym: It's called *AWIPS*—for Advanced Weather Interactive Processing System. Over a hundred locations across

Weather-Speak

AWIPS is the Advanced Weather Interactive Processing System that is the new communication nerve center of operations at all the Weather Forecast Offices and River Forecast Centers. It combines information from ASOS and NEXRAD.

the United States have an AWIPS. It collects NEXRAD Doppler information, GOES data, ASOS, as well as other data sources such as river gauges. Forecast guidance information is also fed into the system, so that at the tip of a forecaster's fingers, a complete picture of the atmosphere can be seen. The next figure shows the location of AWIPS installations across the United States.

Location of AWIPS in the United States.

So, Are the Forecasts Going to Be Better?

We've come a long way from just having a thermometer and barometer. If the volume of data is directly proportional to forecast accuracy, then forecasts should seldom go astray. There's no doubt we're observing the weather better and in more detail than ever before. These detailed observations are helping detect storms with greater precision. All of this should help the accuracy of the forecast—but stay tuned for more. The jury is still out. The leap from observation to forecast is still precarious.

The Least You Need to Know

➤ Great advances in weather technology have occurred in the late twentieth century.

➤ Conventional radar modified for weather operations has been replaced by Doppler systems.

➤ Doppler radar provides excellent resolution and can accurately depict areas of violent weather by indicating air flow.

➤ The modern weather station receives data from radar, satellites, and a world-wide network of automated stations.

➤ Although the technology is dazzling, questions remain about forecast accuracy.

Chapter 23

Let's See How It's Done

In This Chapter

➤ A day in the life of a television meteorologist

➤ A look at the makings of a weather forecast

➤ The basic tools of an operational forecaster

➤ The use of surface and upper-air data

➤ Tapping into computer products

You've gotten this far. You know the basics of what makes our weather click. You've learned how the weather is observed and measured. As far as weather forecasting is concerned, I'm convinced that the rest is really on-the-job training. After the basic principles have been mapped out, the remainder becomes a learning-by-doing process.

The best way for you to learn the skills of weather forecasting is by coming to work with me. By doing that you'll learn far more than reading more technical stuff. So let's take a look at a day in the life of Dr. Mel, and see how I go about coming up with and delivering a forecast in front of a blank blue wall before 100,000 or so viewers.

Sunday Night—The Night Before the Forecast

Although I return to work on Monday morning, my preparation for the forecast begins with some careful thought about the weather the night before. Late Sunday, I begin to think about what has occurred during the weekend.

The particular weekend in mid-October that I wrote this was pleasant, but changeable. On Saturday, the sky was crystal clear and deep blue. The visibility seemed to go on forever. I could look out from the Connecticut shore, and clearly see Long Island's hills on the southern horizon, about 15 miles away. There was absolutely no haze, and the waves were hardly a foot. The weather vane pointed to the north, and because the tree limbs were just barely in motion, I knew that the wind speed was under 10 knots. All the ingredients of a dry, polar air mass were present. The temperature just reached 60 degrees that afternoon, about three degrees below normal. The deep blue sky and excellent visibility were dead ringers for a continental polar air mass. Also, the wind was light, indicating a center of high pressure was nearby. Because of that system's clockwise circulation, a north wind would indicate that the high-pressure center was still to the west, but again, the light winds suggested that the center wasn't very far—250 miles or less.

Weather Words

"I'm in prediction, not production."
—Dr. Mel

On Sunday there were some definite changes. Skies became partly cloudy, with clouds of the high and middle type. Cirrostratus, altostratus, and altocumulus clouds were in view. At the same time, the wind shifted to the south, and it became gusty. I could hear the waves breaking on the shore as far as 120 yards. The waves were building to about three feet. No longer was the visibility crisp and clear. A summer-like haze covered the sky. As the day progressed, the visibility dropped to five miles or less and I could see no more than a third of the way across Long Island Sound. A major change in air masses had occurred, and instead of continental polar air, a tropical air mass seemed to have moved in. Later that afternoon, the temperature reached the 70s, about 10 degrees above normal. The barometer was falling steadily, indicating that the bright high-pressure system of the previous day was definitely moving away to the east.

Braving the Elements

Did you ever wonder how weathercasters stand in front of a blank wall and point to weather maps? The innovation they use is called chromakey, where the computer weather graphics are electronically merged with the blank wall. The weather anchor knows where to point on the wall by looking into television monitors to see the on-air image. I know from experience never to wear a shirt the same color as the blue chromakey wall at Channel 8— that blue shirt would come out blank on television, and instead of my shirt, you would see the computer graphic.

The clouds increased later in the afternoon, and it seemed that more changes were on the way, but I had no way of knowing without looking at a bigger picture, beyond my own horizon. I turned on the television and the radio. There was no mention of rain for Monday, but there was a major story about heavy rains moving into Texas. The floods were extensive and took the lives of more than a dozen people. Something very dynamic was going on, and I remembered from the previous week that there were some signs of a major push of colder weather for the coming week. I thought for sure that those rains were on the leading edge of that polar air. A pretty strong cold front seemed to be out there, but I would learn more when I got to work Monday morning.

But before we go to early Monday, isn't it amazing what you can learn about the weather, just by looking and observing? With the slightest effort, you can tell what type of air mass is present and understand the factors contributing to the sky's appearance, the character of distant objects, even the nature of sounds, such as the breaking of waves. The more you look at the weather, the more you really see, and the more you really understand.

> **Weather Words**
>
> *"Here, in this little Bay,*
> *Full of tumultuous life*
> *and great repose,*
> *Where, twice a day,*
> *The purposeless, glad ocean*
> *comes and goes,*
> *Under high cliffs, and far*
> *from the huge town,*
> *I sit me down."*
>
> —Coventry Patmore

Early Monday Morning—Getting In to Work

The forecast you hear or watch in the morning has been hours in the making. I usually get up around 2:30 a.m., but on this particular Monday, I woke a bit earlier to the sound of rain. My first reaction was, "What's that about?" Nobody had called for pouring rain that morning, but I guess that southerly flow of moist air and the approaching front meant business. On my way to work, the combination of falling leaves and the rain made for some slick and slippery going. I made a mental note to mention that to viewers when I got on the air. But as I was traveling the seven miles to the studio, the rain stopped, and when I went out of the car, I looked up, and saw some stars poking through the cloud cover. I thought, "That is a fast-moving front! Is that all there is?" Although the rain came down heavily, it couldn't have been more than a tenth of an inch.

Now for the Real Work

So far, most of what I knew about the weather on that day in October consisted of my own observations. Now, it was time to look at other observations taken at locations over a wide area and see how this data was mapped out.

Checking Out the Data

I arrived at the weather center at 3:30 a.m. My first task was to examine the flow of information and make sure I had a handle on what was really happening. Our television station has a network of automated weather stations installed at schools throughout our area. The instrumentation is quite sophisticated, even if it's not the caliber of the National Weather Service ASOS network. I immediately polled those stations by punching in a computer command. Within the hour, a vast amount of data would be available. I had a detailed picture of temperature, dew point, wind, pressure, relative humidity, and precipitation. That data is combined with the coded information from the National Weather Service, and what I learned was that very little rain fell with the front. No station reported more than .01 inch of rain—the threshold of "measurable" precipitation.

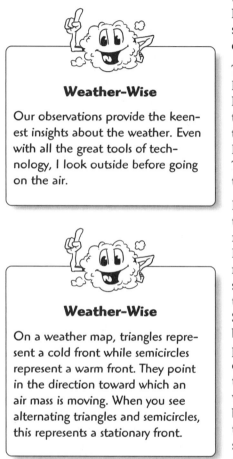

Weather-Wise

Our observations provide the keenest insights about the weather. Even with all the great tools of technology, I look outside before going on the air.

Weather-Wise

On a weather map, triangles represent a cold front while semicircles represent a warm front. They point in the direction toward which an air mass is moving. When you see alternating triangles and semicircles, this represents a stationary front.

The temperatures were mild for that time of year. Readings were close to 60 degrees, almost the normal high of 63 degrees. In mid-October, early-morning temperatures should be 20 degrees lower. The clouds and the south wind kept temperatures up during the night. By 4:30 a.m., all stations were showing a major change. The wind had shifted into the west, although the temperature remained relatively mild.

In addition to the data from the various weather stations, I looked at Doppler radar, and saw that the early rain had completely raced across Connecticut at 40 mph. By the time I got into the weather office, the last of the rain was located in the extreme eastern portions of the state. Then I checked the satellite imagery and saw that the clouds, too, had raced eastward at express speeds. Skies became mostly clear at the New York–Connecticut border, and nothing especially solid or ominous was present farther west. It sure looked like the weather was clearing. It would seem that a cold front had moved through because winds moved into the west, but where was the colder air? Actually, cold fronts don't always bring about a sharp change in temperature; sometimes the air can even be warmer, as is the case during the summer. In the case of this cold front, it seemed that the cooler turn was going to be a gradual one.

Looking at the Surface Maps

The National Weather Service prepares an entire array of charts and maps that help analyze and forecast the weather. One map I studied closely early that Monday morning was a surface chart, as shown in the figure on the next page. It consists of lots of numbers, lines, and more lines. Appendix C breaks down the format used for these charts, but I can explain some of the important things here.

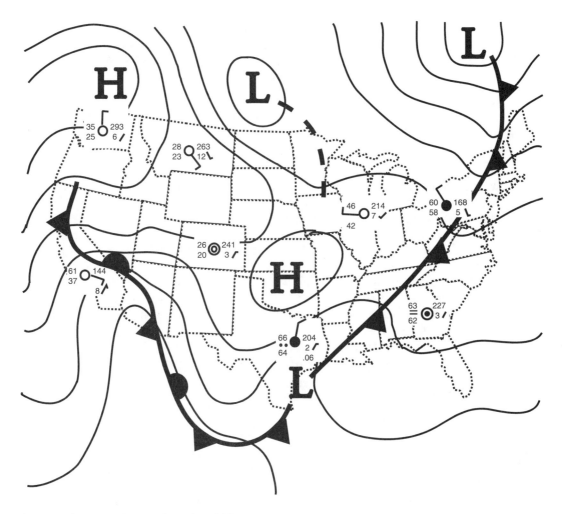

Surface weather map for October 19, 1998.

Each major National Weather Service station is represented and the data is recorded according to a special station model. The temperature is in the upper left of the station model. The number in the lower left represents dew point. Also, a short line extends out from the station position representing the direction the wind is coming from. A line extended into the northwest means the wind is coming from the northwest. Barbs, or flags, are attached perpendicularly to those lines to represent wind speed. A longer line represents 10 knots, or 10 nautical miles per hour. A shorter line represents 5 knots.

In the upper right, barometric pressure is listed in code. The pressure is given in millibars, or hectopascals. For example, a number of "207" means that the pressure is 1020.7 millibars. A coded number of "980" indicates that the pressure is 998.0

295

millibars. The pressure is always around 1000 millibars. The station location is shown as a circle filled in according to the degree of cloudiness. A circle that's completely filled indicates mostly cloudy skies; an open one indicates mostly clear conditions. If any precipitation is occurring, that's indicated between the temperature and dew point with a special code, which is also shown in Appendix C.

Fronts are shown according to a standard format. The lines that look like contours are *isobars*, lines of constant pressure. Those lines enclose areas of high pressure (H) and areas of low pressure (L). Notice how the areas of high pressure tend to have clear skies, while the areas of low pressure have overcast conditions. No surprises here.

Now, the surface map for this Monday morning showed a cold front extending from eastern New York to eastern Texas. The time of the map was listed as "06z" in the lower left-hand portion of the chart. That means the map was prepared from data collected at 0600 Greenwich Mean Time, or 2 a.m. Eastern Daylight Time. Based on all the other data that I looked at from local stations, I could safely assume that the front that had been in eastern New York at 2 a.m. had moved east of Connecticut by 5 a.m. By the way, the heavy rain that occurred in Texas was associated with the southern portion of the front. Evidently, as the drier, cooler air ran into the pure tropical air of the Gulf states, the weather became explosive. So, the surface weather map confirmed that a cold front was moving to the east. It also showed a huge high-pressure region extending from the Pacific Northwest to the Midwest. Something so extensive could result in an extended spell of sunny weather, even if temperatures did change.

Going Into the Upper Air

The ground-level data nicely shows what's occurring outside your window or outside the window of a weather station a thousand miles away. Sometimes that's enough to make a forecast for the next few days, but usually, we need to dig deeper—or, in this case, go to a higher level. In Chapter 21, we looked at radiosonde balloons that are launched twice daily around the world. The data these balloons provide is invaluable. From that information, maps representing different levels of atmospheric conditions are put together. These show the true multi-dimensional character of the atmosphere.

One of my favorite maps is called the 500-millibar (mb) map, which shows the flow of the atmosphere at a level where the pressure is about half the pressure of the surface. On these constant pressure charts, the pressure is the same in New York as it is in Los Angeles, but the elevation at which that pressure is found is different. Contours that show the elevation of the surface are drawn. The figure on the next page shows the 500-mb chart that I used in the weather office. On the upper-air charts, contours are drawn every 60 meters. A contour labeled 576 means that the 500-mb surface is 5,760 meters above the ground.

The notations "L" and "H" indicate locations of low and high elevation of the pressure surface. The dashed lines indicate the temperature in degrees C. Those lines of constant temperature are called *isotherms*. The station locations are represented, with the temperature reading in the upper left of the data array, the dew point-temperature difference in the lower left, the elevation in the upper right (add a zero for height in meters), and the standard wind barbs indicating wind direction and speed. (See Appendix C for the coding of these upper-air observations along with the coding for the surface observations.)

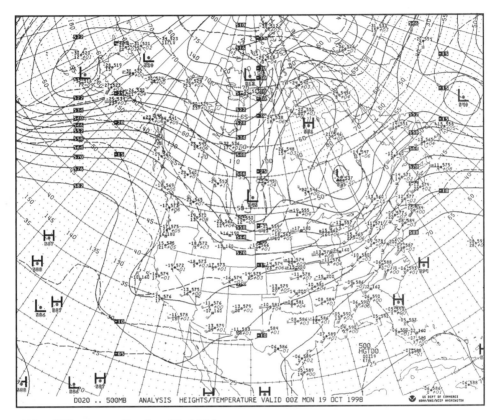

500 millibar map, October 19, 1998.

But let's not get lost in all this symbolism. What I was looking for on this map this Monday morning was the general flow of the atmosphere. The 500-mb chart is great for that. It shows the general direction of weather. Although the jet stream itself is located at a much higher level, above 10 kilometers, the flow at around 5 kilometers is indicative of the way weather systems are moving. Notice how the flow is generally along those contours. In this case, the weather that was heading for Connecticut originated in southern Illinois and southern Indiana. Also, the flow was generally from west to east, but there was a big "High" anchored off the southeast coast.

This told me a lot. First, the front moving through eastern New York and New England had some pretty good push behind it. The west-to-east flow would move it along, which seemed to agree with the satellite and Doppler pictures. Also, the flow was not from the north, so any change toward cooler weather would probably be gradual. If that flow had been sweeping down from central Canada, the temperature would have dropped sharply, but in this case, the weather was more moderate immediately behind the front.

The flow at 500 mb usually represents the average flow in the atmosphere, and surface weather systems move at an average of half the speed at this level. The wind flow between New England and the Midwest is about 60 knots. So, surface weather will move along at a rate of 60 divided by 2, or 30 knots. Now, if the pattern is changing slowly, and it often is, then the air is pushing along at 30 knots, and over a 24-hour period the air will cover a distance of 720 miles (30 times 24).

If I want to see what type of air mass is arriving, I will go back from the air stream to a position 720 miles away. That would place me in southern Illinois. The air mass arriving on this day was over southern Illinois about 24 hours ago. This is far from exact and loaded with problems, but as a first and often best estimate of conditions for the upcoming day, it works. So, what was it like yesterday in southern Illinois?

The following figure shows the high temperatures for the previous day, Sunday, across the entire country, and I saw that in southern Illinois, the temperature reached the upper 60s, close to 70 degrees. I know that I'll be predicting a high temperature close to that. But to get a second opinion of the high temperature, I looked at another upper-level chart.

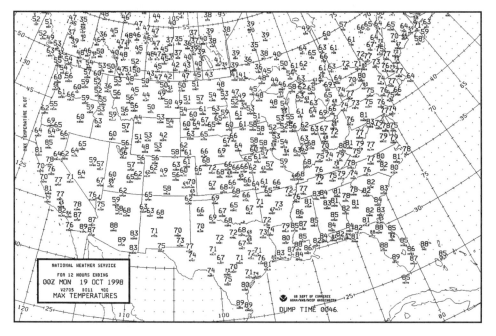

High temperatures observed for October 19, 1998.

This one is at the 850-mb level. This 850-mb chart is useful in many ways (see the following figure). The coding and format are exactly the same as the 500-mb chart, but this chart shows a pressure surface that is closer to the ground, usually about 1,500 meters. This chart is useful for predicting precipitation. Normally, precipitation occurs when the temperature-dew point difference is 5 degrees or less. The smaller the difference, the closer that layer is to saturation. At 5 degrees or less, the difference is small enough to support condensation at a level that's frequently near the base of clouds. I quickly saw that the difference was large overhead, but upwind, in southwest Pennsylvania, the difference was just 1 degree. This chart was prepared from data taken at 8 p.m. on Sunday. Evidently, the showers that raced into the region overnight came from that region of moist air in western Pennsylvania, just 12 hours earlier. Now, for that particular Monday morning, I used this data to help determine the upcoming day's high temperature.

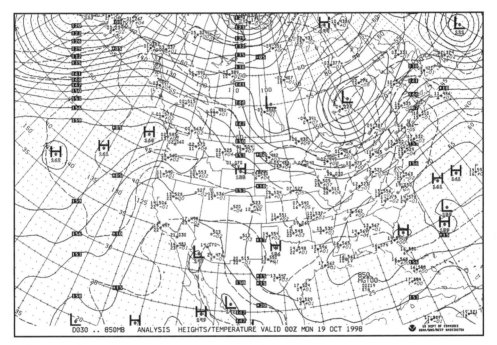

850 millibar for October 19, 1998.

I have a trick. If the atmosphere is stirred up, and if there's maximum sunshine without any strong air mass being blown into the region, I'll add 28 degrees F to the 850-mb temperature to arrive at the day's maximum. In this case, the trajectory of air is coming from southern Illinois, where the 850-mb temperature is 10 degrees C, and that converts to 50 degrees F. If I add 28 degrees to that, the temperature becomes 78 degrees, and that would be the absolute highest the temperature could go. The 28-degree figure comes from the temperature change that a bundle of air would undergo if it sank from about 5,000 feet to the surface. The rate of warming, called the *adiabatic lapse rate,* comes to 5.5 degrees for every thousand feet. (I rounded up from 27.5 to 28 degrees.) It's not an exact technique, and on that day, the 850-mb surface was at 1,500 meters, less than 5,000 feet above the ground. But for a quick, upper limit for the temperature, the technique works. So, the surface maps suggest a high near 70, and this chart suggested the upper 70s. I took an average and put in a high temperature forecast for the mid-70s.

At this point, I felt confident enough to go on the air. All indicators pointed to a day without rain, and a temperature in the 70s. The skies will probably have some cloudiness, but plenty of sunshine was expected. Colder weather will eventually develop, but it will arrive slowly during the day. But of course, perfection is the aim, and we could do some fine tuning. Let's check out the assortment of computer information that's readily available.

Weather-Speak

Adiabatic lapse rate is the rate of temperature decrease due to expansion or contraction without any loss or gain of heat. As a pocket of air rises, it will expand, and that expansion alone causes a cooling, regardless of any heat exchange.

Bring on the Machines

Computers make forecasting easier, although not necessarily more accurate. One can simply *rip and read* a computer product and be correct in a 24- to 36-hour forecast about 85 percent of the time. Yet, I never feel sure until I take a good look around and examine the basic charts such as the surface, 850 mb, and 500 mb, but computers really do make forecasting almost a breeze.

Appendix D gives a rundown and description of many of the computer products. For now, let's start with the one that's most helpful—and easy to interpret. The following table shows an array of data for Bridgeport (BDR). It's called "NGM MOS GUIDANCE." The "NGM" portion stands for the nested grid model. It's one of the computer models used to project the weather, and in the next chapter we'll get into these computer models. But we can easily interpret this data now.

Weather-Speak

Rip and read meteorologists are people who just rip and read the computer outputs and then deliver the forecast as written by the machines.

This computer product shows the high and low temperatures expected for the next two days. The row labeled "MX/MN" gives those readings. From October 19 to October 20, the maximum is 71 degrees. The overnight low is 47. The next day's high temperature is 64 degrees and the low is 42. So there we go—the temperature forecast for the next 48 hours. Other rows of data include clouds (CLDS), wind direction (WDIR), wind speed (WSPD), and probability of precipitation in 6- and 12-hour periods (POP06, POP12). If the data is missing or not available, the numbers (999...) are printed. This model includes the straight output from the computer along with some climatological adjustment for specific locations. Those adjustments are automated, too.

```
                                                        BDR.txt
□BDR   E    NGM MOS  GUIDANCE   10/19/98   0000 UTC
DAY /OCT   19                    /OCT   20                  /OCT   21
HOUR    06 09 12 15 18 21 00 03 06 09 12 15 18 21 00 03 06 09 12
MX/MN                       71              47              64           42
TEMP   999999 60 65 69 68 62999999999 49 59 62 61 55999999999 44
DEWPT  999999 54 50 46 45 47999999999 41 41 40 39 40999999999 34
CLDS   CL CL SC SC CL CL CL CL CL SC SC SC SC SC SC CL CL CL CL
WDIR   99 99 28 29 28 29 29 29 99 99 30 30 28 30 30 31 99 99 31
WSPD   99 99 08 12 13 13 07 05 99 99 07 11 12 13 09 10 99 99 08
POP06        2     0        0        1        0        0        0        0
POP12                       0                 2        0               0
QPF          0/     0/     0/0     0/     0/0     0/     0/0     0/     0/0
TSV06        9/ 1  0/ 0  0/ 3  0/ 2  6/ 5  2/ 0  0/ 7  0/ 3  4/ 5
TSV12        6/ 0        0/ 4        7/ 5        0/ 8
PTYPE  R  R  R  R  R  R  R  R  R  R  R     R     R     R     R
POZP   1  2  0  0  0  0  0  0  0  0  0     0     0     2     1
POSN   0  0  0  0  0  0  0  0  0  0  0     0     0     1     0
SNOW         0/     0/     0/0     0/     0/0     0/     0/0     0/     0/0
CIG    7  7  7  7  7  7  7  7  7  7  7     7     7
VIS    5  5  5  5  5  5  5  5  5  5  5     5     5
OBVIS  N  N  N  N  N  N  N  N  N  N  N     N     N
```

The computer guidance for Bridgeport, October 19, 1998.

The amount of information is huge. The row indicating clouds lists the cloud cover as clear (clr), scattered (sct), broken (bkn), or overcast (ovc). In this case, the conditions are clear or just with scattered clouds. The machine is looking for a sunny day and a pretty quiet spell through 48 hours. The probability of precipitation doesn't even reach 5 percent—but it did rain early in the day and overnight, which the computer completely missed. The machine isn't perfect, but the trend toward dry weather is supported by all the other charts we've looked at. So, at least from the morning on, the computer seems reasonable.

The row indicating wind direction shows the flow to be from the west or northwest. We add a zero to that number and the direction of the wind is given in degrees of a compass. The wind in this case is from around 280 or 290 degrees. The speed isn't outrageous. Again, that "999" represents missing data, but what is available shows speeds up to 12 or 13 knots, and that isn't especially fast. A similar output is shown on the following page for Hartford on that day. The Hartford station is located at Bradley Airport (BDL).

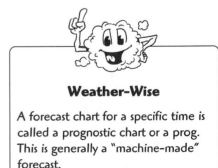

Weather-Wise

A forecast chart for a specific time is called a prognostic chart or a prog. This is generally a "machine-made" forecast.

```
                                          BDL.txt
□BDL   E    NGM MOS GUIDANCE   10/19/98  0000 UTC
DAY /OCT  19                  /OCT  20                    /OCT   21
HOUR  06 09 12 15 18 21 00 03 06 09 12 15 18 21 00 03 06 09 12
MX/MN             72          42          64          37
TEMP  61 58 57 65 70 68 60 53 48 45 46 57 62 60 52 47 43 40 40
DEWPT 54 51 48 46 44 42 44 43 42 40 39 39 37 35 36 35 33 32 32
CLDS  CL CL CL SC CL CL CL CL CL SC SC SC SC SC SC CL CL CL CL
WDIR  21 23 24 25 28 27 24 22 25 25 26 28 28 29 29 29 29 29 29
WSPD  09 09 09 11 15 14 09 04 05 05 07 08 14 14 08 09 09 07 07
POP06     2     0     0     1     0     0     0     0     1
POP12           0           2           0           2
QPF      0/    0/    0/0    0/    0/0    0/    0/0    0/    0/0
TSV06    0/ 1  0/ 0  0/ 5  0/ 2  2/ 3  1/ 0  0/ 6  0/ 3  2/ 5
TSV12       0/ 0        0/ 6        3/ 1        0/ 8
PTYPE  R  R  R  R  R  R  R  R  R  R  R     R     R     R     R
POZP   1  1  1  0  0  0  0  1  0  0  0     1     0     0     0
POSN   0  0  0  0  0  0  0  0  0  0  0     0     0     9    12
SNOW     0/    0/    0/0    0/    0/0    0/    0/0    0/    0/0
CIG    7  7  7  7  7  7  7  7  7  7  7     7     7
VIS    5  5  5  5  5  5  5  5  5  5  5     5     5
OBVIS  N  N  N  N  N  N  N  N  N  N  N     N     N
```

The computer guidance for Hartford, October 19, 1998.

Without much further ado, we can predict that the temperature will reach the 70s, skies will be sunny, and winds will be out of the northwest from 10 to15 mph. Overnight, skies will be clear, the temperature will dip into the upper 40s, and another sunny day will follow for Tuesday, but cooler with temperatures in the mid-60s.

So far, nothing that the computer has presented is out of balance with our expectations from the basic data, and from looking outside. That provides plenty of confidence.

What About the Five-Day Forecast?

Check out the following table which is—a computer projection for not just the next five days, but the next seven. We'd be happy this early Monday morning to get the next two days correct, but everyone likes to look into the distant future, and we have some products that can be put to reasonably predictive use. This particular model is called the MRF—Medium Range Forecast. The name implies that even longer-range forecasts are available. In fact some generalized trend forecasts are available out to 13 months! But for the next five days this MRF gives some useful results.

Weather-Speak

An **operational forecast** is the final forecast product.

In the next figure, each day contains a minimum (MN) and maximum (MX) temperature forecast. On Tuesday, the high temperature for Hartford (BDL) is given as 62 degrees, the morning low is 42. Boston (BOS) and Providence (PVD) are also shown. Notice how the temperature drops through the week—just as we expected from our other data. By Thursday, the high temperature for BDL is given as 47 degrees. The normals are listed in the last two columns under "CIIMO." The prediction of 47 degrees is much lower than the normal 61 degrees. So, when I go on the air, I'll be talking about the chilly turn in a big way.

```
953
FOXE42 KWBC 190000
▨MRF-BASED OBJECTIVE GUIDANCE   10/19/98   0000 UTC

▨BDL   MON 19| TUE 20| WED 21| THU 22| FRI 23| SAT 24| SUN 25| MON 26| CLIMO
MN/MX     71| 42  62| 37  52| 33  47| 31  51| 33  56| 38  61| 40  61| 39  61
POP12      0|  1   2|  3   8| 20  24| 14   7|  9  13|  9  10|  8  11| 19  20
CPOS       1|  0   0|  9  32| 11   8|  8  13|  5   2|  1   2|  0   2|  6   5
CLDS      39| 26  46| 41  54| 61  64| 56  49| 34  44| 38  40| 37  43| 51  54
WIND      12|  6  10|  6   9|  6   9|  7  10|  6   8|  6   9|  7   8|  5   7
POP24         |   2  |   8  |  33  |  17  |  17  |  14  |  14  |  30

▨BOS   MON 19| TUE 20| WED 21| THU 22| FRI 23| SAT 24| SUN 25| MON 26| CLIMO
MN/MX     71| 48  63| 42  54| 37  48| 36  47| 39  57| 44  60| 45  60| 45  60
POP12      0|  0   0|  1   7| 18  24| 19   9| 10  15| 11  12| 10  13| 20  21
CPOS       1|  1   0|  8  25| 10   8|  8  10|  5   2|  1   2|  0   1|  4   4
CLDS      37| 26  45| 37  47| 53  60| 54  46| 31  41| 34  36| 32  38| 46  49
WIND      15| 11  14| 11  12|  9  11| 11  13| 10  11|  9  12|  9  11|  9  11
POP24         |   0  |   7  |  32  |  22  |  19  |  17  |  17  |  31

▨PVD   MON 19| TUE 20| WED 21| THU 22| FRI 23| SAT 24| SUN 25| MON 26| CLIMO
MN/MX     72| 45  63| 38  56| 33  47| 33  48| 36  57| 40  62| 42  62| 41  62
POP12      0|  1   2|  0   5| 18  26| 18   9| 10  15| 13  11| 11  12| 21  20
CPOS       1|  0   0|  6  21|  9   7|  7  10|  5   2|  1   2|  0   1|  3   4
CLDS      37| 26  43| 40  49| 59  62| 58  48| 35  43| 39  38| 37  40| 50  51
WIND      12|  7  10|  7   9|  7  10|  7  11|  6  10|  7  10|  7   9|  7   9
POP24         |   2  |   5  |  34  |  22  |  19  |  18  |  17  |  30
```

Medium Range Forecast (MRF), Long Range Forecast.

Other useful data is the 12-hour precipitation probability (POP12) and the 24-hour precipitation probability (POP24). Any probability above the "Climo" number implies some precipitation is possible. Appendix D describes the additional rows and columns in this product, but for now we can see that the chances for precipitation through the next seven days are slight, except for Wednesday, and the number is just barely above the "Climo" value. I would predict no more than isolated, light showers for Wednesday. My five-day graphic would show plenty of sun, little or no rain, and a definite cooling trend. I may tweak the MRF numbers a bit, based on experience, but any good forecast will come within the ballpark of this output.

Are We Ready?

I think so. I've gathered local data, examined radar and satellite information, checked out numerous charts, and consulted with the oracle of the computer. There are other useful maps, but for this forecast, we've seen enough.

Let's go into the studio—not that I have a choice. It's 5 a.m., and we're going on the air!

The Least You Need to Know

➤ Forecasting is really an application of common sense.

➤ You can learn a lot about future weather patterns by just looking outside.

➤ Surface data and upper-air data are combined to give a complete picture of the atmosphere.

➤ Computers make forecasting a breeze, but they can be inaccurate.

➤ An operational forecast is a mix of computer products and human intervention.

Chapter 24

Prediction by Numbers

In This Chapter

➤ The history of computer weather forecasts

➤ What goes into a computer prediction?

➤ The accuracy of the computer effort

➤ The limits of the machines

The seventeenth and eighteenth centuries really began to put weather on the map. In 1600, Galileo built the first primitive thermometer. Later, his student Torricelli made the first barometer. Mathematicians such as Descartes and Pascal began to explain the principle of the physical world in a special mathematical language. By 1660, the barometer was first used to predict the weather. During the middle of the century, one of the greatest scholars of all time was born. With his work, *Principia*, published during the second half of the century, Sir Isaac Newton laid the foundation of physics for the next 200 years, and provided the scientific framework of weather forecasting.

That was the first Renaissance in meteorology—the second one came in the twentieth century. That's when the tools were developed to actually take Newton's principles and apply them to forecasting tomorrow's weather. The basic laws that made the weather happen were pretty much defined by the end of the seventeenth century. Additional principles were uncovered and refined through the eighteenth and nineteenth centuries, and certainly by the turn of the twentieth century, a completely objective and mathematical forecast could be made. Forget about looking at clouds, looking outside, or trying to sense what could happen next. Just use Newton's calculations and devise a solution from the basic physical laws. It seemed easy enough—until it was tried.

Richardson's Experiment

At the start of the twentieth century, British meteorologist Lewis Fry Richardson had the idea of performing a mathematical solution of the complex mathematical representation of the atmosphere. He divided the world into checkerboard squares and attempted to calculate a 24-hour forecast. Unfortunately, his forecast for "tomorrow"

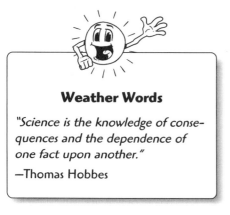

Weather Words

"Science is the knowledge of consequences and the dependence of one fact upon another."

—Thomas Hobbes

wasn't finished for about a year, and by the time it was finally complete, the weather was shown to move backward at the speed of sound! He didn't realize why his forecast went so badly. He was stumped. As a pacifist in World War I, he joined the ambulance corps, and pretty much abandoned meteorology for decades. In 1922, his book *Weather Prediction by Numerical Process* was published. But his vision was far ahead of his time. Although that book was and remains a wonderful basic text in understanding the formulations that make the weather happen, little could be done with concepts. Something went terribly wrong with Richardson's experiment, and he took up a new career in psychology. Later in this chapter, we'll see what went wrong.

Want to Try the Math?

Because the atmosphere is a physical system, it can be represented by mathematics. Ideally, solving that math should provide the weather forecast for tomorrow. Several equations, or mathematical expressions, describe what is happening to the weather.

Newton's Law

The math really isn't that bad. Newton put down the basic laws of fluid motion. Accordingly, if a force is applied to the atmosphere, it should accelerate. For instance, if the pressure is greater at point A than point B, the air will move at an accelerating rate from "A" to "B" (see the figure on the next page). That's all there is to it. In addition to pressure forces, there are other forces such as gravity, friction, and electricity. And a complete representation is needed to get an accurate picture of the atmosphere, although for ease of solution, pressure and gravity are the main players, with friction tacked on later when we develop enough confidence in the process.

So, a particular force exerted in the atmosphere makes it move. It doesn't get simpler than that. The motion is expressed in terms of acceleration, but that really says something about velocity, too, because acceleration is an expression of changing velocity. In any case, if we can measure the forces, we can calculate the velocity of the air—which, of course, is the wind. Newton's laws of motion can be applied to the total wind, or they can be broken up into three components—the wind that moves from west to east, the wind that comes from the south, and the air flow that moves vertically. Therefore, there can be three expressions of Newton's laws: one for west-east motion, another for north-south motion, and the other for up-and-down motion.

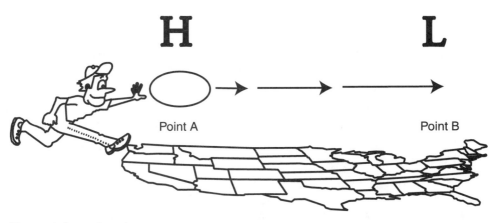

Newton's law of motion.

It sounds okay, but the forces acting on the weather, especially pressure, will undergo change. If we're going to predict future wind from pressure, we need a way of predicting pressure changes. Newton's laws aren't quite enough.

Ideal Gas Law

During the seventeenth century, another important discovery was made. Robert Boyle came up with the assertion that the pressure of a gas depends on volume and temperature: the *ideal gas law*. So now, we have an expression for figuring out future pressure—from the future volume and future temperature. What have we gained? Not a lot, really, because now we need to come up with expressions that show future volume and future temperature.

The volume is related to density, and the density can be derived from the concept of mass conservation. It's the jelly-sandwich principle. If you sit on a jelly sandwich, the jelly will come out at the sides. Similarly, if the air converges horizontally, it will be forced to move vertically. Changes in density can be computed by measuring the convergence. In many situations, that change in density is negligible because of the jelly-sandwich process. The sandwich could be squished, but the density of the jelly remains unchanged because there is a mass flow out the sides. If that flow were prevented, the density would change, but in the atmosphere, there's nothing to restrict that compensating motion, and in most cases, the density change is very small.

Okay, that takes care of density changes, but what about future temperature?

Thermodynamics

Later, in the nineteenth century, expressions that relate heat to temperature and volume were developed. In Chapter 2, we showed how a change in heat brings about a change in volume of a gas, along with a change in temperature. If a can is put on a stove and the burner is turned on, the air molecules inside the can move around. If they hit each other more frequently, the temperature goes up. But the molecules can

307

also bang against the side of the can, and force the can to expand. So if heat is added to a gas, it will expand and reach a higher temperature. Likewise, a change in temperature can be brought about by a change in volume or a change in heat. In other words, you can't get something for nothing—and that tells the story of the first law of *thermodynamics*.

With this thermodynamic expression, the new temperature could be found—but of course that can only be derived if we know the change of heat.

The Dilemma

Okay, let's stop right here. It's getting too complicated. Every time we try to come up with a way of solving one of the variables, we end up introducing another one. You might ask, "What about the second law of thermodynamics?" Well, go ahead, use it. But you'll just introduce yet another unsolved variable—this time, entropy. It just never ends. And this underscores the problem of modern, objective mathematical weather forecasting. There are just too many variables. We always have at least one too many.

Here we have introduced Newton's Laws of Motion in three directions. That gives us three expressions. Then there are the ideal gas law, mass conservation, and the first law of thermodynamics. For these six expressions, we have seven unknowns: the wind blowing west to east, south to north, and vertically, the pressure, the density, the temperature, and the heat. It's an impossible situation, and as soon as you try to simplify, there goes accuracy. No matter how many Doppler radars are available or satellites launched, the problem remains.

Still, we can make the effort, and at least approximate the future weather. Richardson tried and gave up. Another attempt was made about 25 years later, which really did usher in the second Renaissance.

The Computer Age

Richardson's troubles were related to the overwhelming set of variables—along with something else. His checkerboard array of data was too coarse in both space and time. He needed more data points, and he needed to perform many, many more calculations to even approximate tomorrow's weather. He wasn't aware of that problem back in the World War I era. After all, he did spend the better part of a year trying to get one 24-hour forecast together. How many more calculations could he

Weather-Speak

Thermodynamics is the study of heat and its transformation to mechanical energy.

Weather-Wise

I'm often asked about the accuracy of long-range weather predictions. I like to tell people not to depend on the fourth and fifth day of the five day forecast. My reason: There are seven basic variables, and only six equations to solve for the seven unknowns.

reasonably be expected to make? We have to cut him some slack—he and his assistants were only human.

But that was the problem—they were only human and could perform only a modest number of calculations. A mathematical instability set into his experiment, and the entire effort blew up. Let me give you an example of this computational instability.

Suppose you live in Chicago, and the wind is coming from Peoria, a little more than 100 miles away. The temperature in Chicago is 70 degrees and in Peoria, the thermometer reads 80. That's a 10-degree difference in 100 miles, and if the wind is blowing at 20 mph, it might be projected that in five hours the temperature will rise those 10 degrees. That rate of change of temperature is 2 degrees per hour. If you use that rate of change beyond five hours, let's say for 20 hours, you might predict that in 20 hours the temperature will go up a full 40 degrees, to 110 degrees! That's ludicrous, but that's the problem you run into if you make calculations over too large a time interval across a too sparsely defined array of data points.

Through the 1920s and 1930s, nothing could be done to solve this problem. But by the 1940s, a new era was born. The computer arrived.

A Brief History of the Computer

The first widely used commercial electronic computer was the famous *UNIVAC*. CBS television was one of the first organizations to use it. The network wanted it to predict the outcome of the 1952 presidential election. UNIVAC's first prediction of a landslide was right on the money, but the human operators of the machine did not believe the results. So, they reprogrammed it—then it incorrectly predicted a close election. The operators tampered with success, and UNIVAC's revised forecast was way off. This story underscores the reluctant acceptance of computer products, especially in the early days.

The vacuum tube made computers possible in the 1940s. As early as the seventeenth century, Blaise Pascal invented a machine with gears that could add and subtract. Later, in the nineteenth century, British scientist Charles Babbage came up with the concept of a complex mechanical device called the analytical engine. It was designed so that it could perform mathematical manipulations from a set of instructions that were read into it on perforated cards. Still, this device, as visionary as it may seem, could never be completed because of all the mechanisms involved with the operation—just too many moving parts.

Weather-Speak

UNIVAC, or Universal Variable Computer, was built in 1951 and was the first commercially available electronic computer. It stored data on magnetic tape. UNIVACs were sold for about one million dollars each.

That changed in the twentieth century, when vacuum tubes came along and were able to generate electronics in place of the mechanical gears and wheels. During the 1940s, a series of electronic computers were put together. The need for new technology during World War II helped spur the computer development along. One early version known as ENIAC (electronic numerical integrator and computer) was finished in early 1945. This computer contained 18,000 vacuum tubes. The energy drawn by all the tubes in early computers caused lights to dim in nearby communities. At the same time, the computers generated tremendous amounts of heat, which required ventilation, occupied large rooms, and frequently failed. During the late 1940s, transistor technology solved some of the problems, and after the computer chip was developed in the 1960s, there was no stopping these machines. Desktop home computers of the 1990s have more memory, speed, and power than the grand mainframe computers of the 1950s and 1960s.

Putting the Machines to Work

One of the great contributions to the second Renaissance in meteorology was mathematician John von Neumann of Princeton's Institute for Advanced Studies. He was instrumental in the development of the ENIAC. The machine was hardly out of the box before it became apparent that it was just what meteorologists had needed for decades. Jules Charney and Norman Philips of MIT began to carve out new territory when they revisited the works of L. F. Richardson and saw that it was a high-speed computer that was needed all along to solve the basic fundamental equations of meteorology. In 1950, the ENIAC made the first computerized 24-hour prediction, and this time, the weather did not move backward at the speed of sound. The modern age of weather forecasting was underway.

Of course, the computers were primitive in the late 1940s and 1950s, and the programmable models weren't very sophisticated. Calculations were routinely made for one level, 500 mb, and the very first model made all kinds of assumptions. In order to eliminate the problem of the seventh unknown—heat—no changes in heat were allowed. That is called *adiabatic*. Also, the wind field was non-accelerating, and the wind always blew parallel to the contours. That is called *geostrophic*. Then, the most phenomenal assumption of all claimed no temperature change; the temperature in Florida was assumed to be the same as in Montana. This strange assumption was needed to make the set of equations solvable—even with high-speed electronic computers. This situation of no temperature change is called *barotropic*.

But amazingly, it worked—at least on a constant pressure surface at 500 mb. At that level, the temperature contrast is less than near the ground, and the winds do run parallel to the contours. Such a forecast didn't

Weather-Wise

Among the many computer models, progs, that predict the future positions of weather systems are the baroclinic model, the barotropic model, and the LFM (limited fine mesh) model. They show the flow at 500 mb for 12, 24, and 36 hours into the future.

exactly show where it might rain or snow, but it did surprisingly well in projecting the changes of the 500-mb contour field. From that as well as insight about relationships between weather on the ground and air flow at 500 mb, a better idea of upcoming events could evolve.

All this early barotropic model did was shift the 500-mb wind field around along with the Highs and Lows. It didn't create anything new. How could it? There is no heat input, which is the energy that drives the atmosphere.

Yet this very simple, early barotropic computer model became the mainstay of computer projections for more than 25 years—even when more advanced products were made available. For example, another model, called *baroclinic*, eventually came along, and that did include temperature change. Now, storms could develop and dissipate because there is a source of energy. This model was made possible as computers became more sophisticated. Still, the simple barotropic model proved to be more accurate and more reliable, time and time again.

As computer chips began to replace transistors in the 1960s and computers became more efficient, it became possible for weather engineers to run Richardson's entire experiment on the machine. It was feasible to use the basic set of atmospheric equations and come up with a solution for tomorrow's weather. These basic equations became known as the primitive equations and the model became known as the primitive equation (PE) model. Of course there would still be assumptions. The computers weren't that smart. And there is always a problem with that seventh unknown—heat.

But for the first time, at least, the pure expressions could be tackled with a minimum of approximations. Also, calculations were done at a number of levels, and these provided a good cross-section of what the atmosphere was doing.

During the mid and late 1970s, the PE model was refined further and more refinements followed during the 1980s. The data was now placed on a grid system with a spacing that was less than 60 nautical miles. The first of the finely grid models was called the *limited fine mesh (LFM),* and just like the early experience with UNIVAC and CBS, its products were not initially warmly embraced. But a big snowstorm in 1978 changed that.

On February 3, 1978, the new LFM computer model projected the development of a massive storm in the Atlantic waters southeast of Florida. The storm was projected to move northward and turn into a howling nor'easter. However, even in 1978, the computer models were not used with exceptional confidence. Forecasters still liked to do it the old-fashioned way—they liked to look, sense, and feel their way through reams of hand-drawn charts. The primitive equation products were not

Weather-Speak

The **LFM** (limited fine mesh) is a computer model for predicting weather systems and has a closer grid spacing and more data points than two other models—the barotropic and the baroclinic models.

that widely accepted, so when the LFM projected a massive East Coast snowstorm, it was greeted with a collective yawn. The next day, I was interviewed by a radio station and described a potential blizzard arriving on the following day. Before my snowy interview was played on the air, the station played an interview with a forecaster from the National Weather Service. The forecaster said, "It's going to snow because of a front coming from Ohio, but there's no blizzard coming." Even forecasters from the National Weather Service didn't buy into their own computer products.

Well, as it turned out, snow began to fall just before dawn in western New England on February 6, and the rest became history. The Northeast experienced one of the greatest blizzards of the twentieth century. Winds reached hurricane intensity, massive floods swamped coastal communities, and the average snow depth was more than two feet. That didn't include drifts, which were monumental—five feet or more. Traffic was completely paralyzed. There was no warning issued. There wasn't even a watch issued. To most people, the storm was a total surprise. In the Boston area, commuters were on their way to work when the snow began to fall. Major arteries became snarled with stalled, blocked traffic. The storm raged through the 8th.

On the 9th, the computer products had some brand-new believers. Because of this blizzard, computer products became more and more part of the everyday forecast. Appendix D includes some of the modern computer products and describes their use.

Too Much of a Good Thing

The LFM model of the 1970s was followed by even more sophisticated versions in the following 20 years. Forecasters became more and more dependent on them. As we saw in Chapter 23, it's possible to simply rip and read the computer output, and the forecast will be very presentable. The accuracy of the computer product runs about 85 percent. There's nothing wrong with that. However, the remaining 15 percent can make or break an operational forecaster.

We still have a set of equations that are too few for the number of variables. Heat, the development factor, is still a puzzle. It remains the extra unknown. If the basic set of six equations is expanded, the number of variables expand. There is always one too many variables. No matter how large the computer may become, how fast they may compute, or how much storage they may have, the theoretical stone wall remains. A dynamic, objective, 100-percent accurate solution remains elusive. New technology can feed an infinite amount of data into those machines, but the basic theoretical problem stays with us.

Within that 15-percent error window come the most dynamic weather systems on the face of the earth, the ones that a totally computer-based forecast will have difficulty predicting. And these are the ones that attract the most attention. People are watching and listening when a hurricane approaches the mainland. By the time a forecaster delivers all the options, the viewer is often totally confused. The forecaster might say,

"On the one hand, such and such will occur. On the other hand, this will occur." It goes on and on. The simple fact is that the forecaster and the computer are stumped. Other developing situations such as blizzards fall in the same area. Anyone who just depends on the computer product will miss many of the big ones.

Ironically, in the pre-computer era, in the late nineteenth century, an experienced forecaster would be 85 percent correct. Now, an inexperienced forecaster can have the same level of accuracy by looking at a computer product. But to go beyond that, a forecaster really has to go back to basics—looking, sensing, and even drawing some maps. There's never any substitute for experience, even in the computer age. Just go on TV and try it.

In addition, the atmosphere by its own nature is unpredictable. During the 1960s, another MIT meteorologist, Edward N. Lorenz, developed the concept of chaos, whereby small initial deviations or disturbances, even the flapping of butterfly wings, magnify and become overwhelming in the mathematical solution of the atmosphere. The atmosphere is just too chaotic. A forecaster can't develop a reliable product without a good measure of intellect, intuition, mental analogs, experience, and nerve. Those are the intangibles.

Weather-Wise

Computers project general characteristics of the atmosphere, but they have trouble providing specific local weather predictions. This is where we need the human touch.

The Machines Are Getting Better

Even though a computer forecast for the next day's weather may not be sufficiently accurate to stand alone in critical situations, the computer forecasts have improved over the years. For example, during the 1990s, the 36- to 60-hour forecast of precipitation became at least as accurate as the 12- to 36-hour prediction of the 1970s. Also, during the 1990s, the three-day forecasts of general low-pressure development and position became as accurate as the 36-hour prediction of the late 1970s. In addition, monthly and seasonal forecasts have become more reliable with the increased knowledge gained from understanding features such as El Niño and La Niña.

Still, for small-scale occurrences such as tornadoes, flash floods, and hail storms, along with details of upcoming precipitation patterns, the computer forecasts have shown little improvement. The shortcomings remain linked to the limits of our understanding.

The Least You Need to Know

➤ Computer weather forecasts have improved since the 1950s, but they still have major limitations.

➤ A computer forecast can't stand alone; it requires interpretation by an experienced and skilled forecaster.

➤ The problem with computer forecasting is that there are more variables than can be handled through our current understanding of the atmosphere.

➤ Computer forecasts will fail most often during developing situations when heat becomes a major factor.

➤ A good forecaster should still look outside.

Chapter 25

Making a Career Out of It

In This Chapter

➤ Job opportunities in meteorology

➤ The salaries made by meteorologists

➤ Educational training

➤ Prospects for graduates

Opening the Mail

Dear Dr. Mel Goldstein,

Hi. I'm in Frisbie School with Mrs. Demers for a 5th grade teacher in Wolcott, CT. We are learning about weather and I wanted to ask you some questions about your job and different kinds of weather. To start, how do you make predictions? I'm just wondering, but do you use que cards? Now, what are main types of weather? OK, now what about college did you to, to learn about weather? Can I have a list of about 2 or 3 good weather books?

Still, there? OK, how big can the biggest piece of hail be? Somebody said they saw some hail bigger than softballs. Why does lightning light up the whole sky and not just part? Well, there is all my questions. I know that there are more in the world, but this is what I could think of. Thank you for your time please write back.

Sincerely,
Kristen Holmes

This unedited letter was one of a packet that arrived from Mrs. Demers' class while I was putting this book together, and just shows the fascination that people of all ages have with the weather. Similar mail and telephone calls arrive daily. An estimated 90 percent of the public consult weather forecasts once or twice each day, and they do so for a variety of reasons. I'm not sure if Kristen, or any of her classmates, will pursue a career in meteorology, but just in case, I do have some tips and advice.

What Would I Do?

Almost every single aspect of our lives is affected by the weather. The weather influences our health and well-being. It provides the backdrop and inspiration for art, literature, and music. The weather impacts our economics and politics. It has determined the outcome of wars, and it has always been at the forefront of advances in technology. You can find meteorologists performing a huge number of tasks and working in vast numbers of companies and agencies.

Weather Words

"If you have built castles in the air, your work need not be lost; that is where they should be. Now put the foundations under them."

—Henry David Thoreau

Weather-Wise

Many television meteorologists today have their AMS Seal of Approval. To qualify for this seal from the American Meteorological Society, you must have advanced education in meteorology as well as on-air experience in forecasting.

Forecasting

Most meteorologists do work in weather forecasting, either in government or the private sector. The need is certainly there. Some weather forecasters work for private consulting firms that take care of the needs of electric utilities, construction companies, airlines, movie and film companies, trucking firms, highway departments, and outdoor sporting events. And this is only a partial list of the weather-sensitive fields that depend on daily weather forecasts.

The National Weather Service provides some of the same, but mainly issues general forecasts for the public along with analysis, which is used by all meteorologists. The forecasters in the National Weather Service are responsible for delivering warnings and advisories. Other government agencies also use weather forecasters. The military has always been a major area for forecasters. Overall, the government employs more meteorologists than the private sector, but the private sector grew from about 17 percent of the workforce in 1975 to over a third during the 1990s.

Broadcasting

Another major and visible area of involvement for meteorologists is broadcasting. Many forecasters are also broadcasters. In fact, more private-sector meteorologists are in broadcasting than any other area. The expansion of television into numerous network and cable operations has opened the door of opportunity to a number of meteorologists. Of course, communication skills are at least as important as forecast skills for on-air meteorologists. Some with excellent broadcast skills may not be meteorologists at all, but a forecaster works with the person and helps prepare the broadcast.

Consulting

Many meteorologists don't make it through a day without doing some consulting. The telephone rings, and someone needs some past weather information, advice about traveling, information about the long-range forecast, or advice about whether it's a good idea to do some roof work. And the requests go on. A movie crew needs some advice about an outdoor shoot, a tennis match is threatened by some rain, a utility needs to move crews around based on the forecast, a homeowner needs some information about degree days, another needs some historical information because lightning seemed to have hit the well, a police officer is investigating an accident, or somebody wants to invest in oranges and needs to know the odds of a killing frost. And the requests don't stop there!

Braving the Elements

Weather played a huge factor in the D-Day Invasion. On June 5, 1944, the Allied Invasion of the Normandy beaches into Hitler's Europe was postponed because of deteriorating weather and choppy seas. On June 5, President Eisenhower's chief meteorologist predicted that the weather might clear on the 6th. So Eisenhower ordered the invasion for June 6. Operation Overlord was a success!

If you select meteorology as a career, you'll never be lonely. Because the weather influences nearly every aspect of our lives, consulting opportunities are infinite, and many firms have been set up to do just that. The National Weather Service also provides specific information, but the private sector has taken most of the responsibility for tailoring forecasts and information to individual needs.

Air Quality

Another major area of meteorological involvement is air quality. General consulting might include some pollution work, but the field is quite technical and includes field work, forecasting, and communications as well as research. In the late 1960s, before the passage of the Clean Air Act, very few meteorologists worked in air quality. But the passage of the act accompanied the establishment of federal and state agencies to monitor and predict air-pollution levels as well as administer the new laws coming on the scene.

During this time there was a tremendous shortage of trained technicians, scientists, and administrators. The federal government established special training and scholarship programs for meteorologists who were considering working in the environmental area. Then, just as government agencies surfaced, private companies came on the scene. By the 1990s, air-quality work became the fourth-most common activity of meteorologists, just behind weather forecasting, broadcasting, and general consulting. Meteorologists who work in air quality are responsible for monitoring air-pollution levels, predicting concentrations, and developing computer models to show how the pollution will be dispersed. The concerns of global climate change have only expanded the operations of those involved with pollution monitoring and control.

Weather forecasting is the first love of many meteorologists, but they settle happily into air-quality positions because of the opportunities. In my own experience, I elected to be trained as an air-pollution administrator back in the late 1960s in one of the government-sponsored training programs.

Computer Programming

Of course, computer programming has taken off in recent decades. The atmosphere has been reconstructed on these machines, and numerous models have been developed to explain and predict the behavior of the weather. Some of the most influential meteorologists of modern times are scientists who have worked in atmospheric modeling. Those who are involved with this modeling aren't necessarily meteorologists, but they do need to be familiar with atmospheric process. These modelers have a vision of atmospheric behavior and describe the behavior in the language of computers.

The strides made in weather forecasting are largely the result of the success in reconstructing the atmosphere on machines and having the machines carry out operations that human power could not possibly perform. Computer models are constantly being redefined and refined as computers become more effective. Specialists in computer modeling focus on all scales of the atmosphere—small-scale turbulence, thunderstorms, medium-scale fronts, and low-pressure systems, as well as the general circulation patterns that lead to climate studies.

Research and Development

And where would the field of meteorology be without research and development? Most research is carried out by government agencies, or by universities under government-sponsored research grants. Many meteorologists will devote their working lives to the study of all kinds of atmospheric behavior—circulation, cloud dynamics, precipitation, energy transfer, turbulence, radiation, climate change—you name it. Research is done on everything under the sun, including the sun itself. And the effort is performed with the ultimate goal of developing more accurate prediction techniques.

Teaching

On the subject of universities, teaching is an area that commonly employs meteorologists. Most universities have meteorology courses, and over 100 universities offer degree programs in meteorology. In addition, meteorologists can find their way into earth science teaching programs at the middle- or high-school level. In my own 30 years of teaching, I have found that 30 percent of my students have themselves pursued careers in education.

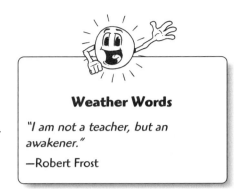

Weather Words

"I am not a teacher, but an awakener."

—Robert Frost

Forensics

Another popular area of work for meteorologists is forensics. This may sound strange, but weather people are often called on to provide historical weather information about legal matters. I have been called to testify in two murder trials when the weather had some influence on the crime. Sometimes the issue revolves around the recollection and reliability of witnesses. Did it really snow that night? Other times, the weather can provide a "cover" for a crime, such as a power outage. Or the brutality of the weather will only add to the pain and suffering of the victim, and that will bear upon the sentence.

Meteorologists are often called on to testify in personal injury cases such as traffic accidents and falls. Was ice on the ground? Could the wind have been strong enough to cause the tree limb to topple onto the car? When did the snow begin and end? In addition, some of this work is related to insurance needs, such as investigating the cause of a roof collapse. The weather has become such an important component in personal injury and damage claims that many meteorological consulting firms specialize in this area.

Other Areas of Specialization

Other areas of specialization for meteorologists include instrument development and remote sensing. These areas have grown in recent decades because of the advances in automated systems, radar, and satellite technology. Also, some meteorologists continue to focus on weather modification work. In addition, because of the great interest in climate change, climatology has become a major area of concentration. Important decisions concerning the environment and energy resources are made based on climate impact. Decision makers need professionals with a solid understanding of meteorology. And because the weather has become a growing business, marketing and managing are two more areas in which meteorologists have begun to specialize. Meteorologists seem to be showing up everywhere.

How Much Will I Earn?

Meteorology has always been at the cutting edge of technology, and in general, meteorologists earn at least as much as any other scientist. Overall, average salaries are skewed on the high side because of the influence of broadcast meteorologists. Some television meteorologists employed in small media markets or on cable networks earn little more than any other meteorologist; but those who work in medium or large markets earn far more. When these salaries are averaged with all the others, it turns out that the average meteorologist actually earns more than any other scientist. Competition in recent years has brought weathercaster salaries down to earth, but most meteorologists in medium markets or higher will earn salaries in the low six-figure area. Those salaries double and triple for primary on-air personalities in larger markets. You might not earn as much as a baseball or basketball star, but you'll do just fine.

Opportunities in broadcasting have expanded in recent decades because of the proliferation of cable stations. That has provided more openings for newly trained and experienced meteorologists, but it has divided the viewer pie. Because a station's revenues are tied to its viewership, management has been less willing to pay the mega-salaries of years gone by. In a number of major markets, salaries have been cut by 50 percent or more. Salaries are still substantial, but not like the pre-cable days. Those who decide to go into broadcasting can expect plenty of competition for the higher paying positions. After all, it is show-biz.

On the low end of the income spectrum are entry-level salaries for those working in private weather-consulting firms. Some of these salaries are just barely over minimum wage, but many of these jobs provide considerable on-the-job training, which translates into more substantial future incomes. The American Meteorological Society did a survey of incomes for those who work in the private sector. The following table shows some of the results. The salaries are in 1995 dollars.

Weather-Wise

A "cooperative observer" for a weather service office is a volunteer who collects weather data and forwards the data to weather service offices.

Incomes of Meteorologists Employed in the Private Sector

Annual Salary Range	Entry Level	1-2 Years Experience	3-5 Years Experience
<$15,000	7.1%	0%	0%
$15,000-$20,000	27.5%	11.5%	2.1%
$20,000-$25,000	28.1%	22%	6.4%
$25,000-$30,000	24.4%	31%	13.8%
$30,000-$40,000	9.9%	29.1%	39.8%
$40,000-$50,000	1.5%	4%	27.8%
$50,000-$75,000	1.2%	1.5%	6.4%
>$75,000	0.3%	0.9%	3.7%

About half of the entry-level positions pay between $20,000 and $30,000 per year. About one-third of the entry-level positions pay less than $20,000. But in three to five years, more than half will be earning between $30,000 and $50,000; only 2 percent will be earning $20,000 or less. Advancement is steady, even if entry-level opportunities are not exactly lucrative.

Salaries within the government are comfortable. Beginning salaries are between $20,000 and $25,000 per year, and experienced forecasters earn in the neighborhood of $75,000.

Those meteorologists who go into management, marketing, or administration earn more. These salaries can approach those of broadcasters in at least medium markets. And for those who own their own weather-related businesses, the sky's the limit!

How Do I Become a Meteorologist?

All of us can become weather-wise. Regardless of your area of work, the weather can be an avocation even if it isn't a vocation. You're already there, just by reading and using this book. Besides, you don't need a college degree to look outside, look up, figure out what the weather will do next, and even tell people about it. Actually, some of the highest paid television weather personalities have no degree in meteorology at all. But that's changing, and if you want to pursue meteorology as an occupation, an education is absolutely essential.

Because meteorology is a broad field that touches on nearly every area of science, a general background in math, science, and technology is included in every meteorological curriculum. In some respects, meteorology has become applied mathematics, so a solid background in math is essential. Young people who plan careers in meteorology should take as many math courses as possible, starting in middle school.

Computer skills are just as important. These skills go far beyond computer games and include the operation and programming of computers.

Communication skills are also important, especially for those dealing directly with the public. For broadcasters, communication skills are more important than anything else. Although television viewers may be somewhat impressed with degrees and credentials, survey after survey has shown that they really just want to be given the forecast. If a weather-caster doesn't communicate well, the audience will reach for the remote. Good delivery is really a talent. It can't be learned, but it can be polished, and very early, a person will learn if that talent is at hand.

Although many schools offer non-degree programs in basic meteorology, the majority of practicing meteorologists hold at least an undergraduate degree in meteorology. The program

Weather-Wise

The National Weather Service has a program called SKYWARN for trained volunteer severe weather spotters. These volunteers are on the lookout for severe storms.

includes basic courses in physics, chemistry, biology, calculus, and computer science. The typical degree program is as vigorous as any engineering program. Most meteorology undergraduates who wish to receive high grades will need to sacrifice some of their social life. But if you use your time wisely and approach the curriculum maturely, there will still be time for a rounded college experience. Because the job market is always competitive, the best opportunities will be waiting for those who perform well during those four short years.

Those who pursue research and teaching will go beyond a four-year degree and seek a masters or doctorate. Some who take the research route may hold an undergraduate degree in one of the sciences or mathematics—but not meteorology. In some cases, a degree in math, physics, or chemistry followed by a masters and doctorate in meteorology is be the best track for researchers. Some of the top graduate schools in meteorology encourage students to receive undergraduate degrees in math or physics rather than meteorology. But for those who love the weather, waiting until graduate school for meteorology courses may be too long. It was for me.

So, for all who want to grow up and be called a "meteorologist," the message is math, science, math, science…. Study hard, make some sacrifices, and the rewards will most assuredly be there. In over 25 years of college teaching, I have never failed to place a student who had a "B" average, or better. Which brings us to the next subject.

Will I Find a Job?

The National Weather Service and other government agencies have historically been the main employers of meteorologists. That has changed. For young people, the modernization of the National Weather Service has been both good and bad. At first, when the effort to update radar, observational, and communications equipment was made in the 1980s, newly trained young meteorologists were in demand. But once the automated systems were set up in the mid-1990s, the National Weather Service stopped hiring, except in rare cases. Then, in the late 1990s, hiring began—about 100 new meteorologists per year to replace employees lost through attrition. The federal government remains the major employer of meteorologists.

As the public sector tightened its belt, the private sector began to grow. By the late 1990s, most private-sector firms were anticipating an increase of 10 to 30 percent in positions over a 10-year period. According to this recent American Meteorological Society survey, that

Weather-Wise

A study tip: If you plan to go into meteorology, you'll have to do all your math homework, and then some. Do every problem. If the odd numbered problems are assigned, do the even numbered ones, too.

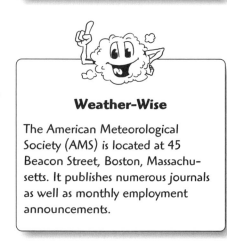

Weather-Wise

The American Meteorological Society (AMS) is located at 45 Beacon Street, Boston, Massachusetts. It publishes numerous journals as well as monthly employment announcements.

translates into a minimum of 360 new entry-level positions each year. That's more than the 100 that the National Weather Service hires. Also, that 360 does not include those who go into education. The general outlook for employment opportunities in meteorology is optimistic.

The opportunities for employment are directly related to one's skills and training. Because meteorology is such a broad and applied field, those seeking employment should have training in many areas. Although forecasting could be the first choice, keep in mind that opportunities may be more likely in air quality work or education. New meteorologists should be flexible. Also, the work environment usually involves irregular hours. The weather never sleeps, and weather people do tend toward insomnia. Shift work is to be expected. Research and teaching provide a more normal schedule, but forecasting is something else entirely. All-nighters go with the territory.

But opportunities aside, for many meteorologists, their occupation is a passion rather than a profession. They simply love what they do. Storms excite them, the howling wind stirs them, and they cannot wait to tell others what the weather will do next. Their real compensation comes from experiencing and observing the infinite number of changes the weather puts on display, almost daily. Then, there is the satisfaction of getting tomorrow's forecast right.

Yet, you really don't need a Ph.D. in meteorology to share in that wonderment and excitement, and that is what this book is all about. The weather belongs to all of us. Just by looking out and looking up, we can learn and understand the weather and its many ways.

Happy Weather!

Weather Words

"On bravely through the sunshine and the showers, Time hath his work to do, and we have ours."

—Ralph Waldo Emerson

The Least You Need to Know

➤ Meteorologists are employed in numerous, fascinating areas.

➤ The educational programs for meteorologists are vigorous and well-founded in the basic sciences, as well as mathematics.

➤ Although the field is competitive, employment opportunities are strong.

➤ Meteorology is at least as lucrative as any other field of science.

➤ Those who do well in their educational programs will most likely find the best entry-level positions.

Weather-Speak Glossary

absolute zero   The point where all molecular motion is presumed to cease. It is the coldest possible temperature: –273 degrees C or –459 degrees F or 0 K.

absorption   The process by which molecules coming from a gaseous phase are retained by the surface of a substance.

adiabatic lapse rate   The rate of temperature decrease due to expansion or contraction without any loss or gain of heat. As a pocket of air rises, it will expand, and that expansion alone causes a cooling, regardless of any heat exchange.

adsorption   The process by which molecules coming from a gaseous phase are retained by the surface of a substance.

air mass   A very large body of air that has uniform moisture and temperature characteristics. One air mass can cover one-half of the United States.

ASOS (Automated Surface Observing System)   Over 850 of these systems are being installed in the United States to serve as the nation's primary surface weather observing network.

aspiration psychrometer   Similar to a sling psychrometer, but rather than being whirled, air is drawn past it with an electric fan.

AWIPS (Advanced Weather Interactive Processing System)   This is the new communication nerve center of operations at all the Weather Forecast Offices and River Forecast Centers. It combines information from ASOS and NEXRAD.

baroclinic zones   Areas of temperature contrasts and available potential energy.

barometer   An instrument used to measure the pressure of the atmosphere. The two kinds of barometers are aneroid and mercurial. The aneroid has a metallic surface and a pointer, with a graduated scale. The mercurial has mercury in a graduated glass tube.

blizzard   According to the National Weather Service, a blizzard is characterized by low temperatures, winds greater than 35 mph, and snow heavy enough to restrict visibility to less than a quarter-mile. In earlier days, the temperature had to be in the teens, but no longer.

bombogenesis   Has been used to describe extreme cyclogenesis of an explosive nature. This development is sometimes seen off the east coast of the United States. Gale force winds and heavy precipitation develop.

boreal forest   Also known as taiga, this is a forest that's made up of conifers and birches.

Carbon dating   The process used to date formerly living plants and animals by measuring the radioactivity of the remaining carbon-14 isotopes.

Carboniferous Period   This includes the Mississippian and the Pennsylvanian Periods under the Paleozoic Era. There was lush vegetation and dense swampy forests, caused by a moist and warm climate.

Celsius (C)   A temperature scale based on 0 degrees as the freezing point of water and 100 degrees as the boiling point of water at sea level.

chlorosis   The condition where plants do not develop enough chlorophyll.

circulation   A condition in which the atmosphere moves in a closed path. Because the earth is rotating, the atmosphere also rotates, and that rotation creates circulations of different sizes.

cirrus   Thin, wispy, high clouds. Derived from the Latin, meaning "thin, wispy," these clouds contain ice crystals.

climate   An average of weather conditions as they've occurred over decades. Sometimes incorrectly used interchangeably with weather. The 30-year average of temperature will define the climate normal for temperature. The same is true for precipitation.

cloud seeding   A process that introduces silver iodide or dry ice into a cloud for producing rain.

coalescence   The joining together of small droplets into larger droplets.

cold front   A front in which a colder air mass overtakes and replaces a warmer air mass.

condensation   The point at which the atmosphere is filled to overflowing.

convergence   A condition that occurs in the atmosphere when air comes together at a particular location. That would take place if opposing winds meet over that point. Convergence would also occur if more air enters a region than departs.

Coriolis force   An apparent force due to the rotation of the earth. Moving objects, such as wind, are deflected to the right in the Northern Hemisphere and to the left in the Southern Hemisphere.

cumulus   From the Latin for "puffy," these are the fleecy-looking clouds that paint the sky on a pleasant, quiet day.

cyclogenesis   The development or intensification of a cyclone.

dew point   The temperature at which the vapor in the atmosphere becomes liquid.

divergence   The process opposite from convergence, where more air leaves than arrives.

dog day season   The period of weather that's usually the hottest of the year. It occurs from early July to early August.

Doppler effect   The change in frequency of sound waves when an object is moving toward or away from you.

eccentricity   Relates to the shape of the earth's orbit as it revolves around the Sun. More elliptically-shaped orbits will have a higher eccentricity than circular-shaped orbits.

echo   This is an on-screen image of a radar target.

El Niño   A periodical warming of equatorial ocean water. It disrupts weather and causes all kinds of havoc, from droughts to floods and landslides.

El Viejo   A relative of El Niño and La Niña, El Viejo occurs when ocean currents in the Pacific Ocean are close to normal.

Fahrenheit (F)   A temperature scale based on 32 degrees as the freezing point of water and 212 degrees as the boiling point of water at sea level.

frontal cyclone   A storm that forms on a front. In the Northern Hemisphere, it has a counterclockwise circulation, and it covers an area of several hundred miles, occasionally 1,000 miles.

frostbite   A condition that occurs on exposed skin when the winds are high and the air is below freezing, characterized by skin that freezes.

geostrophic   A balance between the pressure force and the Coriolis force. The pressure force causes the air to move from high to low pressure. In the Northern Hemisphere, the Coriolis force causes that motion to turn to the right. When that right-directed motion is balanced by the pressure force, the flow is geostrophic.

GMT (Greenwich Mean Time)   The local time in Greenwich, England. It is measured on the prime meridian (0 degrees longitude). Meteorological and navigational clocks are set to GMT so there will be uniformity in reporting the time of data observation and collection.

GOES (geostationary satellites)   These satellites orbit the earth but remain in a fixed place because they revolve around the earth at the same rate as the earth rotates.

greenhouse gases   The gases in the atmosphere, especially water vapor and carbon dioxide, that give it the capacity to retain heat.

ground blizzard   When blowing snow restricts visibility to below a quarter-mile, even after the snow stops falling.

hail   Ice particles that form during thunderstorms when small ice crystals collect vapor and slowly descend through the cloud. Because of the turbulence within a thunderstorm cloud, these ice particles can be tossed up and down, allowing successive layers of ice to form.

half-life   The time it takes for the decay of one-half of the atoms of a radioactive substance. The half-life of carbon-14 is about 5730 years. The half-life of uranium-238 (a uranium-bearing rock) is 4.51 billion years. The half-life of uranium-235 is 713 million years.

heat capacity   The amount of heat required to raise the temperature of a substance.

heat index   An index that describes what the air feels like given the combination of temperature and humidity.

heat syndrome   A severe disturbance of the human thermoregulatory system. It ranges from heat stress to heat stroke.

hurricane   A violent storm of tropical origin in which winds exceed 73 mph. In the western Pacific, hurricanes are called typhoons; in the Indian Ocean, they're called cyclones.

hurricane seeding   The use of silver iodide in the clouds just outside the eye wall of the storm. The eye wall is the ring of squalls wrapped around the center of the hurricane. This seeding is an attempt to diffuse the storm's winds.

insensible perspiration   Perspiration that evaporates before it becomes visible on the skin.

inversion   A reversal in the normal temperature rate, when the temperature increases with elevation, rather than falling.

IPCC (Intergovernmental Panel on Climate Change)   This organization was established by the United Nations in 1988. It is composed of many of the world's leading atmospheric scientists.

jet stream   Made up of relatively strong horizontal ribbons of wind found at the earth's tropopause, which is 6 to 10 miles above the ground.

Kelvin (K)   Also called the absolute scale, this is a temperature scale that has intervals equivalent to the Celsius scale, but begins at absolute zero.

lake effect   Snow squalls that occur when local snowstorms form on the lee side of a lake as the cold dry air picks up moisture from the lake. The air runs into hills and rises. It then releases moisture in the form of snow squalls.

La Niña   The cold phase of the El Niño oscillation. The waters of the Pacific near the equator and off the west coast of South America are much colder than normal during the La Niña. La Niña is the cold water sibling of El Niño.

lapse rate   The change in temperature with elevation. If a pocket of air is dry, it will cool at a rate of 5.5 degrees for every thousand feet it rises. That's called the dry adiabatic lapse rate.

latent heat   The heat that is absorbed or released during a substance's change of state, such as during evaporation or condensation.

lee side   The shore toward which the wind is blowing. If the wind is from the west, the lee side would be on the eastern shore.

LFM (limited fine mesh)   A computer model for predicting weather systems, it has closer grid spacing and more data points than two other models—the barotropic and the baroclinic models.

melatonin   A hormone produced by the pineal gland, a cone-shaped structure in the brain. Melatonin is related to seasonal depression.

mesocyclone   The intense rotating region of air containing a severe thunderstorm.

mesopause   The layer that separates the mesosphere from the thermosphere; it's about 50 miles high.

mesosphere   The layer above the stratosphere; it's about 50 miles deep.

meteorology   The science dealing with the study of the atmosphere.

monsoon   The term commonly used in reference to torrential rains, but it actually describes the wind that brings this weather. This wind reverses direction between winter and summer and usually causes dry winters and wet summers. The wind blows from the land to the sea in winter and from the sea to the land in summer.

NEXRAD (Next Generation Weather Radar)   The National Weather Service's new Doppler radar network installed in the 1990s. Doppler radar detects precipitation and measures the speed of falling precipitation, like conventional radar. But Doppler also measures the speed at which precipitation is moving horizontally toward or away from the radar.

nimbus   From the Latin for "rain-bearing," these are any clouds that deliver rain.

obliqueness   The tilt of the earth's axis. Precession is the wobbling of the earth's axis.

occluded front   A front that is caused by a cold front overtaking a warm front, when the warm air is lifted above the earth's surface.

operational forecast   The final forecast product.

ozone   A gaseous, almost colorless form of oxygen.

ozone hole   The area in the stratosphere where the ozone is depleted. The ozone hole is a seasonal thing. It reaches its peak during the Antarctic spring, in October and November. It fills by December and January.

persistence   The assumption that weather patterns do not change rapidly. Even in mid-latitudes, where change is always expected, persistence can be surprisingly accurate. If you predict that today's weather will be repeated tomorrow, you'll be correct 67 percent of the time in places like Boston, New York, or Chicago. If you predict that in Los Angeles during the summer, you'll be correct 98 percent of the time.

plasmolysis   Tissue collapse in plants from loss of water. Air pollutants such as sulfur oxides can bring this about.

plate tectonics   The theory that the earth's surface is made up of several individual pieces, or plates, that move in relation to one another. As the plates move, the continents also move. The theory of continental drift has been absorbed by the theory of plate tectonics.

potential energy   The potential to do work, or the potential to move. A deck of cards sitting on the edge of a table has the potential to fall, but its energy will only be released if it's pushed over the edge. Temperature contrasts represent potential energy in the atmosphere. When warm air masses mix with colder air masses, that potential energy becomes available for storm development, and is called available potential energy.

pressure plate anemometer   The oldest type of anemometer. It measures wind speed by a single swinging metal plate rather than the cups of a modern anemometer.

primary center   An initial storm center. Often, a second center will develop as the primary center weakens. The secondary center can become very intense.

primary pollutants   Those pollutants that are directly emitted.

radar transmitter   Sends out pulses, and when they encounter an object, a small fraction of microwaves bounce back to the radar antenna. The object shows up as a pattern on the radar screen.

radiational cooling   Cooling that occurs at night. The ground will cool more quickly than the air above it. It is most effective when skies are clear and winds are light.

radioactive decay   The process by which the atomic nuclei break apart and form other, more stable elements.

radiosonde   A balloon-borne instrument that measures and transmits meteorological data of temperature, pressure, and humidity. A theodolite is an instrument used to track a radiosonde.

rain gauge   An instrument that measures the amount of rainfall at a given time interval.

reflectivity   The measure of radiation reflected by a given surface.

refraction   The bending of light as it passes from one medium into another.

relative humidity   The ratio between the actual amount of water vapor present to the capacity that the air has at a particular temperature and pressure.

revolution and **rotation**   The two principal motions of the earth. Revolution is the movement of the earth in its orbit around the sun; rotation is the spinning of the earth around its axis.

rip and read meteorologists   Meteorologists who just rip and read the computer outputs and then deliver the forecast as written by the machines.

saturation   The point at which the atmosphere is totally filled with water vapor.

sea breeze   A breeze that blows from the ocean. The same kind of breeze that develops on the shore of a large lake is called a **lake breeze.**

secondary center   Forms from the primary center. Often these are very intense and cause heavy snow during the winter.

secondary pollutants   Formed by chemical reactions of the primary pollutants in the lower atmosphere.

sensible perspiration   Perspiration that is visible on the skin.

serotonin   A hormone that affects moods.

severe thunderstorm warning   A warning that's posted if the storm is spotted on radar, or observed, and it's considered imminent.

severe thunderstorm watch   A warning that's issued whenever thunderstorms are expected to deliver winds of at least 58 mph with at least $3/4$-inch hail.

sling psychrometer   An instrument that measures relative humidity. It has two thermometers—a dry bulb and a wet bulb—mounted side by side, and has a handle at one end. You whirl the instrument to get the readings.

stationary front   A front that does not move.

sunspots   Cooler, relatively dark areas found on the surface of the Sun. They are associated with solar disturbances, such as solar flares.

tornado warning   A warning that's issued if a tornado is sighted, or its signature shows up on radar. Information is given about where the storm is occurring and its direction of movement.

tornado watch   A warning that's issued if conditions favor tornado development.

sleet   Frozen rain that occurs during the winter. As rain falls into a cold layer near the ground, it will sometimes refreeze into ice pellets, or sleet.

storm surge   A moving wall of water that races to the shore and crushes coastal areas. A hurricane's eye's low pressure causes the sea beneath it to rise measurably, usually well above the high tide level. The strong winds force additional piling up of the water.

stratosphere   The layer next to the troposphere; it's about 30 miles high.

stratus   From the Latin for "layer," these clouds are flat and stay close to the ground.

subsidence   The sinking of air, usually associated with a high pressure area.

suspended particulates   Solids that have a very small diameter and are suspended in exhaust gases. They can be discharged into the atmosphere.

temperature inversion   This occurs when the air near the ground is much colder than the air above. Instead of falling with elevation, the temperature rises with elevation. This takes place most often during a calm, dry, and cloudless night.

thermodynamics   The study of heat and its transformation to mechanical energy.

thermograph   An instrument that continuously measures and records temperature.

thermosphere   A region of the atmosphere from about 50 miles to 300 miles. The temperature increases with elevation here. It lies above the mesosphere.

Tornado vortex signature (TVS)   The image of tornadic wind shear found on a Doppler radar screen. It shows up inside a mesocyclone.

trade winds   The steady east winds found between latitudes 23.5 degrees, north and south. They marked popular sailing routes for commercial sailing vessels.

tropical cyclone   A term that generally refers to all organized tropical circulations.

tropical depression   A storm system with winds under 39 mph.

tropical storm   A storm system with winds between 39 and 73 mph.

troposphere   The bottom layer of the atmosphere, extending from sea level to seven miles high.

UNIVAC (Universal Variable Computer)   Built in 1951, this was the first commercially available electronic computer. It stored data on magnetic tape. UNIVACs were sold for about one million dollars each.

upwelling   The rising of cold water from the deep regions up to the surface.

uranium dating   This can be used for both very old, as well as non-living things. Isotopes of uranium will decay in predictable ways, and the remaining isotopes give clues of the sample's age.

urban heat island effect   The effect of temperatures in urban areas, or cities, being higher than in surrounding rural areas.

warm front   A front in which a warm air mass overtakes and replaces a cold air mass.

weather   A term that refers to current conditions of temperature, precipitation, humidity, and wind. Sometimes incorrectly used interchangeably with "climate."

wind shear   The rate of change of wind direction or speed, especially when it is a sudden variation. It can be dangerous to aircraft when landing or taking off.

Earth and Climate History

Earth's history can be described within certain time intervals. The largest of subdivisions are called *eras*. The Precambrian is the oldest era within which the first organisms appeared between 700 million and 3.4 billion years ago. Then there is the Paleozoic era, which is further divided into periods. These periods include the Ordovician period, when the first vertebrate fossils appeared. That was 400 to 500 million years ago. The first amphibians appeared during the Devonian period, about 400 million years ago.

The Paleozoic era extends up to 200 million years ago, when the first reptiles are indicated. Then the Mesozoic era takes over and extends to 65 million years ago. Within this era, dinosaurs and birds appeared. From 65 million years ago to the present is the Cenozoic era. Mammals and humans characterize this era.

The following figure shows the geologic time scale.

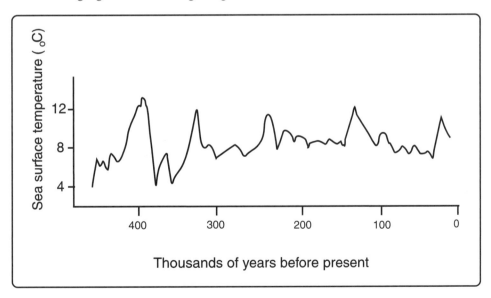

Geologic time scale.

Throughout the periods of the Cenozoic, dramatic climate changes have taken place. The Pleistocene period represents the famous Ice Age, which began about 2.5 million years ago and lasted up until 10,000 to 15,000 years ago, when the last continental glacier receded from North America. The entire Pleistocene period was characterized by numerous glacial advances and retreats even though the entire period is known as the Ice Age. Currently, we consider ourselves in a glacial recession of that Ice Age. The ice will return.

Other glacial periods occurred during Earth's long history. Major ice ages took place 2 billion, 600 million, and 250 million years ago.

Weather Maps

The data is plotted in a standard fashion. The station model is as follows:

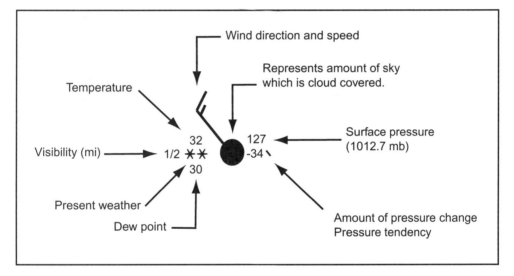

Surface station model.

Each observation provides temperature, dew point, wind, pressure, sky conditions, and precipitation. That data is then recorded on a map according to the model. The coding may seem complicated, but it's really quite basic. The temperature is placed in the upper left of the station plot, the dew point is in the lower left. The pressure is in the upper right.

The amount of cloudiness is depicted by shadings within a center circle. The circle is open if the sky is clear, and it's completely filled in if the sky is overcast. If the weather is partly cloudy, the circle is only partially filled in.

Wind is shown with a line that radiates out from the circle and points in the direction from which the wind is coming. The speed of the wind is shown with flags attached to the end of these lines. A long flag represents 10 knots; a small flag indicates 5 knots. The speed is represented in a way similar to Roman numerals. Two long flags and a short flag would indicate a speed of 25 knots.

Precipitation is shown in coded form between the temperature and dew point. That's all there is to this. Here's a table of precipitation types:

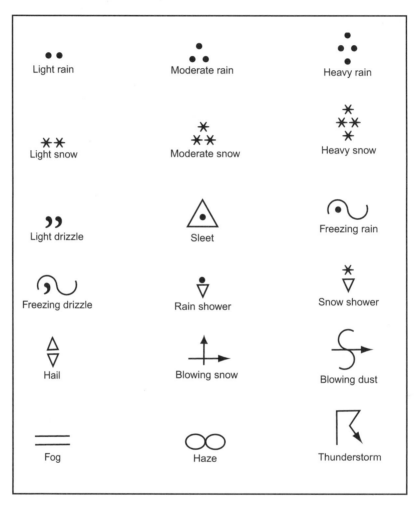

Precipitation types and coding.

A couple of other elements: Visibility is the number between the temperature and dew point, next to the precipitation type; and the pressure change over the past three hours is shown by the symbol beneath the pressure reading. For example, a "+33" would mean that the pressure changed 3.3 mb in the past three hours.

So, in our example, the temperature is 32 degrees and the dew point is 30. Light snow is falling (indicated by **). The sky is overcast with the wind from the northeast at 15 knots. The pressure fell 3.4 mb in the past three hours and the pressure is 1012.7 mb. The various pressure symbols shape up like this:

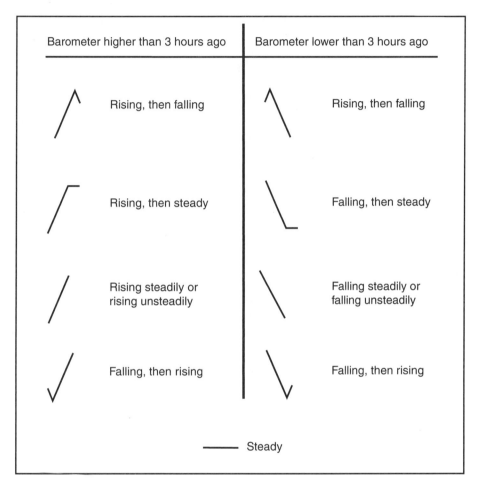

Barometer higher than 3 hours ago	Barometer lower than 3 hours ago
Rising, then falling	Rising, then falling
Rising, then steady	Falling, then steady
Rising steadily or rising unsteadily	Falling steadily or falling unsteadily
Falling, then rising	Falling, then rising
Steady	

Pressure change symbols.

Surface Weather Maps

After the data is plotted, a surface weather map is drawn. See Chapter 23 for specifics.

Upper Air Charts

These are very much like contour maps. The data is collected from radiosonde balloons and plotted on constant pressure surfaces with this format:

337

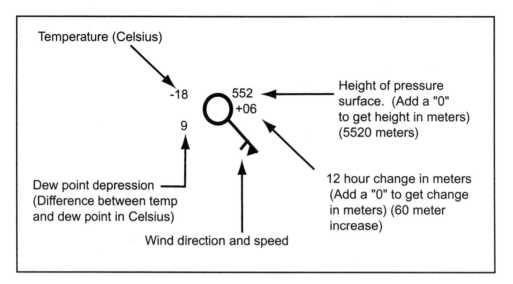

Station model for upper-air observations.

In our example, the temperature is –18 degrees, the temperature dew point difference is 9 (the dew point would be –27), the height of the surface is 5,520 meters, and the height change was +60 meters during the past 12 hours.

The 500-millibar chart is excellent for determining the flow of weather systems. Fronts and high and low pressure systems will generally move in the direction of the flow at about half the speed of the wind at 500 millibars. Refer to the 500 millibar figure in Chapter 23.

Computer Forecasting

Computers have completely revolutionized the way we look at the weather. Forecasting has been assisted by numerous computer products. The two most popular models have been the nested grid model (NGM) and the ETA model (ETA stands for the coordinate system, which uses the Greek letter as a variable). These models generate outputs that look like this:

```
828
FOUS61 KWNO 191200
OUTPUT FROM ETA 12Z OCT 19 98
TTPTTR1R2R3 VVVLI PSDDFF HHT1T3T5    TTPTTR1R2R3 VVVLI PSDDFF HHT1T3T5
ALB//862919 -3010 142920 59100505    BTV//794419 -2910 102720 54100201
0000862321 -2010 142914 59110307    06000913021 -3712 122816 54090102
12001882620 -1411 162814 56090306    12000923125 -2513 142813 52070202
18000893324 -1010 152614 51080300    18001964224 -2308 122311 47070499
24000913420 -2108 122518 46070497    24000955819 01404 082418 41070396
30000814222 -2305 122818 42090295    30005884523 -1205 102817 37070093
36002884225 -2705 142915 40070194    36000883921 -1609 122917 34049891
42000844130 -3709 163012 39050094    42000873723 -1812 152816 33029692
48000844728 -2910 163010 37039994    48000863925 -2113 152815 32009692
48000844728 -2910 163010 37039994    48000863925 -2113 152815 32009692
BOS//742707 -0406 092620 64161309    LGA//752826 -0408 152813 66161310
06000622625 01411 122817 62150708    06000612519 -1011 162914 63160909
12000642521 00613 142917 59130608    12000612028 00112 173016 60140708
18000662631 01113 152814 54120405    18000652442 00314 182912 56120504
24000703319 00411 132417 49100601    24000782715 -0211 162617 52100802
30000633720 -0805 102622 46130699    30000532621 -1709 152821 49140600
36000593524 -3907 122820 42110497    36000583232 -3109 162818 47120698
42000633833 -2210 142918 40090295    42000774051 -0809 182816 45110597
48000624031 -1712 152917 39070097    48000854846 -0608 172712 44090598
48000624031 -1712 152917 39070097    48000854846 -0608 172712 44090598
PHL//644849 -1606 162714 67181410    IPT//842824 -3313 183013 61100706
06000573719 -0109 172913 64181209    06000761920 00812 183013 60110406
12000613436 -0411 173114 61161007    12000791623 -0711 192814 57100403
18000683342 00713 193110 57130704    18000892917 00912 182715 52080600
24000782313 -0313 182817 54100903    24000912520 -0711 172819 48060499
30000482320 -2111 172920 51150702    30000682925 -2907 182918 46100297
36000522735 -2512 182918 50130600    36000873935 -2407 182816 45090396
42000683152 -0212 202916 48110599    42001924547 -1207 192714 44080396
48000784350 -0711 182716 46090699    48003955036 -0806 172811 42070295
48000784350 -0711 182716 46090699    48003955036 -0806 172811 42070295
```

Computer output from an ETA model.

There are a lot of numbers, but the code breaks down like this:

TT represents the time interval in hours from the initial data input. For example, 06 refers to a six-hour forecast; 12 is the 12-hour forecast, and so on. **PTT** represents the precipitation projected in six-hour blocks. The units are in inches. If the block comes out with a 001, then 0.01 inch of precipitation is expected during the six-hour block. In the example of the ETA output, Burlington, Vermont (BTV), has 0.01 inch projected for between 12 and 18 hours out from the initial computer run. Another 0.05 inch is predicted between 24 and 30 hours.

The columns, **Rl**, **R2**, and **R3** represent the relative humidity in three layers—one near the surface, another in the upper atmosphere, and one that is intermediate. At LaGuardia Airport (LGA), the relative humidity is 61 percent, 20 percent, and 28 percent for the three levels at 12 hours.

The *vertical velocity* is given under the header **VVV**. A "–30" would be a downward vertical velocity of 3.0 microbars/sec. A 130 would be an upward motion of 1.30 microbars/sec; about 1.3 cm/sec. Any positive vertical velocity is significant for clouds and precipitation. A 2 or 3 cm/sec vertical velocity is enough to generate a rainy day. If the vertical velocity reaches over 5 cm/second, the weather could be violent. In our example, the vertical velocities are slight, although Boston (BOS) does indicate 014 at six hours, or 1.4 microbars/sec, about 1.4 cm/sec.

The column **LI** shows a stability index called the *lifted index*. If a pocket of air is lifted to 500 millibars, and its temperature is colder than its surroundings, the pocket will be heavier than its environment and will tend to sink. The atmosphere is stable. The lifted index is the difference in temperature between its surroundings and the pocket. A *positive lifted index* shows stability. The environment is warmer than the pocket, and the difference in temperature between the environment and the pocket would be positive. If the difference were negative, the pocket would be warmer, and it would continue to rise. The atmosphere would be unstable and clouds would build, possibly into thunderstorms.

In the code, any LI listed as 99, 98, 97, and so on, refers to a lifted index of –1, –2, –3. Positive lifted indices are read directly, so for Williamsport (IPT), the lifted index at six hours is +12. The atmosphere is very stable.

Pressure at the surface is shown by **PS**. In Philadelphia (PHL), the surface pressure at 30 hours is listed as 17, or 1017 millibars.

Wind direction is shown as **DD,** and *wind speed* is shown as **FF**. For Albany (ALB), in 48 hours is "30" which is decoded as 300 degrees. The wind is from the northwest or 300 degrees at 10 knots—the speed being given under the column of FF.

The average temperature of the atmosphere from near the ground to 500 millibars is shown indirectly under the heading **HH**. That actually represents the thickness in meters of a layer between 1000 and 500 millibars. A thicker layer represents warmer temperatures. For Albany (ALB) in 36 hours HH is given as 40, and that is decoded as

5,400 meters. During the winter, a thickness of 5,400 meters or less often indicates an atmosphere cold enough to support snow. A thickness below 5,100 meters indicates arctic air; thicknesses of 5,700 meters or more show summertime heat.

Specific temperature projections at three levels are given by **T1, T3,** and **T5.** The T1 is very close to the surface, T3 is about one kilometer above the surface, and T5 is approximately two kilometers above the ground.

For Burlington, Vermont (BTV), the 12-hour forecast shows T1 as 7 degrees C, T2 as 2 degrees C, and T5 as 2 degrees C. Negative temperatures are given in the 90 or 80-group. For example, in 30 hours at BTV, T5 is 93 or –7 degrees C. At 36 hours, T3 would be –2 degrees C, and T5 –9 degrees C.

The data can also be placed in another format that's called **MOS** (*model output statistics*). The data shows the character of weather through the next 48 hours. The temperature at three-hour intervals is shown, along with the anticipated high and low for each 24-hour period. The dew point temperature, precipitation probability, and various other parameters are printed out. This output is a combination of direct computer projection modified with local climatology. If a person had no other information but this output, a reasonable forecast could be made. Please refer to Chapter 23 for a sample of the MOS forecast.

In addition to the text data, the information is placed in a map format. A vast amount of information is displayed on the maps, which come in sets of four for 12-hour periods through 48 hours.

Index

Symbols

1938 New England
   hurricane, 96
1998 El Niño, 113
500-mb charts, 296, 338
850-mb charts, 299

A

A class climates, 208
abbreviations for air mass
   types, 71
absolute zero, Kelvin
   scale, 269
absorption
   of light, 182
   pollution control, 159
adiabatic lapse rate, 300,
   310
adsorption, pollution
   control, 159
advection fog, 25
aerovanes, 273
Africa, highest
   temperature recorded,
   18
air
   capacity for water
      vapor, 15
   rising columns,
      rainfall, 37

air masses, 69
   arctic, 73
   available potential
      energy, 78
   baroclinic zones, 78
   boundaries, 81
   cold fronts, thunder-
      storms/tornadoes, 80
   continental polar, 72
   continental tropical, 75
   equatorial, 75
   formation, 70
   frontal cyclones, 81-82
   fronts, 75
      cold fronts, 76
      occluded fronts, 77
      stationary fronts, 77
      warm fronts, 76
   maritime polar, 73
   maritime tropical, 74
   occluded fronts, 81
   potential energy, 78
   radiational cooling, 70
   stationary fronts, light
      precipitation, 81
   temperature, 70
   tropical, 73
   types, 71
   warm fronts, steady
      long-lasting rain, 80
   weather type
      associations, 72

air pollution
   bronchoconstriction,
      143
   carbon monoxide, 144
   chlorosis, 144
   costs of control, 164
   environmental law,
      153
   high-pressure systems,
      163
   horizontal dispersal,
      161
   hydrocarbons, 147
   increased precipitation,
      140
   linear effect, 142
   methods for control,
      158-159
   nitrogen oxides, 146
   ozone, 149, 156
   particulates, 138-140
   photochemical smog,
      149
   plasmolysis, 144
   primary pollutants,
      137
   regulations for control,
      154
   secondary pollutants,
      138
   sulfur oxides, 141
   threshold effect, 142
   vertical mixing, 162
   volatile organic
      compounds, 147

Air Pollution Control Act, 154

air pressure, measuring via barometer, 11

Air Quality Act of 1967, 155

air quality and pollution, 156

air quality careers, 318

albedo, 182

allergies, relationship between weather and health, 133

altimeters, 272

altocumulus clouds, 24

altostratus clouds, 24

ancient approaches to forecasting, 10

anemometers, 273, 276

aneroid barometers, 45, 271

anomalous propagation, weather radar, 283

Antarctic ozone depletion, 171

aphelion, 178

arctic air masses, 71-73

ASOS (automated surface observing stations), 289

aspiration psychrometer, 274

Atlanta climate example, 220

Atlantic ocean, impact of El Niño, 122

atmosphere
  Azores High, 193
  Bermuda High, 193
  capacity for water vapor, 15
  circulation, 192

Coriolis effect, 48
  geostrophic balance, 50
  global air circulation, 195
  horse latitudes, 193
  inter-tropical convergence zone, 193
  mid-latitude, 42
  ozone, formation process, 168-170
  polar easterlies, 192
  polar fronts, 194
  prevailing westerlies, 192
  relationship to oceans, 114
  structure, 168
  trade winds, 192
  tropical, 204
  wind, 51

atmospheric modeling, 318

atmospheric pressure, 42
  average sea-level, 45, 271
  causes, 43
  effect on health, 129
  hectopascals, 271
  measuring in millibars, 271
  normal variation, 45

atomic mass number, 228

atomic number, 228

aurora australis, 166

aurora borealis, 166

automobiles and air pollution, 144, 160

autumnal equinox, 180

available potential energy, air masses, 78

average sea-level air pressure, 45, 271

average world temperature, 184

AWIPS (Advanced Weather Interactive Processing System), 289

Azores current, 200

Azores High, 193

B

B class climates, 210

balancing of weather extremes, 8

ball lightning, 62

balloons, upper air observations, 277

baroclinic zones
  air masses, 78
  computer model, 311

barographs, 271

barometers, 11, 45, 271
  aneroid, 271
  hurricane path forecasting, 94
  placement for accurate readings, 276

barometric pressure, 45-46
  average sea-level, 45, 271
  causes, 43
  effect on health, 129
  hectopascals, 271
  measuring in millibars, 271
  normal variation, 45

barotropic computer model, 310-311
Beaufort scale, measuring wind speed to object motion, 273
Bermuda High, 193
bi-cell air circulation theory, 198
blizzards, 100-101
    Blizzard of 1888, 102
    bombogenesis, 104
    primary center, 103
    record breakers
        Blizzard of 1888, 102
        Midwest, 100
        Southern, 101
        Storm of the Century, 104
    secondary center, 103
    Storm of the Century, 104
blue color of sky, 8
Blue Sky aphorism, 8
bombogenesis, nor'easters, 104
boreal forests, 211
boundaries, air masses, 81
broadcasting, meteorology careers, 316
bronchoconstriction, 143
buoyancy, 57

C

C class climates, 210
California current, 201
Candlemas Day, *see* Groundhog Day

carbon dating, 229
carbon dioxide
    ground seepage, 255
    increase in levels, 259
    understanding climate changes, 250
carbon monoxide, air pollution, 144
Carboniferous Period, 231
careers in forecasting, 317
cars and air pollution, 144, 160
catalytic converters, 161
categories of hurricanes, 92
Celsius (C) temperature scale, 268
Cenozoic era, 333
centigrade scale, 268
centrifugal separators, 158
CFCs (chlorofluorocarbons), ozone depletion, 172
chaos, 313
chinook, 51
chlorosis, air pollution, 144
chromakey, 292
Cincinnati climate example, 224
circulation
    atmosphere, 192
    oceans, 199
        Azores current, 200
        California current, 201
        El Niño, 199
        Gulf Stream, 200
        gyres, 199

Japanese current, 200
Labrador current, 201
north Pacific current, 201
Peruvian current, 201
Sargasso Sea, 201
wind, 52
cirrocumulus clouds, 23
cirrostratus clouds, 23
cirrus clouds, 9, 22
classification of clouds, 21
    cirrus clouds, 22
    convective clouds, 25
    cumulonimbus clouds, 26
    cumulus clouds, 22
    fog, 25
    high clouds, 23
    low clouds, 24
    middle clouds, 24
    nimbus clouds, 22
    stratus clouds, 22
Clean Air Acts, 155
climate, 191
    continent zone examples, 204-206
    economics of relocation, 216-217
    evidence of change over time, 232
    examples
        Atlanta, 220
        Cincinnati, 224
        Denver, 221
        Fresno, 224
        Houston, 219

Las Vegas, 223
Orlando, 222
Phoenix, 220
Raleigh-Durham region, 223
Salt Lake City, 222
Koppen classification scheme, 207-208
A (tropical moist), 208
B (dry), 210
C (mid-latitude moist subtropical), 210
D (moist continental), 211
E (polar), 211
H (highland), 212
tropical island example, 203
understanding changes, 239
carbon dioxide levels, 250
changes in Earth's orbit, 241
fluctuation of solar output, 244
greenhouse effect, 249
obliquity of Earth's axis, 243
volcanism, 248
climatic optimum, 234
climatology, 5, 93, 319
cloud seeding, smaller hail generation, 35
clouds
cirrus, 9, 22
classification, 21

altocumulus, 24
altostratus, 24
cirrocumulus, 23
cirrostratus, 23
cirrus, 9, 22
convective, 25
cumulonimbus, 26
cumulus, 22
fog, 25
nimbostratus, 24
nimbus, 22
stratocumulus, 24
stratus, 22
fog, 20
formation, 20
groups, 22
observing types for forecasting, 26-27
seeding, 34-35
coalescence, rain formation, 30
cold fronts, thunderstorms or tornadoes, 76, 80
coldest places on earth, 212
colds, relationship to weather, 131
color of sky, 8
color-coding, weather radar readings, 282
comfort index, dew point, 217
comfort indicators, 17
computer forecasting, 306, 309-312
computer weather modeling, 318, 339-341
condensation, 17

condensation nuclei, cloud formation, 20
consulting meteorologists, 317
continental air masses, 71
continental polar air masses, 72
continental tropical air masses, 75
continents, climate zone examples, 204-206
continuity, ocean currents, 118
controlling pollution, 158
convection, 24
convective clouds, 25
convective precipitation, 25
convergences in atmosphere, 48, 194
conversion from Fahrenheit to Celsius, 268
cool water surfacing, La Niña, 122
cooling degree days, 217
Coriolis force, 48-49, 177
cosmic rays, 228
costs of pollution control, 164
cumulonimbus clouds, 26
cumulus clouds, 22
cup anemometer, 273
cyclogenesis, 104
cyclones, 64, 87-90, 158

D

D class climates, 211
dating age of items, *see* carbon dating; uranium dating
degassing, 159
degree days, cooling/ heating seasons, 216-217
dendrochronology, 232
Denver climate example, 221
depletion of ozone, gradual cessation, 173
development opportunities in meteorology, 318
Devonian period, 333
dew point, 16
    deriving heat index, 20
    index of comfort, 17, 217
disease, increase due to greenhouse effect, 261
divergence
    air currents, 48
    high-pressure systems, 70
doldrums, 193
Doppler effect
    radial velocity, 284
    TVS (tornado vortex signature), 285
    weather radar, 284
Doppler weather radar, 281
    anomalous propagation, 283
    color-coded readings, 282

Doppler shift, 284
    frequency, 282
    horizontal scan of precipitation, 283
    period, 282
    reflectivity, 283
    vertical scan of precipitation, 283
    wavelength, 282
driest inhabited location, 37
droughts, 75
dry adiabatic lapse rate, 59
dry downslope winds, health affects, 136

E

E class climates, 211
earnings potentials in meteorology, 320
Earth
    changes in orbit, understanding climate changes, 241
    eccentricity of orbit, 242
    geologic time scale
        Carboniferous Period, 231
        Paleozoic era, 231
        Precambrian era, 230
    obliquity of axis, understanding climate changes, 243
    precession, 243
east wind aphorism, 9
echoes, weather radar, 281

ecological impact, greenhouse effect, 262
economics of relocation, 216-217
eddies, 53
effects of heat syndrome, 130
El Niño, 199
    impact
        Atlantic Ocean, 122
        California, 119
        marine life, 118
        South America, 120
        southern North America, 121
        Western Pacific region, 120
    lack of winter weather in U.S., 121
    life cycle, 117
    of 1998, 113
electric hygrometer, 274
electrical force, 228
electrical thermometers, 269
electrostatic precipitators, 158
employment opportunities in meteorology, 322
enhancements, hurricane potential for damage, 96
ENIAC (electronic numerical integrator and computer), 310
ENSO (El Niño Southern Oscillation), 117
environmental lapse rate, 60
environmental law, air pollution control, 153

EPA (Environmental Protection Agency), 155
equatorial air masses, 71, 75
equatorial weather satellites, 288
equinox, autumnal, 180
eras of Earth's history, 333
ETA model, 339
Europe, highest temperature recorded, 18
eye of hurricanes, 90

F

factors causing rain, 36
Fahrenheit (F) scale, 268
fair weather field, 60
February 2nd, Groundhog Day, 7
First Law of Thermodynamics, 59, 308
flooding, hurricane damage, 94
fluid motion laws, 306
fog, 20, 25
Fohn, 51
forecasting, 3
    500-mb charts, 296
    850-mb charts, 299
    adiabatic lapse rate, 300
    ancient approaches, 10
    as a profession, 316-317
    computer-based, 306, 309-312

difficulty using math expressions, 308
    hurricanes, 93
        barometers, 94
        climatology, 93
        persistence, 93
    Medium Range Forecast, 302
    observing
        clouds, 27
        jet stream, 84
        sky, 26
    radar, 281
    typical day, 291
        observations, 292
        viewing surface maps, 294
    watching frontal cyclones, 84
forensic meteorology, 319
forked lightning, 62
formation
    clouds, 20
    hurricanes, high-pressure systems, 89
    lightning, 60
    rain, 29
        coalescence, 30
        ice crystals, 31
        particle suspension, 31
freezing rain, 33
frequency, weather radar, 282
Fresno climate example, 224
frontal cyclones, 81
    forecasting, 84
    life cycle, 82

nor'easter, 83
occluded phase, 83
sou'westers, 83
fronts, 75
    available potential energy, 78
    baroclinic zones, 78
    cold fronts, 76
        thunderstorms/ tornadoes, 80
    occluded fronts, 77, 81
    potential energy, 78
    stationary fronts, 77
        light precipitation, 81
    warm fronts, 76
        steady long-lasting rain, 80
Fujita Scale, tornado size/ damage measurement, 64
funnels, thunderstorms, 63

G

Galveston storm surge, 106
gases, atmospheric pressure, 43
general circulation, 191, 198
geologic time scale, 333
    Carboniferous Period, 231
    Paleozoic era, 231
    Precambrian era, 230
geostrophic balance, 50, 310
glacial periods, 233

global heat budget, 184
global wind circulation, 53, 192, 195
GMT (Greenwich Mean Time), 278
GOES (geostationary satellites), 288
Great New England Hurricane, 106
greenhouse effect, 168
　debate over impact, 253, 258-260
　decrease in rain, 262
　ecological impact, 262
　effect on troposphere, 255
　increase in disease, 261
　measured control policy, 263
　negative impact, 261
　positive effects, 262
　positive-feedback concept, 251
　rise in sea level, 261
　understanding climate changes, 249
　validating effect, 254
greenhouse gases, 184
Greenwich Mean Time (GMT), 278
Groundhog Day, 7
groupings of clouds, 22
Gulf Stream, 200
gyres, 199

H

H class climates, 212
haboob, 51
hail, 33

hair hygrometer, 274
half-life, radioactive decay, 228-230
halos/rings around Sun and Moon, 9
hardest rainfall records, 37
health, relationship to weather, 128
　allergies, 133
　atmospheric pressure, 129
　common cold, 131
　heat waves, 129
　respiratory infections, 131
　Seasonal Affective Disorder, 134
heat
　effect on land, 185
　effect on oceans, 185
heat capacity, 185
heat cramps, 17
heat exchange, El Niño formation, 114
heat exhaustion, 18
heat indexes, 18
heat lightning, 62
heat radiation and absorption, 183-184
heat stroke, 18
heat syndrome, 130
heat waves, 16, 123, 129
heat-stress index, 217
hectopascals, 271
hi-volume sampler, particulate measuring, 140
high barometric pressure, sunny days, 48
high clouds, 23

high pressure areas, clockwise rotation, 48
high-pressure systems
　air pollution, 163
　cause of wind, 193
　divergence, 70
　hurricane formation, 89
　synoptic circulation, 53
highest atmospheric pressure recorded, 45
horizontal dispersal of air pollution, 161
horizontal scan of precipitation, weather radar, 283
horse latitudes, 193
hottest locations on Earth, 212
hottest temperatures recorded, 18
Houston climate example, 219
humidity, 13
　deriving heat index, 18
　effect on health, 129
　measuring via hygrometer, 11
　relative, 16, 273
Hurricane Andrew, 97
Hurricane Hugo, 109
hurricanes, 88, 107-108
　Andrew, 97, 110
　Camille, 108
　categories, 92
　enhancements, 96
　eye, 90
　eye wall, 90
　flooding, 94

349

forecasting
    barometers, 94
    climatology, 93
    persistence, 93
formation, 89
Galveston storm surge, 106
Great New England Hurricane, 106
Hugo, 109
intensity scale, Saffir-Simpson scale, 92
names, 92
New England Hurricane of 1938, 96
of the '50s and '60s, 107-108
rotation, Coriolis force, 89
seeding, 36, 97
spiral rain bands, 90
synoptic circulation, 53
tracking, 93
wave surges, 96
wind damage, 94
hydrocarbons, pollution, 147
hygrometer, 11
hygroscopic particles, cloud formation, 20
hypothalamus, countering excessive heat, 130
hypothermia, 218

I

Ice Age, 334
ice crystals, rain formation, 31
ice storms, 34, 121
ideal gas law, 307
Ides of March, 101
impact of greenhouse effect, 261
impact of El Niño
    Atlantic Ocean, 122
    California, 119
    marine life, 118
    South America, 120
    southern North America, 121
    Western Pacific, 120
inches of mercury, barometric pressure, 45
index of comfort, dew point, 217
index of heat-stress, 217
indicators of comfort, 17
infrared imagery, weather satellites, 287
insensible perspiration, 130
interglacial periods, 233-234
Intergovernmental Panel on Climate Change, *see* IPPC
inversions, 162
IPCC (Intergovernmental Panel on Climate Change), greenhouse effect debate, 253
IR radiation (infrared), 167
isobars, surface maps, 296
isotherms, 500-mb charts, 296
isotopes for dating, 228-230

ITCZ (Inter-Tropical Convergence Zone), 193

J

Japanese current, 200
jet stream
    forecasting, 84
    sub-tropical, 115
jobs in meteorology, 316-317

K

Kelvin (K) temperature scale, 269
khamsin, 51
Koppen climate classification scheme, 207-208
    dry, 210
    highland, 212
    mid-latitude moist sub-tropical, 210
    moist continental, 211
    polar, 211
    tropical moist, 208

L

La Niña, reversing trend of El Niño, 122
Labrador current, 201
lake effect, 72
land
    breezes, 53
    heating, 185
lapse rate
    dry adiabatic lapse rate, 59

environmental lapse rate, 60
moist adiabatic lapse rate, 60
Las Vegas climate example, 223
latent heat, tropical cloud formation, 88
laws of fluid motion, 306
lead particulates, air pollution, 140
leftward motion of atmosphere, southern hemisphere, 50
letter abbreviations for air masses, 72
LFM (limited fine mesh) model, 311-312
life cycles
El Niño, 117
frontal cyclones, 82
light precipitation, stationary fronts, 81
light spectrum, 167
lightning, 60-61
avoiding, 62
types, 62
linear effect, air pollution, 142
Little Ice Age, 235
local heat budgets, 185
long-range forecasting, 4
low barometric pressure, rainy weather, 48
low pressure areas, counterclockwise rotation, 48
low-pressure systems, synoptic circulation, 53
lowest sea-level atmospheric pressure, 45

M

mackerel sky, 23
major cloud groups, 22
mare's tails, 22
marine life, impact of El Niño, 118
maritime air masses, 71
maritime polar air masses, 72-73
maritime tropical air masses, 72-74
mathematical expressions, describing weather, 306-309
Maunder minimum, 246
maximum thermometer, 271
measured control policy, greenhouse effect, 263
measuring
atmospheric pressure, 271
rain, 275
relative humidity, 273
snow, 276
temperature, 267-270
wind speed, 272
medium scale circulation, 53
melatonin, Seasonal Affective Disorder, 135
mercurial barometer, 271
mesocyclone, 285
mesopause, 168
mesoscale convective complexes, 63
mesoscale wind circulation, 53, 57
mesosphere, 168

Mesozoic era, 333
meteorology, 11
as a profession, 316-317, 321-322
earnings potentials, 320
methods for pollution control, 159
microscale wind circulations, 53
mid-latitude atmosphere, 42
Midwest snowstorms, 100
millibars, measuring atmospheric pressure, 45, 271
minimum thermometer, 271
mistral, 51
modern weather trends, 54
moist adiabatic lapse rate, 60
moisture, 13
monsoons, 186-188
Moon, halos/rings around, 9
MOS (model output statistics), 341
Motor Vehicle Air Pollution Act, 155
mountain breezes, 188
MRF (Medium Range Forecast), 302

N

NAAQS (National Air Quality Standards), 155
National Environmental Policy Act, 155

National Weather Service, career opportunities, 316, 322
natural disasters
    Blizzard of 1888, 102
    Galveston storm surge, 106
    Great New England Hurricane, 106
    Hurricane Andrew, 110
    Hurricane Camille, 108
    Hurricane Hugo, 109
    hurricanes of the '50s and '60s, 107, 108
    snowstorms, 100
    Storm of the Century, 101, 104
negative impact of greenhouse effect, 261
New England hurricane of 1938, 96
Newton's law of fluid motion, 306
NEXRAD (Next Generation Weather Radar), 284
NGM model (nested grid model), 300, 339
nimbostratus clouds, 24
Nimbus weather satellite, 287
nimbus clouds, 22
nitrogen oxides, air pollution, 146
nor'easters, 83, 102, 186
    bombogenesis, 104
    primary center, 103
normal variation, atmospheric pressure, 45

north Pacific current, 201
northern lights, 166
NOZE (National Ozone Expedition), 172
nuclear binding force, 228

O

obliquity of Earth's axis, 243
observations
    clouds, 26-27
    typical day of forecaster, 292
    upper atmosphere, 276
occluded fronts, 77, 81
occluded phase, frontal cyclones, 83
oceans
    circulation, 199
        Azores current, 200
        California current, 201
        continuity, 118
        El Niño, 199
        Gulf Stream, 200
        gyres, 199
        Japanese current, 200
        Labrador current, 201
        north Pacific current, 201
        Peruvian current, 201
        Sargasso Sea, 201
        upwelling, 119
    heating, 185

relationship to atmosphere, 114
Ordovician period, 333
Orlando climate example, 222
oxidants, pollution, 149
oxygen-16, 232
oxygen-18, 232
ozone
    air pollution, 156
    benefits in atmosphere, 165
    formation process, 168-170
    photochemical smog, 149
ozone depletion, gradual cessation, 173
ozone hole, 171

P

Paleozoic era, 231, 333
Pangea, 240
particle suspension, rain formation, 31
particulates, 138-140
PE (primitive equation) model, 311
perihelion, 178
period, weather radar, 282
permafrost, 211
persistence, hurricane path forecasting, 93
perspiration, 130
Peruvian current, 201
Phoenix climate example, 220

photochemical smog, 149
pilot balloons, 277
plasmolysis, air pollution, 144
plate tectonics, 240
Pleistocene period, 334
PM-10 particulate, 138
polar air masses, 71
polar easterlies, 192
polar fronts, 194
polar snow-forest climate, 211
polar-orbiting weather satellites, 288
pollution
  carbon monoxide, 144
  costs of control, 164
  environmental law, 153
  high-pressure systems, 163
  horizontal dispersal, 161
  hydrocarbons, 147
  methods for control, 158-159
  nitrogen oxides, 146
  ozone, 149
  particulates, 138-140
  photochemical smog, 149
  precipitation increases, 140
  primary pollutants, 137
  secondary pollutants, 138
  sulfur oxides, 141
  vertical mixing, 162
  volatile organic compounds, 147

positive effects, greenhouse effect, 262
positive lifted index, 340
positive-feedback concept, greenhouse effect, 251
potential energy, air masses, 78
Precambrian era, 230, 333
precession, 243
precipitation
  cloud seeding, 35
  factors causing rain, 36
  freezing rain, 33
  hail, 33
  increase due to air pollution, 140
  sleet, 32
  snow, 32
preponderance of tornado occurences in United States, 64
pressure of atmosphere, 42
  measuring in millibars, 271
  see also atmospheric pressure
pressure plate anemometer, 272
pressure symbols, 337
prevailing westerlies, 192
prevailing wind, continent climate example, 204
primary center, snowstorms, 103
primary pollutants, air pollution, 137
private nuisances, 153

process of rain formation, 29
  coalescence, 30
  ice crystals, 31
  particle suspension, 31
profiles of temperatures
  last 3,000 years, 235
  last half-million years, 234
  last two million years, 233
  twentieth century, 236
prominences, 244
pseudo-adiabatic lapse rate, 60

R

radar, Doppler weather radar, 281
  anomalous propagation, 283
  color-coded readings, 282
  Doppler shift, 284
  forecasting uses, 281
  frequency, 282
  horizontal scan of precipitation, 283
  period, 282
  reflectivity, 283
  upper air observations, 278
  vertical scan of precipitation, 283
  wavelength, 282
  see also weather radar
radial velocity, Doppler radar, 284
radiation fog, 25

radiation of Sun
  absorption, 182
  radiation budget, 183
  reflection, 182
  scattering, 181
radiational cooling, 25, 70
radioactive decay, common isotopes for dating, 228-230
radiometers, 278
radiosonde, 277
rain
  decrease due to greenhouse effect, 262
  factors causing rain, 36
  hardest rainfall records, 37
  measuring, 275
  process of formation, 29
    coalescence, 30
    ice crystals, 31
    particle suspension, 31
  warm fronts, 80
rain gauges, 275
rainmaking, 34
Raleigh-Durham region climate example, 223
recent weather trends, 54
record-setting ice storms, 34
Red Sky aphorism, 7
reflection of light, 182
reflectivity, weather radar, 283
refraction, 10
regulations for air pollution control, 154

relationship between weather and health, 128-129
  allergies, 133
  atmospheric pressure, 129
  common cold, 131
  heat waves, 129
  respiratory infections, 131
  Seasonal Affective Disorder, 134
relationship of oceans and atmosphere, 114
relative humidity, 16
  indicator of comfort, 17
  measuring, 273
research opportunities in meteorology, 318
respiratory infections, relationship of weather to health, 131
rhinoviruses, 131
Richardson's experiment, 306
rightward motion of atmosphere, northern hemisphere, 50
rings around Sun and Moon, 9
rockets, upper air observations, 278
rotation and Coriolis force
  atmosphere, 48
  rotation of hurricanes, 89

S

SAD (Seasonal Affective Disorder), 134
safety and tornadoes, 67
Saffir-Simpson scale, hurricane intensity scale, 92
Salt Lake City climate example, 222
Santa Ana winds, 51
Sargasso Sea, 201
satellites, weather forecasting, 286
saturation, 17
scales of motion, wind, 52
scattering of light, 182
scrubbers, 158
sea breezes, 53, 185
sea level
  atmospheric pressure, 45
  rise due to greenhouse effect, 261
sea-surface temperature, variation over time, 234
seasons, 179
secondary center, blizzards, 103
secondary pollutants, air pollution, 138
seeding
  clouds, 34-35
  hurricanes, 97
sensible perspiration, 130
serotonin, 136
settling chambers, 158
severe thunderstorm watch, 66

shamal, 51
sheet lightning, 62
Siberian Express, 73
silver iodide
    cloud seeding, 35
    hurricane seeding, 97
sirocco, 51
sky, blue color, 8
sleet, 32
sling psychrometer, 273
smog, 142
snow
    formation, 32
    measuring, 276
    squalls, 72
snowstorms
    Blizzard of 1888, 102
    bombogenesis, 104
    historical greats, 100
    midwest, 100
    primary center, 103
    secondary center, 103
    southern, 99
    Storm of the Century,
        101, 104
solar constant, 166
solar flares, 244
sound travel aphorism,
    10
South America, impact of
    El Niño, 120
southern North America,
    impact of El Niño, 121
southern snowstorms, 99
sou'westers, 83
spectrum of light, 167
spiral rain bands, 90
St. Elmo's Fire, 62
stable air pockets,
    environmental lapse
    rate, 60

stationary fronts, 77, 81
storm chasing, 67
Storm of the Century,
    101, 104, 248
storms, historical greats,
    99
stratocumulus clouds, 24
stratosphere, 169
stratus clouds, 22
structure of atmosphere,
    168
subsidence, 39
subsidence inversion, 163
subtropical high-pressure
    systems, 194
subtropical jet stream,
    115
Subvortex project, 67
sulfur oxides, air
    pollution, 141
summer solstice, 180
Sun
    absorption of light,
        182
    aphelion, 178
    effects on weather, 165
    fluctuation of solar
        output, climate
        changes, 244
    greenhouse effect, 168
    halos/rings around, 9
    IR radiation, 167
    perihelion, 178
    prominences, 244
    radiation budget, 183
    reflection of light, 182
    scattering of light, 182
    solar flares, 244
    sunspots, 245-246
    UV radiation, 167

sunspots, 166, 245-246
supercells, 64
surface maps
    forecasting, 294
    isobars, 296
surface station model,
    335
surface weather maps,
    337
surges
    Galveston storm surge,
        106
    Hurricane Camille, 108
    hurricane damage, 96
suspended particulates,
    138
sweating, 17
synoptic wind
    circulation, 53, 69

T

taiga climate, 211
teaching meteorology,
    319
techniques for pollution
    control, 159
temperature
    average world
        temperature, 184
    departure from norm,
        El Niño periods, 114
    deriving heat index, 18
    effect on moisture, 14
    Fahrenheit (F) scale,
        268
    hottest recorded, 18
    measuring, 11, 267-270

profiles
  last 3,000 million years, 235
  last half million years, 234
  last two million years, 233
  profile for twentieth century, 236
sea-surface, variation over time, 234
wind chill, 218
world record, 18
temperature inversions, 10, 162
theodolite, 277
thermistors, 269
thermodynamics, first law, 308
thermographs, 269
thermometers, 11, 267, 276
thermosphere, 168
threshold effect, air pollution, 142
thunder, 61
thunderstorms, 57
  cold fronts, 80
  funnels, 63
  lightning, 60-62
  mesoscale convective complexes, 53, 63
  supercells, 64
  wind shear, 63
tilt of the earth's axis, reason for seasons, 179
time scale of Earth, 230-231
tipping bucket rain gauge, 275

TIROS (Television and Infrared Observation Satellite), 286
TOMS (Total Ozone Mapping Satellites), 172
topography and heat distribution, 188
tornadoes, 63
  mesoscale wind circulation, 53
  preponderance of occurrences in United States, 64
  safety, 67
  size/damage comparison, Fujita Scale, 64
  warnings, 66
  watches, 66
TOTO (Totable Tornado Observatory), 67
tracking hurricanes, 93
trade winds, 117, 192
tri-cell air circulation theory, 197
Tropic of Cancer, 88, 180
Tropic of Capricorn, 88, 180
tropical air masses, 71-73
tropical atmosphere, 204
tropical cyclones, 88-90
tropical depressions, 90
tropical moist climates, 208
tropical storms, 90-92
tropics, 88
troposphere, 170, 255
TVS (tornado vortex signature), Doppler radar, 285
twisters, 64

types of lightning, 62
typhoons, 87, 90
typical day of forecaster, 291-293
  500-mb charts, 296
  850-mb charts, 299
  examining weather data, 294
  Medium Range Forecast, 302
  observations, 292
  surface maps, 294

U

understanding climate changes, 239
  carbon dioxide levels, 250
  changes in Earth's orbit, 241
  fluctuation of solar output, 244
  greenhouse effect, 249
  obliquity of Earth's axis, 243
  volcanism, 248
unicell global circulation theory, 196
United States
  highest temperatures recorded, 18
  preponderance of tornado occurrences, 64
UNIVAC, 309
Universal Time (UT), 278
unstable air pockets, 58
upper air charts, 337
upper air observations, 276

upward motion
  air currents during rainfall, 37
  thunderstorms, 57
upwelling of ocean currents, 119
uranium dating, 230
urban heat island effect, 257
UT (Universal Time), 278
UV radiation (ultraviolet), 167

V

valley breezes, 188
vaporous water, transformation into visible water, 15
variation in atmospheric pressure, 46
vernal equinox, 180
vertical mixing of air pollution, 162
vertical scan of precipitation, weather radar, 283
vertical velocity, 340
VOCs (volatile organic compounds), 147
volcanism, understanding climate changes, 248

W

warm fronts, 76, 80
warm water surfacing, El Niño, 122
water
  humidity, 13

temperature, El Niño periods, 114
wave surges, hurricane damage, 96
wavelength, weather radar, 282
weather
  associated rising air currents, 38
  atmosphere, 193
    Azores High, 193
    Bermuda High, 193
    capacity for water vapor, 15
    circulation, 192
    Coriolis effect, 48
    geostrophic balance, 50
    global air circulation, 195
    horse latitudes, 193
    inter-tropical convergence zone, 193
    mid-latitude, 42
    ozone, formation process, 168, 170
    polar easterlies, 192
    polar fronts, 194
    prevailing westerlies, 192
    relationship to oceans, 114
    structure, 168
    trade winds, 192
    tropical, 204
    wind, 51
  balancing of extremes, 8
  blizzards, 100-101
    Blizzard of 1888, 102
    bombogenesis, 104

    primary center, 103
    record breakers, 100-104
    secondary center, 103
    Storm of the Century, 104
  climate, 191
    continent zone examples, 204-206
    economics of relocation, 216-217
    evidence of change over time, 232
    examples, 215, 219-224
    Koppen classification scheme, 207-212
    tropical island example, 203
    understanding changes, 239-244, 248-250
  describing via mathematical expressions, 306-309
  disasters, 16
  forecasting, 3
    500-mb charts, 296
    850-mb charts, 299
    adiabatic lapse rate, 300
    ancient approaches, 10
    as a profession, 316-317
    computer-based, 306, 309-312
    difficulty using math expressions, 308
    hurricanes, 93-94

Medium Range Forecast, 302
observing clouds, 27
observing jet stream, 84
observing sky, 26
radar, 281
typical day, 291-294
watching frontal cyclones, 84
instruments, 267, 276
modification methods, 34
natural disasters
Blizzard of 1888, 102
Galveston storm surge, 106
Great New England Hurricane, 106
Hurricane Andrew, 110
Hurricane Camille, 108
Hurricane Hugo, 109
hurricanes of the '50s and '60s, 107-108
snowstorms, 100
Storm of the Century, 101, 104
recent trends, 54
relationship to health, 128
allergies, 133
atmospheric pressure, 129
common cold, 131
heat waves, 129
respiratory infections, 131
Seasonal Affective Disorder, 134

weather lore, 6
Blue Sky aphorism, 8
Groundhog Day, 7
halos/rings around Sun and Moon, 9
Red Sky aphorism, 7
sound travel aphorism, 10
White Christmas aphorism, 8
wind direction aphorism, 9
weather maps, surface station model, 335
weather nuts, 66
weather radar, 281
anomalous propagation, 283
color-coded readings, 282
Doppler shift, 284
frequency, 282
horizontal scan of precipitation, 283
period, 282
reflectivity, 283
vertical scan of precipitation, 283
wavelength, 282
weather satellites, 286-288
west wind aphorism, 9
Western Pacific region, impact of El Niño, 120
wettest places on Earth, 37, 212
wind, 51
cause, 185
direction and weather severity, 9
doldrums, 193
hurricane damage, 94

Inter-Tropical Convergence Zone, 193
measuring speed, 272
mesoscale circulation, 57
microscale circulation, 53
polar easterlies, 192
polar fronts, 194
prevailing westerlies, 192
scales of motion, 52
synoptic circulation, 53
trade winds, 192
wind chill, 218
wind direction, 340
wind direction aphorism, 9
wind shear, 63, 285
wind speed, 340
windsock, 272
winter solstice, 180
WMO (World Meteorological Organization), 278
world record temperatures, 18
WSR-88 (Weather Surveillance Radar-1988), 284

Y-Z

Year Without a Summer, 248
zero point, Fahrenheit scale, 268
zones, continent climate examples, 205-206